Chaucer's Italian Tradition

Chaucer's Italian Tradition

Warren Ginsberg

Ann Arbor
THE UNIVERSITY OF MICHIGAN PRESS

For Shira
and
for Sam

PR
1912
.A3
G56
2002

Copyright © by the University of Michigan 2002
All rights reserved
Published in the United States of America by
The University of Michigan Press
Manufactured in the United States of America
⊗ Printed on acid-free paper

2005 2004 2003 2002   4 3 2 1

No part of this publication may be reproduced, stored in a retrieval system, or transmitted in any form or by any means, electronic, mechanical, or otherwise, without the written permission of the publisher.

A CIP catalog record for this book is available from the British Library.

Library of Congress Cataloging-in-Publication Data

Ginsberg, Warren, 1949–
    Chaucer's Italian tradition / Warren Ginsberg.
      p.   cm.
    Includes bibliographical references (p.   ) and index.
    ISBN 0-472-11234-1 (cloth : acid-free paper)
    1. Chaucer, Geoffrey, d. 1400—Sources.   2. Chaucer, Geoffrey, d. 1400—Knowledge—Literature.   3. Chaucer, Geoffrey, d. 1400—Knowledge—Italy.   4. Boccaccio, Giovanni, 1313–1375—Influence.   5. Petrarca, Francesco, 1304–1374—Influence.   6. Dante Alighieri, 1265–1321—Influence.   7. English poetry—Italian influences.   8. Italy—In literature.   I. Title.

PR1912.A3 G56 2001
821'.1—dc21   2001002842

Contents

Preface   vii

Acknowledgments   xiii

1. Introduction: Chaucer's Italian Tradition   1
2. Dante's Ovids: Allegory, Irony, and the Poet as Translation   29
3. Chaucer's Canterbury Poetics: Irony, Allegory, and the Manciple's Prologue and Tale   58
4. Dante and Boccaccio, Boccaccio and Petrarch: The Italian Tradition   105
5. "Medium autem, et extrema sunt eiusdem generis": Boccaccio's *Filostrato,* the Voice of Writing, and the Italian Tradition   148
6. Boccaccio, Chaucer, and Early Italian Humanism: The *De casibus virorum illustrium*   190
7. Petrarch, Chaucer, and the Making of the Clerk   240
8. Envoy/*Congedo*   269

Bibliography   275

Index   291

Preface

The title of this book is peculiar enough to warrant a prefatory word of explanation. Throughout the later fourteenth century, Italian customs and conventions had neither a history nor an audience to sanction them as precedents in England; Chaucer was the only poet of his day who visited Italy and created poems that were based on works by its most renowned authors. In what sense, then, can one speak of Chaucer's Italian Tradition?

The various answers I give this question proceed from the same cardinal premise: the social, municipal, and literary forms Chaucer encountered in Genoa, Florence, and Milan all differed significantly from those he was accustomed to in London. However knowledgeable an English traveler may have been about war, capital, and wool,[1] cities that were also sovereign states were uncharted ground to him; aristocrats who gave up family name and title to become guildsmen, merchants who defined themselves by the contributions their professions made to the welfare of their commune, were not the aristocrats and merchants he knew. However conversant an English poet was with *lais* and *ballades* in the *langue d'oïl*, Dante's metamorphosis of Provençal conventions in his "new style," Boccaccio's rhetorical scrutiny of that style, and Petrarch's transformation of it were developments he was not versed in.

Unfamiliar political, cultural, and artistic traditions made Italy a "somewhere else" for Chaucer; the interpretive schemes he carried with him there, which conditioned what he would see as meaningful, could not fully elucidate what he observed. By 1373, even Florentines

---

1. War, wool, and capital, of course, are the three commodities that David Wallace contends mediated Chaucer's understanding of Italy. See *Chaucerian Polity: Absolutist Lineages and Associational Forms in England and Italy* (Stanford: Stanford University Press, 1997).

found many historical figures and aesthetic demands of a work like the *Comedy* perplexing; a foreign writer visiting Dante's *città* for the first time would especially need a guide to appraise crucial elements of his poetics, such as the "new style," that were at once peculiarly Italian and already obsolescent. The guidance Chaucer got, I will argue, came chiefly from Boccaccio, whose poems he read as a gloss to Dante's. These poems in turn posed problems of their own for an English reader; to meet them, Chaucer pondered texts like the *Filostrato* and *Teseida* with the *Comedy* in mind. Through this process of reciprocal interrogation and transposition, which prompted him to study the *trecento* authors he knew not separately but in conjunction with one another, Chaucer generated an Italian tradition.

The topography of this tradition, however, was determined as much by what Chaucer did not attend to as by what he did. Dante's artistic forebears were not his;[2] Petrarch's lyrics and his humanistic writings caused Boccaccio to reinvent Dante at diverse times in ways unfathomable to someone not well educated in the civic life of their city. The literary and social history of these poets' reception of one another was part of a native tradition that Chaucer knew at most only obliquely. This Italian tradition was like a path Chaucer followed when he made his own, but one he walked as a stranger, not entirely aware of where it started or where it led.

In its simplest form, my thesis is that Chaucer's Italian Tradition is the conversation that emerges when these two traditions translate each other. Because this conversation stems from and will always give voice to literary assumptions and social practices that remained unassimilated in Chaucer's appropriations of Italy, I have adopted Walter Benjamin's idea of translation to steer my inquiries. Briefly put, Benjamin maintained that the translator's task is not to duplicate a text's meaning but to re-create its mode of meaning—the way, that is, its language is oriented to the material differences of sound and letter that constitute language in its "pure" state, prior to the assignment of significance. Once a corresponding mode has been fashioned, the adaptation will simultaneously illuminate the different orientation of the source and reveal its language to be as partial and secondary as that of the retelling. For Benjamin, translation and original are equally derivative;

---

2. I mean, of course, Dante's vernacular heritage; had Chaucer been able to read the *De vulgari eloquentia*, he would not have known the poets Dante quotes.

each achieves its intentional integrity as the consequence of the other's disclosure that it is a fragment of language per se.

Even though I believe Benjamin's notion of *reine Sprache* unnecessarily distances itself from history, his theory does recognize the need to regard what remains untranslated in Chaucer's translation of Italy. Accordingly, the tradition I delineate will be lodged neither in Chaucer's response to the authors he used nor in their responses to each other but in the manner in which their literary and social modes of meaning echo and disarticulate one another. This tradition, Chaucer's Italian Tradition, will express itself, in other words, not in the interaction of individual talents with accredited authorities (Chaucer and Dante, Boccaccio and Petrarch, etc.), but as shifts in tension that occur when the civic engagements and disengagements of Florence's poets are brought into contact with Chaucer's growing metropolitanism and his increasingly evident reluctance to make London the locus of his poetic art.[3] This tradition will reveal itself as the wobble in poetic trajectories one detects by reading what I will call Chaucer's Canterbury style as a translation of the play of irony and allegory in Dante's revisions of Ovid and Boccaccio's revisions of Dante's. Like multiple suns circling one another, the gravitational pull of each writer's manner of meaning follows and modifies the orbit of the others. However odd it seems, I will insist that Chaucer's experience becomes legible as an event in English and Italian cultural history only in the wake of such a trepidation of the spheres.

This is the argument that all others in this book return to; I have developed it by organizing my chapters into three sections, each of which takes as its focal point one of the authors Chaucer adapted. After an introductory chapter, in which I set forth in much greater detail the ideas just outlined, I turn to Dante and his famous definition of himself as poet in the *Purgatorio*. In order to safeguard his existence as an allegory of Love, Dante realized he had to neutralize the propensities of irony that threatened to subvert his claim to be an embodiment of God's creative breath. His strategy is twofold: he represents himself as a kind of Benjaminian translation of Amor's inspiration; and he recalls his previous silencing of Ovid, the satiric spokesman of a very different

---

3. As an orthographical way of distinguishing this tradition, which I designate Chaucer's Italian Tradition, from the tradition he made when he read Dante, Boccaccio, and Petrarch in conjunction with one another, I will mark the former by capitalizing it.

kind of love, which he had staged in the corresponding cantos of the *Inferno*. Together these strategies, I will suggest, constitute the *Comedy*'s *modo di dire;* in the following chapter I examine what I take to be Chaucer's translation of it. In "The Prologue to the Manciple's Tale," the thieving steward incarnates the negations of irony; the Cook's fall from his horse, however, which he instigates, opens into an allegory of Paul's conversion on the road to Damascus. Ovid figures meaningfully in these events and in the tale the Manciple subsequently tells; rather than expunging him, however, as Dante did, Chaucer embraced his ironies, which he translated into parables of salvation. His mode of meaning, which I contend is the mode of meaning of *The Canterbury Tales,* diverges from and perturbs Dante's at the very moment when Chaucer is most Dantesque.

My purpose in this first section of *Chaucer's Italian Tradition* is to provide a broad demonstration of the dynamics I see at play in crosscultural translation. The focus of the second section is Boccaccio, who more than anyone else is responsible for the intertextuality of Chaucer's reception of Italian literature. In each of three chapters I explore one of the various ways Boccaccio read Dante at different times in his life. In chapter 4 I give an overview of these responses by considering key works in conjunction with the political, social, and cultural institutions of Florence. These institutions changed in greater and lesser ways between 1341, when Boccaccio came to Florence from Naples, and 1374, when he left the city for the last time; I demonstrate how the coexistence of old and new forms complicated Boccaccio's view of his great predecessor. In the first part of the following chapter I take up an early work, the *Filostrato,* which I examine as, among other things, a radical revision of Dante's *stil novo;* I then turn briefly to Chaucer's extraordinary translation of its manner of meaning in the *Troilus.* Finally I look at Boccaccio's first major Latin text, the *De casibus virorum illustrium.* At two strategic points in this massive collection of catastrophes that overwhelmed famous men, Dante and Petrarch make decisive appearances; reading these passages in tandem furnishes a unique perspective from which to view how the uses Chaucer made and did not make of Boccaccio's work enable "The Monk's Tale" to challenge the *De casibus* and be challenged by it.

My goals in this section are to establish a tradition that can stand as the Italian counterpart of Chaucer's and to consider the effects of seeing it and the tradition Chaucer made as translations. Allegory and irony will again be at the center of my discussion: Boccaccio's mode of meaning, I will show, rewrites Dante's largely through the way the relations between these figures are renegotiated in his works. By tracking the various Dantes that appear in them, the limitations and insights of Chaucer's accommodation of both authors become more readily apparent. By looking at Chaucer's Italian manner of meaning, which emerges as the interplay between Dante and Boccaccio yet is unlike anything in either, presuppositions and ideologies of his sources become visible as well.

Because my analysis of the *De casibus* inaugurates a discussion of early Italian humanism, it also belongs to the third section of *Chaucer's Italian Tradition*. In my final chapter I continue this investigation by considering Petrarch's translation into Latin of the tale of Griselda, the last story in the *Decameron*, and Chaucer's translation in "The Clerk's Tale." When Petrarch rescued Griselda from Dioneo's scorn by clothing her fortitude in the dignity of Latin *cola*, he brought to a close a long-standing colloquy with Boccaccio about the role of literature in forming the autonomous, moral self. By aligning Griselda's constancy, which is exemplary, with her patience, which is allegorical, Petrarch established an analogy between the historical dialectic through which he assured the independence of his public and private soul in time and his univocal faith that he will be one with God in eternity. Petrarch's dialectic, as Boccaccio well knew, involved the simultaneous excavation and burial of classical works; by imitating their style, Petrarch sought to let the yearning for greatness that drove Virgil and Cicero animate everything he wrote and did. Even though Roman virtue had to be brought into conformity with the truth of revelation, Petrarch believed the Christian became great-souled only by emulating the antique zeal for justice, prudence, fortitude, and temperance. For him, Griselda in Latin would embody these aspirations far more completely than Boccaccio's vernacular heroine ever could.

For the most part, I think Chaucer was quite unaware of the extent to which Petrarch's Griselda is early humanism's answer not only to Boccaccio's claim that the *Decameron* is ethically neutral but to Dante's insistence that the *Comedy* is the poetry of salvation. Petrarch despised logicians in general and sophistical *Brittani* in particular; if the Clerk presented himself in Padua as an Oxford Aristotelian, he more likely would have found himself being shown the door than invited in as a disciple. Nevertheless, by organizing the various secular and ecclesiastical discourses that constitute the Clerk's character around the general figures of allegory and irony, Chaucer brilliantly reinstituted Petrarch's concerns. The Clerk who finds in Griselda a paradigm for the soul's devotion to God speaks in an elevated style that is genuinely Petrarchan. But the Clerk who formally enters into debate with Alice of Bath sings in a register Petrarch never sounded. The "Envoy" of course is French in form, but its tone is not unlike Boccaccio's. All this, I will argue, makes the Clerk, who could not be from anywhere but England, the most Italian of the Canterbury pilgrims and the first true translation of Petrarch.

These are the propositions that inform *Chaucer's Italian Tradition* and how I have organized them. Let me add that, unless otherwise noted, all translations in this book about translation are mine. I should mention as well that this volume has a companion, *Dante's Aesthetics of Being*, which the University of Michigan Press published in 1999. My original plan had been to include much that appears in that book in this one. But I discovered that what I wanted to say about Dante was self-contained and distinct enough from my arguments about what he meant to Chaucer to justify separate treatment. In the event, I have tried to write this study so that a reader who has not read the previous one will be at no disadvantage; even though I devoted considerable space to Dante's poetic manifesto there, my comments here are directed to an entirely different end and, while obviously allied with the earlier discussion, do not rely on it.

Although I had written a substantial part of this book before David Wallace's *Chaucerian Polity* appeared, many readers will already recognize that my study enters into conversation with his from the start. In a number of instances, Wallace covers the same material I do and has anticipated my lines of inquiry; in general, however, because he assumes the boundary between English and Italian customs was far more permeable than I think was the case, his representation of Italy and Chaucer's reception of it varies greatly from mine. Nevertheless, I would like to insist that I neither conceived nor wrote this book as a review of his, nor do I feel it should be read that way. From my vantage point, *Chaucer's Italian Tradition* participates with Wallace's work in a dialogue about Chaucer and Italy; if that dialogue is not quite a translation, I do think the modes of assessing meaning in each differ enough to enliven the colloquy in interesting ways.

Acknowledgments

In a sense, I have been writing this book from the time I took courses in Chaucer from Talbot Donaldson and Dante from John Freccero at Yale. But it was only in 1984, during unforgettable weekly lunch conversations with Giuseppe Mazzotta, that I began to understand why I felt any discussion of Chaucer's translations of Dante, Boccaccio, and Petrarch should begin by acknowledging the different literary and cultural traditions of England and Italy. Since then, in developing my ideas, I have received much advice and encouragement from many friends and colleagues. It gives me great pleasure to be able to thank Teresa Kennedy, John Fyler, Michael Hanly, and Howell Chickering, all of whom read essays that, sometimes in very different form, became part of various chapters in this book. Karla Taylor has been a constant interlocutor and good friend over the years; beyond what she has taught me in her own books and essays, she read the entire manuscript and made many crucial suggestions. I would also like to thank an anonymous reader for the Press who offered much helpful advice. Robert Hanning, Winthrop Wetherbee, and Giuseppe Mazzotta have all been counselors to this project from its inception; each of them has given me more time, encouragement, and invaluable commentary than anyone could have expected or hoped for.

I had the very good fortune of being able to present early versions of some chapters at a number of institutions; I would like to express my gratitude to my hosts in the Department of English at Mary Washington University, the University of Oregon, and the State University of New York at Stony Brook, the Departments of English and Comparative Literature and the Casa Italiana at Columbia University, the Italian Department at Yale University, and the Medieval Colloquium at Cornell University. The comments I received at each gathering helped me immeasurably.

I also wish to acknowledge my indebtedness to Deans and Vice Presidents of the College of Arts and Sciences, the Office of Research, and the Provost's Office at the University at Albany, State University of New York, all of whom provided support that enabled me to conduct research in Italy. I especially want to thank the John Simon Guggenheim Foundation for the fellowship that allowed me to complete this book.

Parts of some chapters have appeared, sometimes in substantially different form, in a number of professional journals and volumes of essays. I gratefully acknowledge permission to reprint from the editors and publishers. Sections of chapter 2 first appeared as "Ovidius ethicus? Ovid and the Medieval Commentary Tradition," in *Desiring Discourses: The Literature of Love, Ovid through Chaucer*, ed. James Paxson and Cynthia Gravlee (Selinsgrove, Pa.: Susquehanna University Press, 1998), 62–71, and as "Ovid and the Problem of Gender" in *Medievalia* 13 (1989): 9–28. Most of chapter 3 appeared as "Chaucer's Canterbury Poetics: Irony, Allegory, and the 'Prologue to the Manciple's Tale'" in *Studies in the Age of Chaucer* 18 (1996): 55–89. Part of chapter 5 appeared as "Medium autem, et extrema sunt eiusdem generis": Boccaccio and the Shape of Writing," *Exemplaria* 5 (1993): 185–206. An early version of chapter 7 appeared as "Petrarch, Chaucer, and the Making of the Clerk," in *The Performance of Middle English Culture*, ed. Lawrence Clopper, James Paxson, and Sylvia Tomasch (Cambridge: Boydell and Brewer, 1998), 125–41.

Finally, as always, I want to thank Judith Baskin, whose life and love translates me into something more than I am each day. And to our children, Samuel and Shira, to whom I have dedicated this book, no words, certainly not these, can match what you have given me.

1
Introduction: Chaucer's Italian Tradition

Perhaps the two most significant literary events in Chaucer's career were his reading of French and Italian poets. Certainly Boethius was a long-standing influence; Ovid, Virgil, and Statius were all important authors for him. But the contours of Chaucer's verse, its soil, atmosphere, and climate, were formed from vernacular rather than from Latin texts.

Chaucer's experience of French poetry, however, had to have differed greatly from the way he engaged Italian works. Guillaume de Lorris, Jeun de Meung, Machaut, Froissart; in the last half of the fourteenth century, these were the writers whose language and style gave literature its complexion and carriage in the sophisticated courts of England. Fashionable and authoritative, they were the literary forebears Chaucer claimed to secure his standing in aristocratic culture. They were, as Charles Muscatine has famously put it, a tradition, an "école des textes," so to speak, in which Chaucer learned the techniques and the ideology of poetic refinement.[1]

Dante, Boccaccio, and Petrarch, however, were another matter entirely. Although England maintained economic, political, and intellectual contact with Italy throughout the Middle Ages, Chaucer was the only poet who was well acquainted with works by these writers. As controller of the wool custom at the port of London, Chaucer inevitably dealt with merchants from Liguria, Lombardy, and Tuscany on a regular basis; he likely had many opportunities to meet diplomats and soldiers at court as well. These Italians may have proved valuable *ciceroni;* nevertheless, both the country Chaucer visited twice and the literature

---

1. Charles Muscatine, *Chaucer and the French Tradition* (Berkeley and Los Angeles: University of California Press, 1969).

he acquired there probably always retained some sense of remoteness for him. A land without a ruling sovereign, in which independent cities, each differently governed, fiercely competed with one another (and with the pope) for hegemony, surely was unfamiliar terrain.[2] Genoa and Florence, where Chaucer conducted the king's business in 1373, and Milan, where he went with Edward Berkeley in 1378 to discuss "aucunes busoignes touchantes lexploit de nostre guerre," were all larger than London;[3] not only did complex municipal, social, and cultural institutions vary from city to city, their forms had been determined by histories and principles that an Englishman, even if he had ample opportunity to observe them, may still have found peculiar or baffling. In Florence, to let one instance serve for a host of dissimilar practices, powerful aristocrats had long been active participants in trade and commerce; indeed, since 1293, the equally active role they played in communal government depended not only on their membership in one of the city's guilds but on their having relinquished their title as magnates. No doubt the civic structures Chaucer knew afforded some insight into those he observed; Florence's *sesti* and *arti* certainly could be compared to London's wards and misteries. But the scope and the pace of political life in Florence would have amazed any English visitor. The chief executive officer of the commune, the *podestà*—a nobleman from a different city!—was chosen every year. The Signoria, with its eight priors and Gonfaloniere of Justice, was elected every two months. The two colleges that advised them stood for election almost as often: the sixteen standard bearers of the guilds were chosen every three months; the College of the Twelve every fourth month. Twice a year three hundred citizens were elected to the Council of the "Popolo," two hundred to the Council of the Commune. One wonders whether Chaucer, after learning of such activity, returned to England with newfound respect for London's biennial wardmotes, or whether he came to regard the less frenetic selection of the mayor, aldermen,

---

2. In Chaucer's day, many of the merchants in London were from Florence and Lucca. For a good account of Italian and English interactions, see Wendy Childs, "Anglo-Italian Contacts in the Fourteenth Century," in *Chaucer and the Italian Trecento*, ed. Piero Boitani (Cambridge: Cambridge University Press, 1983), 65–87.

3. See Robert Lopez, *The Commercial Revolution of the Middle Ages, 950–1350* (Englewood Cliffs, N.J.: Prentice-Hall, 1971), 93. The quotation is from a warrant to cover the expenses of Chaucer's journey to Milan; see M. Crowe and C. Olson, eds., *Chaucer's Life-Records* (Oxford: Clarendon Press, 1966), 54.

sheriffs, and councillors as quaintly provincial.[4] What is clear is that a city in which butchers and noblemen legislated not only the affairs of their guilds but domestic and foreign policy was not a place where Chaucer would immediately feel at home.[5]

No less important than administrative differences such as these are the cultural differences that attended them. Even a century before Chaucer's journeys a fully developed intellectual class comprised of jurists, notaries, doctors, merchants, and bankers had emerged throughout Italy. These citizens frequently justified their "dignity and their social motivation" by the relation their professions bore to the welfare of their cities.[6] Often poets or chroniclers, they were, as Franco Cardini has said, in many ways "the creators of urban cultural self-consciousness."[7] By the late fourteenth century, literate Florentines of both the greater and lesser guilds were similarly civic-minded, as were a growing number of wellborn who determined their allegiances on political or economic grounds rather than on familial ties.[8] When an

---

4. Of course Chaucer did not attend the London meetings because he never became a citizen of the city. He would, however, have attended the Aldgate wardmotes while he lived there; these met four times a year.

5. By the close of the fourteenth century, no member of those lesser guilds represented in *The Canterbury Tales* seems to have been elected alderman. See Sylvia Thrupp, *The Merchant Class of Medieval London* (1948; rpt. Ann Arbor: University of Michigan Press, 1962), 321–77. See also Paul Strohm, *Social Chaucer* (Cambridge: Harvard University Press, 1989), 89–90, 211. The fact that a city would debate foreign policy was surprising in itself. That that policy was constantly shifting and bewilderingly complex would have made it difficult to understand. To give one instance: when Chaucer visited Florence in 1373, he may have heard that the pope, traditionally the ally of the commune, was yet again seeking its aid in his war against their common enemy, Bernabò Visconti. When Chaucer went to Milan to discuss matters of war in 1378, his hosts would likely have informed him with considerable satisfaction that Florence and the pope were now at war with each other. Petrarch obliquely refers to the earlier war in the letter to Boccaccio that contains his translation of the story of Griselda, which I discuss in chapter 7. The later turn of events, along with the fact that Richard presumably had sent Chaucer to Milan to enlist Visconti's aid, whatever the form that aid might have taken, in England's war against France, should complicate our inclination to position Chaucer as an undeviating proponent of Florentine liberty against the "tirauntz of Lumbardye." For the latter position, see Wallace, *Chaucerian Polity*.

6. See Franco Cardini, "Intellectuals and Culture in Twelfth- and Thirteenth-Century Italy," in *City and Countryside in Late Medieval and Renaissance Italy*, ed. Trevor Dean and Chris Wickham (London: Hambledon Press, 1990), 19.

7. Cardini, "Intellectuals and Culture," 19.

8. Literacy in general was more common in Italy than in England. By the end of the fourteenth century nearly every small town throughout the peninsula had a communally

educated poet wrote in his own tongue, it was increasingly this enfranchised polity that he addressed. Though the relations that determined Chaucer's varying station as an esquire in King Richard's affinity were similarly contractual,[9] though the circle of friends whom Paul Strohm has identified as his core audience were equally intellectual, Chaucer's Londoners do not represent themselves in such terms.[10] Indeed, as David Wallace has noted, London is chiefly conspicuous in Chaucer's works by its absence;[11] it is a city still in search of a civic discourse. Far more than France, then, Italy was a "someplace else"; in all probability the hierarchic and associational forms of polity that Chaucer observed in Italian city-states were an education in chiaroscuro, where the light of what he found familiar was given depth by the shadows of what remained strange.

Another way to say this is that Chaucer's Italy was a translation. As Rita Copeland has shown, the medieval *translatio* was both a hermeneutic and a cultural dialectic: the authority of the source was simultaneously acknowledged and displaced by the copy that made it available for appropriation by different social groups.[12] Throughout this book I will argue that similar negotiations shaped Chaucer's reception of Dante, Boccaccio, and Petrarch; in this case, however, these negotiations will need to account not only for Chaucer's adaptations of his "originals" but for the considerable perplexity they almost certainly caused him as well.

---

appointed and salaried grammar teacher; in Genoa, Chaucer may have heard that the private teachers there had formed their own *arte*. See Peter Denley, "Government and Schools in Late Medieval Italy," in Dean and Wickham, *City and Countryside*, 93–107; and especially Paul Grendler, *Schooling in Renaissance Italy: Literacy and Learning, 1300–1600* (Princeton: Princeton University Press, 1988). On the Genoan guild, see Giovanna Petti Balbi, *L'insegnamento nella Liguria medievale. Scuole, maestri, libri* (Genoa: Tilgher, 1979); and Denley, "Government and Schools," 99.

9. For an analysis of the different positions Chaucer held in the king's affinity, and the nature of the ties that bound him, see Strohm, *Social Chaucer*, 1–46. See also Richard F. Green, *Poets and Princepleasers: Literature and the English Court in the Late Middle Ages* (Toronto: University of Toronto Press, 1980).

10. On Chaucer's core audience, see Strohm, *Social Chaucer*, 47–83. Recently Ann Astell has argued for a clerical audience; see *Chaucer and the Universe of Learning* (Ithaca: Cornell University Press, 1996), 32–60.

11. Wallace, *Chaucerian Polity*, 156–81.

12. Rita Copeland, *Rhetoric, Hermeneutics, and Translation in the Middle Ages* (Cambridge: Cambridge University Press, 1991).

To illustrate what I mean, let me compare apprehending Chaucer's Italian Tradition as a kind of hermeneutic and cultural translation to Hans Robert Jauss's notion of a horizon of expectations and the role it plays in his theory of *Rezeptionästhetik*.[13] For Jauss, no work is singular in itself; it gains individuality only in relation to an undifferentiated background of prevailing conventions and ideologies. This horizon of expectations consists of "pre-understandings of the genre . . . the form and themes of already familiar works, and . . . the opposition between poetic and practical language."[14] Jauss constructs his horizon in this way because he wants it to serve two masters, one phenomenological, the other cultural. He believes that the historical consciousness of a given period never exists as a set of propositions that can be openly stated. The new work for Jauss is therefore like a question, but one that achieves its interrogative status not through its own syntactic structure but from the free-floating set of received ideas against which it is silhouetted. At the moment of its inception, the new work and the preexisting conditions that are its setting are connected only by their contemporaneity; through its reception, however, the work will, to a greater or lesser extent, alter the contextual environment, just as a question can disrupt answers that have become common knowledge by making us aware that they were once questions, discrete responses to an earlier, collective answer. By charting the ways successive readings of a work make it part of a revised horizon of expectations, against which new works will subsequently stand out, Jauss constructs a theory of tradition that he can claim comprehends both aesthetic perception and social history.

There is much that is useful in Jauss's conception of the way a work queries its horizon. In the end, however, the epistemology that underwrites his theory is dubious. As Paul de Man has said, Jauss posits "the condition of existence of a consciousness" that "is not available to this consciousness in a conscious mode."[15] In effect, the name Jauss gives this unavailability that darkens knowledge is history, which he consti-

---

13. See Hans Robert Jauss, *Toward an Aesthetic of Reception*, trans. Timothy Bahti (Minneapolis: University of Minnesota Press, 1982), and *Alterität und Modernität der mittelalterlichen Literatur* (Munich: W. Fink, 1977).

14. Jauss, "Literary History as a Challenge to Literary Theory," in *Toward an Aesthetic*, 22.

15. Paul de Man, introduction to *Toward an Aesthetic*, xii.

tutes as the retrospective marking of a text as a query to preconditions that, paradoxically, will have changed the moment the new work is recognized to have interrogated them. Jauss insists, in other words, that the recovery of medieval texts is a historical process, but one that depends on a transcendental state of mind, which acts in a timeless time where things no longer are what they were but are not yet what they will be. This etiolation of temporality clearly concerns Jauss; he attempts to restore the bulk and heft of social experience to literature by viewing the horizon of expectations as if it were the genre that the work joins by means of its reception at various historical moments. But the law of genre, Derrida says, unmarks the texts that participate without belonging to it.[16] Ultimately, Jauss's *Erwartungshorizont* and his notion of consciousness remain metaphysical inventions; because they are, they hobble his program to historicize aesthetic production and perception.

Perhaps, then, rather than entirely dismissing the notion of a horizon, we should instead release it from the burden of expectations, generic or otherwise. If we do, however, we then are obliged to reconsider its composition and how we say we understand it. Certainly the backdrop that enabled Chaucer to pose the *Troilus* as a question to the land he visited and the literature he acquired there was not limited to an unstructured collection of preunderstandings of standard commonplaces and accepted ideologies. We cannot even say it was a cultural or historical interpretation of such conventions (for all horizons, I would contend, are always interpretations) that a London-based court poet, heavily influenced by his reading of French literature, might have arrived at in the last decades of the fourteenth century. The horizon of the *Troilus* was these things in conversation with Italian literary and cultural formations such as the *stil novo* that themselves were part of traditions Chaucer did not know well, if at all. Within its precincts we have to include the strangeness of the history of the vernacular that Dante had foregrounded in the *Commedia*, that Boccaccio had responded to in the *Filostrato* and *Teseida*, that Petrarch had addressed in the preface to his translation of the story of Griselda.

Chaucer's Italian experience, then, is not circumscribed by one but

---

16. Jacques Derrida, "La Loi du genre/The Law of Genre," in *Glyph* 7, ed. Samuel Weber (Baltimore: Johns Hopkins University Press, 1980), 176–232: "En se marquant de genre, un texte se démarque" (185); in Avital Ronell's translation, "Making genre its mark, a text demarcates itself," "demarcates" conveys the sense of "de-marks."

by two horizons, both of which I propose to construct as intertextual dialogues. The first of these consists of the insights Chaucer gained by reading the three Italian writers not as separate texts but in the light one could throw on the other. For when he could, Chaucer, I will argue, turned to Boccaccio to gloss what was odd in Dante, just as he used Dante to supplement Boccaccio. The second voice in this dialogue gains its tonality from the differences between Chaucer's customs and conventions and those he encountered in Florence and Milan. By establishing a colloquy between these literary and social configurations we can map the aesthetic and cultural topography of the Italian tradition Chaucer made.

To mark the boundaries of this dialogue, however, we have to articulate a different horizon, one that will allow us to ask how Chaucer did not read Dante, Boccaccio, and Petrarch in addition to how he did. This horizon entails our construing these Italian authors in their "native" state, so to speak, by reading Dante as he read himself as well as by reading him as Boccaccio read him. Largely a contest between Latin and vernacular eloquence, this Italian tradition starts with Dante's rejection in the *Vita nuova* of Sicilian and Tuscan attenuations of the manner and matter of Provençe and the startling metaphysical claims he advances for his new poetry of the mind in love. It then moves to Dante's reformation of this "new style" and its triumph over Virgilian Latin in the *Comedy*.[17] From there it passes to the early poems of Boccaccio, who subjected the high-minded conceits of "stilnovism" to a rhetorical inquiry into the ethics of motive and agency. Once Boccaccio fell under Petrarch's sway, however, Dante became the Galeotto through whom he attempted, with a spirit that grew more crabbed as he grew older, to reconcile his vernacular works with the Latin humanism of his master. For his part, Petrarch forged a style that also moves along the doubled trajectories of originality and revision; as we shall see, these trajectories form the context of his translation into Latin of Boccaccio's Griselda, the last tale of the *Decameron*.

This literary-cultural history is, as it were, the "original" that the Italian tradition Chaucer made translates. When we read it, models of interpretation are revealed—Boccaccio's rhetorical ethics, for instance, or Petrarch's historical hermeneutics—that illuminate the modes of intertextuality Chaucer deployed in adaptations like the *Troilus* or "The

---

17. I chart and comment in detail on these developments throughout *Dante's Aesthetics of Being* (Ann Arbor: University of Michigan Press, 1999).

Clerk's Tale." By charting Dante's conversion of the scholastic epistemology of the *stil novo* into his poetics of being, we gain a sense of the *Comedy*'s alterity—how Chaucer's representation of character and selfhood belongs to a different aesthetic synthesis even when Dante's influence is strongest. By examining why Boccaccio used Dante in the ways he did, we can see how social ideology might shape the qualities of fiction one way in Florence and another in London. We install Chaucer as a historically situated reader of the *trecentisti* only when we acknowledge these differences.

I therefore will conceive of Chaucer's Italian Tradition not as the accumulation of localized borrowings from Dante, Boccaccio, or Petrarch, important as these are, but as a translation that emerges out of the two horizons that traverse and demarcate Chaucer's experience of Italy. We will find evidence of this translation less in this or that instance of Dante-like allegory or Boccaccian irony than in the inseparable interplay of allegory and irony in *The Canterbury Tales*. We will see it not so much in the specific changes Chaucer made to Italian texts as in the development of what we might call his urban style, a style that made Chaucer metropolitan in ways Gower or Hoccleve were not. It will be observable more in the array of social discourses that comprise the Clerk than in those that comprise his tale.

Chaucer's Italian Tradition, in other words, is a translation of his translations. In order to give some sense of the models of reading I believe this kind of translation solicits, I will enlist ideas that Walter Benjamin introduced in his essay "Die Aufgabe des Übersetzers." For Benjamin, the translator's task is to express "the central reciprocal relationship between languages."[18] This relationship resides "in the intention underlying each language as a whole—an intention, however, which no single language can attain by itself but which is realized only by the totality of their intentions supplementing each other: pure language."[19] What a language as a whole intends, the end it aims at, is never contained within the language itself. Its intention only becomes apparent when a language is seen in relation to other languages, such as happens when it is translated. But in supplementing the original, a translation displaces its language from any proprietary claim of being the final word. *Brot* and *pain* "intend the same object," Benjamin explains, but disparities in sound and affinity make the way each

---

18. Walter Benjamin, "The Task of the Translator," in *Illuminations*, trans. Harry Zohn (New York: Schocken, 1969), 72.
19. Benjamin, "Task of the Translator," 74.

means "bread" entirely distinct. Because the German and the French word each excite different chains of associations, they cannot be interchanged without disclosing the intention of each language as a whole—how it is pointed, one might say, the particular cultural trajectory along which it moves.[20] The aggregation of such disclosures, which are revelations of discrepancies between the intent to name and the words themselves as conglomerations of consonants and vowels, is what Benjamin calls "reine Sprache." For him, "pure language" does not denote some anagogic fullness of meaning that a transcendent consciousness, in Jauss-like fashion, can encompass, but language that exists as such, completely divorced from the burden of signification. In this state, language is sheerly exterior, the "networking," as Tom Cohen has put it, "of prefigural material linguistic differences, including agencies of sound, letteration, grapheme."[21] The relation of the language of the original to this pure language is the mode in which it expresses its intention, and it is a language's mode of intention that translations translate:

> instead of making itself similar to the meaning, to the *Sinn* of the original, the translation must rather, lovingly and in detail, in its own language, form itself according to the manner of meaning *(Art des Meinens)* of the original, to make both recognizable as the broken parts of the greater [pure] language, just as fragments are the broken parts of a vessel.[22]

In finding a manner of meaning that forms itself according to that of the original, the translation disarticulates the source, estranges it to itself,

---

20. See further de Man's elaboration of Benjamin's point. When *Brot* is translated as *pain*, a fundamental discrepancy is revealed between the intent to name *Brot* and the word *Brot* itself as a conglomeration of sounds and letters. In the context of Benjamin's essay, de Man notes that the word *Brot* causes him to hear *Wein* with it because Hölderlin's *Brot und Wein* seems everywhere present in Benjamin's meditation. *Pain et vin*, the French equivalent, moves in an entirely different direction; if one translates the one phrase with the other, one has translated meaning but ignored the materiality of *Brot*, the mode by which the word means. See "Conclusions: Walter Benjamin's 'The Task of the Translator,'" in *The Resistance to Theory* (Minneapolis: University of Minnesota Press, 1986), 87–91. Like everyone else who has rehearsed Benjamin's theory of translation, I have greatly relied on de Man's essay.
21. Tom Cohen, *Ideology and Inscription* (Cambridge: Cambridge University Press, 1999), 13.
22. This sentence is translated (far more accurately than in Zohn) by de Man in "Conclusions," 91.

by exposing the fact that both texts, by virtue of their passage through pure language, have always been fragments. A succession of parts that remain broken, the translation and translated texts disenchant the fantasy that there was a whole vessel that the one or the other ever constituted, separately or together. Instead of projecting an image of that wholeness, the unassimilable materiality of pure language makes evident "a permanent disjunction which inhabits all languages." Indeed, de Man has shown how as phoneme, as letter, "reine Sprache" resists the inclination to see hermeneutics and poetics as complementary, grammar and significance as compatible, the symbol and what is being symbolized as adequate to each other.[23] In refusing these correlations, translation, Cohen notes, opens the possibility of "passing from one system of manufacturing history and meaning (passive, reactive, mimetic, 'humanist,' . . .)" to another, "at war with the first, yet inhabiting it . . . a pro-active mimesis without model or copy."[24] That is to say, translation for Benjamin is a mode of writing that disrupts the ways mimetic narratives make meaning by installing alternative itineraries of signification next to one another; it suspends received constructions of the past and sets other ways of managing time and memory alongside them.

However we ascribe the disruptiveness, whether to language in its presignifying state or to those immanent aberrations that make a culture "foreign" to itself, the various translations that configure Chaucer's Italian Tradition will illuminate manners of meaning within and across the two horizons that frame it. Since every other argument in my book is subordinate to this one, let me offer a preliminary demonstration here. In the twenty-fourth canto of the *Purgatorio*, Bonagiunta of Lucca asks if he sees before him the man who brought forth the "new rhymes," beginning with "Donne ch'avete intelletto d'amore." Dante responds by describing what we well might call the mode of intention of the *Comedy*:

I' mi son un che, quando
Amor mi spira, noto, e a quel modo
ch'e' ditta dentro, vo significando.

(52–54)

---

23. De Man explains the first of these disjunctions in his discussion of *Brot* and *pain*, "Conclusions," 87–91.
24. Cohen, *Inscription and Ideology*, 11.

[I am one who, when Love inspires me, takes note, and in the manner he dictates within goes signifying.]²⁵

Although Bonagiunta immediately says he understands this answer, almost everyone else has welcomed some explanation. Before a reader tries to unpack these words, however, he very likely will be struck by how uncomfortably the moods they juxtapose consort with one another.²⁶ On one hand, by so obviously stage-managing the conversation, Dante appears to trumpet his own achievement in an extraordinary transformation of poetic discourse; the style he proclaims here defines him not merely as a poet but as a living person. On the other, he seems to disclaim all title to authorship in this new aesthetics of being. Such a display of prideful deference is not unfamiliar to Dante's readers; from the *Vita nuova* on, this posture has often been the one he adopts when he discusses his verse. Nevertheless, Dante has lodged together attitudes that usually live far apart; given the solemnity of the setting in which he answers, he could not allow his audience to think he was being ironic, as we tend to think Chaucer is when he simultaneously flaunts and deprecates his craftsmanship. In the next chapter, I will show that Dante in fact secures his integrity as existential allegory against the subversions of irony by marking himself as a twofold translation. An "original," constituted by Love's inspiration, is translated by Dante's noting, which, as we will see, textualizes it; this event then is itself translated when Dante textualizes himself as embodied signification according to the mode of meaning of Amor's inspiration. Even so, the yoking of arrogance and humility remains to unsettle the reader; its untowardness is a signal, I will argue, of an abiding irresolution that frustrates Dante's intent to unify himself as poet and poem.²⁷

However, the most vivid evidence Chaucer had that not even Dante could be master of his own mode of signification probably came from Boccaccio's translation of it. At the end of the *Filostrato*, the narrator revisits the declaration to Bonagiunta as he contemplates the genesis of his own poetic performance:

---

25. Here and throughout, citations and translations of the *Comedy* are from Charles Singleton, ed. and trans., *The Divine Comedy* (Princeton: Princeton University Press).

26. For a full discussion of Dante's declaration, see *Dante's Aesthetics of Being*, 78–95. I will treat this passage as a translation in the next chapter.

27. The yoking of contrary attitudes renders as a matter of temperament the paradox that for Teodolinda Barolini characterizes the *Comedy*'s *modo di dire:* "quel ver c'ha faccia di menzogna" [that truth that has the face of a lie] (*Inf.* 16:124). See further her analysis in *The Undivine Comedy* (Princeton: Princeton University Press, 1992), 58ff.

Sogliono i lieti tempi esser cagione
di dolci versi, canzon mia pietosa,
ma te nella mia grave afflizione
ha tratto amor dell'anima dogliosa
contra natura, né ne so ragione
se non venisse da virtù nascosa,
spirata e mossa dal sommo valore
di nostra donna nel trafitto core.

Costei, sì com'io so, ché spesso il sento,
mi può far nulla e molto da più fare
che io non sono, e quinci l'argomento
della cagion del tuo lungo parlare
credo che nasca . . .

(9.1–2)[28]

[Happy times usually produce sweet poems, pity-filled song of mine, but in my heavy affliction Love has unnaturally drawn you forth from my sorrowful soul. Nor can I account for this, unless it came from a hidden virtue, breathed and moved in the transfixed heart by the highest valor of our lady. She, as I know, for I often feel it, can make me nothing and far more than I am: this I believe is the reason for your long speaking . . .]

When Love inspires Boccaccio, it seems, almost in a programmatic way, to engender effects that are exactly the opposite of those it brings about in Dante. If a power, "spirata e mossa dal sommo valore di nostra donna," was indeed responsible for the production of the poem, the narrator neither knows nor notes it: the "virtù" was and continues to be "nascosa." If such power was not responsible, however, the work is a miracle anyway, but of a sour sort, since it is "contra natura" that Amor, who fosters sweet poems in happy times, should have elicited this love song from his sorrows. In either case the *Filostrato* is a bittersweet prodigy, begotten by one or another prime mover, whose influence has made its existence inexplicable to the man who wrote it, though for reasons that appear to be at cross-purposes.

The speaker then confesses that his own being hangs on a similar

---

28. I quote from *Tutte le opere di Giovanni Boccaccio,* ed. Vittore Branca, vol. 2 (Florence: Mondadori, 1964).

contradiction in himself. He may be uncertain about how his poem came to be, but he is sure that his lady elevates and annihilates him in turn: "sì com'io so, ché spesso il sento, / mi può far nulla e molto da più fare / che io non sono." Yet even this conviction is at once cast into the subjunctive and strengthened when he says he believes ("credo che nasca") that his alternate experiences of extinction and bliss are in fact ("e *quinci* l'argomento") the efficient cause of his "lungo parlare."

Like Dante, Boccaccio would establish a resemblance between himself as a person and the poem that Amor has drawn from his soul. Decidedly unlike Dante, however, he is not about to recruit this resemblance as evidence that human existence and his writing ultimately share the same ontology. Boccaccio's motives are far more selfish. His narrator juxtaposes antithetical qualities in both himself and his poem, I will argue in chapter 5, because the opposition rehearses his divided feelings for Filomena, the lady to whom he writes the poem, who has removed herself from Naples, where the narrator is, and has gone to Sannio. By identifying Filomena with Criseida, he can plead in the same breath that, like Troiolo, his unwavering love makes him worthy of her return, and that if she does not, she, like her Trojan surrogate, is a whore. Prosecuting these desires in tandem is, to say the least, underhanded; even Boccaccio's narrator feels he has to offer some justification for writing the *Filostrato,* which is the instrument he hopes will achieve his ends. His strategy, these concluding verses suggest, is to conscript Dante's poetics of love and turn the abashed pride that is its effect into high-minded cover for his lust and his anger. Of course, the moment the narrator chose to say, "I love you, I hate you" at once, irony became his language's intentional mode. The *congedo* is quite explicit about this. Filomena can make him nothing and something far more than he is. This antiphrasis, in his eyes, becomes "l'argomento della cagion" of the poem—not the cause, but the argument of the cause, the persuasive structure by which it expresses itself as cause: in short, its manner of meaning.[29] My argument will be that when the *Filostrato* translates Dante's metaphysics into the rhetoric of erotic persuasion, it also disarticulates the *Comedy*'s language of love by repatriating the irony it had tried to banish. Boccaccio exposes the fact that a sexual

---

29. *Argomento,* of course, often means "subject" or "topic" in medieval Italian. In the *congedo,* however, and especially in this phrase, where it is coupled with "cagion," it seems likely that Boccaccio was pointing to the more rhetorical sense of "argument" as persuasive structure.

potency animates Dante's allegoresis from within, always ready to convert the spirit into a pander for the flesh. Indeed, when Boccaccio transformed his poem's moral—his concluding stanzas begin as a warning against the evil appetites of amorous desire but quickly turn into an "ars amatoria" (8.29–33)—he revealed what Dante knew he specifically had to repress in order for him to speak the words he speaks to Bonagiunta. For Dante's manifesto, as I will show in the next chapter, itself rests on two prior revisionary acts, his translation of Ovidian metamorphosis and his suppression of Ovid's irony.

Chaucer never formally translated Dante's words to Bonagiunta; at the end of the *Troilus*, however, which is a translation of the *Filostrato*, he did quote the *Comedy*:

> Thow oon, and two, and thre, eterne on lyve,
> That regnest ay in thre, and two, and oon,
> Uncircumscript, and al maist circumscrive,
> Us from visible and invisible foon
> Defende, and to thy mercy, everichon,
> So make us, Jesus, for thi mercy digne,
> For love of mayde and moder thyn benigne.

In the *Paradiso*, just before Dante ascends to the heaven of Mars, Beatrice asks Thomas Aquinas to tell the pilgrim whether the light of heaven will always remain with the blessed the way it is now, and if it will, how their sight will not be hurt by it after they have recovered their bodies. When Thomas answers, he explains, with a voice perhaps like Gabriel's when he spoke to Mary, that their love will always radiate such a garment around the redeemed, but that once they are clothed again in their flesh, they will be more acceptable for being complete, and the light God gives them will be greater. This response is intriguing, less for its content, which is unexceptionably orthodox, than for the reader's perception of it. Thomas seems to say yes and no: the light of love will always be as it now is, but after the resurrection it will be different. In fact he says yes and yes: the light of love will always be the light of love, but there will be more of it.

Chaucer ignored both the manner and matter of this interchange. Before Thomas responds, however, the spirits in the circle of the Sun, inflamed by Beatrice's question, revolve with added joy and sing the praises of the Trinity three times in the *terzina* that Chaucer's first three lines translate word for word. Dante tries to evoke the increased rapture of this dance and song in a striking manner; he represents the reason why he is unable to represent it:

> li santi cerchi mostrar nova gioia
> nel torneare e ne la mira nota.
> Qual si lamenta perché qui si moia
> per viver colà sù, non vide quive
> lo refrigerio de l'etterna ploia.
> Quell' uno e due e tre che sempre vive
> e regna sempre in tre e 'n due e 'n uno,
> non circunscritto, e tutto circunscrive . . .
>
> (14.23–30)

[The holy circles showed new joy in their revolving and in their marvelous melody. Whoso laments because we die here to live there on high has not seen there the refreshment of the eternal rain. That One and Two and Three which ever lives and reigns in Three and Two and One, uncircumscribed and circumscribing all things . . .]

On earth ("qui") the only way to understand the souls' new joy is by analogy to the feeling we have when we regain some cherished thing that we thought was irretrievably lost. The access of happiness can be so exhilarating, every sadness is obliterated by it, even the sadness of death. A Christian can only suppose that the greatest joy of this sort will come when the body is rejoined with its soul. But in heaven ("quive"), there is no absence or sorrow; after the resurrection there will be an intensification of a bliss that from a worldly point of view already is absolute. Reason dictates that "more" cannot be added to "most"; Dante's impatience with those who lament their deaths, which adumbrates the "no" we hear in Thomas's exposition, reflects the inability of human understanding to measure the blessedness of beatitude. That impatience with our limited condition, however, is transcended as soon as it is acknowledged; Dante predicates it on a fully embodied experience that resides entirely in the capacity of tropes of faith to convert no to yes. They only grieve their mortality who have not *seen*, with their living eyes, "lo refrigerio de l'etterna ploia"—no one, that is, who is alive, everyone who reads the figures of the *Comedy* as Dante intends, by inscribing them on the fleshy tables of the heart.

Chaucer undoubtedly chose to conclude the *Troilus* with Dante's hymn in order to underscore the Christian moral he feels readers should draw from the poem. But he does not write this moral as one who has seen the refreshment of the eternal rain. He writes as one who believes in it yet still mourns Troilus's death. His narrator does not summon up the sanctification of the flesh; he asks instead for God's protection against foes who prey on its lamentable weakness. His eyes are still watching Criseida, who, betrayed and betrayer, is such a foe and one who has always stood in need of such defense.

Along with his lauds, then, Chaucer has also translated Dante's mode of meaning. For him earthly flaws, and the metaphors that are their linguistic equivalents, are not made "umbriferi prefazi" (*Par.* 30.78), whose sole purpose as shadow-bearing prefaces is to hint by their imperfections at a superabundance of being, beyond the power of words to convey, which abolishes every ill flesh is heir to. Chaucer remains in the world, where circumstance and judgment are always in dialogue, each querying the other, even after all the verdicts have been recorded. He remains, that is to say, in the world of motive and history, which is the world of Boccaccio's *Filostrato*. Of all the passages from the *Comedy* Chaucer could have adopted to end his tragedy, he chose this description of the Trinity because the uncircumscribed union of Father, Son, and Love breathed between them provides a perspective that reveals how very circumscribed the love of Troilus, Criseida, and Pandarus's huff and shuttle between them really is. In a similar fashion, in place of Dante's stress on Gabriel's annunciation ("una voce modesta, / forse qual fu da l'angelo a Maria"), Chaucer invokes Mary as "mayde and moder," recalling Criseida, who also combined two incompatible natures in one person, not to excoriate her, but in a prayer for mercy that obligates the audience to ponder one last time her failure to match a woman who was matchless.

Chaucer's Englishing of Dante, one sees, is really a translation of Boccaccio's own rewriting of the *Comedy*'s mode of meaning; the morality of the *Troilus*'s peroration is certainly Dantesque, but the narrator's continuing disposition to see the same event from different sides is an outgrowth of the *Filostrato*. At the close of Chaucer's poem, however, allegory no longer functions as a screen for personal gratification, which is what Boccaccio had threatened to make it; neither is it the master discourse it is in Dante. Instead, contradiction and metaphor translate each other's manner of meaning: a contrary stands as a figure of its opposite and cancels it. The continuous adjustments in the *Troilus* that make Chaucer's negotiations between both modes a translation of Boccaccio's and Dante's comprise one aspect of what I am calling Chaucer's Italian Tradition.

The colloquy on the terrace of the gluttons in Purgatory is perhaps the most prominent of many places in the *Comedy* where Dante insists that we read his poetics in Italian. Because he feels his artistic development and the history of his salvation are both enunciations of the Word, Dante constitutes himself as an allegory in which outward forms of expression and inner content of being are analogies of one another. The form of Dante's expression, we learn in the *Purgatorio* and elsewhere, is Virgilian Latin that goes speaking the soul's redemption in the vernacular of Florence. As a Christian poet who wrote in English, as poet of the *Troilus* and *The Canterbury Tales*, Chaucer had to have been deeply impressed by this assertion. Indeed, I am not alone in feeling that Chaucer thoroughly appreciated the classical foundation of Dante's Christian *sermo*, which the presence of Virgil and the converted Statius, who witness the exchange with Bonagiunta, is meant to signal.[30] I will in fact propose that Chaucer reworked Dante's synthesis in the Manciple's prologue and tale by joining together Ovidian irony and Pauline allegories of conversion. But how was Chaucer to recover the Italian element Dante locates at the heart of his poetic selfhood? What was the *stil novo* Bonagiunta goes on to mention? When Chaucer visited Florence, it was out of style, nor do we have any indication that he knew the *Vita nuova*, which chronicles how Dante became its foremost practitioner. My contention is that the answers Chaucer found to these questions—questions the *Comedy* makes difficult to avoid—he found as much in Boccaccio as in the "sacro poema."

On Sunday, October 23, 1373, Boccaccio presented the first of his "esposizioni sopra la Comedia di Dante"; although Chaucer had left Florence some six months before, in a sense he was in the church of Santo Stefano in Badia that day. Like many members of the audience, Chaucer stood in need of a literary commentary. Nothing Machaut or any other French poet had written prepared him to meet the interpretive challenges of Dante's answer to Bonagiunta. But in the *Filostrato*

---

30. See especially in this regard Winthrop Wetherbee, *Chaucer and the Poets: An Essay on Troilus and Criseyde* (Ithaca: Cornell University Press, 1984).

and *Teseida* he would discover a critique of poems like "Donne ch'avete"; insofar as Chaucer saw a representation of love in which phantasm and spirit played a far more profound role than they did in French poetry, a window to the "new style" opened for him. Chaucer could have followed Dante's prompting and have reconstructed a version of his sacramental poetics from these texts; whatever that version was, however, its Italian element was mediated by Boccaccio.

As it happens, the *Filostrato* did bring Chaucer into direct contact with the *stil novo:* in lamenting the loss of Criseida, Troiolo recites almost word for word Cino da Pistoia's most famous *canzone*, "La dolce vista e 'l bel guardo soave." In the *Troilus*, however, Chaucer severely truncated this passage: five stanzas of Boccaccio's *ottava rima* became the seven lines of the "Canticus Troili" in book 5. The reduction is important for what it implies about the translational dynamics of the tradition Chaucer made.

At first glance, the abbreviation seems to support the notion that Chaucer would have found the "new style" problematic no matter how well he had known it. Chaucer's problem, however, may not have been just the *stil novo* but the form Boccaccio had given it in the *Filostrato*. From Criseida's first appearance, Troiolo's pursuit of her is blatantly carnal; for this reason, the perceptual conceits of Cino's *canzone*—the "spirito angoscioso," the loss of power of the soul's faculties in the face of her "gentil atto di salute"—these conceits, as I say, though heartfelt, sound off-key coming from his lips. This dissonance is deliberate; in keeping with the rhetorical protocol of arguing both sides of a proposition, Boccaccio has his characters consistently endorse the sublimations of the *stil novo* and just as consistently sexualize its intellectual arrogations. Chaucer certainly heard the dissonance; he dealt with it by making his Troilus someone who could sing Cino's poem without striking a false note. Yet Chaucer truncates the song nonetheless, even though the *canzone* is one Dante could have written. In his *proemio*, Boccaccio explicitly framed the *Filostrato* as a debate between the poetry of the mind and the body; at the very moment Chaucer would join it on Dante's side, he reveals he is "somdel deef" to the *Commedia*'s vernacular poetics. As much as Chaucer would continue to read Boccaccio through Dante, Boccaccio remained instrumental to his reading of Dante. The long-winded eagle of *The House of Fame* on one side, the closing prayers of the *Troilus* on the other, are both translations that reveal modes of meaning in the now worshipful, now irreverent appropriation of the *Comedy* that Chaucer found in the *Filostrato* and the *Teseida*.

If Chaucer chose not to differentiate his prince from Boccaccio's by turning him into a Dante who thinks Criseyde is Beatrice, we should ask where Troilus's virtue did come from. The most persuasive answer, I think, is the one C. S. Lewis gave long ago: Chaucer ennobled Troilus by imbuing him with the sensibilities of fourteenth-century French verse.[31] To counteract Boccaccio's license and the social coarsening it implied, Chaucer imported the values of texts in which, as Jacqueline Cerquiglini-Toulet has noted, an overwhelming nostalgia for order and continuity constantly took the form of pensive melancholy and the adoring return to older texts as places of refuge.[32] In an era of war, plague, a contracting economy, and an increasingly influential commercial class, these were the qualities aristocrats in France and England prized in the literature that represented them. By reproducing these values in the *Troilus*, Chaucer shows how much the Italian tradition he made was shaped by the French tradition he inherited.

Once he had read Dante and Boccaccio, however, Chaucer had to view the matter of France with new eyes. However much the *Filostrato*'s earthiness shocked Chaucer, the courtly nostalgia of the *Troilus* is so hedged about with its own impossibility, no one could suppose it had a French source. Would Chaucer have made "The Knight's Tale" the critique of chivalric identity in England Lee Patterson has argued it is, if Froissart had written the *Teseida*?[33] No one believes Gower would have been Chaucer had he read Dante and Boccaccio, but the fact that he did not is one reason why their poems differ in the ways they do.

In this way, Chaucer was made a closer observer of his own literary and cultural practices as much by what he found strange (and estranging) in Florence and her writers as by what he could immediately assimilate. One year after Chaucer had returned from his first Italian journey he moved to London to take up his post as controller. Even though he would maintain his ties to the court, Chaucer was now an

---

31. C. S. Lewis, "What Chaucer Really Did to the *Filostrato*," *Essays and Studies* 17 (1932), 56–75.

32. Jacqueline Cerquiglini-Toulet, *La couleur de la mélancolie: La fréquentation des livres ai XIVe siècle, 1300–1415* (Paris: Hatier, 1993).

33. Lee Patterson, *Chaucer and the Subject of History* (Madison: University of Wisconsin Press, 1991), 165–230.

esquire *en service;* the change in the nature of the relation that bound him to the king may well have made Chaucer take note of the differences between the social habits and institutions of the city and those of Edward III's household, where he had been page and esquire before. But from the time Chaucer moved to Aldgate in 1374, London-life itself would not seem quite what it had seemed in his youth. Chaucer had, after all, just returned from Florence; although his time there was brief, what Chaucer saw initiated a dialogue between his and Italian urban culture. If the fact that Dante presumed a municipal rather than a courtly readership was at first a surprise, it would become an ever more understandable and empowering one. As London increasingly impinges on his poetry, even if only as a launching platform and point of return, what we can call the civic mode of intention of Chaucer's Italian tradition was formed in the space between his surprise and his understanding.

From this point of view, the Italian tradition Chaucer made is a transnational conversation that is as much social as it is literary. This conversation took place when he brought the civic and cultural canons he had observed in Italy into contact with those that pertained to his standing as a man with ties to city and court. The impulse that prompted Chaucer to gather his pilgrims at an inn in Southwerk is, in this sense, Florentine, though his guildsmen and their cook, his merchant, his manciple, are thoroughly English.

This dialogue becomes a translation, however, when we read it against Boccaccio's reception of Dante and "stilnovism," a reception that is also social and literary, but in an entirely different manner. We have already seen that in early works like the *Filostrato* Boccaccio treated the conceits of the "new style" as if they already required updating. Perhaps he sensed before he returned to Florence from Naples in 1341 that the city Dante was forced to leave four decades earlier in large part no longer existed. That Florence was unquestionably only a dim memory twenty years later, when Boccaccio left the commune again to retire to Certaldo. Hard times and economic retraction had led to the failure of leading commercial houses even before the plague; the *gente nuova,* whose influx from the countryside Dante deplored, had permanently altered the city's political landscape; black and white had become little more than colors to partisans of the Parte Guelfa. By the time Boccaccio returned to Florence to begin his lectures on the *Comedy,* the literary public Erich Auerbach says Dante created was, from one point of view, superannuated, since the style that created it, to the extent that it was related to the *stil novo*, had long since lost its currency.³⁴ In the meantime, Petrarch had plotted a new course for the vernacular lyric; among the learned, Ciceronian eloquence had begun to contest Aristotelian philosophy as virtue's discourse of choice. All these factors figure in Boccaccio's various reconstructions of Dante. Though the central texts here are the *Trattatello in laude di Dante* and the *De casibus virorum illustrium*, which I will treat in separate chapters, we can glimpse how the modes of making meaning in Florence differed from those in London by comparing a series of sonnets Boccaccio wrote to an unknown detractor of his lectures on Dante and Chaucer's "Envoy to Scogan."

Boccaccio's squibs take part in a long-standing literary tradition known as the *tenzone*; indeed, Dante's own response to Bonagiunta is enmeshed in two such contentious poetic exchanges, his own with Forese Donati, and Bonagiunta's with the founder of the "sweet new style," Guido Guinizzelli.³⁵ In each of his sonnets, Boccaccio acknowledges the validity of his critic's complaint that an unbridgeable gulf separates the excellences of Dante's "alto ingegno" and the meanness of the rabble to whom Boccaccio now reveals them:

S'io ho le Muse vilmente prostrate
nelle fornice del vulgo dolente,
e le lor parte occulte ho palesate
alla feccia plebeia scioccamente . . .

(CXXII, 1–4)³⁶

[If I have vilely prostituted the Muses in the brothels of the lamentable masses, and have foolishly laid open their secret parts to the dregs and the scum . . .]

It is a moot point, Boccaccio continues, that his interlocutor reproves his effrontery, for Apollo himself has taken vengeance by afflicting him with a malady that has turned him from a man into a goatskin. Dropsy and ill health, however, seem not to have been sufficient retribution for

---

34. Erich Auerbach, *Literary Language and Its Public in Late Antiquity and the Early Middle Ages*, trans. Ralph Manheim (Princeton: Princeton University Press, 1965), 312.
35. I discuss these *tenzoni* in *Dante's Aesthetics of Being*, 82–88, 97–102.
36. All quotations are from Giovanni Boccaccio, *Le Rime, L'Amorosa Visione, La Caccia di Diana*, ed. Vittore Branca (Bari: Laterza, 1938).

his carping gadfly; in a second sonnet, Boccaccio evidently felt he needed to mount a more thoroughgoing defense for undertaking his "lettura":

> Se Dante piange, dove ch'el si sia,
> che li concetti del suo alto ingegno
> aperti sieno stati al vulgo indegno,
> come tu di', della lettura mia,
> ciò mi dispiace molto, né mai fia
> ch'io non ne porti verso me disdegno:
> come ch'alquanto pur me ne ritegno,
> perché d'altrui, non mia, fu tal follia.
>
>   Vana speranza e vera povertade
> e l'abbagliato senno delli amici
> e gli lor prieghi ciò mi fecer fare.
> Ma non goderan guar di tal derrate
> questi ingrati meccanici, nimici
> d'ogni leggiadro e caro adoperare.
>
> (CXXIII)

[If Dante weeps, wherever he may be, that the conceptions of his high genius have been revealed to the masses unworthy, as you say, of my lectures, I am extremely sorry, nor will I ever not scorn myself for it, even though I hold myself only partially responsible, since such folly originated not with me but with others. Vain hope and real poverty and the blinded wisdom of friends and their prayers for it made me do it. But they will not enjoy such wares for long, these ungrateful mechanicals, enemies of every refined and precious act.]

Although Boccaccio again agrees with the charges filed against him, the many allusions to Dante in this sonnet at the same time launch an ironic counterstatement against his inquisitor. The masses to whom he lectures are undoubtedly rude and uncouth, but such captious attacks on him hardly emanate from a noble soul. By mentioning the "blinded wisdom" [l'abbagliato senno] of his friends, Boccaccio alludes to Dante's interchange with the Sienese alchemist Capocchio, who includes among the wastrels of his city "l'Abbagliato [che] suo senno proferse" [Abbagliato (who) showed his wit] (*Inf.* 29.132). Boccaccio implies that his critic's censures are equally senseless, while his immoderate tenacity—Boccaccio had to write at least three replies—is shameful. Not only are Capocchio's words in the *Comedy* a response to Dante's opinion that even the French are less vain than the Sienese, they also stand as a prelude to the contretemps between Master Adamo and Sinon, whose extended give-and-take fascinates Dante to his regret in the next canto. Boccaccio subtly associates his controversialist's prolonging the debate with the boorishness of the rabble he despises.

A complicated set of competing social and cultural commitments underlies these ripostes. The "others" who must share in the folly of the lectures are not merely Boccaccio's friends, whose sense, if "abbagliato," at least was dimmed by kind concern for him, but the Council of the Commune and the Signory, who unanimously approved a fee of one hundred florins for the readings, a rate one chronicler called remarkable.[37] Their judgment, Boccaccio implies, was not at all fuddled; in endorsing the yearlong presentations, they were affirming that the dedicated study of literature and philosophy is as much a public virtue as a private pursuit. The noun Boccaccio chooses to characterize his labor is "adoperare." Although not an uncommon term, I would argue that the word resonates here with its scholastic overtones; the *esposizioni* on the *Comedy* are the end product of an intellect that has worked to realize a specific goal. The adjectives that modify this operation of the mind, however, situate it in the social world by conferring nobility on it. Boccaccio uses "leggiadro," I would suggest, to invoke Dante's "Poscia ch'Amor del tutto m'ha lasciato," the great *canzone* on *leggiadria* or aristocratic charm and gracefulness. By "caro," Boccaccio clearly means the worth of industrious erudition. For all their disillusionment, these sonnets still register a revival of Boccaccio's often dashed hope that the roles of poet and citizen might yet prove compatible in his city. That the masses proved themselves vulgarians did not at all compromise his identification with the political structures of Flor-

---

37. The chronicler is Filippo Valori; quoted in Branca, *Boccaccio: The Man and His Works*, trans. Richard Monges and Dennis McAuliffe (New York: New York University Press, 1976), 182. The document that records the honorarium, from the account books of "la camera del comune di Firenze," is printed by Giuseppe Gerola, "Alcuni documenti inediti per la biografia del Boccaccio," *Giornale storico della letteratura italiana* 32 (1898): 355–60.

ence. In agreeing to deliver the lectures, Boccaccio had every right to see himself a latter-day Cicero revivifying the precepts of the *De officiis*. On the other hand, the Petrarchan contempt for the "meccanici," by whom Boccaccio means all guildsmen who ply any of the practical arts, directly contradicts his allegiance to Florentine republicanism. The particular scorn of the final lines simultaneously elevates Boccaccio to the rank of a cultural magnate and disenfranchises the artisanal populace from participating in humanistic endeavors. For them the commentaries on Dante are no more than "derrate." The expression, as Ricci notes in glossing the word as "merce" (wares), is "grossolana."[38] Its coarseness comes from the way it transforms the refinement of Boccaccio's values into the crude cravings of getting and spending. Guildsmen who live only to satisfy their hunger for wealth are peasant-minded even if they reside in the city; such vulgarians could never prize the sustenance of work that nurtures the soul, for in their churlish ears, "leggiadro" can only mean "profitable," "caro" "costly."[39] These sentiments, then, amount to something more than Boccaccio biting the hand that was feeding him. Chaucer was quite capable of harboring class snobberies, but the blend of communal disenchantments and intellectual superciliousness that produced this brand of contempt for the "vulgo indegno" was very different from anything he expressed.

Precisely because the modes of meaning in Boccaccio's sonnets are peculiarly Florentine, they can provide a context for us to read the analogies of a poem even as topically English as Chaucer's "Envoy to Scogan."[40] The premise of this *jeu d'esprit* is that Scogan has left his

---

38. In Giovanni Boccaccio, *Opere in versi*, ed. Pier Giorgio Ricci (Milan: Ricciardi, 1965), 15.

39. In this context, "derrate," I would argue, probably carries its modern sense of "foodstuffs."

40. Here and throughout my citations from Chaucer are from *The Riverside Chaucer*, ed. Larry Benson, 3d ed. (Boston: Houghton Mifflin, 1987). For commentary on the "Envoy to Scogan," see the variorum edition, *The Minor Poems*, ed. George Pace and Alfred David, vol. 5 of *A Variorum Edition of the Works of Geoffrey Chaucer* (Norman: University of Oklahoma Press, 1982), 149–51. In particular I am indebted to Alfred David, "Chaucer's Good Counsel to Scogan," *Chaucer Review* 3 (1968–69): 265–74; and to R. T. Lenaghan, "Chaucer's *Envoy to Scogan*: The Uses of Literary Conventions," *Chaucer Review* 10 (1975–76): 46–61. See also P. M. Kean, *Chaucer and the Making of English Poetry* (London: Routledge, 1972), 33–38; Strohm, *Social Chaucer*, 72–75; Jay Rudd, "Chaucer's *Envoy to Scogan*: 'Tullius Kyndnesse' and the Law of Kynde," *Chaucer Review* 20 (1986): 323–30; John Scattergood, "Old Age, Love, and Friendship in Chaucer's *Envoy to Scogan*," *Nottingham Medieval Studies* 35 (1991): 92–101.

lady's service because she has ignored him: "for thy lady sawgh nat thy distresse, / Therfore thow yave hir up at Michelmesse." This profanation of Love's law has already brought in its wake a veritable distempering of the spheres:

> Tobroken been the statutz hye in hevene
> That creat weren eternally to dure,
> Syth that I see the bryght goddis sevene
> Mowe wepe and wayle, and passioun endure,
> As may in erthe a mortal creature.
> Allas, fro whennes may thys thing procede,
> Of which errour I deye almost for drede?
>
> By word eterne whilom was it shape
> That fro the fyfte sercle, in no manere,
> Ne myght a drope of teeres doun escape.
> But now so wepith Venus in hir spere
> That with hir teeres she wol drenche us here.
>
> (1–12)

Besides these torrential downpours, Scogan's blasphemy will also, Chaucer fears, cause Cupid to take appropriate vengeance not only on the reprobate himself but on those who associate with him. Love will pay Scogan's lady the compliment of imitating her by ignoring them:

> He wol nat with his arwes been ywroken
> On the, ne me, ne noon of oure figure;
> We shul of him have neyther hurt ne cure.
>
> (26–28)

But if Cupid banishes them by indifference, Chaucer says he will have no reward for his efforts to help folk succeed in love: Love will exile ("the wreche of Love")

> alle hem that ben hoor and rounde of shap,
> That ben so likly folk in love to spede.
> Than shal we for oure labour have no mede.
>
> (31–33)

Completely cut off from the god, he will be unable, one supposes, to write poems that can give lovers hope by persuasively depicting the hurts and cures they experience.

This is the basis of the indictment Chaucer brings against his friend's conduct. As soon as he gives voice to it, he imagines Scogan will respond by claiming that his recanted devotion has offended nothing more than Chaucer's poetic fancy: "Lo, olde Grisel lyst to ryme and playe!" (35). Chaucer replies that he is serious:

> Nay, Scogan, say not so, for I m'excuse—
> God helpe me so!—in no rym, dowteles,
> Ne thynke I never of slep to wake my muse,
> That rusteth in my shethe stille in pees.
> While I was yong, I put hir forth in prees;
> But al shal passe that men prose or ryme;
> Take every man hys turn, as for his tyme.
>
> (36–42)

Chaucer does not, I think, claim here that he has altogether stopped publishing his verse (something the "Envoy" itself would immediately contradict); rather I imagine he is saying that since he has grown "hoor and rounde of shap," he has given up writing the kind of lyrics he wrote when he was young and in love himself. By assuming this stance, Chaucer can adopt the same unsentimental attitude toward his muse that Scogan has adopted toward his lady. He too has ceased to call on her, since age has simply eliminated his need to seek her inspiration. Unlike Scogan, however, Chaucer has remained true to Cupid, whom he still invokes when he writes for the sake of other lovers. Chaucer therefore can tell Scogan, in effect, that poetry may be "of imagination compact," but composing it has material consequences. Even though the "diluge of pestilence" he attributes to Venus's tears may indeed be a figure of speech, the ruin it represents is no less damaging than that caused by the storms that drenched London in 1390 or 1393.[41] If Love turns his back on Chaucer, Scogan's recreancy will deprive him of

---

41. On the controversy over the date of these rains, see the *Variorum*, 155–56. I like Fisher's suggestion that Chaucer may have had in mind the great storm of March 1390, since it would coincide with the idea that Chaucer, who oversaw the repair of damaged docks and wharves at Greenwich, was personally affected by Scogan's offense and therefore entitled to ask him to intercede on his behalf. See *The Complete Poetry and Prose of Geoffrey Chaucer*, ed. John H. Fisher, 2d ed. (New York: Holt, 1989), 703.

"mede" for his "labour." The loss for Chaucer will be real—as real as the request that issues from it as the poem's envoy. "Put in a good word for me at Windsor," he concludes; by doing so Scogan might obtain a favor at the king's court to balance the harm Chaucer will incur if he is banned from Cupid's because his friend has transgressed.

The primary conceit of "Scogan," the disillusioned lover, is entirely conventional; Machaut's ballade "Puis qu'Amours faut" has been suggested as an analogue.[42] As a verse epistle, the "Envoy" recalls Deschamps's "balades en manière de lettre." Nothing in the French tradition, however, matches either the verve or the local particularity of Chaucer's dismay at the consequences of Scogan's inconstancy. One need not look for a specific Italian source either, although the opening lines of the poem may echo Virgil's words to Cato at the beginning of the *Purgatorio*.[43] But the inspiration to have Scogan cast a brusque decision to cut his losses, so businesslike and everyday it invites the specificity of a date for its execution, as a ruinous violation of cosmic order and eternal law owes something to Chaucer's translation of Italy; one way he became a master of this sort of epic exaggeration of the quotidian was by reading Dante and Boccaccio together.

Neither Boccaccio nor Dante, however, could have written this poem. Though it was a commonplace for Love's servants to swear their loyalty to their lord in feudal terms, indenturing themselves for life, Scogan clearly thinks he has made himself part of Cupid's retinue by contract, which expired on September 29, Michaelmas last, and which he has no intention of renewing. Scogan has converted one idea of retainership, permanent and unaffected by circumstance, into one in which it is renegotiable and based on the self-interest of both parties. Both forms of service, as Strohm has shown, coexisted at the end of the fourteenth century in England;[44] Chaucer's appointment as clerk of the king's works in 1389 and to a royal commission "of walls and ditches" in 1390, the year a storm caused great damage along the Thames, were of the second sort. But Chaucer subtly evokes the abiding nature of the first by locating Scogan at Windsor as a member of Richard's household. These social relations give Chaucer's artful upbraiding a cutting edge. In rebelling against the Lord of Love, Scogan has offended more

---

42. See James I. Wimsatt, "Guillaume de Machaut and Chaucer's Love Lyrics," *Medium Aevum* 47 (1978): 68–87.
43. *Purgatorio* 1.46, 76; Skeat was the first to cite Dante in Chaucer, *The Minor Poems* (Oxford: Clarendon, 1888), 388.
44. Strohm, *Social Chaucer*, 1–23.

than fictional decorum; he has failed to uphold, in a peculiarly English way, an existing ideal of duty.

To laugh his dereliction out of court, Scogan tries to dismiss his friend's chidings as a jongleur's whimsy. Chaucer's parry is irresistible: he gives Scogan a course in the nature of poetry, which, like love, is the gentle art of accommodating lofty principle and pragmatic self-concern. The truly noble response to a lady's rebuff is not to quit Love's service; it's to find a different way of serving. Chaucer illustrates this point by offering his own deportment as an analogy. Even though he is old and portly himself, he has not renounced his allegiance to Cupid; instead of furthering his own cause, he takes up his pen to speed others in love. Chaucer makes his age and its release from passion the temporal counterpart of Scogan's recasting his bond as a limited contract. But Chaucer also maintains that fealty in love has no date. "Olde Grisel" will indeed "ryme" that he has lost his "mede"; in no way does that lessen his need for it. In fact Chaucer asks Scogan to do at Windsor Castle what he does through his poems: courters and courtiers both, so long as they serve as they ought, merit aid.[45] But whereas Scogan announced his disengagement in the curt tones of a man who no longer will throw good money after bad, Chaucer's appeal, which is just as pecuniary-minded, comes bestrewing rhetorical flowers with open hands: "Scogan, that knelest at the stremes hed / Of grace . . ." (43–44). Just as an actual storm was translated into Venus's flood of tears at the beginning of the poem, King Richard is elevated into liquid allegory at its end. As much as Scogan, Chaucer is a person who looks to his own advantage; but for Scogan to be the poet Chaucer is, he must learn to honor timeless as well as conditional allegiances.

By reading the poetic and political transactions of the "Envoy to Scogan," which are grounded in the hierarchies that relate subjects and their king, alongside the reciprocal interrogations of the ideal and the communally pragmatic in Boccaccio's sonnets, where the city is his patron and the source of his discontent, we do see more clearly what is most distinctive in Chaucer's style. Thoroughly English yet unlike any other in England, courtly and social and typical at once, this style is not Dante's, or Boccaccio's, or Petrarch's. Yet it is, I submit, unimaginable without theirs. In the following chapters, I will attempt to account for this unimaginability by examining those translations that constitute Chaucer's Italian Tradition.

---

45. As John Scattergood notes, Michaelmas was the date when annuities were renewed ("Old Age," 98).

2
Dante's Ovids: Allegory, Irony, and the Poet as Translation

Almost everyone who asks, with Piero Boitani, what Dante meant to Chaucer, answers by saying, in effect, "just about everything."[1] I exaggerate, of course, but only to a point. Winthrop Wetherbee has discussed the profound influence Dante's manner of "inspiriting" classicism had on the *Troilus*.[2] Karla Taylor has argued that Chaucer's perspectivalism, his insights into the relation between the discourses and temporality of the self and of history, owes much to his reading of the *Commedia*.[3] Richard Neuse has identified the marriage of the transcendent with the social realia of the everyday in *The Canterbury Tales* as a Chaucerian version of Dante's allegory.[4] Chaucer, as R. A. Shoaf has put it, was a great interpreter of Dante;[5] almost every aspect of his poetics deepened, sometimes to the point of transformation, as a result of his engagement with the *Comedy*.[6]

Many arguments in each of these readings are, I think, perceptive and persuasive. In some respects, however, the collective image of Chaucer that emerges from them seems to me to comprehend Dante's poem too well. History did not lose its opacity when Chaucer read the *Comedy*. The Italy Chaucer journeyed to differed in profound ways

---

1. Piero Boitani, "What Dante Meant to Chaucer," in *Chaucer and the Italian Trecento*, 115–39.
2. Wetherbee, *Chaucer and the Poets*.
3. Karla Taylor, *Chaucer Reads "The Divine Comedy"* (Stanford: Stanford University Press, 1989).
4. Richard Neuse, *Chaucer's Dante* (Berkeley and Los Angeles: University of California Press, 1991).
5. R. A. Shoaf, *Dante, Chaucer, and the Currency of the Word* (Norman, Okla.: Pilgrim Books, 1983).
6. The most recent addition to this group of critics is Edward Condren, *Chaucer and the Energy of Creation* (Gainesville: University Press of Florida, 1999).

from the England he had come from; some seventy years separated the Florence he visited and the city Dante saw for the last time in 1302. Customs Dante had recorded were now obsolete, figures and incidents whose fame he takes for granted had passed from memory; even native Florentines felt the need for topical commentary. Nor did the complex aesthetic principles that governed the disposition of the *Comedy* become suddenly transparent. Chaucer's acuity as a reader is beyond doubt, but the perspicacity we sometimes grant him makes that of Boccaccio, commissioned by Florence to lecture on Dante, seem shallow and pedestrian by comparison. By itself this should give us pause; as the *Trattatello in laude di Dante* and *Esposizioni sopra la Comedia di Dante* make clear, Boccaccio knew crucial texts, such as the *De vulgari eloquentia* and the "Epistle to Can Grande," that Chaucer did not.[7]

Few poets have understood better than Chaucer how easy it is to misunderstand. The more Chaucer pondered the *Comedy*, the more its reach and its grandeur impressed him, the more he would feel its remoteness as well. In a sense, Chaucer registered the inaccessibility of the *Comedy* in the fact that he addressed it less as an integrated narrative than in piecemeal fashion. To a large degree the three canticles *were* an encyclopedia of images or treasury of memorable scenes for Chaucer, which he adapted as the occasion warranted, always with meaningful effect, but without evident regard for the role they played in the intellectual or representational architecture of Dante's poem.[8] I do not mean that Chaucer failed to perceive the overarching design of the *Comedy*; quite the contrary. But I do maintain that he knew only obliquely elements that Dante thought were fundamental to how he executed his design. One of these elements I will call the poetic ambience of the vernacular—not so much the Italian of the poem as its *eloquentia*. Because he was not fully aware of the literary history that to Dante's mind had made the language of the *Comedy* a "volgare illustre," Chaucer's Dante had to be a Dante of fragments.[9]

---

7. I leave aside completely the debate on the authenticity of the letter; the relevant point for this study is that Boccaccio knew it.

8. For an assessment of Chaucer's borrowings from Dante, see Howard Schless, *Chaucer and Dante* (Norman, Okla.: Pilgrim Books, 1984). Judging from responses to the *Roman de la Rose*, if Chaucer read the *Comedy* in piecemeal fashion, he would be following the custom of most medieval readers when they approached long texts. See Sylvia Huot, *The "Romance of the Rose" and Its Medieval Readers* (Cambridge: Cambridge University Press, 1993).

9. The phrase, of course, comes from Dante's *De vulgari eloquentia*, ed. Aristide Marigo (Florence: Le Monnier, 1968).

Lacking this history, which Dante foregrounds throughout his poem, Chaucer would have to look beyond the *Comedy* itself for a guide to read its Italian poetics. He would quickly discover that none of the narrative or lyric conventions of the French literature he knew could afford him an easy passage through the *Inferno, Purgatorio,* and *Paradiso*. Chaucer needed a Virgil closer to Dante, and he found two: Boccaccio's poems and Boccaccio's Florence. In the former he discovered at one and the same time a version of Dante's "new style" and a very un-Dante-like way to appropriate its psychologism; in the latter he discovered a city and people whose customs and attitudes might give local habitation to the otherwise immaterial names scattered throughout the *Comedy*. But Chaucer's encounter with both Boccaccio and Florence was too circumscribed for either to mark out a "straight way" to Dante. The ethos of Boccaccio's poetry was problematic, and the city was complex and foreign enough to limit the insights Chaucer might have gained during his brief stay there. Indeed, the Florence Chaucer visited in 1373 was one even Florentines were finding it difficult to know: with accelerating ferocity older forms of social organization centered around the family competed with new civic structures to define the ways citizens saw themselves and their city. These ideological relations found inverted counterparts in Boccaccio's aesthetics, which were also in transition: he found his belief in the dignity Dante had bestowed on the communal vernacular increasingly hard to maintain in the face of the elevated gravitas of Petrarch's Latin humanism. All these considerations must figure in any account of Chaucer's reception of Dante. To acknowledge their scope and consequence, I will undertake a series of readings of the *Comedy* as one or another kind of translation. My purpose in this chapter is to revisit the declaration to Bonagiunta in order to argue that the manner in which Dante defines the intentional mode of his poem anticipates in uncanny ways the precepts Benjamin outlined in "The Task of the Translator." In the next chapter, I will turn to what I see as the culminating example of Chaucer's translation of that mode, the Manciple's prologue and tale. This translation, which takes the form of a meditation on the relation between allegory and irony, helps to expose strategies of containment, such as the suppression of Ovid, that Dante had to employ to vindicate the claims he makes for the "non falsi errori" of his poetry. (*Purg.* 15.117). But the gaps and occlusions in Chaucer's telling also reveal that his manner of meaning was formed as much in response to the Dante he could not see as to the

Dante he did. In the three subsequent chapters, therefore, I will follow the history of Boccaccio's response to Dante. The political and artistic crises this history embraces form the Italian tradition that Chaucer translated when he read Dante and Boccaccio each as the other's gloss, and when London, also a city in social transit, began to claim an ever greater conceptual place in his poetics.

In light of Chaucer's lifelong fondness for Ovid, it is easy to imagine that he would track with interest the uses to which Dante put the Roman poet in the *Comedy*. If we leave aside the *Tristia* and the *Ex Ponto*, however, there were for Dante not one but two Ovids. The first was the one he calls "Ovidio maggiore," the poet of metamorphosis.[10] This Ovid Chaucer saw Dante silence in the twenty-fifth canto of the *Inferno*:

> Taccia di Cadmo e d'Aretusa Ovidio,
> ché se quello in serpente e quella in fonte
> converte poetando, io non lo 'nvidio;
> ché due nature mai a fronte a fronte
> non trasmutò sì ch'amendue le forme
> a cambiar lor matera fosser pronte.
>
> (25.97–102)

[Let Ovid be silent about Cadmus and Arethusa, for if he poetically converts the one into a serpent and the other into a fountain, I do not envy him; for two natures face to face he never so transmuted that both forms were ready to exchange their matter.]

The other Ovid was the erotic poet whose *Amores* created a scandal in Rome and whose *Ars amatoria* gave Augustus an excuse to banish him. This was the Ovid whose "maestria" in love allowed Brunetto Latini at the end of the *Tesoretto* to return to the way he had lost,[11] the Ovid

---

10. See, for instance, *Convivio* 3.3.5: "Onde si legge . . . ne l'Ovidio Maggiore," where the text is clearly the *Metamorphoses*. This was the normal designation in the Middle Ages, but see the next note.

11. After meeting Nature, Philosophy, Virtue, and Love, Brunetto turned aside and saw, cloaked "in a rich mantle," "*Ovidio maggiore,* who expounds *(rasembra)* in poems and verse the acts of love, which are so diverse" (2356–62). Thanks to Ovid's art, Brunetto was able to return to the true way ("vera via"): "Ma Ovidio per arte / mi diede maestria, / sì ch'io trovai la via / com'io mi trafugai" [But Ovid, by means of art, gave me the mastery

whose exile gave his medieval vita an unsettling likeness to Dante's own.[12] This Ovid Dante expunged: except for one passing (but significant) mention in the twenty-fifth chapter of the *Vita nuova* (and this to the *Remedia amoris*), the pornographic Ovid never appears in Dante's pages.

The violence that these acts of silence and erasure share in common suggests Dante's responses are related; they are, but not because they have the same moral or philosophical agenda. The mumming of Ovid actually turns out to be part of Dante's program to recuperate him. A poet who would begin the *Paradiso* by invoking Marsyas, Apollo, and Daphne, after all, has not rejected Ovid so much as he has translated the import of metamorphosis. The infernal apostrophe "Taccia . . . Ovidio" in fact makes visible the nature of Dante's translation. At the same moment that he commandeers Ovid's silence, he summons his narrative presence by evoking the alterations of Cadmus and Arethusa. The address so openly contravenes the muteness it decrees, one suspects Dante wanted to call attention to its status as a figure. Indeed, a little later, Dante goes out of his way to re-mark the stylistic bravura of his performance in this *bolgia* by apologizing for it with an equally eye-catching flourish: "e qui mi scusi / la novità se fior la penna abborra" (25.143–44): "and let the novelty be my excuse here if my pen goes a little astray." Nowhere in the *Comedy* does Dante more provocatively multiply rhetorical devices than in the cantos of the thieves. One reason he does so, I will propose, is because tropes, as locutions that transgress the boundaries of the literal, encode the logic by which he reclaims Ovid. Whenever a sinner in hell is punished by changing into a snake or some unidentifiable miscegenation of matter, Dante corrects and supplements Ovidian metamorphosis by making it a metaphor for Christian ideas of justice, the Incarnation, and the Resurrection, all of which theft deforms.

---

so that I found the way I had strayed from] (2390–93): This "greater Ovid" seems to be the poet of the *Ars*. I quote from *Poeti del duecento*, ed. Gianfranco Contini, vol. 2 (Milan: Riccardo Ricciardi, 1960). On this passage, see Peter Hawkins, "The Metamorphosis of Ovid," in *Dante and Ovid: Essays in Intertextuality*, ed. Madison Sowell (Binghamton, N.Y.: Medieval and Renaissance Texts and Studies, 1991), 19–34.

12. Readers will recognize that I am conflating the erotic and the exiled Ovid for rhetorical purposes only. As Michelangelo Picone demonstrated in his paper "Ovid and the *exul inmeritus*," which he delivered at the Dante 2000 conference (<http://www.italianacademy.columbia.edu/lectures/dante2000/index.html>), Dante knew the *Tristia* and *Ex Ponto* well.

The first part of my argument, then, will be that Dante baptizes Ovid's "forms changed into new bodies" ("in noua ... mutatas ... formas corpora," *Met.* 1.1–2) by reducing their transformations to a figure of speech in his discourse of salvation.[13] In order to highlight what is at stake in this reduction—in my view, nothing less than the integrity of the manifesto that Dante issues in his response to Bonagiunta—I will consider Ovidian metamorphosis in general as a kind of Benjaminian translation. The second part of my argument, however, is that Dante is able to incorporate a redeemed poetics of transformation into his allegories of being only by suppressing the Ovid who made himself the "praeceptor amoris." The effacement of this amatory Ovid, unnoted and unremarked, looms as a trauma in the *Comedy*, a trauma whose trace perhaps is embedded in the very equivocations of Dante's apology for the flamboyance with which he had muzzled his predecessor. "Se fior la penna abborra," Dante says: not only does the "se" cast in doubt his concession that his pen has strayed a bit, his *justificatio*, the strangeness of what he has seen, makes present the errancy it disavows, just as his apostrophe had previously invoked Ovid in silencing him. These movements toward self-cancellation suggest that Dante did not find Ovid's obscenity as threatening as his irony. The *Ars amatoria* in fact so thoroughly dismantles the logic of love it professes to teach that it directly imperiled Dante's own understanding of himself as a poet. For if Dante thought he existed on earth as an embodied metaphor of the Love that inspired him to write, Ovid raised the possibility that all figurative language, including the incarnational tropings of the *Divine Comedy*, emerges not from the doubled speech of allegory but from the nullifications of irony.

In many ways, the transformation of Daphne can stand for all the metamorphoses of Ovid's poem; it is the first that occurs after Deucalian and Pyrrha repopulated the world Zeus had flooded in anger at Lycaon's wickedness. When Apollo clasps the just-changed laurel in his arms, however, he does not embrace Daphne so much as his interpretation of her transformation:

hanc quoque Phoebus amat positaque in stipite dextra
sentit adhuc trepidare novo sub cortice pectus

---

13. All quotations from the *Metamorphoses* are from *P. Ovidii Nasonis Metamorphoses*, ed. William S. Anderson (Leipzig: Teubner, 1977).

conplexusque suis ramos, ut membra lacertis
oscula dat ligno: refugit tamen oscula lignum.
cui deus "at quoniam coniunx mea non potes esse,
arbor eris certe" dixit "mea. semper habebunt
te coma, te citharae, te nostrae, laure, pharetrae.
tu ducibus Latiis aderis, cum laeta triumphum
vox canet et visent longas Capitolia pompas.
postibus Augustis eadem fidissima custos
ante fores stabis mediamque tuebere quercum,
utque meum intonsis caput est iuvenale capillis,
tu quoque perpetuos semper gere frondis honores."
finierat Paean: factis modo laurea ramis
adnuit utque caput visa est agitasse cacumen.

(1.553–67)[14]

[Phoebus still loves her, and, putting his hand on the stock, he feels the heart still beating under the bark. And with his arms he embraces the branches as if they were arms, and kisses the tree. Yet the tree refuses the kisses. At which the god said, "Since you cannot be my bride, you shall certainly be my tree. You my hair, my lyre, my arrows shall always hold, O laurel; you shall be with the generals of Rome, when joyful voices sing their triumph and the Capitol witnesses long processions. You shall stand a most faithful guardian before the doors of Augustus's palace and watch over the oak between. And as my head is always youthful with uncut locks, you also shall keep the never-changing beauty of your leaves." The god of healing was done: the laurel nods with her new-made branches, and the treetop seems to shake like a head.]

Though the nymph has escaped Apollo, he takes her anyway by unilaterally imposing a new meaning on the tree she has become. Translators have often understood the god's hair, lyre, and arrows to "intertwine" with the laurel. The verb Apollo actually uses, though, is "habebunt": "habebunt te coma, te citharae, te nostrae, laure, pharetrae." His accouterments literally will "have," "possess," "hold mastery over," as well as "be situated with" the laurel. Apollo still desires to possess Daphne, but possession for the god is nothing less than a verbal appropriation

---

14. For bibliography and a fuller discussion of Apollo and Daphne, see my "Ovid and the Problem of Gender," *Mediaevalia* 13 (1989): 9–28.

so complete Daphne must cease to exist. Apollo's wish "to have and to hold" leaves her with nothing of her own, erases even her name, so that Apollo may make the newly defined "laurus" an extension of himself.[15]

Such an imposition of meaning, however, is an assertion of power Ovid neither fully sanctions nor denies.[16] It seems that Daphne assents to the new offices Apollo has defined for her: "finierat Paean: factis modo laurea ramis / adnuit utque caput visa est agitasse cacumen." But the language of trees is quite as equivocal as the language we speak. Even as tree, Daphne refuses Apollo's kisses: "refugit tamen oscula lignum." Indeed, "refugit" conveys the sense that the laurel still flees the god, at least in word, as Daphne had in fact when she was a nymph. So when she appears to consent ("adnuit"), we remember that she nods as a tree, and a treetop shaking in the wind means nothing. We, like Apollo, may take it that she says yes. It is equally possible that Daphne says no.

In fact, in a world where nothing is so singular it can't turn into something else, every assertion of proprietary meaning, or attempt to establish one interpretation as authoritative will encounter resistance. Since each change begets a new form, we are invited to follow Apollo and become neologists, dictating a new definition for each new being. But in Ovid, nothing is completely new. Something of the creature that has undergone the change survives its metamorphosis to upset all efforts to designate anything univocally.

In order to understand Ovid's position fully, I would like to examine Apollo's definition of the laurel in light of Roman linguistic theory about the imposition of meaning on words. Here the notion of propriety plays a central role. For Cicero, words had either an original or a transferred sense:

> Ergo utimur verbis aut eis quae propria sunt et certa quasi vocabula rerum paene una nata cum rebus ipsis; aut eis quae transferuntur et quasi alieno in loco collocantur; aut eis quae novamus et facimus ipsi.

---

15. One almost feels tempted to recall another meaning of *habere:* "illam suas res habere iussit" [he ordered her to take her things], which was the traditional formula for divorcing a wife. See *Oxford Latin Dictionary*, s.v. *habeo*, 1.

16. Ovid leaves no doubt that this displacement is political; as the exercise of power, however, politics in the *Metamorphoses* become a metaphor of the way metaphors operate. See my "Ovid and the Politics of Interpretation," *Classical Journal* 84 (1989): 222–31.

[The words we employ then are either the proper and definite designation of things, which were almost born at the same time as the things themselves; or terms used metaphorically and placed in a connection not really belonging to them; or new coinages invented by ourselves.]¹⁷

Quintilian's restatement of this doctrine is also worth quoting:

Propria sunt verba, cum id significant, in quod primo denominata sunt; translata, cum alium natura intellectum alium loco praebent.

[Words are proper when they bear their original meaning; metaphorical ("translata"), when they are used in a sense different from their natural meaning.]¹⁸

This distinction between the literal and figurative connotations of a word is part of a long debate that reaches back, as Plato's *Cratylus* confirms, to at least the pre-Socratics. The idea of proper meaning, by which a term seems to share the nature of the thing it designates, competed with the idea that all meaning was conventional, the result of use.¹⁹ In Rome, the orator was counseled to sidestep the controversy: whether language was primarily natural or conventional mattered little so long as a speechgiver knew the effects of using the proper or metaphorical sense of a word. But for a poet like Ovid, who told old stories in new ways, the issue must have seemed designed expressly for him to join—on both sides. As upholder of Daphne, Ovid lends his voice to those who said nature defines a word's proper meaning. For the laurel was a nymph before it was a tree. Its proper meaning, therefore, would be consonant with Daphne's nature. But after her transformation, the tree has taken the place of the nymph; Daphne now stands as a metaphor of the laurel. Daphne's propriety, it seems, does not depend on its distinction from metaphor; it is a metaphor. Nor is Daphne unlike any other noun. "Look at your own definition," we can

---

17. Cicero, *De Oratore*, 3.37.149; trans. Horace Rackham, Loeb Classical Library (Cambridge: Harvard University Press, 1960).
18. Quintilian, *Institutio Oratoria*, 1.5.71; trans. H. E. Butler, Loeb Classical Library (Cambridge: Harvard University Press, 1953).
19. For a survey of the debate, see H. R. Robins, *Ancient and Medieval Grammatical Theory in Europe* (1951; rpt. Port Washington, N.Y.: Kennikat Press, 1971), 7–17 and passim.

imagine Ovid saying to Cicero. "To express the 'proper and definite designation of things,' you not only use a metaphor, but seem driven to mark your usage—the natural meaning of words, you say, was *'born, as it were'* ("quasi . . . nata") with the thing itself."

On the other hand, as citizen of the empire, Ovid is also a son of Apollo; he knows that convention and power do define meaning. As tree, the laurel is no longer Daphne; Apollo seizes the occasion to determine a new nature for the word to express as its proper meaning. For that is what Apollo tries to do; the extent to which the god speaks for one of Rome's most powerful strategies of authentication is illustrated by a brief instance from Pliny.[20] In the fifteenth book of the *Naturalis Historia,* Pliny says that the laurel is especially assigned to triumphs; the way he says it, however, reveals that Rome, by his time, almost naturally would give an "original" meaning to whatever it had assimilated: "Laurus triumphis proprie dicatur vel gratissima domibus, ianitrix Caesarum pontificumque" (15.39.127). Pliny's language is the language of the grammarians; he means that the laurel in its primal and proper sense ("proprie")—its first imposition—is used for triumphs; its other uses, to decorate houses, to guard the portals of the emperors and high priests, are set off from this ("vel . . .") and comprise what linguists called its declined or metaphorical senses. Pliny, of course, knew that laurels existed before there were military triumphs, but the function the laurel has come to perform in the constitution of the Roman empire actually denotes the original meaning of the word for him. For the natural historian, use is nature.

But for Ovid, use is not primary. The very fact that he has made Apollo's pronouncements an *aetion* of Roman custom labels it an imposition of meaning by convention. Indeed, we can see just how much Ovid counters Apollo's assertion of propriety by looking more closely at the conditions that accompany what Varro calls "declinatio voluntaria," the arbitrary creation of new significance for a word according to the will of the neologist.[21] In the *De Lingua Latina* (9.37), Varro says

---

20. My text is Pliny, *Naturalis Historia,* 10 vols., ed. and trans. H. Rackham and W. Jones, Loeb Classical Library (Cambridge: Harvard University Press, 1957).

21. On Varro, see Daniel Taylor, *Declinatio: A Study of the Linguistic Theory of M. T. Varro,* Amsterdam Studies in the Theory and History of Linguistic Science, 3 (Amsterdam: John Benjamins, 1975). My text is Varro, *De Lingua Latina,* ed. and trans. R. G. Kent, Loeb Classical Library (Cambridge: Harvard University Press, 1957). The translations in my text are by Taylor.

these conditions are fourfold: two concern the thing signified, two the signifier:

> There must be an underlying referent which is designated ("quod debeat subesse res quae designatur"); this referent must be in use; the signifier must be such that it can be inflected ("et ut vocis natura ea sit quae significavit, ut declinari possit"); it must take such form as would make it a member of a definite morphological class ("et similtudo figurae verbi ut sit ea quae ex se declinata genus prodere certum possit").

In other words, if one would arbitrarily define a meaning for a new word, there must be a something the word refers to, and this something must still be in use. In addition, the form of the word must be such that if, for example, it is a noun, it takes case endings, and these endings conform to one of the five declensions of nouns that Latin recognizes.

In defining the laurel, Apollo clearly satisfies Varro's conditions: he creates both a form, "laurus," and the meaning of the laurel according to his will.[22] But the nature of the tree that "laurus" is supposed to denominate naturally is more complex than Apollo allows. The laurel, after all, has its form as a tree only because the tree itself has a referent, Daphne, who balked Apollo's will. Indeed, Daphne is still in the laurel and constitutes a nature that we might call not-tree:

> hanc quoque Phoebus amat positaque in stipite dextra
> sentit adhuc trepidare novo sub cortice pectus
> conplexusque suis ramos ut membra lacertis
> oscula dat ligno: refugit tamen oscula lignum.
>
> (553–56)

Consequently, whatever Apollo would have the laurel mean, enough of Daphne remains to prevent his definition from being "proprie dicta."

Similar difficulties extend even to the signifying form itself. Apollo addresses the tree in the vocative, "laure" (559): this is a form of "laurus," a noun of the second declension. Later, however, Ovid uses a dif-

---

22. The form "laurus" is Apollo's creation, even if we assume it predates Daphne's transformation, since the word, born at the time Daphne became a tree, now properly expresses the nature Apollo has defined for the laurel.

ferent word, "laurea," a first-declension noun: "finierat Paean: factis modo laurea ramis . . ." (566). And still later, in a number of manuscripts, the laurel appears as a noun of the second declension with endings of the fourth: as he hangs himself, Iphis says to Anaxarete that she may now rejoice and triumph: "laetos molire triumphos / et Paeana voca nitidaque incingere lauru!" [Celebrate joyful triumphs and sing "paean," and bind your head with shining laurel] (14.720).[23] This proliferation of forms for a single thing confounds Apollo's effort to absorb Daphne into himself, since they disrupt that singular congruity of object and sign that distinguishes natural meaning. So too do the complications of gender that arise with the multiplication of declensions. For genders, as Varro defines them, "are named from *generare*, 'to generate.' For whatever *gignit*, 'begets,' or *gignitur*, 'is begotten,' that can be called a *genus* and can produce a *genus*."[24] As something born at the same time as the thing itself, gender would therefore belong to proper meaning. "Laurea" is a feminine noun: coming as it does at the end of the story, it preserves Daphne, so to speak, even after Apollo's verbal rape of her. Apollo's "laure," on the other hand, situates the laurel as a second-class feminine noun with masculine endings—a perfect linguistic correlative of Apollo's hermeneutic act. But here too, as inflectional grammar smoothly assimilates the laurel into the masculine world of the second declension, the word remains feminine.[25] Its gender substantiates Daphne's resistance even as Apollo subjugates it by overlaying his case endings on her "root" form.

On a more general level, gender problems such as these, together with the pullulation of forms, exemplify how Ovid hobbles every attempt to stabilize hermeneutics by appealing to linguistics. Propriety would guarantee the integrity of definition by aligning an object with the uninflected nominal form of the word that is engendered with it: the connection between a noun and its referent is saved from equivocation even when the declined senses "curve away" and become metaphorical, in the sense that the genitive, the dative, the ablative,

---

23. Anderson is virtually alone among modern editors in choosing the *lectio facilior* of "lauro." Both endings have manuscript support, though a majority read "lauro." See Anderson's edition, ad loc., and Franz Bömer, *P. Ovidii Nasonis Metamorphosen: Kommentar*, 5 vols. (Heidelberg: Winter, 1969–86), vol. 5, ad.17.720: 220–21.

24. *De Lingua Latina*, Librorum XI–XXIV Fragmenta, 7a.

25. Indeed, the ambiguous nature of the word extended beyond language to become part of Roman life: as Pliny says, the laurel was the only tree whose name was given to a man ("unius arborum Latina lingua nomen inponitur viris" [15.138]).

were thought to substitute or stand in for the nominative. In the world of the *Metamorphoses*, however, an object is never sui generis, since everything new both continues and ends something old. Consequently its meaning is always in flux: the laurel is and is not what Apollo says it is. Even the signifier, supposedly born with the thing itself, lacks a fixed nominal case; is Apollo's tree "laurus" or "laurea"? Proper meaning, Ovid suggests, has lost all title to propriety: it exists only as the subtle dissonances one hears in the dialogue between words themselves and their momentary significance.

Perhaps the most surprising consequence of such a radically figural conception of transformation is its materiality. By making meaning metaphorical, Ovid can maintain that his metamorphoses are not. Because Daphne's persistence disrupts the definition Apollo would have stand for her, we collaborate in his violence if we say she is like a laurel or is a laurel. Daphne's survival obstructs whatever significance we assign her as laurel, since any such imposition of meaning will itself be, in de Man's phrase, an exercise of the "totalizing power of tropological substitutions."[26] Indeed, to the extent that the transformed Daphne is not laurel or nymph, we cannot identify what she is by appealing either to nature, where trees are trees and nymphs nymphs, or to a language that is supposed to imitate or copy it. Instead Daphne and the laurel cohabit as metonomies; Ovid's account of her rape and Apollo's definition abide side by side as the facticity of language that vouchsafes the distinctness of each even as it joins both. The metamorphosis of nymph to tree is a troping of bodies that conserves their integrity as bodies. Mimesis and propriety play no part in it because there is no indivisible object to depict or literal sense to turn away from. To speak appropriately of Daphne, then, when she changes, we should not say that she becomes the laurel; we ought rather to say that it translates her.

In many respects, Ovidian metamorphosis is a theory of translation; "laurus," after all, is Latin for Greek "daphne." Precisely because Ovid does not rely on an extralinguistic model of correspondence or referentiality to account for the generation of new forms from old, his transformations seem to coincide with Benjamin's conception of translation. Indeed, the laurels Ovid says crown Augustus's head ultimately interrogate Benjamin as much as they do Roman power: they cause us to ask

---

26. De Man, "Conclusions," 89.

whether any language as a whole can have a single intention that it realizes in one characteristic mode. Ovid's metamorphoses dislodge manners of meaning from within a language; rather than looking to another tongue to divulge the asymmetry between tropes and what they signify, Apollo's definition argues that meaning is already itself a translation, a palimpsest in which the fragmented contours of prior usage continually break the smooth surface of current definitions. In this sense, when Ovid trumps the archival claims of the *Aeneid* by saying his poem spans all time, from the world's beginning to the present day in Rome (1.3–4), he is not being entirely facetious; his transformations *are* profoundly historical, if by history we mean to include the recognition that when we recollect something, it no longer is what it was. Precisely because it beats with two hearts, Ovidian metamorphosis is the one form destined always to haunt allegory, the other discourse of history that speaks with two mouths.

When Dante determined the status of the sinners in hell, he synthesized scientific traditions of anthropology and pneumatology, derived largely from Aristotle, with the biblical and theological idea that the damned are indeed lost souls because they have died the second death. I have argued elsewhere that metamorphosis underwrites every element of this synthesis: it not only informs the constitution of the doomed spirits and how we understand them, but is an instrument in the general distribution of divine justice throughout the *Comedy*.[27] If these arguments carry any weight, little wonder Dante would feel he had to distinguish his transformations from Ovid's. With its apparent balance of old and new forms, metamorphosis should be an analogue of justice, and so an expression of the *contrapasso*, the fitting of retribution to offense that sustains the typology of the *Inferno*.[28] But since the linguistic materiality of Ovid's transformations subverts the power of any trope to make fungible the things it associates, it directly threatened the spiritual materiality of Christian allegory. Instead of functioning as a metaphor of the Incarnation, Ovidian metamorphosis would translate it into the idiom of Arianism: the mystery of the consubstantiality of human and divine in Jesus would become nothing more than a metonymy, a yoking together of disparate natures. Instead of serving

---

27. *Dante's Aesthetics of Being*, 115–59.
28. See, for instance, Kenneth Gross, "Infernal Metamorphoses: An Interpretation of Dante's Counterpass," *MLN* 100 (1985): 42–69.

as a figure of the Resurrection, metamorphosis would cleave the perfected communion of body and soul, rendering each a shard that never could be reassembled into a whole. Instead of being a way to comprehend how the sacraments of the Mass became the body and life of the Christian God, transformation would render the Eucharist bread and tissue, wine and blood, a concatenation that would horrify Wyclif no less than Aquinas.

Ovid's metamorphoses clearly posed challenges that no Christian poetics could ignore if it modeled itself after the Word made flesh. Dante, it seems to me, was aware of these challenges; he sought to meet them by coordinating the transformations of the thieves, which exemplify the general dissolution of body and soul in the damned, not only with his definition of himself as poet and Statius's explanation of how a body of air is generated for souls, which occupy cantos 24 and 25 of the *Purgatorio*, but with his examination on faith, hope, and charity in the corresponding cantos of the *Paradiso*, in which Dante's answers are anchored in his belief in the Resurrection. Each of these linkages deserves extended discussion; in a sense, however, they all subtend Dante's famous declaration of himself as a poet in the *Purgatorio*.[29]

When Bonagiunta asks whether he sees before him the author of the "new rhymes," his question is straightforwardly literary. Dante's answer, however, is ontological; he equates his identity as a poet with his existence as a human being:

I' mi son un che, quando
Amor mi spira, noto, e a quel modo
ch'e' ditta dentro, vo significando.

As I said last chapter, Dante marks his assertion of poetic selfhood as a twofold translation; an "original," constituted by Love's inspiration, is translated by Dante's noting, which textualizes it; this event then is itself translated when Dante textualizes himself as embodied signification according to the mode of meaning of the original. What is remarkable about both these enactments of (or movements toward) textualization is how closely they conform to Benjamin's program of translation; in each Dante acknowledges a verbal materiality that disarticulates systems of reference and resemblance in ways that are similar to what

---

29. I have discussed the connections that link these cantos in *Dante's Aesthetics of Being*, 115–59.

occurs with the passage through "reine Sprache." "Noto," Dante's word for the intellection of Love's breath, is usually glossed as "I take note." With a glance at Augustine's "notitia," the word recalls the scholastic explanation of understanding as an operation that proceeds by abstracting the universal from matter. But "noto" here also carries the sense of "notating"; it is as this act of writing, of making a mark, that Dante's registering of Love translates it. Amor's breath in him, after all, is a metaphor of inspiration that he insists is not metaphorical; it creates Dante as the person he really is. The Spirit that is the Word, however, configures him in such a way that his mind, having become aware, instead of being able to elicit Love's essence, is "en-mattered" by it. When the intellect extracts the unindividuated form from its material object, it produces the *verbum mentis*, the completely abstract idea that determines how we know something in respect to its nature.[30] In this instance, however, no sense organ has played a role in making Dante conscious of the breath he feels, nor does reason have the power to comprehend its nature. Under such circumstances, the word Dante's mind speaks forth as its apprehension can announce no more than its own vocalization. Instead of conceptualizing Amor, his noting will be able merely to stand to it in the same relation that physical substances stand to their essences in ordinary acts of intellection. In this way, by presenting his awareness as a scene of notation, Dante does not equate himself with the Love that inspires him. Rather than copying or substituting for Love, he generates meaning in the same mode as its breathing; he makes understanding, a process that works by dematerializing sense impressions, sensible.[31]

---

30. For a full elaboration of the *verbum mentis* and the role it plays in Dante's poetics, see my *Dante's Aesthetics of Being*, 28–29 and passim.

31. As Teresa Kennedy has made me realize, the musical implications of "noto" are equally material. When Dante asks his readers, for instance, to believe he really did see Geryon come swimming through the air "per le note / di questa comedìa" (*Inf.* 16.127–28), these notes refer not to melody or its markings but to the harmony of sound of the words themselves. As Dante makes clear in the *De vulgari eloquentia*, this harmony, constituted by the actual vocalization of the words, was an entity in its own right. It was not subordinated to meaning as something that it was supposed to imitate or express. If anything, in Dante's lyrics, "It is not that the 'sound' must seem an echo to the *sense*, but the sense must seem an echo to the *sound*" (John Stevens, "Dante and Music," *Italian Studies* 23 [1968]: 1–18). Thus Dante defines the *canzone* as "the completed action of writing down, according to art, harmonized words for a musical setting" (2.8). Perhaps Dante's best exemplification is in the Second Eclogue (written late in his life): instead of a melody, the opening verse of Mopsus's new eclogue issues from Melibeus's flute.

This corporealization of the mind's word is Dante's way of acknowledging that when Love breathes, it breathes with the spirit of "pure language." The poet does not say that he inscribes what Amor says when it is present. That is uninscribable, a speaking Dante can never note; on the contrary, Love's spiration effects an erasure. All prior discourses of philosophy and poetry are emptied of their conceptual power. Faculty psychology stands mute; it cannot explain what Dante says happens to him. Love poetry falls silent: Dante voids the truth-claims not only of other vernacular writers, most famously Guittone d'Arezzo and "il Notaro," Giacomo da Lentini, but, as I and others have argued, the claims Dante had made himself as "stilnovist"—the poetry of the "sweet new style" is not the poetry he writes in the *Comedy*.[32] Literary history is canceled as well; Dante renounces his *tenzone* with Forese Donati here.[33]

Dante thus sets aside all prior discourses, including his own, in the caesura that separates Love and his noting of it in order to signal the essential difference between himself, his poetry, and the Amor that begets both. Human beings never can stand in for the Word of God; translation, which is what happens when they come into contact, reveals the unnameable gulf between them. Nevertheless, Dante did believe that people are made in God's image; just as the Spirit, Father,

---

James Wimsatt shows that Dante's sense of the materiality of the verbal music of the *canzone* corresponds perfectly to what Eustache Deschamps will in his *Art de dictier* call the "natural music" of poetry, in contrast to an accompanying melody, which he labels "musique artificiele." Chaucer shared these ideas. See *Chaucer and His French Contemporaries* (Toronto: University of Toronto Press, 1991), 12–22.

32. By mentioning Giacomo da Lentini, Dante alerts his readers that he has translated the idea of notarial authenticity here as well. As Armando Petrucci has explained, throughout *trecento* Italy the document that the notary produced was recognized as a "public instrument"; the notary's autograph, which had come to replace the signatures of the involved parties, authenticated the legitimacy of a transaction. To the extent that he makes himself Amor's notary, Dante similarly authenticates himself; as he goes signifying, this manner of being becomes the substantive, material evidence of Love's mode of dictation, for which it substitutes. But Dante limits this act of authentication to the social world he moves through as embodied signification. It depends entirely on Dante's previous assertion that his noting cannot even claim to be a signature to the breath that notarizes him by its inscription of the Word in him. In Dante's diplomatics, the value of writing in this world is its defect in the next. This is a truth he feels "Il Notaro" did not recognize; it is also a reason why he had to expunge the ironic Ovid. Among other essays, see Petrucci's "The Illusion of Authentic History: Documentary Evidence," in *Writers and Readers in Medieval Italy*, ed. and trans. Charles Radding (New Haven: Yale University Press, 1995), 236–50.

33. For a full elaboration of these arguments, see *Dante's Aesthetics of Being*, 78–95.

and Son are the same person, so flesh and soul are conjunctive because they are assimilable. Thus, even as he translates to acknowledge the gap between God and his creatures, Dante somehow also had to establish a resemblance between them. More specifically, Dante had to save mimesis, for his poetics as much as his belief depended on the possibility of imitation. He therefore manufactured likeness by retranslating. After he notes Love's breath in him, Dante states: "e a quel modo / ch'e' ditta dentro, vo significando." What Love dictates again is uninscribed; instead Dante reports that he is transmogrified into *homo significandus*, traversing the world according to the mode in which Love speaks. As poem and person he goes signifying his translation of his noting (of) Love. The same textual materiality that breached the possibility of parity between Dante and Amor now becomes the means to notarize his claim that he and his art are God's offspring (*Inf.* 11.105).

This second incarnation as text both copies the first and stands beside it; Dante's going signifying is a metaphor of his noting Love, and it is a metonymy that occupies its own place next to it. In this Dante implies that when Love takes possession of him, he is transformed in ways that make him not unlike Apollo's laurel, in which Daphne remains Daphne but which is something different as well. Love first wipes clean the fleshy tables of Dante's heart, but it also causes his mind to undergo a metamorphosis as the abstracting operations of intellection take on the materiality of inscription. Then his body and the poem that is its extension also undergo their own metamorphosis, in which bones and letters are inspirited so that they signify in a manner that conforms with the mode of Love's inner dictation. In this way, Dante institutes a double relation between translation and metamorphosis: when he sees metamorphosis as translation, he preserves the individuality of flesh and matter against loss through change; when he sees translation as metamorphosis, he recuperates resemblance by making the transformations that Love effects analogies of one another. With Apollonian audacity, Dante embraced Ovid's disruptions to redefine them; alongside all the languages and systems of meaning he silenced in silencing Ovid, Dante installed a new aesthetics of being, a discourse of analogy that, situated between the abstractions of intellect and the particularities of sense, subsumed both. Metamorphosis is the privileged figure of this aesthetic in which flesh and spirit translate the other's manner of meaning. It is the figure that allows Dante to make the mutations of the thieves an analogy of justice's operations in the seventh *bolgia* of the *Inferno*, the formation of bodies of air an analogy of the Incarnation in canto 25 *Purgatorio*, Dante's sudden blinding in canto 25 *Paradiso*, when he tries to see the body of St. John, an analogy of the Resurrection, when, in the twinkling of an eye, each soul shall be changed ("immutabimur" is Paul's word), as it merges again with its flesh, at the last trumpet's final note (1 Cor. 15:51).

Dante signals the centrality of translation to his poetics of transformation by dramatizing a mistranslation just a little before his declaration to Bonagiunta. Both Statius and Virgil witness Dante's aesthetic self-definition; their presence prompts readers to recall Statius's own account of how he became the poet-soul he is. The pivotal event in his life was his conversion, which came about, Dante has him report, as the result of a double translation of Virgil. Statius was first moved to frequent Christian preachers when he found that their sermons accorded with Virgil's famous prophecy in the Fourth Eclogue (5–7):

magnus ab integro saeclorum nascitur ordo.
iam redit et Virgo, redeunt Saturnia regna;
iam nova progenies caelo demittitur alto.

[The ages begin again; now the virgin returns, the reign of Saturn returns, now a new progeny descends from high heaven.]

Dante made two notable alterations when he had Statius translate these words; he glossed Virgil's "Virgo" as "giustizia," and he transformed "redeunt Saturnia regna" into "primo tempo umano" (*Purg.* 22.71). If we understand this latter phrase to mean "the first age of man" (Singleton's translation), Ovid peeps out from behind it, but only long enough to be rendered a cipher. His famous description of the Golden Age disappears into the history of Adam and Eve. But even if Ovid does not lurk in Dante's line, when Eden supplants Arcadia, Virgil is no more exempt from erasure than the poet of metamorphosis: Astrea has vanished; Justice stands in her place.

An even more radical grammar of conversion underwrites the other Virgilian verse that changed Statius's life. In the *Aeneid* (3.56–57), Polydorus had said, "Quid non mortalia pectora cogis, / auri sacra fames": "to what do you not drive mortal hearts, o cursed hunger for gold." Statius vocalizes this as "Per che non reggi tu, o sacra fame / de l'oro, l'appetito de' mortali?" (*Purg.* 22.40–41): "why do you not govern, o blessed hunger for gold, the appetites of mortals." Here Christian meaning alters the words Virgil actually wrote so that they become able to spur Statius to turn his back on avarice.[34] By translating, Dante allows his reader to behold the metamorphosis of the Latin of empire into the vernacular of redemption.[35]

Indeed, throughout the *Comedy*, whenever Dante explicitly represents the relation of his art to God's, he displays the transformative intentionality of his language by showing that even the basic elements out of which it is compounded are translations of Love's mode of speaking. The acrostic in *Purgatorio* 12 is perhaps the most prominent case in point. By beginning each of four consecutive *terzine* with the same word, Dante turns graphemes into glyphs. Solely through repetition and their placement on the page, the *V* of "Vedea," the apostrophe "*O*," and the *M* of "Mostrava" generate *man* from their own matter, as it were. This graphing of meaning in space would risk making an idol of writing, however, if it did not correspond to the *visibile parlare* of the terrace's reliefs. In these tableaux, graven images of insensate marble move and speak to remind the contumacious of the humility they owe the God who gave them life. When Dante spells out U-O-M in his own denunciation of the pride human beings mistakenly think makes them who and what they are, his letters mean in a manner that is congruent with the synaesthesia of the sculptures, which is their *Art des Meinens*.

---

34. Dante's translation, of course, has created contested interpretations from the earliest commentators on. For a review, see Charles Singleton's note to the passage in *Purgatorio 2: Commentary*, in his translation, *The Divine Comedy* (Princeton: Princeton University Press, 1970–76), 521–24. No matter how we translate Dante's translation, the fact remains that he has transformed Virgil's verse.

35. After Dante has defined himself as poet, Bonagiunta says he now sees why he and other poets fell short of the sweet new style. In a famous crux, he continues, "I see clearly how 'le vostre penne' follow close after him who dictates, which certainly did not happen with ours." Does "le vostre penne" mean "your pens," as almost all commentators have it, or "your wings," as Lino Pertile has recently strongly argued? (See "Il nodo di Bonagiunta, le penne di Dante, e il Dolce Stil Novo," *Lettere italiane* 46 [1994]: 44–75.) The need to opt for one or the other reading disappears once we realize that Bonagiunta's response itself translates what Dante has said. What makes his words a translation, however, is not the content of the lesson he derives but the materiality of the letter that conveys it. It is the metamorphosis of "penne" from pens to wings, from wings to pens, that finally enrolls Bonagiunta as a member of Dante's school. When two meanings inhabit Bonagiunta's one word, when literal and figural have become indistinguishable, and linguistic propriety a fantasy, then the poet from Lucca follows the mode of meaning that translates Dante into the poet he is—the poet whose desire flies without wings ("sua disianza vuol volar sanz' ali," *Par.* 33.15) at the end of his journey to see all creation bound by the universal knot ("la forma universal di questo nodo," *Par.* 33.91) of love in one single volume.

In the process, both forms, the one textually, the other in three dimensions, disclose that the final goal they tend toward is not epistemological or ethical but ontological: Dante's intention, quite literally, is to incarnate his poetry with the substance of being. Writing and the plastic arts shape their synchronic appeals to intellect and will according to the material differences of their media; for Dante these different modes of realization become analogous and translate one another the moment they are both oriented toward the pure speech that is the Word made flesh. Translation as such is the *modo di dire* by which his *Comedy* is transformed into an *ars essendi*.

The clearest evidence we have, of course, that Dante configures all alphabets of salvation under the sign of metamorphosis is the transformation of the *M* of "terram" into the eagle of just rulers in *Paradiso* 18, and its translation as the other famous acrostic of the *Comedy*, the spelling out of L-U-E (pestilence) in *Paradiso* 19. In these cantos, Dante recalls and alludes to his definition to Bonagiunta through all the extraordinary mutations he records, beginning with his awareness that he has left the heaven of Mars and entered the sphere of Jupiter, which he compares to "'l trasmutare" one sees when the blush fades and a lady's face changes from red to white (18.64–66), through the souls' skywriting of "DILIGITE IUSTITIAM QUI IUDICATIS TERRAM," each letter formed after they sang and moved to their own notes ("Prima, cantando, a sua nota moviensi," 79), each letter noted by Dante as he inscribed this visible speech in his mind ("e io notai / le parti sì, come mi parver dette," 89–90), to the astonishing composition of the eagle itself.[36] With this climactic demonstration of the essence of the staves God uses to write his Word, Dante discovers the cause why all mimetic modes of representation will finally be of no use to him in paradise: "Quei che dipinge lì, non ha chi 'l guidi" [He who paints there has none to guide him] (110–11); because God designs without a model, Dante cannot copy the principle by which He creates. But, Dante continues, "He Himself does guide, and from Him is recognized that virtue which shapes nests" [ma esso guida, e da lui si rammenta / quella virtù ch'è forma per li nidi]. It is God's guidance that Dante seeks to represent; his poetry depicts neither the nest nor the God we can infer from its construction but the instinct that causes it to be built. The nature of this instinct is metamor-

---

36. For an excellent reading of Dante's simile see Alison Cornish, "Getting There: The Physics of Moral Advancement in Dante's *Paradiso*," *Dialoghi: Rivista di Studi Italici* 1 (1997): 73–85.

phosis per se, without regard to the objects changed: the production of something where before there was nothing. Metamorphosis is Dante's translation of God's *modo di dire:* it is what permits him to say with all conviction:

> O dolce stella, quali e quante gemme
> mi dimostraro che nostra giustizia
> effetto sia del ciel che tu ingemme!
>
> (115–17)

> [O sweet star, how many and how bright were the gems which made it plain to me that our justice is the effect of the heaven which you engem.]

The acrostic Dante interweaves into the next canto is his translation of just this virtue that converts causes into effects; the submerged yet visible presence of L-U-E is a linguistic exemplification of the way justice changes the world by making the crooked straight.

All Dante's translations, however, are not the last word; although he has silenced the Ovid of the *Metamorphoses,* the voice of the other Ovid, the erased Ovid, still reverberates as the white noise of irony that always will accompany the transformation of letters into figures of the spirit. By briefly examining the *Ars amatoria,* I will show why Dante had good reason to associate this self-negating voice of irony with the pornographic Ovid, and why he had to expunge it if he were to preserve the consistency of his definition of himself as poet and allegory of love.[37]

In all his amatory poems, Ovid called into question every principle that literature, philosophy, or politics might offer to guide action. In *The Art of Love,* for instance, morality is not something Ovid merely laughs at; it becomes the occasion of his eroticism, the very "thing" his poem makes its object of desire. The wit with which Ovid executes this surprising volte-face makes it hard to resist; once a reader nods and smiles, however, he or she is not far from asking whether ethics is at all able to

---

37. For a fuller exposition of the following ideas in relation to the medieval commentary tradition on Ovid, see my "Ovidius ethicus? Ovid and the Medieval Commentary Tradition," in *Desiring Discourse: The Literature of Love, Ovid through Chaucer,* ed. J. Paxson et al. (Selinsgrove: Susquehanna University Press, 1998), 62–71.

establish itself as a rational practice. Ovid begins his art of how to win a lover, after all, by retelling the rape of the Sabine women; he ends it by giving the following counsel:

> uim licet appelles: grata est uis ista puellis;
> quod iuuat, inuitae saepe dedisse uolunt.
> quaecumque est Veneris subita uiolata rapina,
> guadet, et inprobitas muneris instar habet.
> at quae, cum posset cogi, non tacta recessit,
> ut simulet uultu gaudia, tristis erit.
>
> (1.673–78)[38]

[You certainly can call on force: that kind of force women like. What delights them they often pretend to have given unwillingly. A woman violated by sudden rape feels joy and holds the wicked deed a form of tribute. But a woman who has retired untouched, when she could have been forced, will be sad, though she pretends to be glad.]

Today, any defense of the brutishness of this passage by pointing to the glib jocularity of its tone will rightly be rejected as quickly as the woman's protests are brushed aside by the speaker. But Ovid's flippancy here masks an irony that is far more thoroughgoing and dangerous, because it really does work to prevent taking what he says seriously. To frame instruction on how to win women by describing rapes is to underscore the irrelevance of any formalized *techne;* what need is there for an art if from start to finish all winning amounts to is seizure by force?

Similarly, the second book of the *Ars* purports to teach men how to hold a lover once she has been won. Yet the initial story of Daedalus and Icarus seems to suggest the impossibility of holding what won't be held. It is no more in the nature of love than it is in the nature of youth to be ruled by sensible advice. The first tale in this book, like the story of the Sabine women in the previous one, again appears to be at loggerheads with the lesson it wants to teach. Few readers will need more prompting before they notice that all the instruction Ovid will now offer his apprentices is directly opposed to what they had learned

---

38. I quote from *P. Ovidi Nasonis Amores . . . Ars Amatoria, Remedia Amoris,* ed. E. J. Kenney, Oxford Classical Texts (Oxford: Oxford University Press, 1961).

before: if love can be held, how can anyone else, even if tutored by the *Ars*, win it?

Nor are matters clarified when Ovid resolves these conflicts by concluding book 2 of the *Ars* with a description of sexual intercourse:

> conscius, ecce, duos accepit lectus amantes:
> ad thalami clausas, Musa, resiste fores
> sponte sua sine te celeberrima uerba loquentur,
> nec manus in lecto laeua iacebit iners;
> inuenient digiti quod agant in partibus illis,
> in quibus occulte spicula tingit Amor . . .
> crede mihi, non est Veneris properanda voluptas
> sed sensim tarda prolicienda mora.
> cum loca reppereris, quae tangi femina gaudet,
> non obstet, tangas quominus illa, pudor . . .
> sed neque tu dominam uelis maioribus usus
> defice, nec cursus anteeat illa tuos;
> ad metam properate simul: tum plena uoluptas,
> cum pariter uicti femina uirque iacent . . .
> (2.703–8, 717–20, 725–29)

[Now the knowing bed has received the two lovers. Stand by the closed doors of the bedchamber, O Muse. Without you the lovers will spontaneously speak a host of words, nor will the left hand lie idle on the bed. Fingers will discover what to do in those parts whose tips Love bedews in secret . . . believe me, pleasure mustn't be hurried, but gradually slow delay should coax it forth. When you have found where a woman delights to be touched, do not let modesty make you caress her less . . . neither do you want through greater exertion to leave your mistress behind, nor let her run the course before you. Hasten to the goal together; pleasure is complete when both man and women lie equally overcome.]

In a stunning peripety, we now discover that instead of being at odds with winning love, holding it requires winning it, not once, but again and again: the "art" of love turns out to be the act of making love. Goals Ovid had led us to believe were in opposition actually turn out to be in collusion: in the parodic dialectic of the *Ars*, thesis and antithesis, pedagogy and delight, happily collapse into one another, just as its version of men and women do. Ovid only seems to set gaining and holding against one another, since, despite appearances, his purpose is not to achieve the closure of philosophical synthesis but to generate pleasurable rhetorical friction by continuously arguing for both.

The consequences for ethical behavior of turnabouts such as these are devastating. Desire exists only when it is resisted; when we recognize the autonomy of the person we seek, her or his right to refuse us, we can, on a traditional reading, legitimately call our desires just. If the *Ars* actually acknowledged the otherness of women, Ovid could claim that its project to teach men how to love them was a moral one. But Ovid suggests instead that desire is always resisted from within, and that this resistance is already complicit with the desire that engenders it. For this reason, women in a real sense do not exist in the *Ars*; they have neither the substance nor the presence to obstruct desire *or* to be its object. Rather they are only the occasion for desire's fulfillment, and it is fulfillment that the *Ars* actively strives toward and just as actively defers.[39] The final lesson in holding love does not end Ovid's book so much as it returns to the poem's opening directions on how to win it. In the same way, the reversals of the third book, which purports to teach women how to win and hold men, reverse nothing. The instruction is the same as in the first two books; to imagine women would follow it is as much a fantasy as to imagine men would follow the previous book's advice about how to hold love. Everywhere in the *Ars*, Ovid quite morally shows how desire narcissistically fashions the objects it seeks in its own image, in order to extend its existence; desire becomes artful when it resists itself for its own sake.

Of course one would be right to say this sort of subordination of women to the perpetuation of desire is a peculiarly masculine strategy, but if in some sense women do not exist in the *Ars*, neither do men. Because Ovid's erotics depend on the deferral of gratification, there is a

---

39. Medieval commentators also recognized, albeit for different ends, that the *Ars* was not concerned with fulfillment. In an accessus to the *Amores* we read that the *Amores* need to be distinguished from the *Ars:* "Ovidius de Amatoria Arte dat precepta amantibus ut sint cauti, hic autem de Amore et in semetipso complet precepta" [In the *Ars* Ovid gives precepts to lovers so that they may take care; here in the *Amores* he fulfills the precepts himself]. The text appears in R. B. C. Huygens, *Accessus ad auctores, Bernard d'Utrecht, Conrad d'Hirsau "Dialogus super Auctores"* (Leiden: Brill, 1970), 37, "Ovidii sine titulo [II]." The same distinction is found in another accessus discussed by Ralph Hexter, *Ovid and Medieval Schooling*, Münchener Beiträger zür Mediävistik und Renaissance Forschung, 38 (Munich: Arbeo Gesellschaft, 1986), 18.

consistent elision of all bodies in the poem. The most illustrative instance of this occurs between the end of the first book and the beginning of the second. During this time, the pupil has won his beloved:

> Dicite "io Paean" et "io" bis dicite "Paean":
> decidit in casses praeda petita meos.
> laetus amans donat uiridi mea carmina palma
> praelata Ascraeo Maeonioque seni.
>
> (2.1–4)

[Cry "Io Paean," and cry it again; the sought-for game has fallen into my snares. The joyful lover gives green palms to my poem, which he prefers to old Hesiod and Homer.]

This celebration of the poem's effectiveness is typically broad and self-congratulatory, but it cannot keep us from noticing that there is no description here of what the words say the *Art of Love* has achieved. The graphic record of going to bed must be postponed until the end of the book, because, as we have seen, once it has been reported, there is nothing more an *ars amatoria* can say.[40] In Ovid the poem's the thing: its writing displaces men and women both.

Because Ovid does not delineate the body and its desires so much as represent their textuality, he removes his poems from the orbit of any ethics that assigns values to actions based on gender. Indeed, Ovid has called into question whether it is possible to decide if the *Ars* can be ethical in any sense. If intercourse is the point of the *Ars*, representing it demands literal explicitness; in fact, once it has been discovered to be the end that coordinates the set of practices Ovid describes, pornography becomes the book's "recta ratio factibilium," its raison d'être.[41] For the *Ars* to be an "art," it must be pornographic. But precisely because sex is the most fleeting, least perdurable aspect of love, Ovid's lubricity is also a declaration of his morality. Not only does the gaining of love seem, Icarus-like, simultaneously the occasion of its loss, holding it by

---

40. Perhaps in his own way the author of the accessus in ms. clm 19475 (in Huygens, *Accessus*, 33) recognized this: he clearly expresses Ovid's aim as if the *Ars* ended with its second book: "Intentio sua est in hoc opere iuuenes ad amorem instruere, quo modo debeant se in amore habere circa ipsas puellas."

41. An art, as scholastic commentators on Aristotle's *Metaphysics* (981a24–b7) would say, was defined as a rational disposition concerned with making that reasons truly, a "recta ratio factibilium" that lies at the heart of all purposeful activity.

repeatedly retiring to the bedroom is a prescription less apt to lead to a lasting relationship than to exhaustion: in the *Remedia amoris,* in fact, Ovid will counsel repeated copulation as one way to fall out of love. From this a moralist could conclude that *The Art of Love* is ethical in that it demonstrates how desire and fulfillment, by exposing the other's excesses and deficiencies, are both temptations to be avoided.[42] The hedonist, though, could say with equal force that the *Ars*'s worth is its incitements to sexual consummation. What one must seek is the very thing one must avoid; if a principle to guide human conduct can be recovered under such conditions, Ovid has shown there is no reason to think reason will discern it.

For Dante, the scandal of Ovid's amatory poems, I would therefore suggest (for in this the *Ars* can stand for the others), lies not in their content but in their manner. No less for the Roman than for the Christian poet, love is a mode of writing that makes the man. In the *Comedy*, however, Amor's breath is heart and glue; it endows letter and figure with substance and intention so that in translating each other they also translate the Word. In Ovid, the opposite occurs: love exists solely as the effect of his poem's art of codifying it. In the *Comedy,* Dante grounds his conviction that his poetry is ontological in the Incarnation. In the *Ars,* textual solipsism, which turns physical consummation into the echo of writing's deferral, lets Ovid dismantle the same claim to presence in the very breath that he makes it. Even as the *Ars* proclaims by its title that it has made love rational and knowable and thus a pragmatic enchiridion of personal relations for Romans, it subverts the pretense that it is educative, or that it mimetically represents the social world.[43] And as Ovid's irony cancels the very program the *Ars* enacts, love gains the

---

42. In this sense, Ovid also authors the moral repudiations of him in the Middle Ages: one striking instance of this is the inclusion of *Ars amatoria* in Jankyn's book of wicked wives in Chaucer's "Wife of Bath's Prologue." See further Michael Calabrese, *Chaucer's Ovidian Arts of Love* (Gainesville: University of Florida Press, 1994), 81–109.

43. On the ironic, rhetorical turn away from the simultaneously advanced claim to mimesis in the *Amores,* see my *The Cast of Character* (Toronto: University of Toronto Press, 1983), 20–47; on the *Metamorphoses,* see *The Cast of Character,* 7–14, 56–70. The affinity of the *Heroides* to rhetorical *suasoriae* would have been apparent to any Roman: Ovid, however, has hobbled the letters' rhetorical effectiveness from the start. How can persuasion succeed when it has been deliberately robbed of its immediacy? Once again irony works against the work's professed intentions. That the same thing occurs in the *Remedia amoris* would seem to be obvious. Yet this poem was especially prized in the Middle Ages precisely because the commentators said it really does work to undo the effects of carnal love!

solidity of an object in the real world, in the sense that no other figure can serve as a trope for it because a space no longer exists for a metonymy to stand beside it, for a metaphor to substitute for it, for a referent to be the thing it points to. But for Dante, despite the laughter it provokes, Ovid's irony could only be a figure of mortality, its negations as real as death because they short-circuit translation and metamorphosis by interposing between the form that was and the form that replaces it the nothingness that is the residue of self-cancellation.[44] In the face of such dissolution, which frustrates in advance any effort to turn love into an allegory of being, what else could Dante do but (ironically) eradicate it?

In a sense, Dante broke most decisively with his literary heritage when he made allegory and irony, once merely rhetorical figures for saying more than one thing at once, the forms of discourse through which he translated the poetry of antiquity. In the *Comedy*, Virgil and Ovid become antagonists in the debate these two forms of polysemous meaning always stage to stand as the source of figurative language. Chaucer certainly paid attention to this debate; one can only imagine his reaction when he saw Dante resolve it by claiming his vernacular was not merely the equal of Latin, no matter whether that Latin was Virgil's or Ovid's, but was in fact the language of a poem that pronounced itself sacred. By the time he began *The Canterbury Tales*, however, Chaucer had also read the *Filostrato* and *Teseida*; in these verse chronicles of Troy and Greece, he watched the young Boccaccio take the palms Dante had given himself through Virgil and, blithely eroticizing his predecessor's baptism of the *Aeneid*, bestow them on Ovid. At the end of the *Tales*, where Chaucer cast his coldest eye on his own poetry's virtues and vices, he revisited the issues these Italian texts had raised *tout ensemble*. In the next chapter I will show that, like Dante, Chaucer considered the connection between irony and allegory in conjunction with Ovid; in the Manciple's prologue and tale, however, rather than efface the Roman love-poet's self-asserting cancellations,

---

44. As John Freccero has noted, writing is a form of idolatry in the *Inferno*. The damned in fact are dead matter; they exist as if a reification of irony. In the terms of my argument, I would recast Freccero's point, which informs all I have said and will say about irony in this and in the next chapter, by calling the damned untranslatable metamorphoses. See "Infernal Irony: The Gates of Hell," in *Dante: The Poetics of Conversion*, ed. Rachel Jacoff (Cambridge: Harvard University Press, 1986), 93–109.

Chaucer embraced them. His embrace, though, was less Boccaccian than one might have expected; as we will see, at the same moment that Chaucer endorses his steward's call to silence, he transforms it into a multiply-voiced narrative of conversion. As his pilgrims neared Canterbury, Chaucer, I will argue, made Dante and Boccaccio his Virgil and Ovid; he seems to summon them as authorial spirits to witness how, by translating their translations of irony and allegory, he has generated the mode of meaning of the *Tales*. Perhaps, had they heeded his call, they would have understood and approved; perhaps not. It is, though, at such a séance that one makes contact with Chaucer's Italian Tradition.

3

Chaucer's Canterbury Poetics: Irony, Allegory, and the Manciple's Prologue and Tale

For a long time, irony and allegory have occupied prominent but opposing places in the lexicon of criticism on *The Canterbury Tales*; recently, however, readers of Chaucer have grown suspicious about granting either one the status of a first principle that governs the organization and reception of the *Tales* and the pilgrims who tell them. New Critical and exegetical interpretations virtually defined themselves according to the ways in which they deployed these figures; commentators such as Lee Patterson have demonstrated how adherents of one or the other approach, by burying their political commitments in what they assumed were unchanging operations of language or belief, presented a Chaucer strangely detached from the economic, social, and political conditions of late medieval England.[1] From a different quarter, textual critics have interrogated the use of these or any concepts to promote ideas of order and unity the manuscripts will not sustain. To tease out Chaucer's global intentions from the uncertain disposition of tales becomes a high-risk game of assumption and inference: whether "The Parson's Tale," for instance, was meant to be the last tale told, or whether Chaucer even intended it should be part of the *Tales*, much less provide a retrospective gloss for them, are questions scribal evidence warrants asking.[2]

---

1. Lee Patterson, *Negotiating the Past* (Madison: University of Wisconsin Press, 1987), 3–39; see also Derek Pearsall's comments, *The Canterbury Tales* (London: George Allen and Unwin, 1985), 318–19.

2. A number of critics have relied on the uncertainty of textual evidence to call into question the assumption that the Parson's rejection of fiction in his prologue and emphasis on penance in his tale coincides with Chaucer's final vision of the scope and purpose of *The Canterbury Tales*. See Charles Owen, *Pilgrimage and Story-Telling in the Canterbury*

It is an irony of history that allegory and irony should have become identifying characteristics of antagonistic approaches to Chaucer, since in medieval rhetorical theory both figures were closely related. Because it simultaneously negates what it asserts, irony in fact was considered a kind of allegory, which was the name for any language that said more than one thing at once. It is equally ironic that these figures should have been dissociated from history, since, as I hope to demonstrate, irony and allegory virtually constitute the style of the social and the historical in the *Tales*. Moreover, even though tales and blocks of tales are fragmentary, the prologues and endlinks to them show that Chaucer did conceive of them as parts of a whole. While we cannot in many cases say a particular order is his, *The Canterbury Tales* do subscribe to the idea of order, an idea that irony and allegory—the figures that join negation and plenitude together—help to realize.

I want to argue these propositions by examining the Manciple's prologue and tale. Many feel the performance of the thieving steward Chaucer describes in "The General Prologue" hastens what James Dean has called the dismantling of the Canterbury book.[3] In the Manciple's tale, not only irony but speech itself yields to a cynicism so alienated, words clot and sour on the tongue; with its closing injunctions to silence, Chaucer seems to disengage from his fiction and confront "the limits of poetic utterance."[4] Chaucer's renunciation of his craft then becomes unequivocal in the affectless prose of the Parson's tale of penance and the repudiations of the "Retraction" that follow: all poetry that is not part of the discourse of the spirit is explicitly revoked.

Although the Manciple's tale does indeed move toward "alienation and silence," the portrait of the man and the prologue to his tale do not. In "The General Prologue," Chaucer explicitly links the Manciple to irony; in the prologue to his tale, the Manciple seems to embody it, once

---

Tales (Norman: University of Oklahoma Press, 1977; A. J. Minnis, *Medieval Theory of Authorship* (London: Scolar Press, 1984); and especially David Lawton, "Chaucer's Two Ways: The Pilgrimage Frame of *The Canterbury Tales*," *Studies in the Age of Chaucer* 9 (1987): 3–40. More generally, Norman Blake especially has argued against basing critical assumptions on the Ellesmere order: see *The Textual Tradition of the Canterbury Tales* (London: Edward Arnold, 1985). I argue below that the Parson's monological view of language dialectically engages the dialogic style of the Manciple's prologue and tale, in which allegory and irony collide; together the tales constitute a satisfying sense of ending for Chaucer's book, even if we cannot say that this sequence represents his final intention.

3. James Dean, "Dismantling the Canterbury Book," *PMLA* 100 (1985): 746–62.

4. The quotation is from Stephen Knight, "Chaucer and the Sociology of Literature," *Studies in the Age of Chaucer* 2 (1980): 51.

when he excuses the Cook from telling a tale, and again when he offers him his gourd of wine. In each case, however, ironic negations and reversals rehabilitate and vindicate Chaucer's fiction. They do so in two ways: first, by evoking a host of voices related to the Manciple's, whose polyphony counters his desire to reduce language's capacity to mean to his own denial of its truthfulness, and second, by evoking allegorical contexts, through which the antinomies and rivalries that give the material world its structure at the same time cancel them by heralding the advent of the spiritual. As the pilgrimage comes ever closer to Canterbury, Chaucer increasingly makes the style of his own fiction his subject; in his poetics, the final silence that completes repentance ironically refutes all the chatter of the world and allegorically justifies it.[5] Both the silence and the chatter are part of a final transformation that lies at the heart of Chaucer's Italian tradition.

The portrait of the Manciple in "The General Prologue" is striking, less for his brand of venality than for the pilgrim Chaucer's attitude toward it. Of this noble "achatour" Chaucer says,

> A gentil MAUNCIPLE was ther of a temple,
> Of which achatours myghte take exemple
> For to be wise in byynge of vitaille;
> For wheither that he payde or took by taille,
> Algate he wayted so in his achaat
> That he was ay biforn and in good staat.
> Now is nat that of God a ful fair grace
> That swich a lewed mannes wit shal pace
> The wisdom of an heep of lerned men?
> Of maistres hadde he mo than thries ten,
> That weren of lawe expert and curious,

---

5. In the following argument, it is clear that I accept the linkage of "The Manciple's Tale" to "The Parson's Tale" and am convinced that together they bring *The Canterbury Tales* to completion. As the editor of the *Variorum* edition of "The Manciple's Tale" says, the textual evidence "strongly suggests that the earliest scribes" thought Fragment H should immediately precede Fragment I. See Donald C. Baker, ed., *The Manciple's Tale, A Variorum Edition of the Works of Geoffrey Chaucer*, vol. 2: *The Canterbury Tales*, pt. 10 (Norman: University of Oklahoma Press, 1984), 44. Even in Hengwrt, whose order constitutes the chief challenge to Ellesmere, the word "Maunciple" seems to have been written, in the scribe's hand, over an erasure at the beginning of "The Prologue to the Parson's Tale." The tales are joined and always stand last in all complete manuscripts.

> Of which ther were a duszeyne in that hous
> Worthy to been stywardes of rente and lond
> Of any lord that is in Engelond,
> To make hym lyve by his propre good
> In honour dettelees (but if he were wood),
> Or lyve as scarsly as hym list desire;
> And able for to helpen al a shire
> In any caas that myghte falle or happe.
> And yet this Manciple sette hir aller cappe.
>
> (A.567–86)

Though Chaucer acknowledges the Manciple's cunning with something like bemused admiration, his purser's malfeasance leaves a disagreeable aftertaste. Chaucer produces this double effect by structuring the portrait as an analogy. As a procurer of provisions, the Manciple's perspicacity makes him an ideal practitioner of his profession, since manciples were charged with overseeing the domestic affairs, especially the table, of a college or Inn of Court. But this particular Manciple pulls the wool over the eyes of the lawyers for whom he procures, masters whose potential stewardship in principle makes them manciples to the lords they would serve.[6] By itself the Manciple's thievery is the dishonesty of a shrewd but small mind; in the context of the portrait, however, it seems to acquire outsized implications, as if his conniving threatens to pull inside out the relations that link and regulate all levels of English society. Were stewards to discharge their obligations to their lords, and lords their duty to the shire, the way the Manciple discharges his, every social transaction from the buying of food to the governing of the realm would become a commodification of deceit.

The Manciple's vigilance in grocery shopping, therefore, is something more than preparation for his quarrel with the Cook; the repetition of "achatours / achaat" is more than a stylistic forecast of the repetitions of his tale ("Whit was this crowe as is a snow-whit swan," H.133, etc.). By superimposing his petty fraud against the larger ideas of stew-

---

6. According to the MED (s.v. (1) a), a steward was "an official or servant in charge of the domestic affairs of a household"; the term came to be applied to a "noble appointed to supervise at a feast; also an officer in charge of provisions." The duties of manciple and steward overlap; at least some of the contempt for the aristocracy that Chaucer's Manciple shows may derive from his envy of better-born men who do what he does. More particularly, his contempt perhaps stems from his association with the lawyers of his temple, who probably were members of the aristocracy. (See note 37 in this chapter.)

ardship, law, and the maintenance of the well-ordered community, Chaucer has implied that, no matter how private, the Manciple's dealings still are part of the public discourse of professions, and that his intentions, no matter how mean, still are comprehended by the civic function they subvert. Yet for all this emphasis on the social formation of the Manciple's character, he is chiefly defined by Chaucer's reaction to him. In his own voice the narrator seems impressed by the Manciple's guile even as he deliberately distances himself from it: "Now is nat that of God a ful fair grace . . ." In its double-edgedness, its approving disapproval, the narrator's irony translates those sly but fraudulent acts that provoke it.[7]

The temptation is strong to see this response as personal, Chaucer's peculiar displeasure for the Manciple's kind of chicanery. But complex as it is, Chaucer's stance here is not really his own; it is Luke's, when he tells the parable of the wicked steward:

> There was a certain rich man who had a steward: and the same was accused unto him, that he had wasted his goods. And he called him, and said to him: "How is it that I hear this of thee? give an account of thy stewardship: for now thou canst be steward no longer." And the steward said within himself: "What shall I do? for my lord taketh away from me the stewardship: to dig I am not able: to beg I am ashamed. I know what I will do, that when I shall be put out of the stewardship, they may receive me into their houses." Therefore calling together every one of his lord's debtors, he said to the first: "How much dost thou owe my lord?" But he said: "A hundred barrels of oil." And he said to him: "Take thy bill, and sit down quickly, and write fifty." Then he said to another: "And how much dost thou owe?" Who said: "A hundred quarters of wheat." He said to him: "Take thy bill and write eighty." And the lord commended the unjust steward *(villicum iniquitatis)*, forasmuch as he had done wisely: for the children of this world are wiser in their generation than the children of light. And I say to you: make yourselves friends of the mammon of iniquity *(de mammona iniquitatis)*, that when ye

---

7. Unlike other instances in "The General Prologue," Chaucer's words here seem to be an instance of irony in the technical sense; we imagine him conveying the opposite meaning of what he says through pronunciation. For this definition of irony, a commonplace of classical rhetorical tradition, see Isidore of Seville, *Etymologiarum libri XV*: I 37, 25: "ironia est sententia per pronuntiationem contrarium habens intellectum." Quoted in Hennig Brinkmann, *Mittelalterliche Hermeneutik* (Tübingen: Niemeyer, 1980), 217–18; for further medieval elaboration, see Brinkmann, 218–19.

shall fail, they may receive you into everlasting dwellings. (Luke 16:1–9)

Chaucer's Manciple has a portion in the special irony of Jesus's commendation. The wicked steward in the Bible does act wisely in a difficult situation; by remitting part of the debtors' liability, he purchases their good will and future entrance to their houses. Nevertheless, the wisdom of this world is pound foolish: the steward's charity to those in debt is one final defrauding of his lord. Thus, as the commentaries explain, when the lord praises the steward's wisdom, he commends not the deception but the shrewdness that inspired it.[8] The steward has forfeited the right to dwell with his master, but the cunning way he has assured admittance to the houses of his lord's debtors nevertheless is an object lesson to those who would walk the path to light.

At the same time, however, Jesus's final embrace of the steward's conduct obliterates it. In his own voice he offers wily, practical counsel, counsel that the faithful instantly reject. "Make friends with the mammon of iniquity," Jesus advises, "enter into the economy that determines social relations on earth, so that when you fail at the end of days you may find dwelling in eternal tabernacles ('aeterna tabernacula')," by which presumably he means the tabernacles of hell.[9] In the face of the eschaton, the success of all worldly maneuvering becomes silly-wise.

Jesus can damn with real, not faint, praise here because his talking at cross-purposes, instead of producing an impasse in meaning, becomes part of allegory's project to speak otherwise. If irony negates the subject it posits, if by saying "I and Not- I" at once it creates a rift of contradiction no logic can repair, allegory transforms such oppositions into analogies of difference.[10] Luke's parable in particular exemplifies the

---

8. See, for instance, Hugh of St. Cher, *Evangelii super Lucam*, 208–9. His comment reflects a long tradition, but, as we shall see, it by no means is the only reading of the steward's foresight.

9. This is Ambrose's reading: "pecuniae uilis usura tabernacula defunctis adquirit aeterna . . ." *Expositio Evangelii secundum Lucam*, VII, 122–23 in *Traité sur l'Évangile de S. Luc*, ed. G. Tissot, 2 vols., *Sources Chrétiennes* 45, 52 (Paris: du Cerf, 1952), 2:255. Most commentators, however, influenced by the positive overtones of "tabernacula," see the eternal dwellings as a metaphor for heaven. I explain the divergence below.

10. In these characterizations of irony and allegory I follow Gordon Teskey, "Irony, Allegory, and Metaphysical Decay," *PMLA* 109 (1994): 397–408; now in *Allegory and Violence* (Ithaca: Cornell University Press, 1996). Drawing on de Man's "The Concept of Irony," Teskey offers a powerful analysis of the inevitable linkage and fundamental incompatibility of irony and allegory in the rhetorical tradition. See also Larry Scanlon, "The Authority of Fable: Allegory and Irony in the *Nun's Priest's Tale*," *Exemplaria* 1

biblical method of taming irony's impulse toward nihilism, toward what Gordon Teskey has called "the absolute, nondialectical oppositions of antiphrasis," which is the form of irony that "derives its name from negation."[11] In one utterance, Jesus twice bespeaks himself. He impersonates the steward's voice of worldly expediency: "Make friends," he says, "with the mammon of iniquity."[12] At the same time this exhortation reformulates the lord's commendation. But though Jesus can speak as master and servant, neither steward nor lord speaks for him. In a voice not theirs—above theirs—Jesus invokes an apocalyptic context, which immediately cancels the literal, opportunistic sense of his words by identifying it as a rhetorical deflection from their ultimate significance. Like the leaves scattered through Dante's universe that are gathered into one volume bound by love, even contrary antagonisms have been made part of an unfolding proliferation of forms already and always unified in the mind of God. Through impersonation Luke domesticates irony's oppositions by extending them into a metanarrative in which this life's husbandries are both canceled by those of the next and reformed in their image. "Not-I" negates "I" and stands beside it; the steward is wise and corrupt; his foresight is and is not a model for the children of light. Instead of being a principle of annulment, contradiction has been transformed into a postulate of simultaneous continuity and fracture between the historical world and the timeless realms of the spirit.[13] Irony's negations have been translated into allegory's concurrent swerve from propriety and promise of return to a truer form of it; single-minded negations have become sites of doubled vision, wherein acts that undermine the social ideal are immoral because they undo the sanctioned material order, and com-

---

(1989): 43–68. Scanlon also briefly treats the connection of irony to allegory; like me he sees in the association a justification of Chaucer's fiction.

11. On antiphrasis, see Quintilian, *Instituto oratoria*, vol. 3: 9.2.47. Quintilian's discussion epitomizes the rhetorical tradition's classification of irony as a species of allegory "in which opposites are shown" (8.6.54). For the medieval transmission of this tradition, see Brinkmann, *Mittelalterliche Hermeneutik*, 214–19; and Teskey, "Irony, Allegory, and Metaphysical Decay," 399.

12. That the steward ("villicus iniquitatis") and Mammon ("de mammona iniquitatis") share the same quality reinforces the impression that Jesus impersonates the servant's voice.

13. Jesus' impersonation in fact makes irony the appropriate figure to mirror the paradoxical, but not self-negating, epistemology of parables in general, which couch the profoundest truth in forms so simple they confound the wise.

mendable because they proclaim every earthly community the shadow of a different, higher sodality that will finally replace it.

Depending on whether one regards this life or the next, therefore, Luke's parable altogether endorses or completely does away with the emphasis classical ethics had placed on the relative and the mean. Formally, however, by joining irony and allegory, the parable is entirely conventional. Because irony says one thing but implies the opposite, in ancient and medieval rhetorical theory it was always considered a species of allegory, which was defined as that general category of language wherein proper meaning is deflected. Whether created through intonation or by verbal means, from Quintilian to Isidore, through Bede and Gervais of Melkley, all forms of linguistic contrariety, rather than bringing discourse to a halt, were seen as a way of doubling it.[14]

In the Middle Ages, parables were the ideal form to exhibit the connection between allegory and irony. By definition, parables sustain a comparison between dissimilar kinds of things.[15] To the extent that one foregrounds the comparison, parables therefore *were* allegories in the rhetorical sense of the word: extended metaphors that say one thing and mean another. Indeed, because they were spoken by Jesus, the Gospel parables were even thought to partake of the mysteries that characterize theological allegory: from the earliest times many details were interpreted spiritually. But Jesus also announced a time when there would be no need to speak in parables (e.g. John 16:25); to the extent, then, that one foregrounds dissimilarity, the parables would tend toward irony, juxtaposing things whose incompatibility increasingly borders on pure opposition.

Medieval commentators recognized the contrary pull of these impulses and did their best to make them companionable; they acknowledged that the literal can have an extended or allegorical sense, but at the same time they emphasized the difference between this kind of polysemy and divine discourse. Parables provided the pattern that demonstrated how human speech could house multiple meanings: by

---

14. For medieval discussions of irony and the other figures of rhetorical allegory, which include *aenigma* (riddle), *charientismos* (euphemism), *paroimia* (proverb), and *sarcasmos*, see Brinkmann, *Mittelalterliche Hermeneutik*, 214–19.

15. "Parabola est rerum genere dissimilium comparatio"; the definition comes from Cicero. For a discussion of the range of meanings parable had in the Middle Ages, see Brinkmann, *Mittelalterliche Hermeneutik*, 164–68.

the time of Aquinas, in fact, figurative meaning generally had been given the name *parabolic* ("parabolicus seu metaphoricus").[16] But because this proliferation of senses was generated by overstepping the bounds of the proper, it could never be more than a rhetorical trope; the resemblance parabolic language bore to the anagogic unity of spiritual allegory was of the lowest order.[17]

Medieval interpretations of the parable of the wicked steward are exemplary in this regard.[18] Not surprisingly, a fault line runs through the logic of the commentaries. Some take the lord's commendation of the steward literally, but in order to do so, they read the steward's actions metaphorically, nearly to the point of allegory: by forgiving our neighbor's debts, we make friends with the angels and saints (Ambrose); by modifying the accounts, the steward shows that a life of penance requires the release of our debtors and almsgiving (Haimo of Auxerre).[19] Others read the commendation metaphorically; to do so, they take the steward's fraud literally, and ironically find moral sustenance by rejecting it.[20] These inconsistencies create little tension, even if the distance they interpose between cause and effect seems to widen almost to the point of contradiction. As Bonaventure explains, the parable obviously mixes literal and parabolic teaching: the lord's praise of prudent behavior is literal, since it speaks to the steward's liberality and mercy, but his fraud is detestable and something Jesus would

---

16. De Bruyne's model of the senses that were ascribed to the literal is still useful. Words can have both proper and figurative meaning; under proper meaning, one understands the denotative definition of words (the "historical" sense), the meaning they bear by reason of their cause ("secundum aetiologiam"), and the meaning they bear by virtue of their proportionate relationship to other elements in the work, through which the unity of thought is conveyed ("secundum analogiam"). Under figurative meaning, one understands the "typical" ("typicus"), that is, the individual representing the universal; the parabolic or allegorical in the rhetorical sense; and the moral, in the sense that beast fables contain a moral that is not conveyed by what they literally say. See Edgar de Bruyne, *Études D'Esthétique Médiévale*, 3 vols. (Bruges: De Tempel, 1946), 2:312. On the relation of beast fables to parables, see below, note 24.

17. Aquinas makes these points in the *Summa Theologica*, 1.1.10.

18. For a complete summary of medieval commentary on this as well as the other biblical parables, see Stephen Wailes, *Medieval Allegories of Jesus' Parables* (Berkeley and Los Angeles: University of California Press, 1987). Wailes documents the pronounced tendency to allegorize details from the parables throughout the Middle Ages.

19. See Wailes, *Medieval Allegories*, 249–50.

20. Augustine is a good example of this reading. He comments that the parable teaches by contraries: not all aspects praised by the lord are to be imitated. *Quaestionum evangeliorum libri duo, Patrologia Latina*, 35:1348. See Wailes, *Medieval Allegories*, 247.

never have supported; it teaches only parabolically, by means of contraries.[21]

Such accommodations, however, cannot entirely put to rest the fundamental struggle between irony and allegory over the nature of figurative language itself. According to Quintilian, whose account, though modified, set the terms of discussion throughout the Middle Ages, language becomes figurative when what is said bends away or deviates from what is meant, much the way nouns in the oblique cases were thought to decline from the "uprightness" of the nominative. Allegory is the home and source of all such expressions; it operates by ordering the divergence of meanings it creates as parts to the whole. Allegory simultaneously produces and repairs the tilt away from the nominative by presupposing an original, "linguistically omnipotent self," a self "that both intends and deflects its intentions in a language that it 'uses.'"[22] Under such a dispensation, which is, as we shall see, very much like Petrarch's, even irony's opposition of same and different will participate in one unifying truth and thereby become a form of likeness.

But if, as Teskey says, the essence of irony is antiphrasis, it, rather than allegory, is the site of the genesis of tropes. Since irony "speaks not from an angular but from an opposite position," it must be part of allegory's arc of deflection, but what is posited there is posited as absolute, nondialectical negation, as I and Not-I at once. Contradiction rather than identity is the limit of divergency; all deflected language is consequently closer genetically to antithesis than to similitude, nor will any interpretation be able to restore to it a prior "uprightness" or propriety. On the contrary, "speaking *against* now comes before, and enables, speaking *other*."[23] Allegory emerges out of irony, which haunts from within every attempt to construct a polysemous system of correspondence. In the primal scene where they meet, figuration, which is the result of their encounter, now looks more toward the meaningless noise

---

21. As Wailes says, Bonaventure therefore allegorizes some elements of the story: the steward's inability to dig, for instance, shows that the weak of spirit will not accept the corporal labor that the perfection of penance requires. Other elements he accepts as literal, such as the adjusted debts; *Commentarius in Evangelium S. Lucae,* cited in Wailes, *Medieval Allegories,* 247–48.

22. The quotation comes from Teskey, "Irony, Allegory, and Metaphysical Decay," 399.

23. Teskey, "Irony, Allegory, and Metaphysical Decay," 399.

and random, unceasing juxtapositions of chaos than toward the transcendental silence of a logos singular to itself.

Far more than medieval commentators perceived, the parable of the wicked steward dramatizes what is at stake in the clash between irony and allegory. Unlike other instances, such as the parable of the mustard seed, allegory and irony here arise from the same utterances. Within the narrative, the lord's commendation of the steward's cunning begets a complementary declaration, which like it is both praise and rebuke: "For the children of this world are wiser in their generation than the children of light." Interpreting these words is difficult, not so much because we need to decide whether they are straightforward or meant to refute what they denote, but because we cannot read the sentence allegorically without reading it ironically at the same time. The figurative language—"the children of this world" and "the children of light"—invites us to take the opposition these terms suggest as a metaphor for the contrast between this life and the next. But if we do, the assertion cancels itself: in the last analysis, when all generations have passed away, only the children of light are wise. So where do these children of light come from: are they begotten from the irony or from the allegory of the statement?[24]

Outside the narrative, interpreting it, we find an exhortation that, instead of drawing a clarifying (and therefore reductive) lesson from the story, repeats its inhering ambiguity: "And I say unto you: make yourself friends of the mammon of iniquity, that when ye shall fail, they may receive you into eternal tabernacles." In most parabolic utterances, the hermeneutic imperative is to establish the hidden likeness that enables the differences to be compared. Here no similarity brought in from beyond the text seems to reconcile those differences; irony runs unchecked, to the point that Jesus seems to turn heaven into hell. Yet even here, as we have seen, Luke does work to limit the effect of the irony by doubling the language from which it arises. In repeating the lord's commendation, Jesus's counsel also subordinates it; as soon as they reiterate one another, the reversals both statements occasion have

---

24. The commentaries reveal the aporia in interpretation very nicely: both the children of this world and the children of light are variously interpreted. Most often, as one might expect, they are contrasted, to the benefit of the latter. But other exegetes reversed the valency (Peter Chrysologus); Innocent III takes both groups negatively! See Wailes, *Medieval Allegories*, 252–53.

been situated in the domain of the same, and (ironically, of course) an order (inside and outside, contained and container) has been established between them.

Because Chaucer saw the Manciple's cunning subversion of his office as a corruption of the entire social order, he fashioned his déclassé steward, who, like Luke's, defrauds the masters he serves by cooking his records of purchase, after that equally sly "villicus iniquitatis."[25] More importantly, Luke's parable furnished Chaucer a set of traditionally connected rhetorical figures to associate with the Manciple, which between them define the range and power, as well as the dangers, of poetic language. Most of all, however, Luke demonstrated how through impersonation these figures can translate without canceling each other. When Chaucer wrote the "Prologue to the Manciple's Tale," he extended his meditation on the inevitable linkage of polysemy and negation, and on impersonation as a means of simultaneously representing their manners of meaning. The Manciple will speak, both for himself and for the Cook, with all the irony an alienating cynicism can command, but what he says does more than deny because he has been otherwise involved in allegories of conversion.

The "Prologue to the Manciple's Tale" begins with a question that asks readers to locate themselves:

> Woot ye nat where ther stant a litel toun
> Which that ycleped is Bobbe-up-and-doun,
> Under the Blee, in Caunterbury Weye?
> Ther gan oure Hooste for to jape and pleye,

---

25. There is a formal link between the parable in general and the Manciple as well: to the extent that his tale is a beast fable, it is first cousin to parables. In discussing *homoiosis*, which is the demonstration of something less known by drawing an analogy between it and something similar but better known, medieval rhetoricians classified both the *apologus* and the *parabola* as kinds of *paradigmae* or exempla, that is, exhortatory or warning examples. The *apologus* introduced its analogies from the beast world, the *parabola* drew them from human interaction. See Brinkmann, *Mittelalterliche Hermeneutik*, 165–66.

Chaucer certainly thought the Manciple a child of this world, wise in his generation: in the tale he endlessly reinforces the association through his exhausting recitation of his mother's injunctions to keep quiet: "My sone, thenk on the crowe, a Goddes name! / My sone, keep wel thy tonge, and keep thy freend" (H.318–19), and so forth. These strictures have rightly reminded many readers of *Proverbs*. *Parabola* and *proverbium* were also synonyms: the Book of Proverbs itself was called *Parabolae Solomonis*.

And seyde, "Sires, what! Dun is in the myre!
Is ther no man, for preyere ne for hyre,
That wole awake oure felawe al bihynde?
A theef myghte hym ful lightly robbe and bynde.
See how he nappeth! See how, for cokkes bones,
That he wol falle fro his hors atones!

(H.1–9)

The straggler, of course, is the Cook, whom the Manciple besmirches while excusing him from telling a tale. In response,

the Cook wax wrooth and wraw,
And on the Manciple he gan nodde faste
For lakke of speche, and doun the hors hym caste,
Where as he lay, til that men hym up took.

(H.46–50)

This is both roadside drama and drama that points to the road beside it. At Bobbe-up-and-doun, the Cook and Manciple travel in two directions at once; as they quarrel, they mark out one path for their souls and a contrary path for the spiritual pilgrimage to Canterbury, for their actions recall and parody Paul's conversion.

Soon after his persecution of Stephen, Saul asked the high priest for letters to the synagogues at Damascus,

ut si quos invenisset huius vie viros ac mulieres vinctos perduceret in hierusalem. et cum iter feceret contigit ut appropinquaret Damasco et subito circumfulsit eum lux de celo et cadens in terram audivit vocem dicentem sibi Saule Saule quid me persequeris. (Acts 9:2–4)

[that if he found any men and women of this way, he might bring them bound to Jerusalem. And as he went on his journey, it came to pass, that he drew near to Damascus: and suddenly a light from heaven shone round about him. And falling on the ground, he heard a voice saying to him, "Saul, Saul, why dost thou persecute me?"]

In the Vulgate account, it is not clear whether Paul went by horse or by foot: medieval iconography of the incident in fact accommodated both possibilities. In the majority of scenes, however, Paul is on horseback or was just before he falls: his horse appears either to have stumbled or has been blinded and has thrown him.[26] With the Host's cry that "Dun is in the mire" (the horse is in the mire), Chaucer announces that this game in his fiction is played in "ernest."[27] The sleepy Cook of London rides the (Pilgrim's) "Weye" to Canterbury, an easy prey for a thief to "robbe and *bynde*": the kind of man a persecutor like Saul would catch on the *way* ("huius vie") and bring *bound* ("vinctos") to Jerusalem. The metaphorical mire, the actual "slough" Harry wants the Cook's horse to avoid (H.64), the heaviness that has overcome Roger (H.22), the real weight of his "dronken cors" (H.67), even his admission that he would now rather sleep than drink, whereas the night before he drank rather than slept (H.22–24): literally and figuratively the scene seems to point to the need for spiritual rebirth.

But as Chaucer stages this allegory of the soul's conversion on the way to the "Jerusalem celestial" that the Parson sees the nearer he gets to Canterbury, his Saul splits into two: one the object, the other the agent, of the nullifying spirit of irony. As object the sodden Cook paradoxically embodies irony's propensity toward noncoincidence by powerfully countering any movement toward change. Unlike his confreres, whom the Pardoner claims "stampe, and streyne, and grynde / And turnen substaunce into accident" (C.537–38), this mormal-ridden maker of blancmange doggedly remains what he was. Accident has become substance in him; crapulent now, he will drink merely to be drunk and hung over tomorrow. Though his anger at the Manciple will soon reduce him to witless "lakke of speche," the night before, when in his cups, he was also something less than the creature God made in the image of his word. If nothing else, the comparison of various grades of inebriation to animals (the Manciple says Roger has "dronken ... wyn ape"), rests on wine's wresting from humans their distinctive power to speak meaningfully.[28] As the Manciple implies, the Cook has fallen away from the place people occupy in God's order. Inert, detached

---

26. In the Princeton Index of Christian Art, there are thirty-four depictions of Paul on horseback in illuminated mss., four paintings, two frescoes, three sculptural portrayals, two in glass, and an ivory diptych, all before 1400. I want to thank Elaine Beretz for providing this information to me.

27. For a description of the game of Dun Is in the Mire, see Baker, *Variorum*, 81.

28. See the helpful note in the *Variorum*, 87–88. Compare the Summoner, who "wolde speke and crie as he were wood" after he had drunk "strong wyn" (A.635–36). This religious figure debases language to the point of stupidity and unintelligibility; he is the other side of the Friar, who perverts language for sexual and monetary ends. Both are presented as adulterers of God's word.

from the others, the Cook resists incorporation into larger communities because, not being himself, he is incapable of being like anyone else. He is at odds with allegory's compulsion to unite through synecdoche; instead he stands as the ironic end-product of what Teskey calls "metaphysical decay," that dropping off from the polysemous unity of God into its counterpoint, a morass of matter nearly exhausted of its form, a singularity that defies intelligibility. More than half-brother to Stevens's snowman, the Cook comes close to being the nothing that is there; sunk in his density, he is irony's version of pure language, sheerly exterior, fallen from the possibility of signification, very nearly the untranslatable.

The thief who catches and binds the Cook is the Manciple. He is ironic in a more insidious way than Roger, since he is the efficient cause, the agent who in speaking for the Cook will intentionally render him the speechless, "hevy dronken cors" he becomes. Indeed, the Manciple cynically forecloses the very possibility of conversion by leveling its contraries. For him, *before* and *after* not only do not mark an essential difference in condition, they are lies that disguise the fact that nothing has really changed. Thus the Manciple politely releases Roger from telling a tale on the one hand (H.25–29), but immediately defames the Cook's character on the other (H.30–45). Though this seems a reversal in behavior, the Manciple is never less than malicious, even when his malice has been cloaked as politesse:

> "Wel," quod the Maunciple, "if it may doon ese
> To thee, sire Cook, and to no wight displese,
> Which that heere rideth in this compaignye,
> And that oure Hoost wole, of his curteisye,
> I wol as now excuse thee of thy tale."
>
> (H.25–29)

Considering how it purchases the audience's complaisance, what is ironic in this *captatio benevolentiae* is its apparent lack of irony. Since his regard for the Cook's "ese" parallels his concern for the Host's "courtesy" and the company's welfare, the Manciple at first reconfederates the laggard with the fellowship. By the time his sentence ends, however, the Manciple has again set Roger entirely apart from the other pilgrims. Similarly, in retrospect, because we know the Manciple holds aristocratic values in contempt—for him "degree" is nothing more than high-toned language that gilds the basest acts (H.212–22)—the sarcasm of his "sirring" the Cook becomes impossible to separate from the respect the title accords him.[29] As he traduces the Cook with a deference that is oh so mannerly, and cheats him, in the name of the greater good of all, of the chance to do penance by telling a tale, the Manciple denies both individual and community the possibility of reformation. His contemptuous irony lets him declare himself the standard-bearer of "nothing that is not there"; his manner of meaning would make translation impossible.

Thus the actual maligning of the Cook, which begins with the Manciple's next word, does not contradict the spirit of what he has just said but continues it. The Manciple's denunciation meticulously follows the same order that his absolving of the Cook had: as before, he moves from Roger himself—focusing on his eyes, which are half-shut; his mouth, which is too open; and his breath, which poses a danger to the company ("Thy cursed breeth infecte wole us alle," H.39)—to a scoffing reprisal of the Host and his courtesy. The Manciple mimics Harry's call of "Dun in the mire" by referring to the equally popular game of fan jousting: "wol ye justen atte fan" (H.42); unlike Harry, however, in his desire to humiliate the Cook, to see him muddied, the Manciple again would soil highborn pursuits by dragging them down to the lowest level.[30] With him graciousness is indistinguishable from venom, and calumny a kind of service to the well-being of the community: a consistent mean-spiritedness enables the Manciple to make bad and good, true and false, versions of each other.

In the first part of the prologue, the Manciple's irony imperils allegory's capacity for weaving opposition into the fabric of the universe. Like Jesus in Luke's parable, the Manciple seeks to speak in two voices: out of seeming care for the Cook, he would become Roger's mouthpiece, yet in his own voice he never stops vilifying him. But unlike Jesus' steward, whose voice is affirmed even as what it says is rejected, the Manciple nullifies Roger *by* impersonating him. His "I" negates its

---

29. The fact that the Manciple uses the familiar "thou" to Roger also is a verbal indication of the irony of the title.

30. On the popularity of the game, see again Baker, *Variorum*, 86–87. To my mind, the Manciple's snide swipe at a game that prepared squires to become knights is set in context by Paul's call to arm the soul with the breastplate of faith and charity, and with the helmet of hope for salvation.

"Not-I," however, not because the Manciple recognizes the Cook as his inimical opposite but because he allocates all space to speak to himself. In the Manciple's manner of speaking, "Not-I" exists only as the denial that it can say something other than what "I" does. In canceling whatever differs from himself, the Manciple's irony makes the man by unmaking the character of everyone else.[31]

Even before Roger topples speechless from his horse, the Manciple has silenced him, left him behind in the unintelligibility of the slough, denied him the possibility of conversion. The pilgrimage itself as a polysemous event, as a scene of divergent subjectivities joined by social play and the possibility for spiritual reform, has thus been put in jeopardy by a spirit of negation that deprives its object of the potential to exist, much less to change, because it eliminates the chance for it to say something different. If allegory operates by establishing likeness even between opposites, the Manciple turns all similarity into alternate forms of emptiness. As his tale of the crow's transformation will make clear, for the Manciple black and white are contraries only in illusion; in truth, the difference between them means nothing.

For Chaucer, however, the Manciple's irony has prepared the ground for allegory; precisely because it makes every peripety an occasion for more of the same, the opposites it levels are able to substitute for one another. The way this watchful, sober child of the world who steals from the lawyers he serves suddenly falls on the tipsy Cook both associates the Manciple with the thief Harry mentions and recalls Jesus' coming as a thief in the night, an event, Paul says, of great significance for the children of light:

> the day of the Lord shall so come, as a thief in the night.... But you, brethren, are not in darkness.... For all you are the children of light, and children of the day: we are not of the night nor of darkness. Therefore, let us not sleep, as others do; but let us watch and be sober. For they that sleep, sleep in the night, and they that are drunk, are drunk in the night. But let us, who are of the day, be sober, hav-

---

31. Louise Fradenburg has also commented on the Manciple's appropriation of Roger's voice; she sees in it a complex reflection of Chaucer's position as court poet. See "The Manciple's Servant Tongue: Politics and Poetry in *The Canterbury Tales*," *ELH* 52 (1985): 85–118.

ing on the breastplate of faith and charity, and for a helmet the hope of salvation. (1 Thess. 5:2–8)[32]

To enable the Thessalonians to understand the second coming, Paul must turn earthly axiologies upside down. Though he returns to bring day and establish the kingdom of God, Jesus will not come in triumph but in stealth, like the highwayman who marauds under the cover of night. Though the waiting children of light would gladly give *this* thief all they have, they must arm themselves as adults to protect themselves from the reprobate who might waylay them whether it is day or night. As if in response to these reversals, after Roger has fallen from his horse, the Host, Cook, and Manciple replay their encounter in reverse. Instead of the hollowness of barren repetition, however, their actions acquire a second sense that inverts the demeaning intent that had impelled the Manciple's previous engineering of them. This incarnation of cynicism now ironically becomes the pilgrim through whom Chaucer multiplies oppositions in order to generate a discourse that is fully able to accommodate them. By showing that irony and allegory can translate each other's mode of meaning, this advocate of silence in others becomes the vehicle through whom Chaucer vindicates the "entente" of his fiction of impersonation: "*Al* that is writen is writen for oure doctrine" (I.1083).

Once the Cook has been remounted through the efforts of the other pilgrims, Harry excuses Roger from telling a tale:

By cause drynke hath dominacioun
Upon this man, by my savacioun,
I trowe he lewedly wolde telle his tale.
For, were it wyn or oold or moysty ale
That he hath dronke, he speketh in his nose,
And fneseth faste, and eek he hath the pose.
He hath also to do moore than ynough
To kepen hym and his capul out of the slough.

(H.57–64)

---

32. These allusions to Paul were first noted by Rodney Delasanta, "Penance and Poetry in the *Canterbury Tales*," *PMLA* 93 (1978): 240–47.

Because the Cook is drunk, he would spout gibberish and therefore talk to no one's profit ("lewedly"): he speaks through his nose, wheezes hard, and seems to have a head cold. For Roger's own well-being, and for the good of the other pilgrims as well, it is enough that he concentrate on staying in his saddle without taking on the additional burden of telling a tale. Point for point and in the same order followed by the Manciple, Harry focuses first on the Cook and then on his relation to his fellow wayfarers. Harry also speaks in two voices, as did the Manciple; but whether he speaks for himself or as the pilgrims' host, when Harry talks of Roger's sorry state, the Cook is part of the group, not split off from it. Just as Jesus' reformulation of the lord's commendation in the parable of the wicked steward allowed Luke to turn the oppositions of irony into the polysemy of allegory, Chaucer's formal doublings act to repair the Manciple's uncouplings.

Yet if the Host can say with the Manciple to the Cook, "Of me, certeyn, thou shalt nat been yglosed," neither will he flatter the Cook's detractor. He reproves the Manciple's too open reproof of the Cook; Roger could "reclayme" the Manciple and bring him "to lure" by raising doubts about the honesty of his reckonings in supplying victuals to his Inn:

> I meene, he speke wole of smale thynges,
> As for to pynchen at thy rekenynges,
> That were nat honest, if it cam to preef.
>
> (H.73–75).

Harry upbraids the Manciple in exactly the way the Manciple had called the Cook to account. He impersonates Roger, but unlike the Manciple, Harry's indirect discourse lends the Cook words that expose the fiduciary indiscretions of the man who has defamed him. And as before, the irony of the situation opens to allegory. Even as Harry catches and binds the Manciple, the figure he corners reminds us of another wily dispenser of provisions who was not quite wary enough in his dealings, the evil servant whom Jesus, coming suddenly, will separate from the righteous:

> Who, thinkest thou, is a faithful and wise servant, whom his lord hath set over his family, to give them meat *(cibum)* in season. Blessed is that servant, whom, when his lord shall come, he shall find so

doing. . . . *But if that evil servant shall say in his heart: My lord is long a coming, and shall begin to strike his fellow servants, and shall eat and drink with drunkards,* the Lord of that servant shall come in a day that he hopeth not, and at an hour that he knoweth not, and shall separate him, and appoint his portion with the hypocrites. There shall be weeping and gnashing of teeth. (Matt. 24:43–51; emphasis added)

By weighing the actions of both the good and the wicked servant, whose hidden thoughts are brought to light by being given a voice, Matthew frames this tableau of justice as if it were a question at law. By using this passage as a model for both the interchange between Harry and the Manciple and, as we shall see, the Manciple's subsequent offer of wine to the Cook, Chaucer counterbalances his recordkeeper's every negation. The same action that the Manciple undertakes to portray himself as a faithful steward to the pilgrims—his attempt to quarantine Roger and keep the company safe from his "infection"—leads Harry to identify the Manciple as a "malus servus." He has become one with the menial he smites with his tongue. This pairing does not result solely in their mutual condemnation, however, as would happen if they had been disposed of according to the Manciple's sense of equity. Rather, both men have been made players in a different, ever more urgent drama of reckonings and accountability: judge not, lest ye be judged. Even as the clever Manciple, who steals from the lawyers of his temple, and the dull Cook are assigned the same portion, a real difference is opened between them and the truly faithful master of provisions. The Manciple's antiphrastic derogations have been "infected" with a likeness that opens into allegory.

Similarly, the Host's metaphor of falcon and lure, pointedly aristocratic in its provenance, rescues the Manciple's contempt for the nobility, not only metaphorically in its suggestion that the Cook will be able to turn the tables on the Manciple, but socially by being a figure of justice.[33] Though the image of the lure is common, if Chaucer remembered Dante's striking use of it in the *Purgatorio,* his transposition of it here would be apt. As Dante is about to leave the terrace on which envy is repented, Virgil explains that the form the penance takes—the sewing

---

33. "The Manciple, who, like the falcon, has been flying free and 'stooping' upon the helpless Cook, is to be 'reclaimed' when the Cook sobers up" (Baker, *Variorum,* 92). Of course, the figure also forecasts the Manciple's association of himself with the crow of his tale; more importantly, it suggests that the Cook and Manciple are birds of a feather.

shut of the former sinners' eyelids—is just because envy is a kind of misdirected seeing.[34] The devil tempts us with worldly goods, Virgil says, and we take the bait:

> e però poco val freno o richiamo.
> Chiamavi 'l cielo e 'ntorno vi si gira,
> mostrandovi le sue bellezze etterne,
> e l'occhio vostro pur a terra mira;
> onde vi batte chi tutto discerne.
>
> (*Purg.* 14.147–51)

[And therefore rein or lure (literally "recall") is of little effect. The heavens call you and circle about you, showing you their eternal splendors, and your eye looks only on the ground; wherefore he who sees all smites you.]

For all the resemblances—the Cook certainly is a man who looks only to the ground, where he tumbles as if shoved from his horse by the Manciple's malice, which one can easily believe is fueled by rivalry and envy—Chaucer may well have been most drawn by the allegorized irony of Dante's figure.[35] The heavens themselves here correspond to the spirals of the falcon, but in reverse. On earth the bird would

---

34. Virgil here and throughout cantos 13 and 14 plays on a very common but false etymology of *invidia* as a form of lack of vision.

35. One should note in this regard that Virgil explains on this terrace the system of scourge and curb, the oppositions that govern penance throughout Purgatory. The scourge goads the penitents toward the virtue that is the contrary of the vice they must repent; the curb deters from the vice itself and so must be of contrary sound to the scourge. Since envy is purged here, "the cords of the whip are drawn from love" [tratte d'amor le corde de la ferza] (*Purg.* 13.39). The irony that makes love a whip is thus an allegory for those acts of envy that had perverted love in the first place; similarly, the system of scourge and curb is an allegory of the "conmensuration" that, for Aquinas, restores the balance that is justice.

Chaucer offsets the Manciple's advocacy of silence with the Parson's penitential meditation and its insistence on confession. As the greatest book on penance the Middle Ages produced, the *Purgatorio* would be an appropriate work for Chaucer to remember here, especially in light of the fact that Harry's metaphor of "reclamation" is essentially a figure of justice, since, as Thomas Bestul says, penance itself "and the satisfaction for sin fulfill the divine requirement for justice." See Thomas Bestul, "Chaucer's Parson's Tale and the Late-Medieval Tradition of Religious Meditation," *Speculum* 64 (1989): 600–619. Moreover, the example of charity that prompts Virgil's explanation is the miracle at Cana, which will figure in the Manciple's offer of wine to the Cook.

descend in ever tighter swoops down to the lure or recall ("richiamo": compare Chaucer's "reclayme"), but this is precisely the opposite way the soul should move. It should spiral upward as it journeys through the ever-increasing orbit of the spheres until finally it rests in the infinite point that is God. Dante simultaneously inverts the valency of down and up and entirely transcends direction and geometry by locating the "richiamo" in God, whose center is everywhere and circumference nowhere. But one need not claim Chaucer took the image from Dante to see that it counterbalances the Manciple's hoodwinking of the masters of his temple, many of whom would have been members of at least the gentry, if not the upper aristocracy.[36] The very class whose efficacy as instruments of equity and truth the Manciple has called into question provides both the practice and the language whereby the Manciple's hypocrisy might be uncovered and judged.

Though the cunning Manciple's insults strike his fellow servant to the earth, he is brought up short; in the face of the Host's challenge to his own probity, he attempts a volte-face and now would "eat and drink with the drunkards" like his counterpart in Matthew. The Manciple implies he would cancel his previous slander of the Cook by maintaining he was joking—"I seyde it in my bourde!" (H.81)—and as if to prove this, offers the Cook a propitiatory pourboire of wine. But the antiphrastic spirit never sleeps in him: "here's 'a good jape,'" he says, as he calls for the pilgrims to witness how the Cook will become the butt of his joke by drinking again, despite his earlier avowal that he would exchange a gallon of Cheapside's best for a place to lie down.

In offering Roger his gourd, the Manciple, both in his professional identity and as a man, acts most like himself. Again he speaks in two voices apparently at odds with each other. The man who slandered Roger, he claims, was not really he, since he was joking; yet the man

---

36. The Inns of Court were a "frequent source of education for the aristocracy"; Christopher Dyer, *Standards of Living in the Later Middle Ages* (Cambridge: Cambridge University Press, 1989), 75. From the twelfth century on, lawyers increasingly were members of the gentry: see E. W. Ives, *The Common Lawyers of Pre-Reformation England* (Cambridge: Cambridge University Press, 1983), 322–29. The great stewards mentioned in "The General Prologue" might well have been royal retainers; see J. R. Mandicott, *Law and Lordship: Royal Justices as Retainers in Thirteenth- and Fourteenth-Century England, Past and Present*, Supplement 4 (Oxford: Past and Present Society, 1978). As noted below, we can imagine that the Manciple developed his scorn for the upper classes from his contact with the lawyers of his Inn.

who presumably now speaks seriously is the man he has just denied being, for he is about to joke again. Once more the Manciple mockingly stages a conversion in which nothing is converted; as in his first intervention, his oblation here is one in which a false show of charity for the Cook becomes a second opportunity to ridicule him in public. But yet again, the Manciple's cynicism evokes an allegorical context: his actions recall Jesus' first miracle, the transformation of water into wine at the wedding in Cana.

After Mary told Jesus that the wine had failed, Jesus ordered six stone jars used in Jewish rituals of purification to be filled with water. He then commanded some liquid be drawn from them and brought to the steward of the feast ("architriclinus," or "chief steward," in the Douai-Rheims translation), who did not know what it was. When the steward tasted it, he went to the bridegroom and said:

> Every man at first setteth forth good wine, and when men have well drunk, then that which is worse. But thou hast kept the good wine until now. (John 2:10)

This event receives its gloss in Jesus' famous admonitions about the proper times to indulge and to fast:

> Can the children of the bridegroom mourn, as long as the bridegroom is with them? But the days will come, when the bridegroom shall be taken away from them, and then they shall fast.
>
> Neither do they put new wine into old bottles. Otherwise the bottles break, and the wine runneth out, and the bottles perish. But new wine they put in new bottles: and both are preserved. (Matt. 9:15, 17; cf. Mark 2:22; Luke 5:37)

As in the parable in Luke, John's steward becomes the agent through whom readers experience the irony of the eschaton. From Augustine on, this miracle was interpreted as a mark of temporal continuity and spiritual rupture. The old dispensation remains but is fulfilled by the new, yet as the steward makes clear, if not to himself then to those who understand, the new order turns the old inside out. For in the eternal dispensation, according to Augustine, Jesus is the bridegroom, whose miraculous marriage to the soul purifies its sins; he is the wine that makes the water of the old prophecies fruitful.[37] The same lesson is taught by the figure of new wine in old bottles: while human beings still reckon years by history's calendar, it is appropriate to preserve both old and new wine, since today the former and tomorrow the latter will be drunk. But in the end of days, only the spiritual wine of fasting will suffice: old bottles and new both will crack if all they contain is wine.

In *The Canterbury Tales,* the Manciple and Cook repeat but do not translate each other: they both remain what they are. The gourd the Manciple proffers to make his joke is filled with worse wine, for it is the wine of spite; when the Cook drinks it, he merely will get drunk again.[38] At Bobbe-up-and-doun, however, Chaucer, by impersonating both, writes a narrative of choice that represents the moment of transformation when the soul sinks or swims. Even if the Cook is a man who, muddle-brained, would totter his way through an epiphany, and the Manciple a man who would shut his eyes to it, their actions outreach their intentions. The kitchen economics that link these servants and perhaps account for the need of the one to exult in the mortification

---

37. Augustine, *Tractatus in Iohannis Evangelium,* tractatus 8 and 9 (*Patrologia Latina,* 35:1450–66). Augustine explicitly sees the miracle as an allegory of history in the form of language, specifically prophecy. The six jars stand for the six ages of the world; Jesus was foreshadowed as the defining event of each age in the prophetic waters of the Old Testament; the miracle at Cana shows that Jesus' coming is both a natural miracle—in the way that the rain nurturing the vines marvelously becomes wine each year ("Sicut enim quod miserunt ministri in hydrias in vinum conversum est opere Domini, sic et quod nubes fundunt in vinum convertitur eiusdem opere Domini," 8.1)—and a miracle that transcends nature and history, performed to show Jesus is God, outside time and place. Miracles themselves embody the irony of allegory.

38. As Andrew Galloway has shown, the setting of the miracle, the wedding at Cana, became the event from which writers of marriage sermons throughout the Middle Ages drew their counsels. Wyclif, for instance, repeats Augustine's interpretation, but places it in the context of marriage (*Johannis Wyclif Sermones,* ed. Johann Loserth, in *Wyclif's Latin Works* [London: Trübner, 1887], part 1, sermon 9, 1:78–86). "Nuptiae factae sunt" sermons in fact were widely disseminated; Galloway has argued convincingly that one sequence by Jacobus de Voragine, which survives in twenty-two late medieval copies of English provenance, closely parallels many features of the Wife of Bath's own discussion of marriage. See "Marriage Sermons, Polemical Sermons, and *The Wife of Bath's Prologue*: A Generic Excursus," *Studies in the Age of Chaucer* 14 (1992): 3–30. In his tale, the Manciple draws on some of the propositions of these sermons, which uphold the institution of marriage and have good things as well as bad to say about women, but unlike them, the Manciple's points are characteristically all uniformly negative. For him, marriage seems no more than an invitation to adultery, woman's nature (and man's) being no different from the "lewedeste" she-wolf's (H.183–86).

of the other yield to the economics of redemption and damnation, in which true opposites are established forever.[39] Despite their motives, the wine that the Manciple has brought to the Cook, by establishing amity where there had been wrath, is better than the wine Roger had drunk the night before.

Harry Bailly seems to realize the irony of the Manciple's irony; like Chaucer he acknowledges the steward's joke, but completely inverts the spirit that prompted it:

> I se wel it is necessarie,
> Where that we goon, good drynke with us carie;
> For that wol turne rancour and disese
> T'acord and love, and many a wrong apese.
>   O Bacus, yblessed be thy name,
> That so kanst turnen ernest into game!
>
> (H.95–100)

Harry's comment is gentle and recuperative; his bemusement at this "miracle" perfectly matches Chaucer's wonder at the Manciple's wit: "Now is nat that of God a ful fair grace." The Host, of course, is in a good position to know the goodness of the wine, even if the Manciple, like the chief steward at Cana, does not. Harry, after all, will undertake to be manciple to the pilgrims, who have appointed him to "sette a soper at a certeyn pris" (A.815) to reward the teller of the best tale. So it

---

39. The Manciple is "wise in byynge of vitaille": his vigilance is such that whether he bought with ready payment or on credit, he was "ay biforn" in his purchases (A.570–73). The Cook, who probably also buys the food he prepares for the parvenu guildsmen who employ him, is "al bihynde" (H.7) the pilgrims at Bobbe-up-and-doun. Certainly Roger is less the Manciple's opposite than his fraternal twin if he is anything like the cooks Langland accuses, along with brewers, bakers, and butchers, of harming the poor by cheating them through fraud: "For þise aren men on þis molde þat moste harme worcheth / To þe pore peple þat parcel-mele buggen" (B.3:80–81). As Bennett explains, it was easy for these tradesmen "to give short weight or measure on small portions, and as the poor can only buy thus, they chiefly suffer." *Piers Plowman*, ed. J. A. W. Bennett (Oxford: Clarendon, 1972), 137.

In this regard, Frederick Tupper, *Types of Society in Medieval Literature* (New York: Holt, 1926), 100–102, argued that the enmity between manciples and cooks was traditional. Robinson cautiously accepted Tupper's "evidence," which has made the conventionality of the rivalry a staple of criticism ever since (see Robinson's note, *The Works of Geoffrey Chaucer*, 2d ed. [Boston: Houghton Mifflin, 1957], 763). In fact, Tupper's evidence is only his inference. Because citations from the *NED* showed that manciples and cooks were both involved with the buying and selling of victuals, Tupper assumed they would cross horns. Professional rivalry almost certainly underlies the quarrel, but the spat seems attributable rather more to Chaucer than to convention.

is appropriately ironic that by recognizing Bacchus as the sociable god who provides good spirits to preserve the community as they journey to Canterbury, Harry distinguishes himself from the Manciple, whose service is divisive because it only serves himself. The harmony and love the Host ascribes to Bacchus, however, Chaucer's readers might ultimately see as attributes of a different deity, whose godhead, revealed in an even more miraculous birth and transubstantiated in a different kind of wine, serves as the foundation of a perfect communion.

Harry's grateful observation that Bacchus can turn "ernest into game" pointedly employs terms Chaucer has used throughout *The Canterbury Tales* to define its status as a work of fiction; by laying less stress on wine itself than on the transformations it effects, the Host's words signal that Ovid figures as prominently in that definition as he did for Dante in the *Comedy*. Certainly the Manciple's sudden hospitality and Roger's surprised gratitude for it are far enough from the ill will each felt for the other to border on metamorphoses; these reversals, whether feigned or real, nicely prepare us for the tale that follows, in which the Manciple gives his version of how the white crow became black. That story, of course, Chaucer originally found in the *Metamorphoses*; the ultimate inspiration for Harry's invocation to Bacchus here, however, I would argue comes from a passage in the first book of the *Ars amatoria*. Even though Ovid's "praeceptor amoris" had earlier counseled his pupil to avoid wine, he now recommends it:

> ecce, suum uatem Liber uocat: hic quoque amantis
> adiuuat et flammae, qua calet ipse, fauet.
>
> (1.525–26)

[Lo, Bacchus summons his poet: he too helps the lover and favors the flame by which he himself is warmed.]

"Suum uatem Liber uocat": just as the key terms Harry used apprise readers that the transactions between Cook and Manciple have a direct bearing on the nature of Chaucer's art, so Ovid alerts his audience that they should attend to his.[40] In typical fashion, he proceeds to illustrate

---

40. Chaucer may well have noted Ovid's substitution of the Italian wine deity for the Greek Dionysus; "Liber" nicely anticipates "Libra," the astronomical allegory of balance that the Host will soon invoke (assuming, of course, that Fragment I follows H) in the "Prologue to the Parson's Tale."

that he is Dionysus's poet by corroborating and discounting the helpfulness of his aid. Soon after Ariadne discovered Theseus had abandoned her at Cnossis, the god appeared to turn her "disese" to "accord." She had just finished crying, "What will become of me," when suddenly she heard the clamor of bacchants' cymbals and caught sight of "old Silenus," who, very Cook-like, was "drunk, scarcely able to sit on his crook-backed mule, holding tightly the pressed mane ("ebrius, ecce, senex pando Silenus asello / uix sedet et pressas continet arte iubas," 543–44). Like the Manciple, the maenads attacked him when they could and fled when he careened toward them, until finally, as bad a horseman ("malus . . . eques," 546) as Roger, he fell off his long-eared mount and had to be helped up again by the satyrs who accompanied him, just as the pilgrims had to resaddle the Cook. Perhaps the fantastical outlandishness of this entourage, together with Ariadne's certain fear of it, distracted her long enough from her grief to make her susceptible to Bacchus's blandishments. In announcing that she will be his wife ("Bacchi . . . uxor eris," 556), the god promises her a faithfulness greater than Theseus's and her apotheosis as the "diadem of Crete" ("Cressa Corona," 558), the crown of stars that guides sailors when they are in peril. In truth, however, Dionysus, like Apollo with Daphne, trusts force far more than he believes in the power of persuasion. Lest the tigers that draw his chariot frighten her, Dionysus dismounts, goes to Ariadne, and, "holding her close to his breast, for she had no strength to fight," bears her away: "in every matter it is easy for a god to do as he will":

> implicitamque sinu, neque enim pugnare ualebat,
> abstulit: in facili est omnia posse deo.
>
> (561–62)

Almost overwhelmed in this triumph of divinity is Ariadne's response to it. Like Daphne, she neither rejects Bacchus nor assents to be his bride. All we are told is that she lacked the strength to resist. But even were she to have struggled—the phrase "neque enim pugnare ualebat" implies she would have—Ovid, by folding her blows between Bacchus's embrace ("implicitamque sinu") and his abduction ("abstulit"), also implies that they would have been useless. Once again the story becomes part of the art of love by showing that art plays no part when love is really an expression of the will's drive to coerce. All Ovid's examples are generated out of this denial and become extended figures of it.

Even in the *Ars*, then, when Ovid combines intentions that are mutually exclusive, contrary positions supplement rather than cancel one another. A story of submission is at the same time a story of resistance; one cannot say the wooing of Ariadne is the former without saying it is the latter. For Ovid, self-contradiction is a mode of procreation; in his hands, irony translates "is not" by rendering it as an alternative form of "is."

In the Manciple's tale, irony also produces an abundance of exempla, but their spirit truly is antiphrastic: his asides invert in order to efface; the goal they aim at is the silence of an evacuation. In each instance, to realize his intention the Manciple also translates, not once, but twice. He first collapses opposites by making both consequences of the same cause; he then renders the cause null and void by denying that it is real or that it matters. Consider the Manciple's comments the first time he intrudes in his narrative. Phebus's jealousy makes him fear that his wife will "byjape" him unless he keeps her under narrow watch. Lost labor, the Manciple says, for a faithful wife should not be treated as if under house arrest, and a shrew will do as she pleases no matter how closely a husband keeps an eye on her. Although the good woman is defended and the bad one censured, the differences between them disappear when they solicit the same response. According to the Manciple, each should be dealt with by doing nothing: "This holde I for a verray nycetee, / To spille labour for to kepe wyves" (152–53).

By itself, such a conclusion would seem sufficiently caustic to make morality a form of cynicism; in context, its corrosiveness is doubled. The Manciple had begun his tale by briskly describing qualities of word and deed that confirm Phebus as a model of knighthood.[41] His prowess in arms has its fit symbol in his bow, with which he slew the python; his mastery of "minstralcie" corroborates his courtly refinement. In short order, of course, Phebus will renounce both these attainments; however, before the Manciple transforms courage and art into vices so that he can dismiss both as delusions, Chaucer's wicked steward conspicuously repeats himself. In rapid succession he tells us once more that Phebus always carried a bow in token of his victory over the python (125–29); that Phebus had a crow ("Whit . . . as is a snow-whit swan," 134) that could speak and sing a hundred thousand times better than any nightingale; and that he also had a wife. By reverting to Phebus's chivalric

---

41. "Sapientia et fortitudo" traditionally defined chivalric excellence; the portrait of the Knight in "The General Prologue" is organized according to his possession of both qualities. The Manciple, I think, very much makes the Knight one of his targets when he tells his tale.

achievements, we expect the Manciple to complete the pattern by referring again to some aspect of gentle breeding. This he does and does not do when he tells us that the crow sings as well as its owner. As in beast fables, the bird has taken on human attributes; by the next line, however, the Manciple already seems to have sneered at the equation, as if to imply that aristocratic manners and animal instinct really amount to the same thing. For the Manciple immediately levels crow and wife by reiterating a syntactic pattern: "Now hadde this Phebus in his hous a crowe" (130); "Now hadde this Phebus in his hous a wyf" (139).

These repetitions make repetition as such the agency of antiphrastic irony. With more than a hint of resentment, the Manciple certifies Phebus's lordly standing by showing that he considers his crow and his wife no more than prized possessions to be kept caged up in his house— much the way we suspect the Manciple feels the great lawyers of his Inn treat him. At the same time, the Manciple abolishes every right of rank by identifying Phebus with his crow and his wife. If each can stand in for the other, what is nobility but a phantasm, a fiction of preeminence where no distinction actually exists? Instead of underwriting the construction of correspondence between dissimilar things, the Manciple's repetitions blot out both. Instead of sponsoring the polysemy of allegory, the Manciple's repetitions homogenize its multiple senses in order to render each a figure of the same emptiness of meaning.[42]

Precisely because the Manciple's redundancy haunts the multivo-

---

42. We can measure the depth of hollowness that the Manciple creates by repetition by comparing Ovid's use of the same device in the story that was Chaucer's ultimate source for the tale. In the *Metamorphoses,* the transformation of the garrulous raven is not one story but two. As the "corvus loquax" flies to tell Apollo of Corinna's infidelity, he encounters a crow, who tries to dissuade him by revealing how she was changed for speaking unwelcome tidings. Her story is the mirror image of the one that the raven is about to learn: by telling both Ovid commits the very fault of talking too much that each story warns against. Ovid luxuriates in this irony. Together his stories ask a flippant question: how can one tell the difference between a raven and a crow, anyhow? Ovid answers, "You can't, you can't" and makes the second response as diverting as the first. Contrary to the Manciple, repetition becomes the way for Ovid to mark stylistically the fecundity of his poetics. He introduces the raven by addressing it, "cum candidas ante fuisses . . . subito nigrantes versus in alas" [when you were suddenly changed to black, though you were once white] (2.534–35) and then announces his moral (540–41):

lingua fuit damno: lingua faciente loquaci,
qui color albus erat, nunc est contrarius albo.

[Talking too much was his undoing; by making his tongue talk too much, the talkative bird who once was white now is white's opposite.]

calic fruitfulness of allegory from within, his reiterations are likewise philoprogenitive. They beget first the counsel that Phebus should confront his jealousy by doing nothing about it. As we have seen, the effect of this little homily is to negate everything that unites the characters and everything that sets them apart by allowing the Manciple to suggest that the god, his wife, and the crow should all be written off. They then breed the three successive exempla that outspokenly justify the repudiation of humankind that to this point the Manciple had been content merely to suggest. People *are* beasts, he now says, for, as he said before, it is wasted effort to restrain the natural impulses that nature (note the doubling) sets in creatures:

> But God it woot, ther may no man embrace
> As to destreyne a thyng which that nature
> Hath natureelly set in a creature.
>
> (160–62)

A caged bird, the Manciple continues, no matter how dainty its food and tender its care, would still rather be free to eat worms "and swich wrecchednesse" in the forest (163–74); give a cat all the milk and meat you will, let it see a mouse and its "lust" and "appetit" will put "discrecioun" to flight (175–82); the she-wolf in heat will couple with the "lewedeste wolf . . . leest of reputacioun" she can find (183–86).[43] In each case, human traits consort and become interchangeable with animal characteristics so that the Manciple can say fie to animal and human both.

Out of repetitions that reveal the vanity of everything on earth this wise child of his generation thus generates a discourse that obliterates the world. Nothing escapes the Manciple's purview, not even his own words. Each of the "ensamples" he has just recited repeats *in parvo* the form of the story he is telling; since all beast-fables carry an interpretive moral, the Manciple will offer his:

> Alle thise ensamples speke I by thise men
> That been untrewe, and nothyng by wommen.
> For men han evere a likerous appetit

---

[43]. In the first two examples, of course, the Manciple ironically implicates himself in his condemnation by emphasizing the importance of supplying provender.

On lower thyng to parfourne hire delit
Than on hire wyves.

(187–91)

The application seems almost defiantly preposterous in the way it contradicts the plain sense of the matter that it glosses; not a second before the Manciple had castigated the she-wolf for its lechery, and Phebus's wife is poised to commit adultery with a "man of litel reputacioun" (199). The Manciple misidentifies the object of his censure, of course, so that he can defend women by extending his contempt for them to men. At the same time, by demonstrating that black and white can be made to repeat each other, he exposes the arbitrariness of all commentary. With one ethical aside he effectively wipes blank all the records of moral philosophy. Men are the same as women, who differ not a bit from wolves in their lewdness: each frictionlessly substitutes for the other in the Manciple's parables of annulment.

Nor does it seem that anything can fill the vacuum the Manciple's denials create except more instances of the same sort of consumptive moralizing. The Manciple's animadversions about the deceitfulness of words work in exactly the same way that his earlier censures work (207–34), and they produce the same sort of torpor that his stultifying profusion of proverbs produces at the end of the tale (309–62), when the Manciple talks much too much about the necessity of not talking too much.

If the Manciple's manner of meaning were the last word, the poetry of *The Canterbury Tales* could have nothing to do with truth or salvation, since all figural language would trope only his mode of self-affirmation through the annulment of others. But in Harry Bailly's mouth, as in Chaucer's, irony does otherwise: by means of its parabolic affiliation with allegory, it creates characters and events in "The Prologue to the Manciple's Tale" that are able to say "I" and "Other-than-I" even when they say "I" and "Not-I" as well. At the same time that his steward uses irony to dispossess, Chaucer transforms it into a principle that draws concord out of discord, sodality out of rivalry. The Manciple's censure of the Cook would unknit the company; the Host's censure of both Manciple and Cook reunites them. These moments, though contradictory, also complement each other, for between them Roger has toppled from his horse and has been remounted through the joint efforts of the pilgrims. In this fall and rise, all oppositions of blood and mire cease merely to oppose; the Cook, the Manciple, the Host, all the pilgrims, have become more than themselves by becoming figures in parables of conversion. Beyond composing events that run counter to one another, irony as a manner of meaning has been given a narrative of its own. The Manciple's desire to alienate and make dumb provides the perfect occasion for Chaucer to demonstrate that in the "book of the tales of Caunterbury," writing all along has aspired to the plenitude that comes from speaking otherwise.

As much as any pilgrim, the Manciple exemplifies what H. Marshall Leicester has called the disenchanted self; indeed, in an irony Max Weber could have appreciated, it is precisely the Manciple's pernicious, calculating cynicism that encourages us to think him less the representation of an autonomous human being than a mode of disillusionment per se.[44] He tricks his masters not so much for self-gain as to pit his "lewed" wit against their "lerned" wisdom, eliminating the difference between honest stewardship and fraudulent service in the process. When accused of keeping crooked accounts, he admits the charge in order to imply it is false: with the Manciple, truth-telling becomes a way to maintain a lie; confession an accessory of obfuscation. He is the kind of man who, in his tale, would make a fabliau the occasion for a sermon, and a sermon the occasion to preach a gospel of silence: he is the kind of man who would say again and again that the truth is better left unsaid.[45] Through the Manciple we see that neither language nor propriety can stand outside the motives of those who use it and are used by it: in his tale he shows that the most fashionable

---

44. H. Marshall Leicester, *The Disenchanted Self* (Berkeley and Los Angeles: University of California Press, 1990). In his introduction" (14–28), Leicester significantly expands Max Weber's notion of disenchantment to distinguish selfhood from subjectivity.

45. "The Manciple's Tale" was I think first characterized as a fabliau by H. E. Ussery, *Chaucer's Physician: Medicine and Literature in the Fourteenth Century,* Tulane Studies in English, no. 19 (New Orleans: Tulane Dept. of English, 1971), 130–34. It has been called a sermon by John Fyler, *Chaucer and Ovid* (New Haven: Yale University Press, 1979), 155. Both I think are right, in that the tale harnesses the impulses of either genre to cancel the expectations of the other. Richard Hazelton, "The Manciple's Tale": Parody and Critique," *JEGP* 62 (1963): 1–31, has characterized it as a moral fable; this too is right, since, as antiphrastic counterpart to the Nun's Priest's tale, the Manciple's carefully maligns both morality and fable.

Beyond this, it is worthwhile to point out that the Manciple's desire to replace interpretation with silence is directly related to his embodiment of irony. As Teskey says, irony's disposition with respect to interpretation is completely negative: "There is nothing objectively there to interpret" ("Irony, Allegory, and Metaphysical Decay," 399). In Chaucer, of course, the irony of the Manciple's peroration is its prolixity: the pullulation of authorities who all counsel curbing the tongue turns the call for muteness into the riot of commentary that is the mark of allegory.

terms can camouflage the meanest acts, that the most moral-sounding discourse can urge complete disengagement from ethical responsibility. Through the Manciple Chaucer demonstrates that every system and institution, however much it offers itself as a reflection of an ideal order, always is realized by the social practice of those who constitute it: in the wrong hands, chivalry is nothing more than an exercise of brute force, courtesy an invitation to adultery, and stewardship, instead of being a way to administer a just society, a canker that assures its corruption from within.

The Manciple's identity is premised on these effects; he becomes a character when we assign them a motive, when we say he is a person who levels contraries in order to cancel them. As such the irony the Manciple embodies directly imperils the entire project of *The Canterbury Tales* since, as we have seen, it abrogates the subjectivity of the character it impersonates by robbing it of its voice. But because even antiphrastic irony in Chaucer is a spoken as well as a speaking discourse, it is self-reflexive by nature; because it does not silence the object that it declares null and void without also locating that denial in the denier, the Manciple cannot escape becoming his own victim. If nothing else, the Manciple delivers his moral exhortations at the end of his tale in the belief that his cynicism has freed him from the mystifications he exposes. But in the prologue, the Manciple has equally depended on mystification to present himself. Like the steward in Luke, the Manciple will no longer be manciple if he is accused unto his masters; he therefore most bespeaks who he is when, to make sure his thieving remains undiscovered, he acknowledges, jokingly to be sure, that Harry's charge of malfeasance is true. As in the portrait in "The General Prologue," the Manciple's "true self" is the revelation of a concealment that continues to remain concealed, a disclosure of defects in his accounts that he neither admits nor compensates. Though the Man-

---

Donald Baker ably summarizes the large literature that assesses the prologue and tale to 1981; see the *Variorum*, 19–38. Among the essays that deal with language, of special note are the following: Wayne Shumaker, "Chaucer's *Manciple's Tale* as Part of a Canterbury Group," *University of Toronto Quarterly* 22 (1953): 147–56; Britton Harwood, "Language and the Real: Chaucer's Manciple," *Chaucer Review* 6 (1972): 268–79; V. J. Scattergood, "The Manciple's Manner of Speaking," *Essays in Criticism* 24 (1974): 124–46. Since Baker's survey, a number of important studies have appeared: Chauncey Wood, "Speech, the Principle of Contraries, and Chaucer's Tales of the Manciple and the Parson," *Mediaevalia* 6 (1980): 209–27; Fradenburg, "The Manciple's Servant Tongue"; Dean, "Dismantling the Canterbury Book"; Mark Allen, "Penitential Sermons, the Manciple, and the End of *The Canterbury Tales*," *Studies in the Age of Chaucer* 9 (1987): 77–96; John Hill, *Chaucerian Belief* (New Haven: Yale University Press, 1991), 63–76.

ciple claims he is "noght textueel" (H.235), we find his personality based not in the "presence" of voice but in the absence and deflections of writing. As befits a man who means the opposite of what he says and does, the Manciple stands in opposition to himself: he has no inner being of his own that can be divulged, since he exists as the record of his masking his attempts to outwit others.

Within the social world of *The Canterbury Tales*, however, Chaucer undoes the Manciple's irony *through* impersonation, by relating his voice to others, both like and unlike his own, to create a discourse in which antiphrasis is an element of polysemy. When the Manciple speaks for the Cook in excusing him from telling a tale, he reduces Roger to speechlessness. After the Cook has fallen, however, Harry Bailly speaks for him with opposite effect. Yet this is the same Harry who early in the pilgrimage had bickered with the Cook and who at the start of the prologue seemed ready to resume the game in the Manciple's spirit of mockery. But the words Harry actually utters to "reclaim" the Manciple are modeled not only on the steward's exchange with the Cook but on words Roger himself had previously addressed to Harry. After all, it was Hogge of Ware who had said in response to the Host's baiting, "sooth pley, quaad pley" ("a true jest is no jest," A.4357), and who then promised, as V. A. Kolve says, that if Harry "comes too near the truth about cooks, he may have to hear some home truths about innkeepers before the journey is over."[46]

Indeed, the Cook's horsemanship recalls so vividly the drunken "chyvachee" of the Miller (A.3120–21) that the quarrel between Robyn and the Reeve seems a country version of the city squabble the Manciple and Roger replay here. We sense that the end of *The Canterbury Tales* reiterates the beginning: Fragment H, at least, repeats Fragment A.[47] Certainly a circle of sinners is joined, leading from the Miller and Reeve to the Manciple, whose portrait stands between theirs in "The General Prologue."[48] Nor is it accidental that the tales they tell seem as connected to each other as they do. If "The Miller's Tale" offers a cri-

---

46. V. A. Kolve, *Chaucer and the Imagery of Narrative* (Stanford: Stanford University Press, 1984), 267.

47. In this regard see Donald Howard, *The Idea of the Canterbury Tales* (Berkeley and Los Angeles: University of California Press, 1976), 303–4.

48. The Miller leads the pilgrims "out of towne" (A. 566); the Reeve always "rood the hyndreste of oure route" (A. 623); the Cook has fallen "al bihynde" (H. 7), which prompts the Manciple to tell the last tale before the Parson's. With Miller and Reeve, Cook and Manciple, it makes no difference whether the first shall be last or the last first. In the case of the Manciple and Parson, the last of the fiction-tellers remains last even when he speaks first.

tique of the aristocratic construction of chivalric identity, if the Reeve's rebuttal puts sex inside and out of marriage in the service of envy and revenge, if the Cook's tale turns on returning a profit on adultery, the Manciple manages in his prologue and tale to cast his jaundiced eye not only on genteel values and the idea of a stable identity but on the very possibility of faithful relations or a justice that rewards and punishes according to the canons of truthfulness.

Again, however, repetition in Chaucer everywhere generates cohering as well as contradictory oppositions. Both the Miller and the Manciple would assume Harry's prerogative of determining who should tell the next tale; but whereas the Host at the start of the pilgrimage had surrendered in exasperation to the Miller's drunken insistence, he now successfully confirms his authority by permitting the Manciple to substitute for the drunk Cook. And whereas the Reeve, who is a bailiff, had tried to call the "thrice-tolling" Miller to account (A.562) because he wished to prosecute a quarrel between Robyn and himself, the "baillie" named Harry here composes his earlier quarrel with the Cook by calling attention to the Manciple's "rekenynges."[49] As a swindling record-keeper given to preaching ("The devel made a reve for to preche," says Harry [A.3903]), the hypocritical Osewold is closely related to the moralizing Manciple; in the Manciple's prologue, however, the corrupt steward—who, as his initial words to Harry reveal, would be friends with this not-so-evil-mammon so that he might be received into his inn—finds himself checked by the crafty publican, a child of this world equally concerned that his account books show a profit.[50] Harry is the Manciple's alter ego; he also is his nemesis.

---

49. On Harry as bailiff, see *MED, baillie* and *bailiff*, B.1. See further Linda Georgianna, "Love So Dearly Bought: The Terms of Redemption in *The Canterbury Tales*," Studies in the Age of Chaucer 12 (1990): 85–116. Georgianna's remarks on penance in general and on the notion of reckoning in particular are especially pertinent to my argument here. Also relevant is the legal notion of an action of account. As Elizabeth Dobbs says, in the case of a lord and his bailiff, such an action "compels the latter to account for the profits of the manor" (36). See "Literary, Legal, and Last Judgments in *The Canterbury Tales*," Studies in the Age of Chaucer 14 (1992): 31–52. Like the Reeve, the Manciple is in an accountable relationship. The idea of justifying one's accounts is central to the exchange between Harry and the Manciple.

50. In this regard, it is of interest to note that in the Wycliffite Bible, the steward of Luke's parable is asked to "ʒelde reckynyng of thi baili" (16:2). Cited in Georgianna, "Love So Dearly Bought," 104. Luke's use of the figure of childhood to describe both the worldly and the spiritual perhaps also lies behind Chaucer's depiction of himself as poet. Lee Patterson has argued that Chaucer's references to himself as "elvyssh" and "a popet" in the "Prologue to Sir Thopas" both represent him as a child: see "'What Man Artow?': Authorial Self-Definition in *The Tale of Sir Thopas* and *The Tale of Melibee*," Studies in the Age of Chaucer 11 (1989): 117–75.

In the frame of the *Tales*, this backward- and forward-looking polyphony of personal relations equates characters who in their particular settings begin and end in the antinomies of rivalry. These antinomies then are reinscribed as the données that propel the fabliaux the Miller, Reeve, Cook, and Manciple tell. As a group these tales circumscribe a large part of the social world of the poem, a world of often contradictory motives that Chaucer represents under the sign of irony; for whatever else it is, the social in *The Canterbury Tales* is never less than the style that simultaneously registers antagonisms and constructs from them a network of similarities. Even the tales that seem to stand outside this circle, those of the Knight and Parson, are part of its circumference through contrariety. The Miller announces with all the fustian of "Pilates voys" that he will "quite" the Knight's tale, which he does by brilliantly debunking its courtly pretensions. But by tilting with the Knight, the Miller ironically copies the rivalry of Palamon and Arcita in the Knight's tale. Robyn may mock them, but the paradigm of conduct the Theban cousins have established is the one we use to judge the Miller's exchanges with the Host and the Reeve.[51] In the same way, even as the Parson sets himself apart from the Manciple and all other fabulists, the affiliations that connect him to his fellow tale-tellers only grow more pronounced. With perhaps the Miller's fervor, though certainly with the opposite intent, the Parson says that unlike the Manciple's tale of the crow, the pilgrims will get "fable noon" from him (I.30–31).[52] But after suffering through the Manciple's sermon, when we "turne over the leef, and chese another tale" (A.3177), we find that the Parson, who says he is "nat textueel" (I.57) and not inclined to "glose" (I.45), is explicitly linked to the Manciple, who has already used the same phrases to declare his "untextuality" and indisposition to "glose." The spiritual steward is everything his too worldly counterpart is not. Therefore, it is no surprise that by preaching about ultimate reckonings, the Parson provides the final textual gloss not only on the Manciple's defalcations but on Harry's concern that each debt be stamped paid as well: on the day of judgment, the Parson says, everyone

---

51. If the Cook is in fact Roger Knight of Ware, as Edith Rickert has suggested ("Chaucer's Hodge of Ware," *TLS*, October 20, 1932, 761), the verbal polyphony I am discussing here becomes that much more complex.

52. To Harry's demand for a fable, "for cokkes bones," the Parson responds "Thou getest fable noon ytold for me" (I.30). Compare the Miller's opening words: "By armes, and by blood and bones" (A.3125).

"shal yeven acountes," as saith Seint Bernard, "of alle the goodes that han be yeven hym in this present lyf, and how he hath hem despended, / [in] so muche that ther shal nat perisse an heer of his heed, ne a moment of an houre ne shal nat perisse of his tyme, that he ne shal yeve of it a rekenyng." (I.253–54)

The dissembling Manciple would bring all tale telling to an end by gagging the tongue before it can utter a word; the Parson believes we will all be forced, like the Manciple's forebear in Luke's parable, to justify our stewardship.[53] The Manciple is everywhere countered by a host of other voices that, sometimes in his own words, speak forth everything he would leave unconfessed.

This polyphony often gives intertextuality in *The Canterbury Tales* the structure of irony, an irony in which opposites negate but negation itself translates allegory's intentional mode. Of all the voices that intermix with and counteract the Manciple's, therefore, the most powerful, and the one most at risk, should be Chaucer's. Throughout the *Tales* the narrator has often asked readers not to blame him for his fiction; in his accustomed manner, the Manciple now threatens to invalidate these apologias by repeating them. If Chaucer would avoid responsibility for the tales he will rehearse by claiming that he will be a false "compilator" unless "the wordes ... be cosyn to the dede" (A.742), the Manciple, who also seeks to avoid responsibility for the false records he reports to his company of masters, is all too ready to claim he too must speak the unvarnished truth.[54] If a noblewoman commits adultery, he says, she should not be called a lady but the wench she is. Just as Chaucer had before him, he appeals (twice, one should note) to a dictum he ascribes to Plato to ask forgiveness for saying so:

The word moot nede accorde with the dede.
If men shal telle proprely a thyng,
The word moot cosyn be to the werkyng.

(H.208–10)

---

53. The parable of the wicked steward was in fact most often interpreted as an allegory of man's failings as God's steward. See Wailes, *Medieval Allegories*, 248.

54. The idea of Chaucer as "compilator" everywhere except in the "Retraction," where he is "auctor," is Minnis's (*Medieval Theory of Authorship*, 206–10). Lawton, "Chaucer's Two Ways," reads "The Parson's Tale" on the supposition that a compiler, who may have been Chaucer, placed it at the end of *The Canterbury Tales*.

Perhaps these quotations are what made Chaucer reject entirely in the *Retraction* the "synne" and "greet folye" of fictions that

> apeyren any man, or hym defame,
> And eek . . . bryngen wyves in swich fame.
>
> (A.3146–48)

These are the words the Reeve directs against the Miller before he tells his tale, but they apply even more to the denigrating Manciple; indeed, they make us recall the similar case of the Miller's preemptive exoneration of himself for his performance. Robyn, of course, asks for forgiveness before he says anything on the grounds that he is drunk. It would be easy to conjure with such a request for pardon if Chaucer did not make the same request in his own name a moment later. Using the terms Harry Bailly will echo, the narrator tries to excuse himself for the "cherles tale" of "harlotrie" by making his readers answerable for it:[55]

> Avyseth yow, and put me out of blame;
> And eek men shal nat maken ernest of game.
>
> (A.3167–86)

In repeating the Miller's words, Chaucer shows that when he says them, they mean more. The "stout carl" looks to his lees for absolution; the narrator looks for it by reminding us that if we are too sober, we will mistake the spirit of the old and new wine that is his fiction.

Just as the Miller's crying in "Pilates voys" had already established a different register in which all possibility of washing one's hands of liability has been eliminated (even as it brilliantly foreshadows the crucial role water will play in the tale), Chaucer has created perspectives here that likewise render him more accountable for everything he has written. He admits double responsibility for the Manciple: first by having the Manciple quote his own defense of poetry, through which Chaucer formalizes the equation in "The General Prologue" of his own ironic attitude and that of the provisioner; and then by turning irony into its

---

55. The similarities between the Miller and the Manciple are striking. The Miller "unnethe upon his hors he sat," "nolde avalen neither hood ne hat, / Ne abyde no man for his curteisie" (A.3121–23); of the lawyers he serves, the Manciple "sette hir aller cappe," and though he does "abyde" Harry's "curteisie," he does so in order to make the Cook tumble from his horse.

opposite by making it, in accordance with rhetorical precept, an allegory in the "Prologue to the Manciple's Tale."

As the pilgrimage nears Canterbury, the covenant Chaucer forges between irony and allegory more and more becomes the subject of his discourse. We can see how much it preoccupied Chaucer's attention if we accept the Ellesmere order and consider the last tales a sequence. The Second Nun introduces her life of Saint Cecilia, itself a narrative of conversion, by allegorizing the martyr's name. It makes sense, then, that Chaucer would couple her hagiography with "The Canon's Yeoman's Tale," in which alchemy proves to be essentially ironic, both as language and as practice, because it is a failed allegory for the conversion of matter.[56] Indeed, in alchemical treatises, the "multiplication" of technical terms for the "conversion" of the elements was explicitly associated with the hermeneutics of biblical allegory; the language of "The Canon's Yeoman's Tale" thus is the inverted image of the "doubled" speech of the Manciple's prologue, in which irony is translated into an allegory of conversion.[57] The Parson, of course, would convert even allegory's figurations into the abstract, univocal language of sacramental penance; but as he pursues rationally the goal that the Second Nun had represented in affective terms, his tale makes conversion itself part of a larger allegory of penance. His "meditacioun" is the verbal act of satisfaction that ironically transmutes the Manciple's mockery of confession and the alchemical Canon's Yeoman's half-contrition of heart into a narrative of redemption.

We might well call this burgeoning of the spiritual out of the material and social Chaucer's Canterbury poetics; it is proper that Chaucer should explicitly foreground the inner and outer constitution of his poetry at the end of the *Tales*, because by doing so he simultaneously recovers and reverses the opening of the poem, where allegory also converges with irony:

---

56. On the linkage of the "Canon's Yeoman's Tale" and the "Second Nun's Tale," see especially Joseph Grennan, "Saint Cecilia's 'Chemical Wedding': The Unity of the *Canterbury Tales*, Fragment VIII," *JEGP* 65 (1966): 466–81.

57. On the association of alchemical language and spiritual hermeneutics, see Lee Patterson, "Perpetual Motion: Alchemy and the Technology of the Self," *Studies in the Age of Chaucer* 15 (1993): 25–57, esp. 45–46. I would also note that the emphasis on blindness and sight in the "Second Nun's Tale," and on bleary vision in the "Canon's Yeoman's Tale," both nicely prepare the ground for Chaucer's reconfiguration of Paul's conversion. As a result of the flashing light, of course, Saul was blinded three days; when he recovered his sight, he was Paul.

> Whan that Aprill with his shoures soote
> The droghte of March hath perced to the roote,
> And bathed every veyne in swich licour
> Of which vertu engendred is the flour . . .

Here again, but for the first time, the sacramental and natural are inseparable. April showers bring May flowers, but the rain, by answering to the metaphorical overtones of "perced" and "veyne," becomes the blood of Jesus, and this blood, which flowed with water after the spear had pierced his side, is transformed with the mention of "licour" into the wine of Christian communion.[58] In like manner, the showers pierce the drought of March to the root (the word functions both naturally and metaphorically at once) before their virtue brings forth the flower: from death comes life, and the downward and upward motions of rain and flower are also the directions of Christian Incarnation and Assumption. So too the showers' sweetness naturally modulates into the mildness of "bathed," which itself seems to call forth the idea of baptism, of waters giving life.

And what we learn from the first four lines of "The General Prologue," the subsequent fourteen confirm:

> Whan Zephirus eek with his sweete breeth
> Inspired hath in every holt and heeth
> The tendre croppes, and the yonge sonne
> Hath in the Ram his half cours yronne,
> And smale foweles maken melodye,
> That slepen al the nyght with open ye
> (So priketh hem nature in hir corages),
> Thanne longen folk to goon on pilgrimages,
> And palmeres for to seken straunge strondes,
> To ferne halwes, kowthe in sondry londes;
> And specially from every shires ende
> Of Engelond to Caunterbury they wende,
> The hooly blisful martir for to seke,
> That hem hath holpen whan that they were seeke.

---

58. That "Liquor" not only means "liquid," but "wine," especially "communion wine," is confirmed by the *MED*, s.v. *liquor*, 2(a).

The syntax of "Whan Zephirus eek with his sweete breeth," which repeats that of the opening line—the doubled "whan," the equating "eek," the clear similitude of "shoures soote" and "sweete breeth"—all this encourages us to read the wind as we have read the rain. There is a spirit, natural and holy at once, that grows the crops, as the waters, and blood, and wine engender the flower. But there is a larger disposition at work here as well. As we move from the waters to the dry land, from the plants to the lights in the firmament, from the birds to people, Chaucer refashions the program of creation almost point for point as we find it in Gen. 1:9–31. *The Canterbury Tales,* in effect, begin with the third day, when the waters under heaven were gathered together and separated from the dry land. The earth then put forth vegetation, plants yielding seed, fruit trees bearing fruit. The next day God made the greater and lesser lights and set them in the firmament as signs for the seasons, days, and years. On the fifth day the waters brought forth living creatures, and God said, "Let birds fly above the earth." The sixth day, after creating creeping things, beasts, and cattle, God made man and woman.

Chaucer begins his book by suggesting there is an analogy between it and what he took to be the beginning of everything. *The Canterbury Tales* opens by invoking an earlier opening; its allegory partakes of both absolute and conditional origins at once. But, as Barbara Nolan has said, once Chaucer locates himself at the Tabard, the poem shifts to "the fallen, historical world, in which chance, change, unpredictability hold sway."[59] This social world is the realm where the absolute and the conditional stand in ironic opposition; it is the world where the saint's helping the sick becomes the Manciple's offer of "charity" to the indisposed Cook. It is a world whose style is irony, but an irony that at any time can be parabolic because as deflected speech it is never other than a form of allegory; the Manciple guides the pilgrims precisely the way Luke would have his wicked steward guide the righteous to eternal tabernacles. And it is a world whose end simultaneously differs from and returns to its rhetorical origins, both in "The Manciple's Prologue," and even more in the "Prologue to the Parson's Tale," where the sense of final balance and justice implicit in Libra, of harvesting and separating the "whete" from the "draf," of knitting up the "feeste," and being

---

59. Barbara Nolan, "'A Poet Ther Was': Chaucer's Voices in the General Prologue," *PMLA* 101 (1986): 159.

"fructuous, and that in litel space," all convey the hurry of a fast-approaching Last Judgment even as they harken back to the springtime fertility of the opening vision of "The General Prologue."[60]

Only the "The Parson's Tale" and the "Retraction" stand apart. As I said earlier, in the face of the Parson's insistence that the language of penance be as forthright as the act is wholehearted, even the doubled speech of allegory seems an equivocation. But in establishing sin as a violation of the *ratio dei* throughout the entire *ordo* of the universe, the Parson's anatomy of penance cancels neither irony nor the fictive sociality of which I have argued it is the defining figure. Rather the Parson's prose seeks out all antonymies so that they may be incorporated into the univocality of salvation. Heaven is a state of "endelees blisse," the Parson says, "ther joye hath no contrarioustee of wo ne grevaunce." Nevertheless,

This blisful regne may men purchase by poverte espiritueel, and the glorie by lowenesse, the plentee of joye by hunger and thurst, and the reste by travaille, and the lyf by deethe and mortificacion of synne. (I.1077, 1080)

Though set squarely in opposition to the poetry that precedes it, the intellective and nonreferential language of "The Parson's Tale" is neither logically nor stylistically discontinuous with that poetry;[61] indeed,

---

60. One might also note in this regard the linkage between the Manciple's portrait, prologue, and tale and the Man of Law, whose tale may well have stood first at an early stage in the construction of the *Tales*. The Manciple is a thieving "achatour" of a temple whose lawyers match the eminence of Chaucer's none-too-honest "Sergeant of the Lawe," who also is a "purchasour," whose "purchasyng myghte nat been *infect*," and whose legal drafts were unimpeachable:

Therto he koude endite and make a thyng,
Ther koude no wight *pynche* at his writyng.
(A.318–26)

The stylistic reminiscences are striking: the Manciple says the Cook's stinking breath "infect wole us alle"; Harry cautions the Manciple that Roger will reclaim him if he were "to pynchen at thy rekenynges." Moreover, lawyers like Chaucer's, who made money from their knowledge of positive law ("Al was fee symple to hym in effect," A. 319), were also characterized as children of this world: Richard of Bury (*Philobiblon*, 11) comments that "the more useful [knowledge of positive law] is to the children of this world, the less it assists the children of light." Quoted in D. W. Robertson, *Chaucer's London* (New York: Wiley, 1968), 204.

61. See Lee Patterson, "The Parson's Tale and the Quitting of the *Canterbury Tales*," *Traditio* 34 (1978): 331–80.

it relies on a rhetoric of irony as much as the Manciple's sarcasm depends on a rhetoric of allegory. Even if it purchases its metaphors from the storehouse of Christian redemption, the language remains figurative, its sense parabolic. Derek Brewer has rightly said that Chaucer fashions his poetics out of the "collisions" between sacred and secular, learned and popular forms of knowledge and narrative; in that poetics, the Manciple and Parson represent two countervailing discourses, each of which presupposes the other.[62] In *The Canterbury Tales,* there is no getting around irony and allegory, nor is there need to.[63]

Even in the "Retraction," language hovers between the final silence of rejection and an all-encompassing embrace of speech. "*Al* that is writen is writen for oure doctrine," says Chaucer, again quoting Paul, "and that is myn entente." Yet Chaucer then revokes those tales "that sownen into synne." Here is a contradiction that is more than mere gainsaying. The repudiation is irrevocable: a fable like the Manciple's would be exactly the kind of "draf" the Parson rejects for the "whete" of "vertuous mateere" (I.35–38). Yet by quoting Paul, Chaucer also quotes himself, since the Nun's Priest has used these words to justify another beast fable, similar to the Manciple's but very different from it as well: "Taketh the fruyt, and lat the chaf be stille" (B2.4633).[64] In the "Retraction," Chaucer defends his fiction and disowns it in the same breath; the structure of opposition, however, is not ironic, but allegorical, because the oppositions are resolved in the inclusiveness of Chaucer's intention. "Al that is writen is writen for oure doctrine . . . and that is myn entente." This is a language where one rejects what one includes, includes what one rejects. It is a language that makes the Manciple not simply the Parson's opposite but his fellow pilgrim as well. It is a language of heaven and earth; it is not at odds with that of *The Canterbury Tales,* but part of it.

Without question Chaucer learned more about the literary uses of allegory from Dante than from anybody else; the Manciple's prologue and

---

62. Derek Brewer, "Towards a Chaucerian Poetic," Sir Israel Gollancz Memorial Lecture, *Proceedings of the British Academy* 60 (1974): 219–52.

63. See Carol Kaske, "Getting around the Parson's Tale: An Alternative to Allegory and Irony," in *Chaucer at Albany,* ed. Rossell H. Robbins (New York: Franklin, 1975), 146–77.

64. On Chaucer's use of St. Paul here and elsewhere in the *Tales,* see Russell Peck, "Biblical Interpretation: St. Paul and the *Canterbury Tales,*" in *Chaucer and the Scriptural Tradition,* ed. David L. Jeffrey (Ottawa: University of Ottawa Press, 1984), 143–70.

tale in particular provide fair grounds to assess the nature of Chaucer's debt to the *Comedy* and to measure the distance that separates him from it. Certainly something more than coincidence must account for the fact that when both poets pondered the relation between language and salvation, each made Ovid the vehicle through whom he linked ideas of theft, conversion, metamorphosis, irony, and allegory. It was, after all, Harry Bailly's surmise that the Manciple is a petty thief that brought about the mock transformation in his behavior toward the Cook. And it was a story from the *Metamorphoses* that the cunning steward used to make a parable of his mockery; to reprove Harry's reproof, the Manciple blackened the blackening of the crow in order to preach his gospel that silence is the better part since the truth rebukes only those who tell it. As I say, I doubt Chaucer would have framed these events the way he did had he not had Dante's metamorphoses cantos in mind. But whether he did or not, in mood and mode of meaning the Manciple's experience and tale remain extraordinary translations of the fate of Vanni Fucci and his fellow thieves in the *Inferno*.

Of the many riveting events Dante witnessed in the seventh *bolgia*, none is more startling than Fucci's blasphemy:

> il ladro
> le mani alzò con amendue le fiche,
> gridando: "Togli, Dio, ch'a te le squadro!"
>
> (25.1–3)

[the thief raised up his hands with both the figs, crying: "Take them, God, for I aim them at you!"]

The obscenity grabs our attention, but cannot hold it because Dante registers the emptiness of Fucci's gesture as soon as he makes it. The "mule" of Pistoia (24.125), as he calls himself, is free to profane, but a Balaam he is not: as a curse, his anathema is powerless. Indeed, among beasts ("son Vanni Fucci / bestia," 24.125–26), Dante sets him far lower than Balaam's ass. The moment he finishes speaking, the serpents that bound him muzzle him so that he may speak no more; as they wind around his neck, they widen to the point of cancellation the gap between the performative potency of Fucci's speech act and its actual effect. In silence these offspring of the creature cursed for his subtle tongue silence the sinner; they, not Fucci, make his curse a curse by making it ironic, not only because through them he becomes the victim of his own pronouncement, but because with the hush of their coils they invert the act of vocalization without which no curse can be a curse. Fucci's curse curses him not when he utters it but when it leaves him dumb. Intention and act totally confound one another; like every soul in hell, Fucci exists, as Freccero has argued, solely as a reification of irony.

In Numbers, immediately before Balak sends for Balaam to curse the children of Israel, Moses ordered a brazen serpent to be forged so that it might be set up as a sign of life; in the cantos of the thieves Dante likewise sanctioned his protracted dalliance with infernal irony by becoming friends with snakes that are figures of justice ("Da indi in qua mi fuor le serpi amiche," 25.4).[65] As they wandered toward Canaan, the people yet again became impatient and spoke against God and Moses ("locutusque contra Deum et Moysen"). The Lord sent fiery serpents ("ignitos serpentes") to afflict them; after they had repented their transgression, God told Moses to make a brazen (or fiery) serpent and set it before them as a standard ("pone eum in signo"), so that everyone who was bitten, when he saw it, should live (Num. 21:6–8).[66] When Dante orchestrated Vanni Fucci's rise from the ashes of his own incineration, this passage furnished a biblical paradigm in which antiphrastic irony is transformed into a *signum* so that it can take part in an allegory of trespass and redemption.[67] For Dante, the snake that saves is the snake that kills when the serpent Moses made becomes a symbol of Jesus, who died to give life.[68] These are the transactions of letter and spirit that Dante re-creates as he watches the serpents curb Fucci's tongue.

---

65. On this passage see further my *Dante's Aesthetics of Being*, 149–50.
66. In the Hebrew Bible, the adjective that always qualifies (or stands in for) the serpents is *saraph*, whose meaning is uncertain. From Isaiah's use of the word (14:29, 30:6), commentators have translated it as "fiery." In the Vulgate, the serpents are fiery when they first appear (21:6), but the "saraph" that Moses makes Jerome says is a "serpentem aeneum" [serpent made of brass] (21.8). Whether or not Dante knew why Jerome made the change, the shift focuses attention on the question of the legitimacy of artistic production, an issue Dante foregrounds in these cantos.
67. In the Vulgate, of course, "signum" is meant in the sense of "standard," but Dante, I would argue, deliberately exploited the semiotic connotations of the word.
68. These events in Numbers were given their gloss in the Book of Wisdom (16.5–7): when the people were destroyed by the bitings of the wicked serpents, God's wrath did not last forever. He gave them a "sign of salvation" [signum . . . salutis], "for he that turned to it was not healed by what he saw, but by thee, the Saviour of all." To Christian exegetes, the brazen serpent was a symbol of Jesus.

They become the model that vindicates his mumming of Ovid by outdoing his metamorphoses.

Chaucer, however, does not silence Ovid, nor does he silence the Manciple, whose ironic volte-faces make him, linguistically at least, the *semblable* and *frère* of Fucci's curse. Indeed, the Manciple is far more dangerous than Fucci, who, dead, damned, and deficient, cannot realize anything; Chaucer's thieving steward is alive and fully invested with agency. Incorporating his voice into the pilgrimage risked crippling permanently the idea that the road to Canterbury also led to "Jerusalem celestial," as the Parson puts it. Chaucer countered the danger, as we have seen, by involving the Manciple with the Cook in an allegory of conversion. This allegory effectively translates the allegory of the *Comedy* by making its intentional mode more readily apparent: when Dante faced the threat antiphrastic irony poses to figural language, he expunged it. Like the earth that fled before the falling Satan to form the mountain of Purgatory, all the senses of Christian deliverance that fill Dante's poem reverberate in the space he created by his excision. After the serpents choke off Fucci's foul-mouthed impiety, their deed is not left to speak for itself. Dante supplies words that, however conditionally, redeem the silence his vipers imposed: "una li s'avvolse allora al collo / come dicesse "Non vo' che più diche" [one then coiled itself about his neck, as if it said, "You shall say no more"] (25.5–6). The law Dante writes under is absolute; because those who have violated it have been blotted out from God's book, he must blot them out from his. In the *Inferno,* ironic cancellation is the manner of meaning that registers the presence of this erasure; Ovid's muting is only one of its more visible traces.

By contrast, in the world of *The Canterbury Tales* no judgment is so faultless, no law so perfect, that it can always say with complete certainty, "This is truth, this justice." Because sin and penance make all earthly choices contingent, Chaucer will be able to stage the contest between the deprivations of antiphrasis and the multivocalic reclamations of allegory without needing to represent his certitude that its outcome was predetermined. Unlike Dante, Chaucer can import the amatory Ovid into his work, even when he is most intensely ironic, because the character who impersonates this voice is only one among many others. Hovering between doctrine and intention, authority and experience, partaking of each, Chaucer's maturest poetry is an aesthetics of earnest and game. By constantly juxtaposing both in the same event, he goes signifying Dante's "once and for all" by translating it as "but not yet."

As Christian poets, neither Dante nor Chaucer believed for a second that all metaphors of the Word were at heart forms of irony. For them, not only parables but a host of passages throughout the Bible proved that the rhetoricians were right: even antiphrasis could be a manner of speaking otherwise. Of course, to convey this conviction, Dante's strategy is the opposite of Chaucer's: where one cuts, the other pastes. The irony of this juxtaposition suggests that the struggle between irony and allegory is inevitable and never settled. It also suggests that Chaucer's translation of Dante did not depend on the *Comedy* alone. In a variety of Boccaccio's works Chaucer found a reading of Dante that also did not hesitate to join his spirituality and Ovid's erotic artfulness in rhetorical embrace. Over the next three chapters I will discuss these translations of Dante; by examining their differences from Chaucer's, we will be able to delineate more securely the tradition that is their outgrowth: Chaucer's Italian Tradition.

4
Dante and Boccaccio, Boccaccio and Petrarch: The Italian Tradition

In an exchange of sonnets, a young Dante Alighieri asked the physician Dante da Maiano what is the greatest suffering that love causes.[1] Since unrequited passion disturbs more faculties of mind and body than anything else, da Maiano responded that a lover experiences nothing more painful than to love unloved. This, he says, certainly has been his own experience. He tried at first to cure himself by reading the *Remedia amoris*; dosing himself with Ovid, however, proved a poor physic. He therefore was left with no choice but to carry on in the hope that pity, patience, and loyal service will someday provide relief.[2]

These prescriptions did not satisfy Dante, who was at once too earnest and too optimistic to find them persuasive. For him the pain of love was far less a somatic condition than a moral imperative. When the heart's ardor is slighted or ignored, he says, the lover should rely on "ingegno ed arte" (natural wit and acquired skill), not to try to fall out of love but to seize the occasion to demonstrate the virtues that conquer the distress it brings.

Had Chaucer read this correspondence or, for that matter, any of Dante's early "rime," he would not have felt he was in very foreign climes. The Provençal and Sicilian-Tuscan poets who influenced the

---

1. For text, translation, and commentary, especially on the problem of attribution of the poems, see *Dante's Lyric Poetry*, ed. K. Foster and P. Boyde, 2 vols. (Oxford: Clarendon, 1967). See in particular the comments in 2:1–3, 6–9.
2. See poem 5a in Foster and Boyde, *Dante's Lyric Poetry*. Even more typical of da Maiano is his response to the vision Dante presents for interpretation in "A ciascun alma presa," the sonnet that later appears as the first poem in the *Vita nuova*. The doctor, alarmed by the vapors that obviously have gone to the sonneteer's head, advises him, in conformity with medical practice of the day, "to give his testicles a good wash" [che lavi la tua coglia largamente]. See Foster and Boyde's note, in which they summarize Bruno Nardi's important article, "L'amore e i medici medievale" (2:29–31).

one and the other Dante and the poets of northern France whom Chaucer emulated differed more in temperament and pitch than in mode of meaning.[3] Both schools subscribed to the central analogy that informed *fin amor:* the appropriate reply to the exalted worthiness of the lover's lady was the utter abjection of his service to her. In Provençal lyric, however, the extent to which the virtues of the *midons* were idealized was matched by the intensity of the lover's ardor to possess her carnally. Even after we understand that the speaker's adoration is an effect of the sublime nature that has caused it, his desire is so visceral it seems to belong to a wholly diverse realm of being. In Tuscan elaborations, poets like Guittone d'Arezzo moralized this tension by setting the claims of the flesh against those of spiritual love.[4] Dante's refusal to accept his namesake's counsel places him squarely in this tradition.

Though I imagine Chaucer would have readily appreciated da Maiano's dry humor, he could have easily embraced the qualities Dante declared will overcome love's woe since he was familiar with the conventions they presupposed.[5] The ideas that generated the complexities of the *dolce stil novo*, however, came from a different order of discourse. These rimes broke decisively from the Sicilian and Tuscan manner by analyzing love according to both the technical epistemology of Aristotelian scholasticism and medieval doctrines of pneumatology.[6]

---

3. I do find telling, however, the absence of any allusion to any Provençal poet, from the prominent meeting with Sordello in *Purgatorio* 6—the canto of "Ahi serva Italia," Dante's famous invective against Italy—to the exchange with Arnaut Daniel in canto 26, which calls attention to itself by granting this "miglior fabbro del parlar materno" (*Purg.* 26.117) the unique privilege of speaking his own language. Chaucer does not show he is either familiar or comfortable enough with the poetry of the *langue d'oc* to quote any of its conventions.

4. For a fine account of the literary traditions that Dante engaged throughout his poetic career, see Teodolinda Barolini, "Dante and the Lyric Past," in *The Cambridge Companion to Dante*, ed. Rachel Jacoff (Cambridge: Cambridge University Press, 1993), 14–33, and more extensively *Dante's Poets: Textuality and Truth in the Comedy* (Princeton: Princeton University Press, 1984).

5. Dante's complete list of virtues is as follows: "Savere e cortesia, ingegno ed arte, / nobilitate, bellezza e riccore, / fortezza e umilitate e largo core, / prodezza ed eccellenza" [Knowledge and courtesy, natural wit and acquired skill; nobility, beauty, wealth; strength and gentleness and generosity; valor and high distinction]. The translation is from Foster and Boyde, *Dante's Lyric Poetry*, no. 5.

6. I discuss Dante's appropriation of scholastic concepts and pneumatological lore in the *Vita nuova* in *Dante's Aesthetics of Being*, 20–77.

To be sure, almost all medieval poets, including Chaucer's French models, introduced the workings of phantasm and spirit into their account of falling in love. But what work by Machaut or any writer of the *langue d'oïl* could have prepared Chaucer for learned intricacies of a *canzone* like Cavalcanti's "Donna me prega"? What then would Chaucer have made of Dante's own "Donne ch'avete intelletto d'amore," or the other momentous poems in praise of Beatrice, whose *stilo de la loda* not only marked an ideological break with Guido but became the theoretical backdrop for the poetics of the *Comedy*?

The *Vita nuova* is Dante's chronicle of his artistic evolution. We have no evidence that Chaucer read or even knew of this indispensable introduction to Beatrice and the poetry Dante wrote about her. But Chaucer did read the twenty-fourth canto of the *Purgatorio*. There, as we have seen, Bonagiunta specifically asks if Dante brought forth the "new rhymes, beginning with 'Donne ch'avete.'" Despite Chaucer's lifelong preoccupation with the form and function of poetry, he nowhere quotes Dante and Bonagiunta's extended conversation. Nor does he cite the entire sequence that surrounds it, beginning with Statius and ending with Arnaut Daniel. In fact Chaucer does not directly engage any episode in the *Comedy* in which Dante deals expressly with artistic craft or vernacular literary history. Arguments *ex silentio* are always suspect; in this case, though, Chaucer's reticence seems to me to indicate that he was not completely conversant with crucial premises of Dante's poesis.

Indeed, given the distance that usually separates high-minded school terms and love-matters in his own poetry, Chaucer may not have embraced the style of "Donne ch'avete intelletto d'amore," had he known it. Perhaps he would not have gone so far as to mock its pretensions with the words of his Dantesque eagle, who ends his disquisition on why all sounds congregate at the House of Fame by saying:

> Have y not preved thus symply,
> Withoute any subtilite
> Of speche, or gret prolixite
> Of termes of philosophie,
> Of figures of poetrie,
> Or colours of rhetorike?
>
> (*House of Fame*, 854–59)

Quite possibly, though, he would have seconded the complaint that Bonagiunta directed at Guido Guinizzelli, the man whom Dante called the father of the *dolce stil novo*. Like Guido, Dante too had changed "la mainera / de li plagenti ditti de l'amore" [the manner of elegant love songs].[7] Rather than reject the subtleties of such "iscuri . . . parlatura" outright, however, I think Chaucer, as was his wont, would have recast them into the more familiar introspections of French courtliness. But for Dante, as the dialogue with Bonagiunta makes clear, one way the "new style" was new was precisely the way in which it had reformed the Gallic (and Tuscan) conception of love.

If Chaucer was unaware of these literary controversies, which Dante foregrounds throughout the *Comedy*, the obstacles he had to overcome to comprehend its vernacular art were formidable. Fortunately, however, Chaucer had more than his French forebears to help him make sense of Dante: he had Boccaccio. Although Chaucer never really was in position to understand the *stil novo* as Dante understood it, he still could see, at least partially, how Boccaccio responded to it. The vantage that poems like the *Filostrato* and *Teseida* gave Chaucer was necessarily oblique since these texts were themselves radical translations of Dante. But by reading them Chaucer did come into contact with the Italian poetic tradition that is the horizon of the one he made.

In one respect Chaucer engaged Boccaccio's poems in a manner that differs markedly from the way he engaged the *Comedy*. The *Troilus* and "The Knight's Tale" both translate Boccaccio's texts and profoundly revise them; the material Chaucer retained as well as the changes he made show that he had pondered continuously not only the parts but the poetics that had joined them into a whole. A significant component of that poetics consists of a reading of Dante; both the *Filostrato* and the *Teseida* deploy an epistemology of love that is entirely Dantesque and entirely unlike anything Chaucer had ever seen in Machaut. In the *Jugement dou Roy de Behaingne*, for instance, a knight and lady argue whether a woman's betrayal or a husband's death causes a lover the greatest anguish. To a great extent, these characters are fleshless ciphers who exist for the sake of the position each supports in the *demande d'amour*. The *Filostrato* turns on a comparable *quistione d'amore:* does thinking about one's beloved or seeing her give the greatest

---

7. On the *tenzone* between Bonagiunta and Guinizzelli, see *Dante's Aesthetics of Being*, 80–81, 86–88.

delight? Boccaccio, however, compacts the conflicting arguments into the psychology of a single character. Criseida in fact embodies both alternatives in Machaut's poem: she is the widow whose husband has died *and* the lady who deserts her knight for another paramour. While Boccaccio did not know the *Jugement* when he wrote his poem, Chaucer certainly did; he drew extensively from it in *The Book of the Duchess*.[8] As he read the *Filostrato*, the elegant speeches of the French debate would all at once seem stiff and contrived compared to the elastic play of Criseida's thoughts and emotions as she passes from the first woman to the second. The way Boccaccio internalized the drama must have seemed a revelation to Chaucer; it was perhaps the principal reason why he gave the *Filostrato* the time and attention he did.[9]

At the same time, however, Boccaccio punctured the intellectual conceits of "stilnovism" with a deflating rhetorical skepticism. Though his protagonists strive to profess their love in the most refined language, Criseida is no Beatrice; as we shall see in the next chapter, she is comprehended by far more than her effects on a mind that perceives her as the idea of virtue. Nor is Troiolo, Pandaro, or the narrator, separately or in combination, any Dante. In each of them, idealism never sidetracks the carnality of his desire; indeed, metaphysics becomes a

---

8. According to the best assessments, Machaut's *Jugement* and Boccaccio's *Filostrato* were both written about the middle of the 1330s. While the two poems were therefore almost certainly conceived independently, we can assume Chaucer noticed their resemblance, especially since Machaut's extended portrait of Jean de Luxembourg, which is one of the high points of the debate, depicts him listening to the story of Troy: "En moult grant joie / Estoit assis sur un tapis de soie, / Et ot un clerc que nommer ne saroie / Qui li lisoit la bataille de Troie" [He was seated in great joy on a silk carpet, and heard a clerk whom I will not name who read to him the battles of Troy] (1472–75). I quote from the first volume of *Oeuvres de Guillaume de Machaut*, ed. E. Hoepffner, 3 vols. (Paris: Firmin-Didot, 1908–21). For a translation of the *Jugement* and a comparison of it and "The Book of the Duchess," see Barry A. Windeatt, *Chaucer's Dream Poetry: Sources and Analogues* (Cambridge: Brewer, 1982).

9. The "newness" of the Italian poetic enterprise would not have been lost on Chaucer. French poetry of the fourteenth century constantly gives voice to what Jacqueline Cerquiglini-Toulet has called "la tristesse du 'déjà dit'." This melancholy knowledge of belatedness stands in stark contrast to the creative confidence of the poetry of the previous century: the *Roman de la Rose* proudly declares its matter is "both good and new" ("La matire est et bonne et neuve"). As Pierre-Yves Badel notes, the poems Chaucer read were written in an "état réflexif," in an age that had passed from the love of the Rose to love of the *Roman de la Rose*. See *Le Roman de la Rose au xive siècle* (Geneva: Droz, 1980), 93. Chaucer also pictures himself in search of new material; in Dante's *stil novo*, as well as in Boccaccio's rhetorical skepticism and Petrarch's humanism, he found it, perhaps in excess of his wish for it.

persuasion to satisfy the demands of the flesh. Boccaccio revivified the Provençal roots of the *stil novo*, in part by introducing the popular conventions of the *cantare*;[10] in his hands, however, sexuality now exposed the universalizing mystifications of love's high moral style. In the *Filostrato*, Troiolo, Criseida, Pandaro, and the narrator all bear witness that no attraction ever remains entirely divorced from selfish purpose.

Boccaccio's juxtaposition of what we might call a Dante-like philosophy of love and an Ovidian rhetoric of motive, which propels the *Teseida* as much as the *Filostrato*, I think appealed to Chaucer. It is rather similar to his own practice of simultaneously embracing and distancing himself from the courtly refinements of Machaut and Deschamps. More immediately, however, Boccaccio's poems provided a point of entry to the *stil novo*, and to the literary influences that lay behind Dante's championing of it. Those scenes in the *Comedy* where perception itself becomes the object of representation—the entire *Paradiso*, for instance, and the "circle of knowledge," to use Giuseppe Mazzotta's phrase, that it constructs—Chaucer read through a Boccaccian filter.[11] Ultimately Boccaccio's appreciation of the particular and the contingency of personal intentions gave Chaucer a way, distinct from Dante's, to humanize the absolute judgment of words and deeds in the *Comedy*. Although Chaucer certainly rejected the values that Boccaccio's rhetorical critique sponsors, at least in the *Filostrato*, part of his tolerance for the foibles of the earthbound in *The Canterbury Tales* can, I think, be traced to it.

Of course, if Chaucer read Dante through Boccaccio, he also read Boccaccio through Dante. Beyond the *Troilus*, where many readers feel the revisionary spirit of Dante is strongest, there is a piece of negative evidence to consider, no less fascinating for being long pondered. When Chaucer visited Florence in 1373, Boccaccio's authority as interpreter of the *Comedy* was at its zenith. The commune would soon vote to sponsor a series of public readings on the *Commedia*. Although Boccaccio's lectures began some five months after Chaucer had returned to

---

10. On the importance of the *cantare* in Boccaccio's early work see Vittore Branca, *Il cantare trecentesco e il Boccaccio del Filostrato e del Teseida* (Florence: Sansoni, 1936); and David Wallace, *Chaucer and the Early Writings of Boccaccio* (Suffolk: Brewer, 1985), 75–93 and passim. Some of Branca's claims have been challenged, but the influence of popular literature on Boccaccio is not in doubt.

11. See Giuseppe Mazzotta, *Dante's Vision and the Circle of Knowledge* (Princeton: Princeton University Press, 1993).

England, critics like to think that he may have heard of the proposal.[12] After all, as Branca notes, Boccaccio himself was the subject of a cult in Florence at this time. His name was linked in honor with Petrarch's: the circle of friends who were vigorously promoting the lectures to the priors and Gonfaloniere of Justice formed the cultural center of humanism in the city. If, however, Chaucer ever did speak to any of these men, their enthusiasm for Boccaccio as a Dantist probably puzzled him in retrospect. For when Chaucer translated the *Filostrato* especially, he would find that the spiritual grandeur of the *poema sacro* had hardly prevented Boccaccio from reconfiguring many of its scenes for far more prurient ends. Chaucer's failure to mention Boccaccio by name has always perplexed his readers; it is hard not to see some deprecation in his silence. Part of that deprecation may indeed stem from the reading of Dante he discerned in Boccaccio.

Such a conclusion, of course, is supposition; Chaucer's silence need not be a judgment at all.[13] It is, though, a fitting emblem for what he did not know about Boccaccio's vision of Dante, about his views on poetry, about his later moral works. No less than Dante, Boccaccio too had a side that, like the moon, always faced away from Chaucer. To gauge the nature of the light he did see the one Florentine throwing on the other, I will therefore examine the history of Boccaccio's shifting ideas about his great predecessor, not only in texts Chaucer knew, but in those he did not know, such as the *Trattatello in laude di Dante*.[14]

There are many instructive instances in the *Trattatello* of how Boccaccio treats the poet he calls "primus studiorum dux et primus fax"; of these,

12. Chaucer left Florence in May, 1373; the petition was presented to the priors and Gonfaloniere of Justice in June of that year. See Padoan's introduction to the *Esposizioni sopra la Comedia di Dante*, ed. Giorgio Padoan, in Boccaccio, *Tutte le opere*, vol. 6 (Milan: Mondadori, 1965), xv.

13. After examining the two versions of the *Teseida* that were in the Visconti library in Pavia, for instance, William Coleman argues that Chaucer's silence in part reflects the fact that both manuscripts lack any attribution to Boccaccio. See "Chaucer, *Teseida*, and the Visconti Library at Pavia: A Hypothesis," *Medium Aevum* 51 (1982): 92–101.

14. The *Trattatello* exists in three versions: the earliest and longest (from Boccaccio's autograph copy); and two later recensions (A and B), called the *Compendio*. Pier Giorgio Ricci has edited both the *Trattatello* and the *Compendio* in Giovanni Boccaccio, *Tutte le opere*, ed. Vittore Branca, vol. 3 (Milan: Mondadori, 1974). Unless otherwise noted, all quotations are from this edition of the *Trattatello* and are identified by paragraph number. For a recent translation of the *Trattatello*, see *The Life of Dante*, trans. Vincenzo Z. Bollettino, Garland Library of Medieval Literature (New York: Garland, 1990); Bollettino gives a full summary of the textual history of the work.

the first meeting between the nine-year-old Dante and Beatrice is exemplary:

> In the season when the heavens' sweetness reclothes the earth with its ornaments and makes it laugh everywhere with varied flowers mixed among verdant branches, it was the custom of our city, of both the men and women in it, to assemble as an associated group, each in its own neighborhood, to hold a festival. Among others, Folco Portinari, a man of great standing among the citizens at that time, happened to have gathered his neighbors at his house for a feast on the first of May. One of the neighbors was [Dante's father] the Alighieri I had mentioned . . . [whose nine-year-old son accompanied him]. After the first course had been served, Dante joined with others his age, playing in his child's way in accordance with his years: there were many boys and girls at the feast.
>
> Among the throng of children was Folco's daughter, whose name was Bice, although Dante always called her by her full name, Beatrice. She was perhaps eight years old, very charming the way children are, extremely courteous and pleasing in her acts, and far more sober and modest in conduct and speech than one would expect in one so young. Moreover, her features were extremely delicate and excellently disposed, and beyond this beauty, she was filled with such integrity and charm, many thought she was a little angel.
>
> So she appeared at the feast, such as I describe her, or perhaps even more beautiful, to Dante—not, I believe, for the first time, but for the first time with the power to make him fall in love. And though he was still a child, he received the beautiful image of her in his heart with such affection it never departed from there while he lived from that day on. (30–33)

Boccaccio concludes his description of their encounter by commenting on its possible causes; his explication is so surprising it needs to be given in his own words:

> Quale ora questa si fosse, niuno il sa; ma, o conformità di complessioni o di costumi o speziale influenzia del cielo che in ciò operasse, o, sì come noi per esperienza veggiamo nelle feste, per la dolcezza de' suoni, per la generale allegrezza, per la dilicatezza de' cibi e de'

vini, gli animi eziandio degli uomini maturi, non che de' giovinetti, ampliarsi e divenire atti a potere essere leggiermente presi da qualunque cosa che piace. (34)

[When this may have happened, no one knows—but either a conformity of temperaments or of habits or the special influence of the heavens that were in the ascendant, or, as we are wont to see at feasts, the sweetness of the music, the general conviviality, the fine food and wine, expand the souls not only of young but also of mature men, and make them apt to be easily captivated by whatever pleasing thing.]

In the face of the symbolic pageantry and unequivocal certainty of the exordium of the *Vita nuova,* Boccaccio's multiplication of reasons is as astonishing as their banality. In Dante's *libello,* the heaven of light had made its circuit nine times when he, just completing his ninth year, saw Beatrice, who was just beginning hers. The elaborate astronomical apparatus fixes the time of his falling in love and establishes its supernal importance. Both Beatrice and the moment of Dante's sighting her are concrete and definite yet somehow unattached to the everyday world. The "gloriosa donna de la mia mente"—Dante's designation is clearly retrospective, even though he is about to see his beloved for the first time—"was called Beatrice, even by those who did not know her name"; from the start Beatrice is a form of knowing, who (or that) seems able to transcend time and understanding. Her appearance immediately causes a threefold epiphany in Dante's vital, animal, and natural spirits. Yet, as extraordinary as these psychic events are, Dante also takes pains to insist that there is an essential difference between himself and the miracle he has been possessed by.[15]

By contrast, in the *Trattatello,* instead of a miracle, we find merely the unusual: one child falls in love with another. Boccaccio does all he can to rob the meeting of special significance. The celestial machinery of the *Vita nuova,* the climactic advent of the God of Love, the intricate staging of the inner motions of the soul: all these have disappeared. Dante's numerical determinism is dismissed with a quick denial, all the more provocative for being so pedestrian: "quale ora questa si fosse, niuno il

---

15. I discuss these differences in *Dante's Aesthetics of Being,* 20–77.

sa."[16] The Beatrice who dazzles him is emphatically a child in this world. Her name, so portentous for Dante, is mysteriously meant in the *Trattatello* only at the level of a nickname: she was called was Bice Portinari, even though the poet always addressed her as Beatrice. And in place of the visionary annunciations of Dante's animal, visual, and vital spirits, by which he registers her effect on him, Boccaccio substitutes his list of explanations, each more likely than the last, all dumbfoundingly drab. Perhaps Dante fell in love because of a "conformità di complessioni o di costumi," perhaps it was the influence of the stars; then again, we do know what parties are like, how their sweet sounds and food and wine loosen the reins of the soul and make men vulnerable to whatever charming thing attracts them. Against the fervent fireworks of the *Vita nuova*, these interpretations are made almost insouciant by their plausibility.

Clearly Boccaccio examines Dante's passion not for its sublimity but for its verisimilitude. The transcendent has been handed over to the circumstantial. Love is emphatically an earthly affair of the bodily senses; its effects always have a material cause, even when they are felt by a child. These are unexpected adjustments, to say the least; disregarding Dante's own commentary, they seem intent on desacralizing the defining event of the poet's life. Our wonder, however, may grow into bewilderment when we realize, as Leonardo Bruni realized long ago, that the mise-en-scène in the *Trattatello* is actually a recasting of Boccaccio's earlier romances.[17] In fact, I think Boccaccio has specifically trans-

---

16. This line so flies in the face of Dante's account, editors and translators have done all they can to make it say anything but what it does. Ricci gives its meaning in a gloss in an earlier edition he prepared of the *Trattatello*: "quando precisamente sia avvenuto l'innamoramento" [when precisely the enamorment may have occurred (no one knows)]; see Giovanni Boccaccio, *Opere in versi, Corbaccio, Trattatello in laude di Dante, Prose Latini, Epistole* (Milan: Ricciardi, 1965), 578. In the Mondadori version, however, he tortuously repunctuates the line to read "Quale, ora, questa si fosse" and says in a note that what "questa" refers to here is the beautiful image Dante received of Beatrice in his mind: "What, now, this [image] may have been . . . ." Ricci clearly wants to eliminate the seeming break in logic between this sentence and the one that follows it, but the extraordinary contortions of his explanation argue against it, as does the fact that when "quale ora" appears elsewhere in the *Trattatello*, it always means "when" in a temporal sense. Bollettino translates, "No one knows precisely why this event took place"; James Robinson Smith anticipates Ricci's second explanation: "Now just what this affection was no one knows." See *The Earliest Lives of Dante* (1901; rpt. 1908, New York: Russell and Russell).

17. In the proem to his life of Dante, Bruni says he had come across the *Trattatello*; much as he admired it on a previous reading, he feels "that our gentle and sweet Boccaccio had written the life and habits of that sublime poet as though he were writing the *Filocolo*, the *Filostrato*, or the *Fiammetta*." The translation is from Smith, *Earliest Lives of Dante*,

formed Dante and Beatrice into versions of his own Troiolo and Criseida.

Both sets of characters fall in love in strikingly similar fashion. As the *Filostrato* begins, it is spring in Troy, that lovely season which reclothes the meadows with grass and flowers, when all creatures become joyful and show their love in diverse acts ("il vago tempo il quale / riveste i prati d'erbetti e di fiori / e che gaio diviene ogni animale / e 'n diversi atti mostra suoi amori").[18] The Trojan elders were preparing to honor Pallas with their customary feast, which both knights and ladies gladly attended. Among those present was the daughter of Calchas, Criseida ("li Troian padri al Palladio fatale / fer preparare li consueti onori; / alla qual festa donne e cavalieri / fur parimente, e tutti volentieri / Tra li qua' fu di Calcàs la figliuola / Criseida ... ," *Fil.* 1.18–19). She was a tall woman whose limbs were all in harmonious proportion to her height and whose face was adorned with celestial beauty. As Troiolo looks at Criseida's "occhi lucenti e l'angelico viso," he falls in love with her.

When we return to the episode in the *Trattatello,* the resemblances, both in wording and in situation, seem too pointed to be unintentional:

Nel tempo nel quale la dolcezza del cielo riveste de' suoi ornamenti la terra, e tutta per la varietà de' fiori mescolati fra le verdi frondi la fa ridente, era usanza della nostra città, e degli uomini e delle donne, nelle loro contrade ciascuno in distinte compagnie festeggiare ... Era intra la turba de' giovinetti una figliuola del sopradetto Folco, il cui nome era Bice, come che egli sempre dal suo primitivo, cioè Beatrice, la nominasse, la cui età era forse d'otto anni, leggiadretta assai secondo la sua fanciullezza, e ne' suoi atti gentilesca e piacevole molto, con costumi e con parole assai più gravi e modeste che il suo picciolo tempo non richiedea; e, oltre a questo, aveva le fattezze del viso delicate molto e ottimamente disposte, e piene, oltre alla bellezza, di

---

81. Bruni's comment has often been echoed. Of modern studies of the *Trattatello,* two above all have influenced mine, though I part company with many of their interpretations: Giuseppe Billanovich, "La leggenda dantesca del Boccaccio dalla lettera di Ilaro al Trattatello in laude di Dante," *Studi danteschi* 28 (1949):45–144; Todd Boli, "Boccaccio's *Trattatello in laude di Dante,* or Dante Resartus," *Renaissance Quarterly* 41 (1988): 389–412.

18. Boccaccio's phrase "Vago tempo," literally "fair season," deserves particular attention. While it has all the trappings of a cliché—as Branca notes, the entire description recalls not only classical traditions and the popular *cantare* but also "subtly echoes" Dante (849)—it is far more than a mere commonplace. It establishes a link between the springtime and Criseida: both are "vago," "lovely" and, drawing on the word's etymology, "wandering" or "passing." Chaucer follows and intensifies this association.

tanta onesta vaghezza, che quasi una angioletta era reputata da molti. (30, 32; translated previously in this chapter)

Both texts use the same conventions to describe spring; in both we learn it was the custom of noble men and women to hold a feast at that time. Each tells us that among the celebrants there was the daughter of an important citizen, who then is named. Criseida and Beatrice both derive their beauty from their features and the harmony their deportment keeps with their condition; each seems an angel of loveliness.

Beyond these similarities, Boccaccio has transported the framing premises of the *Filostrato* into the *Trattatello* as well: sight and thought are again in conflict. Like Troiolo, Boccaccio's Dante becomes Beatrice's "ferventissimo servidore"; nothing gives him pleasure or comfort except seeing her ("se non il vedere costei," 35). He abandoned all his other pursuits, and most assiduously went wherever he thought he could see her ("là dovunque credeva potere vederla," 35). "Oh insensato giudicio degli amanti" (36), Boccaccio then expostulates, "Oh foolish judgment of lovers"; going to see her is to think that by adding wood the fire burns with less heat. Indeed, for Boccaccio, Dante's ardor is completely misplaced since it is inimical to the studies for which his intellectual gifts supremely suited him ("avversario agli sacri studii e allo 'ngegno," 38). The mind, in fact, puts the heart to rout throughout the *Trattatello*: women are persistently denigrated, to the extent that Boccaccio is willing to interrupt his narrative at considerable length to condemn marriage as a distraction to genius (46–59). Virgin or wife, every woman seems to bear the mark of Criseida.

There is a moment in the *Filostrato* that corresponds to Boccaccio's outburst in the *Trattatello*. Just before he sees Criseida, Troiolo delivers himself of a discourse on why it is witless to love. The narrator intervenes, saying "O ciechità delle mondane menti" [Oh the blindness of earthly minds] (1.25). I will argue in chapter 5 that this access of indignation is double-edged: the narrator chastises Troiolo's improvident scorning of love's power, but he doesn't contradict anything Troiolo says. Since the narrator openly admits that he has written the *Filostrato* both to induce his beloved Filomena to return to him and to reprove her if she does not, he simultaneously praises and deplores love. The Boccaccio of the *Trattatello* seems to adopt the opposite position with an assurance that does not admit the slightest doubt: carnal love of any sort deserves only our scorn. In truth, however, this stance of Boccaccio's is just as two-sided and equivocal as his narrator's is in the *Filostrato*.

Boccaccio read in the *Convivio* that Dante regarded the *Vita nuova* as a work of youthful fervor and passion. By no means does Dante wish to disparage his earlier book; now that he is older, however, he says he intends to write in a style that more befits a mature man ("E se ... più virilmente si trattasse che nella *Vita nuova*, non intendo però a quella in parte alcuno derogare," 1.1.16). Boccaccio's adopts exactly the same perspective in the *Trattatello*. He too views Dante's love for Beatrice with all the wisdom of moral hindsight but will not derogate the work that records it. On the contrary, Boccaccio organizes the *Trattatello* so that it makes the *Vita nuova* its palimpsest. If Dante dates the birth of his poetic career with the sonnet "A ciascun'alma presa," his vision of Love feeding Beatrice his burning heart, Boccaccio begins his "vita di Dante" with an equally fantastic vision. He tells of the poet's mother, who while pregnant dreamed she gave birth to her son beneath a laurel; he fed on its berries and was transformed into a peacock (17–18). If the climax of Dante's *libello* is the death and apotheosis of Beatrice, the climax of the *Trattatello* is Dante's. Boccaccio first describes the splendid sepulcher erected for him in Ravenna, then relates the contest among poets to write Dante's epitaph, and finally quotes in full the best of these tributes, "Theologus Dantes nullius dogmatis expers," which was composed by Giovanni del Virgilio (87–91). Such are the obsequies rightfully due a man who overcame so many obstacles to complete his sacred poem that, had he been given the support he merited, Boccaccio says "he would have been a God on earth" [io direi che egli fosse in terra divenuto uno iddio] (83). If Dante's autobiography concludes with a vision of Beatrice in glory and a promise to speak of what he saw when he is more fit to write it, Boccaccio ends his homage by explicating its opening dream. The peacock with one hundred eyes in its tail foreshadowed the *Comedy*'s one hundred cantos, the very work many feel fulfills the pledge of the *Vita nuova* (226).[19] And if, in the most general terms, the central discovery of the *Vita nuova* is the *stilo de la loda*,

---

19. The peacock again enables Boccaccio to coordinate his own work with Dante's. In the *Filocolo* (2.29–35), Biancifiore displays a cooked peacock, which she does not know has been poisoned, to King Felice and his barons; she asks each of them to render homage to the bird ("domandando le ragione del paone"). These vows on the peacock originate with Boccaccio; the elevated "ragione" the bird had provoked in his work made it a fit symbol to prophesy Dante's future "ragionamento."

praise of Dante becomes the raison d'être of Boccaccio's *Trattatello in laude di Dante*.[20]

And yet, despite these analogies, Boccaccio has Dante say, against the clear statement in the *Convivio*, that he was deeply ashamed of having written the *Vita nuova* ("E come che egli d'avere questo libretto fatto, negli anni più maturi si vergognasse molto," 175). To imitate what he makes Dante reprove may seem underhanded as well as contradictory, especially when the only defense Boccaccio can offer for his appropriations of the *Vita nuova* is as mild a commendation of Dante's book as this: "nonetheless, considering his age, it is very beautiful and pleasing, especially for those who only read the vernacular" [nondimeno, considerata la sua età, è egli assai bello e piacevole, e massimamente a' volgari] (175). Boccaccio, however, is not a hypocrite; he is an apologist. He can defend beautiful works written in the "fiorentino idioma" and be ashamed of them at the same time, because the *Trattatello* is more than a review of Dante. As the correspondences with the *Filostrato* make clear, Boccaccio has made his *Vita di Dante* the occasion for a revisionary biography of his own work as well.

In the *Convivio*, Dante submitted passion and poetry to the scrutiny of scholastic logic and moral philosophy; the motor that drives Boccaccio's reassessment of his literary career, however, is the humanism of Petrarch. Boccaccio composed the *Trattatello* sometime between 1351 and 1355; he continued to revise it, directly and indirectly, the rest of his life.[21] He had met Petrarch for the first time in Florence in October 1350; in 1352 Boccaccio journeyed to Padua to tell his magister that the Florentine priors had revoked the confiscation of his exiled father's property and were offering Ser Petracco's son a chair at the newly established Studio. While in Padua Boccaccio spent joyful days avidly

---

20. The title Boccaccio actually gives his tract, one should note, is "De origine, vita, studiis et moribus viri clarissimi Dantis Aligerii florentini, poete illustris, et de operibus compositis ab eodem, incipit feliciter." He refers to the book in the *Esposizioni sopra la Comedia di Dante* as "scrissi in sua laude un trattatello." This has become the title nearly all editors have given the work ever since, though it is often also called the *Vita di Dante*.

21. For the dating of the *Trattatello* and the two versions of the *Compendio*, see Pier Giorgio Ricci, "Le tre redazioni del 'Trattatello in laude di Dante,'" *Studi sul Boccaccio* 8 (1974): 197–214; the essay is reprinted in the Mondadori edition of the *Trattatello*, in Boccaccio, *Tutte le opere*, 3:425–35.

copying Petrarch's works while their author devoted himself to "sacris ... studiis."[22]

As he wrote of Dante, it would have been hard for Boccaccio not to think he was writing about Petrarch as well.[23] Both poets shared a similar temperament and fate. Each struggled mightily to discipline physical appetite by devoting himself to sacred studies; both suffered political exile, Dante directly, Petrarch through his father.[24] And now, just as Boccaccio had been instrumental in arranging Petrarch's repatriation, so he will ask the Signoria to "regain Dante in death" by restoring his citizenship posthumously. At the height of his long rebuke of Florence in the *Trattatello*, Boccaccio exhorts his city "no longer to be enemy but to show her maternal self, to grant her son the tears due him and to give him a mother's love" (101). I will return to this vision of civic nostalgia

---

22. "Tu sacris vacabas studiis: ego compositionum tuarum avidus ex illis scribens summebam copiam." I quote from Epistle IX in Giovanni Boccaccio, *Opere latini minore*, ed. Aldo Massèra (Bari: Laterza, 1938), 136. One of the "compositions" Boccaccio copied was the letter to Gherardo that became *Familiares* 10.4. See note 27 following.

23. This is especially true if Boccaccio drafted his "Life of Petrarch" before 1350, as Massèra thinks (367). Sometime after their conversation in Padua, Boccaccio sent Petrarch a manuscript of the *Comedia* that he had copied in his own hand. He attached to it an "epistola metrica," in which he equates Dante, whose temples "an overhasty, infamous death did not permit to be crowned with merited laurel" [meritis tamen improba lauris / mors properata nimis vetuit vincere capillos] (21–22) and Petrarch, "now acknowledged the honor of Italy, crowned laureate by the leaders of Rome" in the Senatorial Palace on the Capitoline ("Ytalie iam certus honos, cui tempora lauro / romulei cinxere duces" [1–2]). Boccaccio also addresses Dante, telling him there will be one who comes after, also a great poet born in Florence ("Florentia mater"), whom she will joyfully revere just as he will praise and honor her (29–32); Boccaccio ends by asking Petrarch to "receive, read, embrace, honor, and approve" the work of his fellow poet and citizen (37–38). By alluding to Dante's own discussion of the two Guidos (Guinizzelli and Cavalcanti) in the *Purgatorio* ("and he is perchance born that shall chase the one and the other from the nest," 11:97–99), Boccaccio implies what he will make explicit in 1359, when he sent a revised version of the letter-poem to Petrarch: as great as Dante is, Boccaccio esteems Petrarch even more. For the text of Boccaccio's poem (Carme III), see *Opere latini minore*, ed. Massèra, 96–97. See also Massèra's note, 294–96. Boli, "Boccaccio's *Trattatello*," nicely shows how Boccaccio remade Dante so that he might meet Petrarch's standards. I would argue that Boccaccio's remaking extended in the other direction as well.

24. Petrarch would himself claim that his father and Dante went into exile the same day. (Ser Petracco was in fact proscribed in October 1302, Dante in January.) See *Familiares*, 21:15, a long letter in which Petrarch attempts, not very persuasively, to make Boccaccio understand that he does not envy Dante at all. On Petrarch's anxiety about Dante, see, for example, the rather extreme comments of Giocchino Paparelli, "Due modi di leggere Dante: Petrarca e Boccaccio," in *Giovanni Boccaccio editore e interprete di Dante*, ed. Società dantesca italiana (Florence: Olschki, 1979), 73–90.

later; for now I would only note that it looks as much to the future as to the past. When Dante's mother dreams Boccaccio's dream of her son's birth under a laurel, the author of the *Trattatello* could at the same time fondly hope that he was also prefiguring the return of Petrarch, crowned laureate in 1341, to the city, thereby substantially fulfilling the dream of the earlier poet to sleep again in his native "ovile" (sheepfold), having accepted "'l cappello" at the Baptistery of San Giovanni (*Par.* 25.1–9).[25]

As Branca says, the meetings with Petrarch were decisive for Boccaccio. From this time his works increasingly focused on ethical and religious themes, and their language increasingly was Latin.[26] In the *Trattatello* itself, the famous digression on poetry begins with almost a word-for-word translation of passages from a letter that Petrarch had written to his brother on December 2, 1351. Gherardo had recently become a monk; he was worried that the fables of poets he had always loved were inimical to goals of his new way of life. In response Petrarch rehearsed the origin of poetry, which he says arose among primitive people from their desire to worship the divine. With the institution of temples and priests, the ancients felt that in addition to marble altars and beautiful vestments they should praise the gods in noble prayers that were free of vulgar forms of speech and were arranged in rhythmical measures to provide pleasure. Such language was called *poetes* in Greek, and those who used it were called poets. At its source, poetry is thus a form of theology; Petrarch can justly commend it to his Carthusian brother. In fact, if Gherardo would take note of the parables and figurative speech in sacred Scripture, he would have to admit the truth of a further argument as well: "theology is the poetry of God."[27]

---

25. In both versions of the later *Compendio*, the rebuke of Florence has been toned down. Petrarch had been much moved by the offer from Florence, but declined it, perhaps because he had already accepted Clement V's invitation to go to Avignon. In response to what it saw as a snub, the Signoria in Florence revoked its offer. See Branca, *Boccaccio*, 91. Boccaccio deplored the Signory's actions; in retrospect, however, Petrarch's removal to Milan may have been one reason (though not the main one, as I explain below) why he tempered his vehemence against Florence.

26. Branca, *Boccaccio*, 94. The *Corbaccio*, probably written in 1355 (though Giorgio Padoan argues it should be dated a decade later), would be the last literary work Boccaccio composed in Italian. He continued, however, to revise some texts like the *Decameron* until he died.

27. *Familiares*, 10.4. For a translation, see Francisco Petrarca, *Letters on Familiar Matters*, trans. Aldo Bernardo, 3 vols. (Baltimore: Johns Hopkins University Press, 1975–86). Petrarch's defense of poetry against the attacks his brother had heard at his monastery adopts the same manner of argument Boccaccio will use in "Ut huic epistole," the letter

Boccaccio never wavered from Petrarch's belief that, with the corrections of Christian revelation, the superior moral dignity of Latin made it the fit tongue to inherit this legacy from the Greeks.[28] But from 1353 on, Boccaccio was also painfully aware that Petrarch's cultural poetics could be fundamentally at odds with his own commitment to the ideals of the commune. In June of that year, despite his previous disapprobation, Petrarch agreed to join the court of Giovanni Visconti in Milan.[29] This decision scandalized Petrarch's friends in Florence, who thought the archbishop a tyrant and the city he ruled their direst enemy; it precipitated the only crisis in Boccaccio's relations with the man he called his father. He never could bring himself to break entirely with Petrarch; nonetheless, in the *Trattatello*, after he rehearses poetry's origins but

---

he sent to Petrarch to protest his defection to Milan. Petrarch argues that although poetry and theology differ in their subjects, they are the same kind of discourse. Theology deals with God and divine things, poetry with God and man; both, however, clothe their meaning in figurative language. While he will concede that poetry should not be preferred to theology, Petrarch will in no way admit that it should be spurned. He then spends the rest of his letter explicating the hidden meaning of the first eclogue of his *Bucolicum carmen*. In "Ut huic epistole," Boccaccio positions himself in an analogously mediate position. Quoting Walter Map's "Epistola Valerii ad Rufinum," Boccaccio begins by saying, "He fears to speak yet cannot remain silent." He then casts the Paduan conversations he had had a year before with his mentor as an eclogue. Beyond prompting Petrarch to recall both his poetical and his political commitments, Boccaccio implies that they are inseparable. He therefore doubles the character Silvius, who serves as Petrarch's bucolic surrogate. The Silvius who speaks stands for the Petrarch who had denounced Giovanni Visconti. The second Silvius, however, remains silent throughout; he is the Petrarch who now lodges with the archbishop. There is a comparable division in the *Trattatello*, which I discuss below.

28. After distinguishing the vernacular of the *Comedy*, which is "elegant, graceful, and sublime" [ornato, leggiadro e sublime] from the language women use, which lacks these qualities ("delle quali cose nulla sente il volgare delle femine"), Boccaccio writes in the *accessus* to his *Esposizioni sopra la Comedia di Dante* (1373):

Non dico però che, se in versi latini fosse, non mutato il peso delle parole volgari, ch'egli non fosse più artificioso e più sublime molto, per ciò che molto più d'arte e di gravità ha nel parlare latino che nel materno.

[I do not mean that if it (the *Comedy*) were in Latin verse, it would not be far more artful and sublime. Even if the words in the vernacular kept the weight they have, Latin has far greater art and gravity than the mother tongue.] (*Accessus*, 19)

The older Boccaccio is a full-fledged Petrarchan humanist here, not least in his deprecation of the vernacular at the expense of Latin by associating Italian with women. Although Boccaccio follows Dante here, the spirit is quite different, and much meaner, than it is in his source, the *Epistle to Can Grande* (paragraph 10).

29. For a discussion of Petrarch's motives, see Ernest H. Wilkins, *Petrarch's Eight Years in Milan* (Cambridge, Mass.: Medieval Academy, 1958), 9–15.

before he turns to the idea that poets are theologians, Boccaccio inserts a passage that seems to speak directly to his "preceptor inclite":[30]

> E poi susseguentemente cominciarono diversi in diversi luoghi, chi con uno ingegno, chi con uno altro, a farsi sopra la moltitudine indòtta della sua contrada maggiori; diffinendo le rozze quistioni, non secondo scritta legge, che non l'aveano ancora, ma secondo alcuna naturale equità, della quale più uno che un altro era dotato; dando alla loro vita e alli loro costumi ordine, dalla natura medesima più illuminati; resistendo con le loro corporali forze alle cose avverse possibili ad avvenire; e a chiamarsi "re"; e mostrarsi alla plebe e con servi e con ornamenti non usati infino a que' tempi dagli uomini; a farsi ubidire; e ultimamente a farsi adorare. Il che, solo che fosse chi 'l presummesse, sanza troppa difficultà avvenia, perciò che a' rozzi popoli parevano, così vedendogli, non uomini ma iddii. (134)

> [And subsequently, different men in different places, one by one stratagem, one by another, began to raise themselves above the unlearned masses of his region. They settled their rude disputes not according to written law, which they did not yet have, but according to some native sense of equity, which some possessed more than others. Enlightened to a greater degree by nature, they brought order to their lives and manners, and they resisted with physical force any occasion that might rise against them. These men began to call themselves king and to appear before the common people with servants and ornaments until then unused by men to make the people obey and ultimately to worship them. This was not too difficult to bring about, if only one presumed to do it, since to the rude people who saw them they seemed not men but gods.]

---

30. The phrase comes from the opening of "Ut huic epistole." Petrarch never answered Boccaccio's complaints directly; however, what explanations he did offer his other friends seem to have placated them as well as Boccaccio. They all continued their friendships with him. By 1359, the rift between Boccaccio and Petrarch was completely healed. After discussing the matter at length, Boccaccio agreed that Milan was probably the best place for Petrarch to be. At this time Boccaccio again praised Dante, so much so that in a later letter, despite including the revised version of his metric epistle, he excused himself for having said so much. Petrarch should understand, Boccaccio continues, that his praise for Dante implies even higher praise for him, since he values Petrarch even more than he does Dante. Boccaccio's letter has not survived; Petrarch's response, in which he paraphrases his friend's comments, has. See *Familiares*, 21:15.

Such men, Boccaccio continues, used religious ritual to supplement their force; they deified their fathers, grandfathers, and ancestors so that the people would fear and hold them in reverence. All this they could not have done without the collaboration of poets, who

> sì per ampliare la loro fama, sì per compiacere a' prencipi, sì per dilettare i sudditi, e sì per persuadere il virtuosamente operare a ciascuno—quello che con aperto parlare saria suto della loro intenzione contrario—con fizioni varie e maestrevoli, male da' grossi oggi non che a quel tempo intese, facevano credere quello che li prencipi volevan che si credesse. (136)

[to broaden their fame, please their princes, delight his subjects, and induce all to act virtuously, which had they spoken plainly would have had the effect opposite to the one they intended, made various and masterful fictions. These fictions, misunderstood by the coarse today not to mention those of that time, made the people believe what the princes wanted them to believe.]

Because Boccaccio frames the careful modulations and progressions of these sentences with ideas and phrases he borrowed directly from Petrarch, these remarks stand out as an explicit critique of his master's values.[31] The poet who serves a tyrant becomes his henchman, his

---

31. Ultimately the tyrant's use of the arts to secure his power is a perversion of magnificence. Boccaccio's source is the *Nicomachean Ethics;* according to Aristotle, "the magnificent man is like an artist"; his expenditures are "of the kind which we call honorable, e.g. those connected with the gods—votive offerings, buildings, and sacrifices—and similarly with any form of religious worship" (4.2.1, 20 [1122b1]). The same thoughts, obviously given a more benign interpretation, had been in Galvano Fiamma's mind when he wrote his history of the Viscontis (1328–42). To justify the palace Azzone Visconti had built for himself, Fiamma cites both the *Ethics*—"it is the work of a magnificent man to erect a fine dwelling"—and the *Politics:* "for people who see marvelous dwellings are deeply impressed with strong admiration" (6.7.35 [1321a1]). These passages from Aristotle clearly could be put to opposite ideological use: where Boccaccio compacted a tyrant from them, Fiamma saw an ideal patron. By citing the *Politics,* Fiamma ran the risk that his reader might recall, as Boccaccio surely had in his talks with Petrarch, Aristotle's definition of the tyrant as the man who directs his actions to his own good rather than to the welfare of the many. Petrarch, however, could have readily responded that at least in the passage Fiamma quotes, Aristotle was not talking about a tyranny, but about an oligarchic government like Florence's. Fiamma was a Dominican friar; as John Larner says, he may well have been following ideas of patronage that had been elaborated at S. Maria Novella in Florence. See *Culture and Society in Italy, 1290–1420* (New York: Scribners, 1971), 101, where the passage from Fiamma is quoted.

poems perversions of the theology poetry ought to be. In men who seek power, genius degenerates into wily ploy: Boccaccio's word "ingegno" encompasses both the natural superiority of intellect of a man like Petrarch, and the dishonest contrivance of the exceptional man who yields to Augustinian temptation of dominating others.[32] Justice is subverted, and the ordered life Petrarch so eloquently advocated is made the adjutant of brute force: authority no longer resides in the preeminent possession of an innate sense of equity, but in the ability to combine might and imposture to subject others to one's will. At heart, "kings" such as these do not merely dress themselves in the trappings of divinity, they become self-idolaters.

And the poet who, seduced by such power, pledges his allegiance to a dictator's ambition is little more than his ape. He may very well pursue the Petrarchan goal of gaining fame by composing verse that instills virtue. But Boccaccio rips the mask away: no matter the intent, the effect of his poems will be to get people to believe what their rulers want them to believe. Boccaccio in effect invites Petrarch to picture Visconti at his marble altars in his archbishop's robes. Unlike the priest in Petrarch's letter, however, the despot is not God's minister but his imposter, a fraud who would put on his power as easily as he dons the "ornamenti" of divinity.[33] In like manner, the marvelous fictions of his poet will not set forth the "shadow-bearing prefaces" of God's glory. Their artful ornaments will gild the corruption of despotism.

In the *Filostrato*, Boccaccio had proposed that no form of mediation is pure agency; means not only take on the value of the end they are directed to, they have qualities of their own that act to construct the values of the end. In the *Trattatello*, Boccaccio subjects Petrarch's defection to the same rhetorical analysis. Virtue in the service of vice, he suggests,

---

32. After announcing in "Ut huic epistole" that he will cast his letter as an eclogue, Boccaccio tells Petrarch to uncover, if it pleases him, the sense hidden under the pastoral cortex with his understanding: "tu autem que sub pastorali cortice tecta sunt, si libet, *ingenio* percipe" (emphasis added). The admixture of command ("percipe") and deference ("si libet") strikes precisely the attitude Boccaccio takes toward Petrarch in the *Trattatello*; the use of "ingegno" there ties Petrarch to the "king" Boccaccio is now describing.

33. In the letters of explanation he wrote (*Fam.* 16.11, 12, 13; *Epistolae variae*, 7), Petrarch in fact stresses Visconti's faithful devotion to his ecclesiastic duties. Although E. H. Wilkins is perhaps too apologetic, he sounds an important cautionary note: Boccaccio's protests need to be read in light of the general fear of Milan in Florence. See Wilkins, *Petrarch's Eight Years*, 10–12.

can only parody itself; Dante, the man whom Boccaccio says "fosse in terra divenuto uno iddio," is the true poet-king. By choosing to stop in Milan, Petrarch not only revealed himself as the diminished reflection of his great predecessor, he stained his very soul.

Dante's achievement in the "idiom of Florence," therefore, allowed Boccaccio to resist the absolute division Petrarch had by this time made between Latin and vernacular literature. For Boccaccio, part of the *Comedy*'s ethical value lay precisely in its accessibility to the greatest number of citizens. Because Dante wrote in Italian, his poem is useful both to the unlettered, who can appreciate its beauty and artfulness, and to the learned, who can understand the doctrine concealed beneath its surface. Yet the very same Boccaccio also contends that Dante chose the vulgar tongue by default. The liberal arts were in such decline, and classical poets so scorned, that Dante originally began to write the *Comedy* in Latin, the appropriate language for the subject; he stopped after three lines, Boccaccio tells us, because he realized that he couldn't put crusty bread into the mouths that still sucked milk (192). The hauteur that buttresses such sentiments is worthy of Petrarch, even if in the process Boccaccio has made Italian Latin's equal as a medium of learning.[34]

In the *Trattatello*, Dante and Petrarch are like two magnets, each with poles that attract and repel the other's; by locating his own literary history in the intersection of their fields, Boccaccio was able to register the ruptures and insist on the continuity between the moral dictates of Latin humanism and the sensual play of his works in the vernacular. Boccaccio thus associated youthful efforts such as the *Filostrato* and the *Teseida* with the *Vita nuova*, but implies he now judges them, like Dante in the *Convivio*, from a maturer perspective. He disowns their passion, yet commends their beauty and their utility as a vehicle for transmitting classical culture. At the same time, however, Boccaccio also embraced a Petrarchan gravitas severe enough to change the letter of Dante's text by making him more ashamed of his love than he was. In censuring Dante's desire for Beatrice and his marriage to Gemma Donati (whom he does not deign to name), Boccaccio endorsed

---

34. The "source" of this information is the letter of Frate Ilaro to Ugucione da Faggiuola, which Boccaccio probably wrote himself. The letter exists in Boccaccio's own hand in the Zibaldone Laurenziano. See Billanovich, "La leggenda dantesca del Boccaccio," 80–98, 123–28.

Petrarch's devotion to masculine solitude and study.[35] The movement toward the misogyny of the *Corbaccio* is readily apparent in the *Trattatello;* we are not far from its stylistic counterpart, an open renunciation of all fiction inspired by "vaghe donne" and written in the maternal tongue.

Pulling against these tendencies, however, is Dante's commitment to civic justice and liberty in Florence. In order to save Petrarch's appearance, Boccaccio seems to discriminate between politics and poetics; he will swear fealty to "le cantiche della Comedìa di Dante Alighieri fiorentino" in the former if he can take his master's eloquence for his model in the latter. But Boccaccio knows full well that no style is without its political dimension. He subscribed to the idea, a commonplace of the medieval accessus, that poetry is a branch of ethics; for him the beauty of Dante's language, "la bellezza del nostro idioma," derived in part from his ability to praise and reprove the public conduct of Florence's citizens in it.[36] Boccaccio in fact establishes his own tract's status as legitimate preface to the *Comedy* by underscoring its political purpose:[37] the *Trattatello* begins with Solon, whose laws are testimony of the regard the ancients had for justice. Only when good acts are rewarded and those that cause harm are punished can a city stand on solid footing. If it fails in the performance of one of these requirements of justice, it is crippled; if it fails in both, it will not be able to stand at all. Boccaccio's immediate source for these remarks about Solon and the image of the two feet of the republic is a letter that Petrarch addressed to Florence in 1349 (*Fam.* 8.10). In it he had indignantly called on the city to cultivate justice and to keep its roads free of brigands and thieves.[38] Petrarch in turn had drawn his metaphors from Cicero; at the start of the *Trattatello*, however, Boccaccio may well have

---

35. As Ricci notes, when Boccaccio says that "studies in general, and speculative studies in particular, usually need solitude and the removal of care and tranquility of soul," he was following Petrarch's *De vita solitaria*, I, 7.

36. In the *Esposizioni*, the branch of philosophy to which Boccaccio assigns the *Comedy* is "alla parte morale, o vero etica" (*Accessus*, 42).

37. As Ricci has shown, the *Trattatello* and *Compendio* were conceived not as freestanding works, but as a prologue to the *Comedy* ("Introduzione," 426). This fact, rather than lessening the Derridean tensions of the supplement, seems to me to bring them even more into play.

38. Petrarch wrote his letter after two friends, Luca Cristiano and Mainardo Accursio, had both been robbed, and Accursio killed, on the road from the Apennines to Florence. Boccaccio successfully persuaded the priors and Gonfaloniere of Justice to support Petrarch's cry for justice. See Branca, *Boccaccio*, 88.

associated the figure of the "lame" republic less with the *Pro archia* than with Dante's "limp" after his encounter with the three beasts at the start of the *Comedy*.[39] Certainly after 1353 Boccaccio felt Petrarch had made a crippling misstep; instead of embodying the republican aspirations of a Cicero, Petrarch now, in perverse imitation of Dante's fiction, hobbled after the despotic beast of Milan.[40] For Boccaccio, who was actively involved in missions to curb the ambitions of the Viscontis during the 1350s, Petrarch's surrender to the blandishments of tyranny could be nothing less than an act of poetic and ethical self-laceration.

Thus the Dante whom Boccaccio presents in the *Trattatello*, simultaneously sovereign poet and cultural statesman of the *popolani*, reflects his own divided loyalties. Another way to say this is that Boccaccio's Dante is constructed from the collision of two discourses, one political and distinctively Florentine, the other literary and increasingly humanistic. These languages were not altogether compatible; throughout the *Trattatello* we see Boccaccio struggling to subordinate Florence's social dialogue to his literary aesthetics. For all its words about Solon and justice, Boccaccio's *Life*, like the Provençal *vida*, stands as a humble preface to Dante's works. However much the *Trattatello* makes those works more accessible to the general public, Boccaccio also believed that the *Comedy*, like *trobar clus*, addressed the select few who could understand

---

39. In the *Inferno*, Dante is refashioning Aristotle's trope of the feet of the soul, as John Freccero has shown in "Dante's Firm Foot and the Journey without a Guide," *Harvard Theological Review* 52 (1959): 643–72. Although Boccaccio doesn't comment specifically in the *Esposizioni* on the "firm foot which was always lower," he does say of these lines in general:

> E come il nostro corpo infermo senza l'aiuto d'alcun bastone sostener non si puote né muoversi ad alcuno atto utile, così l'anima nostra, dal peccato vinta e stanca, senza alcuno aiuto della divina clemenzia non può cosa alcuna aoperare in sua salute. (1.146)

> [Just as our body, when ill, cannot support itself without a crutch or be engaged in useful acts, so our soul, tired out and overcome by sin, can do nothing to cure itself without some aid from divine mercy.]

In light of these comments, I think it likely that Boccaccio was alluding to the opening of the *Comedy* at the start of the *Trattatello*.

40. Designating Visconti a beast is not a completely fanciful invention on my part. About this time Boccaccio had composed his epigram against the archbishop (Carme IV in *Opere latine minori*, ed. Aldo F. Massèra [Bari: Laterza, 1938], 97): "Nescis posse meum, que sit gloria mea nescis" [You know not my power; what my glory is, that know you not]. He put these words, doubly ironic for someone both a churchman and a tyrant to hear (cf. David's prayer to God when Solomon became king, 1 Chron. 29:10–30), in the mouth of the Florentine lion. See also Branca, *Boccaccio*, 98–99.

both the depth of its doctrine and the technical accomplishments of its form. In much the same way, Boccaccio cast Dante's political life in Florence, his alliance with the Bianchi, and his exile, in the familiar trappings of a Fortune tragedy.[41] From this point of view, justice, with its commensuration of offense and degree, becomes a metaphor for poetic allegory, which, with its dialectic between inner truth and outer tegument, is perhaps the chief mode Boccaccio employs to try to establish the greater and lesser merit of the discourses that compete with one another in the *Trattatello*.

At this moment in his career, however, Boccaccio was well aware that allegory could stabilize values only provisionally. He was close enough to the *Decameron* to remember that in it allegory had been an adjunct, in Giuseppe Mazzotta's words, to "the pornographic imagination."[42] It was, one could argue, precisely this knowledge that allegory can direct the languages it coordinates to different ends that enabled Boccaccio to clear a space in his biography for politics to begin to function as an independent discourse.

In *trecento* Florence, the Signory, the colleges, the deliberative councils, and the appointment of extraordinary commissions *(balìe)* were the center and circumference of enfranchised life. As we have seen, elections were constant. For an act to become law, legislation previously approved by the Signory and the two colleges was sent to the Council of the "Popolo" and the Council of the Commune, who had to pass the measure by a two-thirds majority.[43] Yet even though the exercise of authority was so much a communal affair, Florentines for the most part were uninterested in speculating about their political institutions. As Gene Brucker says, "the merchant or artisan took the same practical

---

41. A typical example of Boccaccio's rhetoric is instructive:

Dante, in un momento prostrato della sommità del reggimento della sua città, non solamente gittato in terra si vide, ma cacciato di quella. (66)

[Dante, in one moment hurled from the height of the government of his city, not only sees himself thrown to the ground, but chased from it.]

Although this rhetoric derives from *The Consolation of Philosophy*, the atmosphere of the *Trattatello* differs completely from that of Boethius's work. The same misogyny that had impelled Boccaccio's digression on marriage drives his remarks here: Lady Fortune is the final ingathering of every deleterious impulse that Beatrice and Gemma Donati had already been made to embody.

42. Giuseppe Mazzotta, *The World at Play in Boccaccio's Decameron* (Princeton: Princeton University Press, 1986), 105–30.

43. For a full description of these offices, see Gene Brucker, *Florentine Politics and Society, 1343–1378* (Princeton: Princeton University Press, 1962), 59ff.

view of his government as he did of his business: he was interested in its efficiency and success, not in its theoretical basis."[44] No one, of course, would claim the *Trattatello* is *Il Principe*. But if Boccaccio does not directly analyze the forces that constantly changed the ideological direction of his city's administration, his disquisitions on justice and public remonstrances of Florence do make the *Trattatello* political in a way that the chronicles, for instance, are not. Like the Villanis or Velluti, Boccaccio consistently turns the events he recounts into occasions for moral sermonizing; unlike them, however, and in stark contrast to his own "Life of Petrarch," which Boccaccio probably drafted in 1349, the *Vita di Dante* records social structures that not only help explain Boccaccio's aesthetic figurations but are involved in their production.[45]

---

44. Brucker, *Florentine Politics and Society*, 72. Brucker, of course, wishes to emphasize the practical nature of Florentine politics; he downplays the political writings of the Dominicans such as Remigio Girolami who commented on Aristotle's *Ethics* and *Politics* at S. Maria Novella in Florence. And Brucker entirely discounts the *Defensor Pacis*.

45. In the fourth book of Matteo Villani's *Cronica*, for instance, one finds attitudes that, at first glance, seem very similar to Boccaccio's:

> Perocche gli antichi moderati e virtudiosi che soleano reggere e governare lo stato della repubblica in grande libertà, e con maturi movimenti e con diligente provvidenza governavano quella in tempo di pace e di guerra, e non perdonando i falli che si faceano contro la patria, né lasciando senza merito l'operazioni che si facevano virtudiose in accrescimento e onore del comune, onde al nostro tempo è da maravigliare come la cittadinanza si mantiene, essendo strana da quella virtù e della provisione di quel reggimento; e in luogo di quelli antichi amatori della patria, spregiatori de' loro propri comodi per accrescere quelli del comune, si trovano usurpatori de' reggimenti con indebiti e disonesta procacci e argomenti, uomini avventicci, senza senno e senza virtù, e di niuna autorità nella maggior parte, i quali abbracciato il reggimento del comune intendono a' loro propri vantaggi.

> [Moderate and virtuous men of old used to rule and govern the republic in great liberty; with mature deliberations and diligent foresight they governed Florence in times of peace and of war. They did not pardon crimes committed against the state, nor did they leave unrewarded virtuous works that contributed to the commune's growth and honor. In light of this, it is a wonder that the citizenry is maintained in our day, estranged as it is from that virtue and foresight of previous government. And in place of those ancestors who loved their city, who disdained their own affairs to make the commune's grow, one finds men who with their unwarranted seizures and trumped up justifications usurp office rather than govern in it; and men of the hour, without sense or virtue or the least authority for the most part, who, having grasped the offices of the commune, intend to ply them to their own advantage.]

(Matteo Villani, *Cronica di Matteo Villani*, ed. F. Dragomanni [1846; rpt. Frankfurt am Main: Minerva, 1969], IV, 69). Like Boccaccio, Villani holds in contempt those *popolani grassi* who regularly misappropriated communal lands and accounts for their own use, and the "new men," who are of lower standing yet are equally greedy. But unlike Boccaccio, Villani's remedy is cast in nostalgia; his justice is that of an antique time, when long-standing residents governed Florence with virtue, before newcomers moved to the

For Florentines in the 1350s, the proem of the *Trattatello* would have had distinct reverberations. In September 1342, the duke of Athens had been installed as lord of Florence for life. The following July, a popular rebellion broke out, which a number of aristocratic families joined. As soon as Walter of Brienne had been driven from the city, these "magnates," as they were called, formed a government in conjunction with the great *popolani*; this was the first time anyone from a magnate family had been allowed to enter the Signory in fifty years.[46] Their joint rule lasted two months; they increased direct taxes, which were levied on everyone, decreased taxes on capital and property, from which only the patriciate derived income, and generally left unpunished the crimes that the *grandi e potenti* perpetrated.[47] As a result the *popolo* rose against them; as one of its first acts, the newly formed government revived the Ordinamenti di giustizia.

These ordinances, first adopted by the commune in 1293, were promulgated to curb the violence of the great clans in Florence. If a magnate murdered a *popolano*, his whole family would be held responsible. The office of Gonfaloniere of Justice was established and made part of the Signoria, from which all magnate families were now proscribed. Unless they were designated *popolani*, the aristocratic houses of Florence, even if intimately involved in commerce, were effectively barred from political power.[48]

By 1343, the Ordinamenti were still a powerful instrument of class politics in the commune, but half a century of prosperity had significantly altered the nature of the struggle. Blood still was at the heart of it, but social distinctions increasingly were defined in terms of the length of time a family had resided in Florence. The *novi cives*, guild members and artisans who had recently come to the city, had grown wealthy; for the next fifty years they would use the Ordinances to protect their political prerogatives against the great *popolani* who were established noblemen. Despite the fact that economic interests brought both groups together—they often joined in business ventures, partnerships, and marriage—the enmity each class felt for the other over the

---

city and brought with them their corrupting hunger for gold. Even though Boccaccio's emphasis on justice and law takes the same form as Villani's, who also invokes Solon, the *Trattatello* is far more "political" and forward looking.

46. One fifth of the Council of the Commune, however, was comprised of magnates.

47. Marvin Becker, *Florence in Transition*, 2 vols. (Baltimore: Johns Hopkins University Press, 1968), 2:109–10.

48. For a description of the enactment of the ordinances, see Giovanni Villani, *Villani's Chronicle*, trans. Philip Wicksteed et al. (London: Constable, 1906), VIII, I.

years varied only in intensity. In the wake of the Black Death, it was at high tide.

In 1349, a wine merchant, a notary, and three other "new men" proposed to alter the Ordinances; the liability of a member of a magnate house who committed a crime would be borne by his kinsmen to the sixth degree. The representatives of the patriciate argued that responsibility should extend only to the third degree. Debates such as these established the tenor of civic life in Florence when Boccaccio began the *Trattatello*. But the political and social landscape was shifting and extremely complex; one cannot point to one bloc and say these people identified themselves with the welfare of the commune, these with the privileges of the magnates. Certainly the great *popolani* who dominated the Signory during these years were no friends of the artisans and members of the lesser guilds. They proposed legislation to exclude from governmental office any citizen who had not been born in Florence or whose father and grandfather were not native residents. Yet these measures received overwhelming support, even from those they hurt the most, the new men who were members of the fourteen *arti minori*. During the Black Death, the representation of these lower guilds in the Signory was significantly reduced to two; the number of guilds themselves was cut in half to seven.[49] On the other side, the *grandi* among the *popolani* were themselves severely divided. The strife between the oligarchic, propapal Albizzi and the populist, antipapal Ricci first gave Florentine politics its distinctive stamp in 1350; the same antagonisms still dictated allegiances even after Uguccione de' Ricci proved himself a hollow demagogue when he turned his back on the people and joined the Albizzi the year before Chaucer visited the city in 1373.[50]

---

49. Though these measures crippled the political power of both the greater and the lesser *gente nuova*, they did not precipitate a crisis. In fact, the number of lesser guilds was restored to fourteen in 1350 on the initiative of the oligarchic Albizzi faction. For the next thirty years, the lower guildsmen were courted by rival cliques for their support. More surprisingly, the *popolo minuto*, the unenfranchised manual laborers in the city, who frequently rose in protest, sometimes violently, during the 1340s, seem to have become quiescent thereafter. As Brucker points out, no documents reflecting discontent among them have been found between 1350 and 1368 (*Florentine Politics and Society*, 123).

50. Uguccione had been for twenty years the most vocal opponent of Albizzi policy. The chroniclers were bitter about his defection: Stefani claimed Uguccione had betrayed the *parte popolare* for promises of rich ecclesiastical benefices for his kinsmen. As a result, the merchants and artisans of Florence were now the slaves of the tyrannical Albizzis and Riccis (cited in Becker, *Florence in Transition*, 2:134–35). Stefani's sentiments were echoed by many others; in the wake of this new alliance, artisans, who were new men, and *popolares*, who were nonfactious independents, joined together to establish what Becker calls "the most democratic of all Florentine regimes" (135). These events and issues would have dominated conversations when Chaucer visited Florence in 1373.

The three decades between 1343 and Boccaccio's death in 1375 were years of deep dissension and profound transition in Florence.[51] Besides a political transformation, which saw the privileges of the great ruling families yield ground to the legislative power of the state, there was a transformation of social values as well. The *gente nouva*, who increasingly were the men who governed the commune, had been scorned by Dante at the beginning of the century (*Par.* 16.49–57); by its end, Salutati was calling them the bulwarks of the republic. The aristocratic attainments of a Cacciaguida, chivalric prowess, courtly wit, were faded flowers of an age that had passed; the last public tournament in Florence was held in 1343. Lineage did remain the predominant force in determining the attitudes and conduct of Florentines of every rank. But a new standard of worthiness began to be articulated as well: devotion to the liberty and justice of the commune. More and more people came to define their status in relation to the republic rather than by ties to a familial clan; many members of magnate families petitioned the Signory to become commoners, even though this meant the petitioner had to divorce himself from his *consorteria* (family group), relinquish his title and coat of arms, and sometimes assume a new family name. Political allegiances became more important than kith and kin in the forming of business partnerships.[52] Even spiritual renovation began to take civic forms: the model of charity Sacchetti urged his lay brethren to follow was that of the man who lends money to Florence without interest.

The way Boccaccio configures justice in the *Trattatello* recuperates these changes and the factionalism that divided his city and his poetics. Boccaccio expected some of his readers to recognize that his remarks about Solon presupposed scholastic distinctions between particular justice, which regulates relations between persons, and general justice, which unites all the virtues and becomes the cement of human society.[53] In Florence, however, two interlocking structures, kinship and the body politic, determined the shape these forms of justice would take. To an extent, these structures function, in Anthony Giddens's words, as "interpretive schemes," commonly held ideas or "standard-

---

51. The statements in this paragraph follow Becker's discussion of the advent of civic humanism in Florence and the political fortunes of the *novi cives* (*Florence in Transition*, 2:25–149).

52. Brucker, *Florentine Politics and Society*, 126–27.

53. For a full discussion of these definitions of particular and general justice in conjunction with the transformation of the thieves in Dante's *Inferno*, see *Dante's Aesthetics of Being*, 115–59.

ised elements of stocks of knowledge" that enable an event to be understandable to those who enact it.[54] As Boccaccio's audience listened to the opening of the *Trattatello*, they would not have forgotten the debates about the Ordinamenti di giustizia and their emphasis on degree of association determined by blood. For them his words would evoke a whole system of social alliance that had dominated Florentine life since the twelfth century: they would remember the *consorterie*, the tower societies of aristocratic clans, the vendettas and the violence that had precipitated the adoption of the Ordinances in the first place. But when Boccaccio related the operation of justice to the well-being of an organic body politic, his audience might begin to discern the shape of a newer, alternative form of organization: the commune itself has become a sodality capable of binding its citizens by means of the laws their representatives have ratified.[55]

Boccaccio feels the pull of both kinds of association. He presents the unjust Florence as lame and halt, since it has failed to administer the statutes that, by punishing wrongdoing and rewarding good deeds, would preserve general justice. Instead, ambition has gained the honors that integrity and probity should have: Boccaccio therefore bids those who "tend the rudder of the ship [of state]" [che il timone governano di questa nave] to bear God's judgment in mind, because men of humbler standing, among whom he includes himself ("noi, più bassa turba"), are borne by the same flood of Fortune even though they do not share the guilt of those who govern badly (3). Such misdeeds clearly unmake Florence from the communality Boccaccio thinks it should be, a city in which citizens promote the general welfare by discharging the duties appropriate to their station. Instead Florence dis-

---

54. Anthony Giddens, *Central Problems in Social Theory* (Berkeley and Los Angeles: University of California Press, 1979).

55. It is significant that, as Brucker notes, in the records that preserve the discussions of the advisory councils to the Signory, the theme of *unitas civium* first appears in July 1351, "and with monotonous regularity in later protocols" (Brucker, *Florentine Politics and Society*, 129).

As we have seen, Boccaccio had little regard for oral custom, since it allowed more powerful men to impose their wills on others ("non secondo scritta legge, che non l'avevano ancora," *Tratt.* 133). Boccaccio's esteem for written law seems more than a reflex of his humanism; it reflects an interesting cultural co-option on the part of what Franco Cardini calls the new "intellectual" class of the commune, the professional notaries, legalists, merchants, and others, who saw in writing, not only of laws but chronicles and personal diaries, a way to preserve their place in Florentine government. See Cardini, "Intellectuals and Culture," 13–30.

members itself; by exiling Dante, it cut from itself one of its worthiest citizens. Boccaccio represents this crippling of the polity, however, as the unnatural breaking of family ties, even though he knows that it was affinity of blood that gave birth to the confederation of magnates that has so threatened the republic.[56] Florence is thus the mother ("la madre") who envies the virtue of her child (101), the fatherland ("patria") that exiles its own son (92). Indeed, Boccaccio finally bases his right to condemn his city's malfeasance in the fact that he is its son:

> Deh! non ti rincresca lo stare con meco, che tuo figliuol sono, alquanto a ragione, e quello che giusta indegnazione mi fa dire, come da uomo che ti rammendi disidera e non che tu sii punita, piglierai. (92)
>
> [Ah! Do not take exception to standing before my judgment for a while, I who am your son, and you will hear what righteous indignation makes me say, not as a man who desires that you be punished but that you make amends.]

Clearly, familial and civic allegiances competed to determine where one stood in Florence at this moment. To fabricate the latter out of the former, however, as Boccaccio's imagery suggests, to join Florence's families to make Florence, as it were, a family, was to generate the body politic from tissue incompatible with its well-being. Boccaccio's language is pointedly juridical: "stare a ragione," as Ricci notes, is a legal expression that means "to allow oneself to render judgment."[57] The idea behind Boccaccio's use of the phrase is evident: when justice is administered impartially, and laws executed without regard to special interests, the people in Florence become the polity of Florence. The very impersonality that enables civic institutions to function as a source of identity thus is at odds with Boccaccio's appealing to them as a son. The one thing the courthouse could not be was a home; the bonds of birth

---

56. By the time of the *Corbaccio*, Boccaccio was referring to the magnates as "rapacious wolves of noble lineage." See Giorgio Padoan's article and rejoinder in *Lettere Italiane* 15 (1963): "Sulla datazione del 'Corbaccio'" (1–27), and "Ancora sulla datazione e sul titolo del 'Corbaccio'" (199–201). Yet the "Epistolaria consolatoria" (1361–62), which I discuss below, was written for Pino de' Rossi, a magnate exiled from Florence for plotting to overthrow the government. In the *Trattatello*, Boccaccio still tries to accommodate his respect for the aristocracy and its values with his championing of democracy.

57. *Trattatello*, 877.

and hearth had no more than a minor role to play in producing the public self. The fact that the officers chiefly responsible for maintaining justice, the *podestà*, the captain of the *popolo*, and the executor of the Ordinances of Justice, were never citizens of Florence, but noblemen summoned from other Italian cities with Guelf traditions, is a telling admission: though a practice other communes followed, Florentines would hardly have called on *stranieri* to adjudicate their disputes if they had not felt blood connections made it impossible for them to do so themselves. Even so, city records are full of charges of subornation and improper influencing of judges by powerful clans; blatantly biased verdicts sometimes provoked violent responses not only from the disenfranchised *ciompi* but from members of the greater and lesser guilds as well.[58]

For the commune to establish itself as an effective agency of civic identity, it had to develop an ideology of virtue that, in addition to superseding the ties of kinship, would also overcome the divisions of class. Boccaccio is able to articulate such an ideology only negatively, by condemning with equal vigor each of the estates in Florence:

> Deh! dimmi: di qua' vittorie, di qua' triunfi, di quali eccellenzie, di quali valorosi cittadini se' tu splendente? Le tue ricchezze, cosa mobile e incerta; ... le tue dilicatezze, cosa vituperevole e feminile, ti fanno nota nel falso giudicio de' popoli, il quale più ad apparenza che ad esistenza sempre riguarda. Deh! gloriera'ti tu de' tuoi mercatanti e de' molti artisti, donde tu se' piena? Sciocamente farai: l'uno fu, continuamente l'avarizia operandolo, mestiere servile; l'arte, la qual un tempo nobilitata fu dagl'ingegni, intanto che una seconda natura la fecero, dall'avarizia medesima è oggi corrotta e niente vale. Gloriera'ti tu della viltà e ignavia di coloro li quali, perciò che di molti loro avoli si ricordano, vogliono dentro da te della nobiltà ottenere il principato, sempre con ruberie e con tradimenti e con falsità contra quella operanti? (93–94)

[Ah, tell me: what are the victories, the triumphs, the virtues, the worthy citizens that make you illustrious? Your wealth is a fleeting

---

58. For a description of how judicial posts were filled, and how justice was often subverted in Florence, see Brucker, *Florentine Politics and Society*, 61–64. The disenfranchised laboring workers in Florence rose in revolt in the *Ciompi* rebellion in 1378, which should be compared to the English Uprising of 1381.

and unstable thing . . . your embellishments, blameworthy and effeminate in themselves, make you renowned in the mistaken judgment of the people, who always look more at how things seem than at how they actually are. Ah, will you glory in your merchants and in the many artisans who fill your city? You will do so foolishly. The former, always driven by avarice, once practiced a servile trade; the same avarice has corrupted each craft and made it worthless, which once was ennobled by men whose genius made their production a facsimile of nature's. Will you glory in the cowardice and indolence of those who, because they can recall their many ancestors, want to hold the highest offices in the city by virtue of their nobility, yet always besmirch it by robbery, sedition, and deceit?]

The "vittorie, triunfi, eccellenzie" and worthiness of the citizenry are the collective attainments that Florence should gather from its *mutatione officiorum*, the circulation of public office that Cicero had said unites various men in securing the general good of the republic. Instead, the classes are joined solely in the scorn Boccaccio heaps on their perverse addiction to greed. Yet even as he chastises them, Boccaccio reinscribes the social distinction between the *popolani grassi*, the merchants and members of the greater guilds, and the humbler artisans of the lesser guilds. He reinstates the right of the nobility to hold the highest offices, so long as they exhibit the integrity proper to their rank and are not the criminal poltroons he savages here. The other groups of people in Florence fare worse. Women, in keeping with the misogyny of the *Trattatello*, are turned into objects, "dilicatezze" fit only for the vulgar. The *sottoposti*, or poor, disenfranchised laborers who were not guild members, and Florence's many slaves, are not even acknowledged in the survey, unless they peep from the "mestiere servile" merchants once followed. The ideals of general justice allow Boccaccio to diagnose some of the ills that class factionalism has produced in his society, but his cure, which one might call the homeopathy of moral indignation, will do little to restore the patient's health.

One doubts, however, whether anything could have made the body politic whole in *trecento* Florence. Perhaps only a decade after Boccaccio composed the first version of the *Trattatello*, attempts to manipulate class divisions began to appear in council debates. During the 1360s, no domestic issue embroiled the commune more than the Parte Guelfa's proscription of men from holding office by declaring they were Ghibelline. The Parte, which was dominated by noble patricians, blatantly politicized their disbarments; the people they indicted often were "new men" who opposed them. Eventually the Parte challenged the right of the Signory to have jurisdiction over its affairs; the captains backed down only when it was clear that if they did not, armed conflict would break out, in which case they would have the most to lose. In 1368, the crisis was about to reach its climax: the city records show that patrician leaders of the Ricci bloc, who opposed the Parte, represented themselves in debates as spokesmen for those businessmen who desired peace so that they could attend to their cloth factories, their druggist shops, and their moneychanging. They said they stood as well for "the middle and lower classes" [mediocrum et minorum concivium] against the "grandi e possenti," whom they painted as wealthy and indolent aristocrats intent on oppressing all those who, though perhaps recently come to Florence, were willing to work with industry for its good. *Justice, unity, ordo, gens, pax civium*, all the terms that Florentines repeatedly invoked as part of their lexicon of *civilitas*, were brought forth by class interests and spoke the language of political partisanship from the start.[59]

In these ways, the *Trattatello* both shapes and was produced by the social and literary ambivalences of the decade in which Boccaccio wrote it. Familial bonds still exerted a preponderant hold over every aspect of life in Florence, but capitalistic enterprise fostered new forms of economic and political confederation and a new ideology of republican virtue to promote them. In the *Trattatello* this ideology is still inchoate and labile, not firmly enough grounded in the actual civic experience of the commune to prevent its subordination to Boccaccio's literary intentions. We have seen that when Boccaccio presents Dante's

---

59. For the material in this paragraph, and an account of the crises that lead to the reform of the Parte Guelfa, see Brucker, *Florentine Politics and Society*, 202–21. It is interesting to note that when tension was highest, those who sought to reconcile the commune and the Parte would adopt a rhetoric similar to Boccaccio's: a spokesman for the merchants' court urged the priors to treat the Guelf captains "as a patient and loving father would deal with his erring sons" (quoted in Brucker, *Florentine Politics and Society*, 219). Almost immediately after the crisis was resolved, the same divisions, greatly intensified by family allegiances, reappeared.

By contrast, the politics of "The Parliament of Fowls" are less political. Each estate is determined by species, not by familial allegiance or by reference to the Parliament itself. Each speaks for itself or criticizes the other; none speaks for itself by pretending to speak for another.

first sighting of Beatrice, he alters the *Vita nuova* by making Folco's festival part of the cultural life in Florence: "era usanza della nostra città, e degli uomini e delle donne, nelle loro contrade ciascuno in distinte compagnie festeggiare" (30). This sort of gathering of the neighborhood at the house of a major noble family in it was one of the ways in which magnate clans consolidated their power and became dangerous to their enemies. But besides providing an identifiable locale for the celebration, Boccaccio gives it a specific date: "il primo dì di maggio." It is hard to believe Boccaccio would speak of a May Day in the *sesto* of Porte San Piero and not recall the fatal consequences of the most famous *calendimaggio* in Florence's history. In 1300, a street fight broke out between members of the Cerchi and Donati families, both of whom lived in Dante's ward. This was the brawl that, for Villani at least, had made the Neri and Bianchi as implacable enemies as Buondelmonte's murder in 1215 made the Guelfs and Ghibellines; from it came Matteo d'Acquasparta's failed mission of reconciliation, the decision during Dante's priorate to banish leaders from both factions, including Guido Cavalcanti,[60] Charles of Valois's nefarious conniving with Corso Donati, the routing of the Bianchi, and Dante's exile.[61] By inventing a date for the first signal event in Dante's life, Boccaccio associates it with the calamities of the second. In all this, however, there is no note of ominous disapproval; in fact Boccaccio elaborates the scene with obvious enthusiasm. The social and political implications are completely muted, in part because Boccaccio probably still felt the association of honorable families is an honorable association, but mostly, I

---

60. From the moment Petrarch decided to live in Milan, Boccaccio may have thought that the Treaty of Sarzana, which ended hostilities between the Viscontis and Florence in 1353, had suddenly become peculiarly ironic. Sarzana was the city Guido Cavalcanti went to after he was exiled on June 24, 1300, by order of the priorate of which Dante was almost certainly a member. While there Cavalcanti, who had been allowed to return to Florence ten days before, contracted the disease he would die from on August 29. Sarzana could serve as self-standing proof for Boccaccio's later rejection of all political contentiousness; at this point in the *Trattatello*, however, Boccaccio has other aims in mind.

61. *Cronica*, 8:39–49. Earlier chronicles, such as Dino Compagni's and the anonymous *Cronica fiorentina*, also see the murder of Buondelmonte and the division between the Cerchi and Donati as comparable events. The May Day festival, of course, was closely allied to religious and civic festivals throughout Italy. For descriptions of the feast of St. John the Baptist, see Cesare Guasti, *Le feste di San Giovanni Battista in Firenze* (Florence: Cirri, 1908); and, more generally, Richard Trexler, *Public Life in Renaissance Florence* (New York: Academic Press, 1980).

think, because he was more concerned to establish the thread that tied Dante's poetry to his own.

By the early 1360s, however, when Boccaccio probably composed the *Compendio*, his far more compact redactions of the *Trattatello*, both the poetic and the civic ideals Dante stood for had undergone severe contraction. In place of the passionate chastening of Florence ("Oh ingrata patria"), which originally stretched across seventeen paragraphs (92–119), Boccaccio substituted a passage remarkable for its curtness:

> Sogliono gli odii nella morte degli odiati finirsi; il che nel trapassamento di Dante non si trovò avvenire. L'ostinata malivolenza de' suoi cittadini nella sua rigidezza stette ferma; niuna compassione ne mostrò alcuno, niuna publica lagrima gli fu conceduta, né alcuno uficio funebre fatto. Nella qual pertinacia assai manifestamente si dimostrò i Fiorentini tanto essere dal cognoscimento della scienza rimoti, che fra loro niuna distinzion fosse da un vilissimo calzolaio ad un solenne poeta. Ma essi con la lor superbia rimangansi; e noi, avendo gli affanni dimostrati di Dante e il suo fine, a l'altre cose che di lui, oltre alle dette, dir si possono ci vogliamo. (66–67)

> [Hatreds usually die with the death of the one who was hated; this did not happen when Dante died. His fellow citizens stood firm and rigid in their obstinate malevolence; no one evinced the slightest compassion for his death, no public tears were shed on his account, nor was any funeral rite performed. By such pertinacity, the people of Florence showed very clearly how far removed they were from recognizing the value of knowledge, since they would not make the least distinction between the basest shoemaker and an august poet. But let them continue to keep company with their pride, and I, having described Dante's travails and his end, wish to turn to other things that can be said of him, beyond what already has been recounted.]

Compared to the molten rhetoric in the *Trattatello*, the temperature of these two paragraphs is gelid; Boccaccio speaks less as a man who has been disillusioned than as one who seeks to be resigned to the loss of his convictions. Once he believed only justice would enable the republic to stand upright; now he has discovered that the ill will of hardened hearts is perfectly able to keep Florence's knees locked in place. No longer does Boccaccio address the city as its son; his voice now comes from someplace beyond it, as distant from it as the exiled Dante, dead in Ravenna, was from the compassion of "suoi cittadini." The time for exhortations has passed; Boccaccio knows his townsmen will not mend their ways—"Ma essi con la lor superbia rimangansi." Even his contempt seems more that of a person who has removed himself from the social fray than one who is still intent on reforming it. No longer does he despise the greed of the several classes because it prevents them from contributing to the common good; instead he vilifies the pertinacity of their pride because it blinded them to the benefits of knowledge and permitted them to treat the worthiest poet as if he were the lowliest cobbler.

These changes, which bespeak a far fuller acceptance of Petrarchan principles, almost certainly proceeded from events that led to Boccaccio's political disgrace.[62] In 1360, a number of leading Florentines plotted to overthrow the government on the last day of the year, the date when the priors were to be renewed. Among the conspirators were friends of Boccaccio: after their "coup" was discovered, one of them, Niccolò di Bartolo di Buono, to whom Boccaccio had dedicated the *Ameto*, was hanged; Luca Ugolino, Andrea dell'Ischia, and Pino de' Rossi all fled Florence to avoid the same fate. Boccaccio too, though driven it seems more by prudence than by necessity, left the city and returned to his ancestral town of Certaldo. Soon after arriving there, he wrote the "Epistolaria consolatoria" to Pino (1361–62).

In many respects, this text, which Boccaccio calls more a book than a letter, glosses the revisions of the *Compendio*.[63] It is an extraordinary palinode to the social and political commitments of the *Trattatello*. Whereas Dante's exile had incited Boccaccio to call for Florence's moral reformation, Pino's banishment becomes the occasion for Boccaccio to urge his friend to endure private and public misfortunes with Senecan disinterestedness. Being removed from the support and consolation of "i cari amici, i parenti, i vicini" [dear friends, relatives, neighbors] is no real loss, Boccaccio says. The letters they can exchange will allow Pino to be one in spirit with those who have proved themselves his true

---

62. I agree entirely with Ricci that Boccaccio probably made the revisions of the *Compendio* after he had left Florence for Certaldo. See "Introduzione," 430.

63. My text of the "Epistolatia consolatoria a Pino de' Rossi" is from Boccaccio, *Opere in versi*, ed. Ricci, 1112–41. Quotations are given their page number within the text.

friends. To take the place of the lands and possessions the Rossi have held for generations, which now have been confiscated, Pino and his family will discover that nature provides true riches and that simple virtues are their own reward. Regarding Pino's concerns for his wife, Boccaccio will venture to say, even though he has never married, that a bad spouse is a heavier burden in prosperous than in lean years; he will grant, however, that a man in adversity can have no greater consolation than a good helpmate.

Public humiliations are similarly of little account. The citizens of Florence brought disgrace on themselves, not on Pino, when they rushed to brand him a traitor and ignored "the blood and life [he had devoted] to the common good and to the exalting of his city" [il sangue e la vita per lo comune bene, per la esaltazione della sua città] (1131). Even had Pino been guilty, justice demanded that a lifetime's good works leaven his sentence. Instead, the envy and ingratitude of Pino's judges have enabled him to share the honorable fate of Solon himself, who had given Athenians their precious constitution yet was forced at the end of his life to flee, an exile, to Cyprus (1132). Nor will the accusation of sedition be able to taint Pino's fame, since he knows he is innocent and has answered every charge against him fully and sufficiently. Even if people of other cities believe he has committed the crimes Florence accuses him of, Pino's good name will remain unsullied. The mistaken opinion of the ignorant is of no concern to the man who is wise.

With the "Epistolaria consolatoria" Boccaccio thus renounces the familial and communal allegiances that just a few years before had given the *Trattatello* its structure and tenor. Public life has been left entirely behind. Both at the start (1114) and at the end of his letter, Boccaccio says the world is a "universal city" for all who dwell in it [universale città] (1136); since in Florence shame redounds to those who honor its customs and honor to those it chases into exile, the city's institutions no longer can offer a man the means to define himself by his relation to them. Solon therefore stands not as the archetype of civic justice, as he had in the *Trattatello*, but as an example of the just man unjustly driven from his homeland. Dante, the most famous of all Florence's exiles, is never invoked as a model; the city simply is not worth hoping to return to.[64] Instead, the whole world finds itself shrunk to fit within the walls of the wise man's house. Here the humbler economics

---

64. Soon after he was exiled, Dante joined a confederation of proscribed "Bianchi" magnates and Ghibellines who plotted to overthrow Florence by force. In light of this collusion, it would, of course, be something of a gaffe for Boccaccio to cite him directly as an

of the hearth can put to scorn the commune's perverse traffic in greed and pride. If Pino learns to be content with what nature provides, he will be rich in poverty, his children a staff unto his old age, and his wife a companion in his labors. Then he shall be able truly to fortify himself with "buona speranza," which is not the farmer's hope for an abundant harvest, or the merchant's for large profits, or the king's for a glorious victory in the field, but the patient man's faith in God's mercy and grace (1136–37). Boccaccio has not quite adopted Petrarch's need to make the unquiet mind the site where every conviction is sifted for its existential virtue. But in moving from Florence to the *contado*, Boccaccio does follow his master by turning his back on the social world and entering the moral universe of the philosopher's study. When he took up the *Trattatello* again, he revised it according to the perspectives of the *vita solitaria*.[65]

Petrarch's influence also likely accounts for Boccaccio's erasure of his own vernacular literary history in the *Compendio*. The description of Dante's falling in love with Beatrice is much abbreviated; nearly all echoes of the *Filostrato*, or of Boccaccio's other Italian works, have disappeared. The abridgment severely diminishes the importance of the *Vita nuova* as well; not only does it no longer serve as a structural model for the *Vita di Dante*,[66] it has lost its function as a calque by which Boccaccio could coordinate his popular writings with his more learned Latin texts. The misstatement that the older Dante was greatly ashamed of the *Vita nuova* has been excised. Boccaccio apparently now feels the less said about Dante's book, and its relation to his own erotic works, the better.[67]

---

example to Pino. But at the end of the letter, Boccaccio does quote the famous verses with which "nostro poeta," as he calls Dante, rebuked Florentines, who are so changeable "che a mezzo novembre / non giugne quel che tu d'ottobre fili" [that what you spin in October doesn't last until mid-November] (*Purg.* 6.143–44).

65. No fact more completely reveals how far Boccaccio had traveled from the values he espoused in the *Trattatello* than this: despite his outspoken hatred of tyranny, he moved quickly to console Pino, a magnate who harbored tyrannical intentions, at least in the minds of the people whose legitimately elected officials Rossi plotted to overthrow.

66. For instance, in the *Compendio*, Boccaccio defers the account of Dante's mother's dream until he explains it at the end of the book; by contrast, in the *Trattatello* the dream is recounted at the beginning and explained at the end.

67. The last time Boccaccio refers to Petrarch's discussion of the origin of poets is in the *Esposizioni* (1.73ff.). Boccaccio explicitly cites the letter that "il mio padre e maestro messer Francesca Petrarca" wrote to Gherardo and summarizes its contents. There is not a hint of reproach in either; the rapprochement between the poets is complete. If Chaucer heard anything about Boccaccio's view of Petrarch's politics, these lines express it.

Conditions change over time, and with them trust in the cogency of political and aesthetic systems. Boccaccio's reading of Dante spans a quarter century of adjustments and realignments; it is a chronicle of conflicting impulses, of backtrackings and revisions, of disillusionments and altered loyalties. The things Boccaccio makes Dante stand for at one moment are at odds with the things he stands for at another. There is the Dante who was the "prima fax," the poet whose light inspired Boccaccio's early writings, his belief in the nobility of the vulgar tongue, his support of communal democracy against the authoritarianism of the tyrant.[68] But there is also the Dante who stands for Boccaccio's contempt for the "mechanical" classes, his abhorrence of money-hungry merchants and ignoble aristocrats, his rejection of the political intrigues of Florence altogether. And there is the Dante who by his failures becomes the vehicle through which Boccaccio expresses his increasingly ascetic devotion to the discipline of private study, his misogyny,[69] and his ultimate allegiance to Petrarch and to Latin humanism. All three Dantes are present in the *Trattatello;* in different proportions they are present in the *Compendio* as well.

Let us return to Florence in 1373 and suppose Chaucer did hear that Boccaccio might soon deliver public readings of the *Comedy.* Let us suppose further that Chaucer heard admirers speak of Boccaccio himself, how in his mature years classical rigor and moral probity had caused Italy's greatest *prosatore* to renounce the very works the English poet would translate a decade or so later. The same year Boccaccio began his lectures, he chided Mainardo Cavalcanti for permitting the

---

68. It is significant that even while Boccaccio tempers his criticism of the commune's subversions of justice in the *Compendio,* he retains the remarks he had made in the *Trattatello* about poets' complicity with kings. Indeed, Boccaccio continued to associate Dante with civic liberty throughout his life. Even after he had reconciled himself to Petrarch's residence in Milan, Boccaccio introduces his biography of Walter of Brienne in the *De casibus virorum illustrium* (book 9) by imagining that Dante himself appeared to Boccaccio, who wanted to write about the poet's exile. As we shall see in chapter 6, Dante excuses himself from inclusion in Boccaccio's book; while certainly a victim of Fortune, he wants Boccaccio rather to write about the duke of Athens, who brought perpetual shame to the people of Florence when they chose him to be their tyrant. That way, posterity will know the kind of man Florence exiles and the kind she welcomes. Though Boccaccio wrote the *De casibus* in the late 1350s, he revised it later, dedicating the final draft to Mainardo Cavalcanti perhaps in 1373. See Carlo Muscetta, *Giovanni Boccaccio,* 2d ed. (Bari: Laterza, 1974), 317.

69. Boccaccio includes his misogynistic digression about marriage in the *Compendio* as well.

women in his house to read his trifling vernacular works ("nugas meas"). Boccaccio urged Mainardo to put a stop to it:

> You know how much in them is less than decent and is opposed to honorable conduct, how many are the spurs to unfortunate love, how many things there are that impel to dissoluteness even hearts steeled against it. Although they do not drive illustrious women to commit lewd acts, and a chaste modesty adheres to most of them, nevertheless an enticing heat goes forth with silent step, and sometimes excites and corrupts immodest souls with the loosening lasciviousness of lust.[70]

Boccaccio adds that the women who read him will think he is a "filthy pimp, an incestuous old man, shameless, foul-mouthed and slanderous, eager to relate the depravity of others."[71]

Had Chaucer heard these attitudes spoken of, he might have understood, even after he read the *Filostrato*, why the commune would commission Boccaccio to lecture on Dante. At the same time, however, Chaucer's surprise probably would not have lessened his sympathy had he also learned that, despite the epistle to Mainardo, Boccaccio continued to polish the *Decameron*. In fact, throughout the 1360s he had maintained the dignity of the "vulgar tongue" in a series of letters to Petrarch, who, given the great care he devoted to shaping the final form of the *Canzoniere*, also seems to have thought his Italian poetry, however nugatory, worth burnishing for posterity.[72] Even more telling than the exchanges with Petrarch, however, is Boccaccio's final poem, which he wrote after his "caro signor" had died. In it Boccaccio envisions his dear master rejoicing in heaven with Lauretta, who sits beside his own

---

70. [Nosti quot ibi sint minus decentia et adversantia honestati, quot veneris infauste aculei, quot in scelus impellentia etiam si sint ferrea pectora, a quibus etsi non ad incestuosum actum illustres impellantur femine, et potissime quibus sacer pudor frontibus insidet, subeunt tamen passu tacito estus illecebres et impudicas animas obscena concupiscentie tabe nonnumquam inficiunt irritantque, quod omnino ne contingat agendum est.] The text of the letter is in *Opere latine minori*, ed. Massèra, letter XXI, p. 211.

71. [Existimabunt enim legentes me spurcidum lenonem, incestuosum senem, impurum hominem, turpiloquum maledicum et alienorum scelerum avidum relatorem.] Most commentators think Boccaccio has the *Decameron* chiefly in mind; I agree, but his attitude extends to all his vernacular works ("nugas meas"). In this passage, and in the passage quoted in the previous note, Boccaccio uses the word "incestuosum" in conjunction with his works. I will discuss the significance of this association in the next chapter.

72. See Branca, *Boccaccio*, 140–42.

beautiful Fiammetta; Petrarch will reside there forever with Sennuccio del Bene, Cino da Pistoia, and Dante. The poem ends with a prayer addressed to Petrarch: "If you held me dear in this wayward world, draw me after you to where I may joyfully see her who first kindled love in me":

Deh, s'a grado ti fui nel mondo errante,
tirami drieto a te, dove gioioso
veggia colei che pria d'amor m'accese.

The Petrarch whom Boccaccio beatifies in paradise is the poet of the *Canzoniere*, not the *Africa*;[73] the boon he asks of him is that he perform the same service, admittedly for a more earthly love, that Pandaro performed for Troiolo in the *Filostrato*. In the same moment that Boccaccio bids his vernacular career a firm but poignant farewell, he reaffirms it as well.

If, as I say, Chaucer heard of Boccaccio's views about his fiction, he likely could have seen his way past their contradictions, which are quite similar to the tergiversations of his own retractions. But Chaucer's introduction to Boccaccio may have been yet more complicated, for it is possible that he heard misgivings about the proposed lectures on Dante as well. Some of these grumblings would have been easy to discount: descendants who thought Dante had defamed their families, clerics who were upset by his heterodoxies, had for many years been vocal in their disparagement of the *Comedy*. Other objections, however, would come from people who shared Boccaccio's humanist assumptions, and these might have puzzled Chaucer less than the fact that Boccaccio agreed with them, as we saw in the *tenzone* with the unknown critic of his *letture*, which I discussed in the first chapter of this book.

Amid such conflicting attitudes, Dante always remained a mode of vision for Boccaccio, a way for him to view his own literary and historical *vita* both from within and from outside the texts and events that comprised it. As poet, he was Boccaccio's "principe Galeotto," a means

---

73. In picturing Petrarch amid a heavenly congregation of vernacular poets, Boccaccio seems to reimagine Dante's welcome among the major poets of classical antiquity in Limbo. Of the many reversals Boccaccio's scene enacts, the most ironic and recuperative is this: even though he can only pray to join "tra cotanto senno," Boccaccio nevertheless corrects Dante and Petrarch both. In paradise, Latin and the vernacular are the same language.

by which he could constitute himself at various moments and in diverse ways as an acolyte of Petrarch who nevertheless valued the vulgar tongue. As citizen, Dante was a medium of social transformation, through whom Boccaccio learned how he could be Florentine by birth but not by custom, a commoner by rank and republican by temperament, but an aristocrat by culture and intellect.

By himself, Dante could never mean these things to Chaucer. Yet, in a sense, Dante *and* Boccaccio could. By reading them each as the other's gloss, he could discern a manner of meaning, both civic and aesthetic, that he would subsequently be able to translate into English. While Chaucer was conducting the king's business in Florence, he may well have dealt with people who expressed their displeasure with the *novi cives* and their confederates, with the laws that allowed them to have any of the *popolani* declared a magnate at the slightest provocation, with their sacrilegious support of the Ghibelline Bernabò Visconti against the pope. Nor is it entirely implausible that Chaucer met others who spoke about the violence and arrogance of the Albizzi, the Ricci, and the oligarchic leaders of the Parte Guelfa, the injustice of their accusations of Ghibellinism, and the danger of their suspected alliances with Gregory XI. These were all issues that greatly concerned the Florentine populace during the first months of 1373. But as he listened, Chaucer would necessarily feel he had missed the beginning of the conversation. These controversies had been given their shape by economic and political pressures and practices even longtime residents may have found difficult to explain; we assume too much, I feel, to think that Chaucer, after a month or so in the commune, had learned enough to understand them in depth. Nor is it likely that he had enough time to assimilate the social hierarchies and class distinctions that, assumed or challenged, propelled his interlocutors' remarks. We can call such dark corners and blind spots the difference of Florence; Chaucer's experience of the city, the experience in any case that we have access to, is his attempt to read that difference. My argument, as I have said throughout, is that he read it as a translation. He may not have had the opportunity to register the pulse and rhythm of Florence's neighborhoods, marketplaces, guildhalls, and palaces, to say nothing of their history, but Chaucer's works show that he did sense something more general, an intentionality, a mode of conduct that referred actions to the city for their value and meaning. To naturalize those formations that were foreign to him, I imagine he would, like any one-time visitor, turn to what did know: his perceptions of life in London-Westminster and in the courts of aristocratic England. Once he moved to Aldgate in 1374 and began to ponder what was comparable and what was dissimilar to Florence, Chaucer would unavoidably look at his own civic institutions from a different perspective, a perspective in which London's presence is increasingly felt but, significantly, rarely seen. Because the *Comedy* encompassed the cities of God and man, it would remain Chaucer's model of a poetry fully able to elucidate how spiritual verities round the diurnal transactions of municipal life. But Dante's Florence, which becomes the domain for all earthly politics, exists only in his poem; it was not the place Chaucer visited. Boccaccio's Florence was. It is no accident, then, that Chaucer first became a recognizably "urban" poet in the *Troilus*. Nor is it oversubtle to think the pains Chaucer took to underscore the alterity of Troy, despite the resemblance between the comings and goings of its knights and ladies and courtly conduct in England, were in part a response to his experience in Italy. In this way, Dante and Boccaccio together spurred Chaucer's development as a reader of cultural traditions. One facet of his Italian Tradition appears in the translated city-space of his poems that is not Florence, nor London, and is both.

In like manner, Chaucer brought the sophistications of French literature to his initial encounter with the distinct world of the *Comedy*. But these could carry him only so far; eventually, he would learn more by reading one Italian writer in the light of the others. Just as in the *Trattatello* Boccaccio read his own early poetry in tandem with the *Vita nuova*, so Chaucer would discover in the *Filostrato* (and, even more, if he knew it, in the cognate *quistione* of the *Filocolo*) another way to read Dante. It was, in short, through Boccaccio that Chaucer's Italian texts entered into conversation with one another. Though the texture of this conversation obviously differed from that of Boccaccio's with Dante, which was, after all, a colloquy of the social, aesthetic, and cultural discourses that formed and reformed Florentine life during the middle decades of the fourteenth century, it would nonetheless demystify texts like the *Comedy*, make them available for appropriation into his own culture, and enable Chaucer to see more clearly the achievements and limitations of the French and English poets he continued to read and reread. It is, then, with Boccaccio reading Dante that we can rightly speak of the making of Chaucer's Italian Tradition.

5

"Medium autem, et extrema sunt eiusdem generis": Boccaccio's *Filostrato*, the Voice of Writing, and the Italian Tradition

"The mean is of the same genus as the extremes": this statement, although drawn from Aquinas's discussion of faith (*Summa Theologica*, 2.2.1.2: contra), characterizes the nature of all agencies that mediate between contraries. Since Thomas's mode of argument is dialectic, the ultimate context from which he takes his rule is logic. To show that faith is complex (that is, that it has the nature of a proposition), Thomas situates it as the mean between science and opinion. Because neither of these is simple, faith too must be complex. Thomas's proximate context, however, is ethics. His discussion of faith introduces his treatise on the theological and moral virtues; moreover, the principle that propels this particular argument has obvious connections with Aristotle's *Nicomachean Ethics*, from which the Middle Ages learned that the means to an end must be judged in relation to that end.[1] Since human beings are creatures of body and soul, they cannot know simple beings like God, who is the object of faith, without a certain amount of complexity; it is therefore proper, indeed necessary, that anyone's experience of faith be "propositional."

A number of linkages here are worth noting. The premises that drive Aquinas's argument are that faith is discursive and that it is rational. Thomas therefore engages the services of logic and dialectic, those arts that determine certainty in language. Yet faith is not solely a matter for the intellect; even if (or perhaps because) the nature of faith takes the form of a proposition, it still needs the commitment of will to become a

---

1. Aristotle, *Nicomachean Ethics*, 1–2 (1094a1–1095b1); see also 2.6 (1106a24ff.).

living act. Thus, if only by its Aristotelian recall, Thomas's discussion of the mean at the start of the disquisition on faith as a virtue extends to ethical means as well.

Ethics, however, is an approximate science, as Aristotle says;[2] the clarity of logic and dialectic would not seem as well matched to its ends as the more oblique hypotheses of rhetoric. Indeed, even as Thomas positions faith between doubtful opinion and unequivocal knowledge, he limits the confidence we can have in human reason. The generic continuity of means and extremes is an incontrovertible principle, part of what Aquinas means by *scientia*, yet its predicate in this article is the impossibility of anyone knowing God as he is. Faith, as a result, comes to "characterize" those who walk in it by calling attention to how it differs from the end that, at the same time, it seeks. This may seem a dangerous disjunction for Thomas to entertain: on the one hand, faith is a means to God; on the other, God is sui generis. We notice, though, that Thomas implicitly repairs on the level of the will the discontinuity he admits on the level of the intellect. For if he employs a law of logic to constitute faith as the mind's space between itself and the Truth that is its destination, God necessarily remains the uninterrupted object of desire for the faithful.

The general lesson one might draw from these operations of faith is that means can never become pure agency since their own qualities tend to obtrude on and affect the very process by which they would be subsumed in their ends. Certainly such a conclusion about mediation would have appealed to Boccaccio as he contemplated and wrote the chronicle of faith and faithlessness that became the *Filostrato*. Indeed, his tale of Troiolo and Criseida, and especially of Pandaro, who plays so central a part in it, seems to me a direct response to the idea of means in those late medieval philosophies of mind and action that formed the intellectual context of the *stil novo*. In particular the *Filostrato* is, I would argue, an incisive revision of Dante's meditation on the place of writing within the realms of psychology and ethics. In the *Comedy*, Dante had made the mediation of the word an act of faith; even though he knows that his poetry can never become so utterly transparent God may be seen through it, that is the goal it still must strive to reach. Boccaccio responded by radically translating Dante's critical imperative; he shows that language always takes on the rhetorical opaqueness of per-

---

2. Aristotle, *Nicomachean Ethics*, 1.2.

sonal motives.[3] It not only derives its value from the use it is put to but gives value to its end as well. For Boccaccio, writing's mediations especially will be felt not only, or even primarily, as disjunctions in the intellect but as persuasive strategies of the will. Not truth so much as truthfulness, not the rational content of a proposition so much as the faithfulness of the one who argues it: these are the issues Boccaccio wishes to debate with his predecessors.

The *Filostrato* is a remarkable poem not only in its revisions of literary history but for the place it occupies in the arc of Boccaccio's own career. The prologue to the poem, which purports to account for its genesis, establishes its textual and intertextual dynamics; besides locating the narrator's entire experience within the confines of a rhetorical love-debate, the particular question he ponders invites us to read the *Filostrato* in conjunction with the *Filocolo*, where it also appears.[4] In the latter work, a raging storm has caused Filocolo to delay his quest for Biancifiore in Naples. On the way to visit the tomb of Virgil, he meets a

---

3. See Mazzotta, *World at Play*, especially the chapter "Allegory and the Pornographic Imagination," 105–30. Although Mazzotta deals primarily with the *Decameron*, I would argue that Boccaccio's ideas about the rhetorical amorality of literature were already established by the time he wrote the *Filostrato*. Janet Smarr, *Boccaccio and Fiammetta* (Urbana: University of Illinois Press, 1986), also sees the *Filostrato* in terms of a revision of Dante, though her analysis and conclusions are quite different from mine. For an account of mediation in the *Filostrato* quite compatible with the one I offer here, see Robert Hanning, "Come In out of the Code: Interpreting the Discourse of Desire in Boccaccio's *Filostrato*," in *Chaucer's Troilus and Criseyde: "Subgit to alle poesie,"* ed. R. A. Shoaf (Binghamton: Medieval and Renaissance Texts and Studies, 1992), 120–37; see as well Hanning's "The Crisis of Mediation in Chaucer's *Troilus and Criseyde*," in *The Performance of Middle English Culture: Essays in Honor of Martin Stevens*, ed. James Paxson et al. (Cambridge: Brewer, 1998), 143–59.

4. The debate over whether the *Filocolo* or the *Filostrato* was written first is not relevant to my argument, even though I am presenting the *Filostrato* as if it were composed after the *Filocolo*. This was the assumption of older critics; Branca and others have shown that it was based on an untenable romantic reconstruction of Boccaccio's biography from his works. Branca, Ricci, Padoan, and others now hold that the poem predates the prose romance. There is, however, as Branca says, no evidence at all that can establish the date of the poem beyond argument (Boccaccio, *Tutte le opere*, vol. 2, *Il Filostrato*, introduction, 3). See also P. G. Ricci, "Per la dedica e la datazione del *Filostrato*," *Studi sul Boccaccio* 1 (1963): 333–47. For a review of the arguments about the date, see Thomas Bergin, *Boccaccio* (New York: Viking, 1981), 105–7. It seems to me that attempts to date the *Filostrato* before the *Filocolo* repeat the gesture they so forcefully discredit. My arguments in any case do not depend on the anteriority of one work to the other: indeed, the apparent development from the *Filocolo* to the *Filostrato* is, to me, just that, apparent.

group of courtly men and women; they all retire to a garden where they debate thirteen questions of love. Graziosa's is the eleventh; she asks whether seeing one's beloved or thinking amorously about her provides the greater delight (*Filoc.* 4:quest.11).[5] Fiammetta responds that thinking gives the greater joy; the terminology she couches her answer in reveals that the literary provenance of the ladies' exchange is the *stil novo*. Fiammetta says, for instance, that

> pensando alla cosa amata graziosamente, gli spiriti sensitivi tutti allora sentano mirabile festa, e quasi i loro accesi disii in quel pensiero con diletto contentano; ma, nel riguardare, ciò non avviene, però che solo il visuale spirito sente bene, e gli altri s'accendono di tanto disio che sostenere nol possono, e rimangono vinti.

> [when one thinks graciously about one's beloved, the sensitive spirits may all experience wondrous joy and seem to satisfy with delight their kindled desires in that thought. But that does not happen when one sees her, since only the visual spirit feels contentment, and the other (spirits) are kindled by such desire that they cannot sustain it and remain vanquished.]

Graziosa then puts forth the case for the superiority of sight in a similar manner, but Fiammetta refutes her arguments by insisting on the triumph of the mind over the eyes:

> Quelle cose, e dilettevoli e noiose, che più all' anima s'appressano, più noia e più gioia porgono che le lontane. E chi dubita che il pensiero non dimori nell' anima medesima e l'occhio a quella si trovi assai lontano, ben che elli per particolare virtù di lei abbia la vista, e convengagli per molti mezzi le sue percezioni all'intelletto animale rendere?

> [Those things, whether delightful or bothersome, that are closer to the soul give greater annoyance or delight than things that are more distant. And who doubts that thought dwells in the soul itself, while the eye is quite distant from it, even though the eye derives sight as

---

5. Giovanni Boccaccio, *Il Filocolo,* ed. Salvatore Battaglia (Bari: Laterza, 1938).

its particular power from the soul and must deliver its perceptions to the intellect by means of many mediations.]⁶

From this it follows, Fiammetta continues, that when one thinks sweetly of one's beloved, the thought and the beloved do not differ in the soul ("Dunque, avendo nell'anima un dolce pensiero della cosa amata, in quello atto che il pensiero gli porge, in quello con la cosa amata essere gli pare"). Thought sees with eyes from which distance cannot hide anything; a lover, therefore, can speak to his lady in his mind, and tell her of the pains love for her has caused, and rejoice with her according to his desire.

For Fiammetta, the experience of love should be even more an affect of the mind than it is an affair of the senses; as I have said, her arguments draw on the technical language of medieval psychology that became the foundational vocabulary of the "rime d'amor . . . dolci e leggiadre" (*Purg.* 26.99). Indeed, from the thirteenth century on, with the recovery of Aristotle through the intermediaries of Avicenna and Averroes, philosophers in the Latin West were preoccupied precisely by the question of the role that the senses and imagination played in understanding. Although the most contested issue concerned the nature and indeed the existence of an agent intellect, the whole debate really took its impetus from the prior question of how the material senses could be the ground of knowledge at all if intellection itself was immaterial and the concepts it had as its object were completely separated from all individualizing matter.⁷

For Boccaccio, the writings of Albertus Magnus and Thomas Aquinas, mediated perhaps by Cavalcanti and Dante, were most important. All agreed with Aristotle that material things act as objects of sensation and, ultimately, knowledge. When we know a thing via sensation, however, we do not know it as it actually exists, as a form united with its matter. Rather we know it by means of an "intention," which is an image of the material object that its form produces in the sense organ. The first level of sensation thus involves the generation of

---

6. The language of this passage, as we shall see, is technical: it seems to have caused scribes some difficulty. See Battaglia's note, *Filocolo*, 578.
7. For a discussion of the role the senses and spirits play in the production of knowledge in Dante, see *Dante's Aesthetics of Being*, 28–35; I repeat the material here because Boccaccio drew on these traditions as well, whereas Chaucer alludes to them, if at all, only in the most cursory manner.

the *intentio* through the abstraction of the sensible form from the matter of an existing thing. We do not sense the stone itself, but a *similitudo* or likeness of it that, in Aquinas's words, is not stony.[8]

The next stage of knowing occurs in the internal senses, which were thought to be four or five in number, depending on whether one followed Averroes, as Thomas did, or Avicenna, as did Albertus.[9] The common sense *(sensus communis)* enables us to be aware that we hear and see; it also allows us compare sounds to textures, scents to sights.[10] The imagination, also called the phantasy, formed and stored images called phantasms. Like the intentions of the outer senses, phantasms are the forms of sensible objects; unlike the outer senses, however, the imagination is able to retain its image of a sensible thing even when the object is no longer present. Phantasms therefore have undergone a second grade of abstraction; they are the forms that the intellective faculties of the soul use to arrive at rational knowledge. There are two other internal senses: the estimative or cogitative power, and memory. In animals the estimative sense perceives phantasms that are not directly known to the external senses and moves them to instinctive judgments: it causes the sheep to sense danger in the presence of the wolf and to flee from it. Aquinas calls this sense in humans the cogitative power

---

8. In this discussion, I am following chiefly the *Cambridge History of Later Medieval Philosophy: From the Rediscovery of Aristotle to the Disintegration of Scholasticism, 1100–1600*, ed. Norman Kretzmann, Anthony Kenny, and Jan Pinborg (Cambridge: Cambridge University Press, 1982), 602–22. See also Nicholas Steneck, "Albert on the Psychology of Sense Perception," in *Albertus Magnus and the Sciences: Commemorative Essays, 1980*, ed. James Weisheipl (Toronto: University of Toronto Press, 1980), 263–90. Aquinas, one should note, agrees with Albert in his account of this aspect of sensation. For sense knowledge in Dante, see Bruno Nardi, *Dante e la cultura medievale* (Bari: Laterza, 1983), 138–41. Nardi generally accepts Dante's own testimony that he undertook a serious study of philosophy only after Beatrice's death, that is, coincident with the writing of the *Convivio*. It would be hard to understand, however, how Dante could have read and admired Cavalcanti, especially "Donna me prega," without a thorough understanding of sensible knowledge. In this regard, see J. E. Shaw, *Guido Cavalcanti's Theory of Love* (Toronto: University of Toronto Press, 1949).

9. Albert followed Avicenna: because the imagination and the fantasy were separate, there were five internal senses. Aquinas followed Averroes; for him there was only the imagination. The difference carries no weight in my reading. On the internal senses, see Nicholas Steneck, "Albert the Great on the Internal Senses," *Isis* 65 (1974): 193–211. For their use in Chaucer, see Kolve, *Imagery of Narrative*, 9–58.

10. Steneck, "Albert on Internal Senses," 197. Aquinas differs from Albert in that he feels the common sense, like the other internal senses, abstracts its intention completely apart from a physical object; for Albert, the common sense made its abstraction as the external senses did, in the presence of the object.

since it makes some rational comparisons among intentions and acts. Finally, memory stores all this information for reference to past time.[11] Because all the internal senses make use of intentions abstracted from sensible things even when those things are no longer present, they all utilize some form of memory.

These operations of the sensitive soul share a structure that is continuous with and analogous to the operations of reason, which begins with the abstracting of a second phantasm from the one that the imagination had produced. These latter phantasms are still individualized by matter; one will be an image of Rover, another an image of Spot. The intellect, however, bears upon the universal; from the particulars produced in sensation it therefore abstracts the essential form, that which makes Rover and Spot both dogs, or dogs and foxes both canines.

The faculties that allow this activity to take place are the passive and the active intellects. The active intellect illuminates the particular thing that is represented in the phantasm and renders it intelligible by abstracting its essential form from the matter and the conditions that individuate it. The resulting universal likeness, called the "intelligible species," is then impressed on the passive intellect, which in response forms its own likeness of the abstracted nature. This is the *verbum mentis* (or, in the Augustinian tradition, *verbum cordis*), the universal concept in the full sense.[12] The abstract concept, expressed by a single word, determines how we know anything with respect to its nature.[13]

Because human beings, however, are a compound of body and soul, the universal concept is not, in and of itself, the object of cognition *(id quod intelligitur)*; rather it is the means by which *(id quo intelligitur)* we come to know the material object, which is the proper goal of human

---

11. For Albert, the imagination stores intentions without reference to past time. See Steneck, "Albert on Internal Senses," 197.

12. The quotation is from Frederick Copleston, *A History of Philosophy*, vol. 2, *Medieval Philosophy*, part 2 (Garden City: Doubleday, 1962), 110. See *Summa Theologica*, 1a.79; see also appendix 7 of vol. 11 of the Blackfriars' edition. On Aquinas's theory of knowledge, see Copleston, *History*, 108–17. In Dante, as Nardi notes, the agent intellect seems affiliated more closely with the Neoplatonic and Augustinian notion of divine light than with Aquinas's idea that it is a faculty of the human soul *(Dante e la cultura medievale*, 149–54). One should therefore emphasize that in Augustine the confrontation of the mind with ideas gave birth to the concept, the mind's representation of the idea, which Augustine calls the "verbum." This word came to be called the *verbum cordis*. See Joseph Owens, "Faith, Ideas, Illumination, Experience," in *The Cambridge History of Later Medieval Philosophy*, 443–44, 453. In either case, however, what is important for my argument is that intellection ends in the production of language.

13. See Owens, "Faith, Ideas, Illumination, Experience," 452.

understanding. Knowing something with respect to its nature alone is not enough, for if understanding stopped here, one could not know anything in particular. To comprehend a thing as it exists therefore requires that the soul return to the phantasms (*se convertere ad phantasma*), armed, as it were, with the abstracted concept, through which it can now form a judgment of the discrete object as true or false. This judgment takes the form of a proposition: not a single word, such as *dog* or *man*, but the concept embedded in a statement that has the form $a = b$, such as "Rover is a dog"; "Socrates is a man." This is what Thomas means when he says that faith is propositional.

For Fiammetta, love is something more than sense and less than intellect.[14] She therefore upholds the superiority of thought to sight by making the former coincide with the rational operations of the internal senses, all of which are distinguished from their external counterparts, as we have seen, by their ability to integrate and make judgments about the intentions that have been abstracted from physical objects. Only in the common sense or the imagination can all the sensitive spirits experience the wondrous joy Fiammetta claims they do in thought. Only in the imagination will the nobility of the beloved herself be preserved, since her intentional image has been brought closer to the soul by having undergone a second degree of rational formulation, without sacrificing her individuality, since she has not yet been subsumed in the concept of womanliness. Indeed, when Fiammetta says that in contrast to thought the eye must deliver its perceptions to the intellect through many mediations, she uses a term, "intelletto animale," that is unusual.[15] By it I think she is referring specifically to the role that the spirits play in the nonintellective knowing of the internal senses.

---

14. Indeed, were such a thing possible (as it is not to Thomas), it would seem that Fiammetta's thoughts of love are completely unaffected by the process of intellection. There are two reasons why Fiammetta, very much in contrast to Dante, would not wish to identify love and the mind. The first is that to do so would render the whole question moot, since thinking is a species of "mental vision," the linking of the imagination's phantasm with the phantasm of the universal to form a proposition. The second is that once a lover has actualized love by comparing the ideal intention of feminine beauty with a real lady, the body experiences pain and desire. While the intention still resides in the internal senses, one experiences nothing sensible because one knows the image is not real. Though Fiammetta speaks of joy and anguish, they seem curiously unreal. Compare Cavalcanti, "Donna me prega," 24–25: Love "in quella parte [i.e., the intellect] mai non ha pesanza, / perché da qualitate non discende." For the appropriate citations from Albert and Aquinas, see Shaw, *Cavalcanti's Theory of Love*, 43–46.

15. The term *intellectus animalis* is not used, so far as I can discover, by any philosopher who is discussing the intellect.

As Nardi, Klein, and Agamben have shown, by the twelfth and thirteenth centuries the phantasm of Aristotelian psychology had been firmly joined to the idea of the warm breath or spirit that the Middle Ages had inherited from Stoic and Neoplatonic pneumatology.[16] In its earliest form, the pneuma was a substance physicians thought caused health and illness. Generated from the exhalation of blood, this invisible "hot breath" flowed through the arteries to all parts of the body, vivifying it and making it capable of sensation. If the equilibrium between its circulation and that of the blood through the veins was maintained, a person remained well; if it was disrupted, he developed a fever.

The Stoics extended these notions; for them the pneuma was nothing less than a material principle of life. Identical to fire, this subtle and luminous body pervaded the universe and penetrated every living thing; besides enabling corporeal reproduction and growth, it also was the "matter" in which the phantasy impressed its images. As such the pneuma functioned as an intermediary between sensation and thought. Neoplatonic philosophers developed this idea; the pneuma became the medium through which the material touched the spiritual.

By the time these doctrines reached Avicenna, medieval doctors had generally distinguished three kinds of spirits. The natural spirit empowered growth; it was formed from exhalations of the blood and administered in the liver. When the natural spirit underwent a series of digestions or purifications in the heart, it became the vital spirit, which animated the body as it coursed through the arteries. The animal spirit (Dante calls it "lo spirito animale" in the *Vita nuova*, 2.5), most subtle of the three, was distilled from the vital spirit when it passed through the three cells of the brain; once purified by the phantasy and memory, it filled the nerves and thus was responsible for sensation and movement. Under the influence of this pneumatic circulation, the sensitive soul

---

16. See Nardi, *Dante e la cultura medievale*; Robert Klein, "Spirito Pellegrino," in *La forme et l'intelligible* (Paris: Gallimard, 1979), translated as *Form and Meaning* by Henri Zerner (New York: Viking, 1979), 62–85; Giorgio Agamben, *Stanze* (Turin: Einaudi, 1977), 71–155; a good English translation, from which I take all my citations, is *Stanzas: Word and Phantasm in Western Culture*, trans. Ronald Martinez (Minneapolis: University of Minnesota Press, 1993), 61–131. See also Patrick Boyde, *Perception and Passion in Dante's Comedy* (Cambridge: Cambridge University Press, 1993), 144–54, and Mary Wack, *Lovesickness in the Middle Ages* (Philadelphia: University of Philadelphia Press, 1990). Further citations from Albertus Magnus are in *Vita nuova*, ed. Domenico de Robertis (Milan: Riccardo Ricciardi, 1980), 29–30; see also Shaw, *Cavalcanti's Theory of Love*, 57–58. In the subsequent paragraphs I generally follow Agamben.

was rationalized in such a way that Fiammetta's "intelletto animale" seems an apt way to describe it: for her "un dolce pensiero" of love can indeed be sweet precisely because it remains individualized and apperceptible even after it has risen above the compulsions of the flesh.[17] In conjunction with the imagination's capacity to combine and synthesize the intentions received in the internal senses, the spirits enable Fiammetta to maintain with no loss of decorum that in thought it is permitted to embrace one's beloved without any fear and sport with her according to one's desires ("Allora gli è licito senza alcuna paura di abbraciarla. Allora mirabilmente, secondo il suo disio, festeggia con essa").

Graziosa asks her *quistione d'amore* in the shelter of a "giardino"; it marks a time out of time, a respite from the harsher realities of Filocolo's quest. One suspects a light irony plays over Fiammetta's answer, for the sublimation of passion it exalts corresponds nicely to the unworldly setting it is given in. But on another level, the abstract quality of Fiammetta's arguments becomes more pointed if we accept, as most readers do, that Caleon, who is in the party that hears the questions, is Boccaccio's surrogate, and that Fiammetta, identified as the daughter of the king of Naples, is his (fictive) love, Maria d'Aquino. Love me, she seems to say, neither for my body nor with your mind, but with and for both through the resources of your imagination; the dispassionate, intellectual character of her discourse, which nevertheless embraces the senses and speaks personally to a particular lover, exemplifies the kind of elegant writing she thinks the young poet should produce.[18]

In the *Filostrato*, however, it seems that a different kind of love calls

---

17. As Albertus says, the imagination does not consider its intention apart from the "appendages or conditions" of the matter of an object. By appendages or conditions, Albertus means "the individual things that are associated with the same object, such as the placement of limbs, the color of a face, age, the shape of a head" (Albert, *De anima* 2.3.4; quoted in Steneck, "Albert on Sense Perception," 281).

18. From the point of view of Boccaccio as writer, the question becomes a veiled declaration of the status of his love: both she and the poem addressed to her are products of imagination. It is clear from the analysis below that I do not accept without qualification the now standard readings of Boccaccio's relation to the sweet new style and to the Dante of the *Comedy*. I think Branca and Padoan, for instance, are right to say Boccaccio's early works constitute "un mondo tutto letterario, nato da suggestioni letterarie per essere letteratura" [a world completely literary, born from literary suggestions in order to be literature]: Giorgio Padoan, "Mondo aristicratico e mondo communale nell'ideologia e nell'arte di Giovanni Boccaccio," in *Il Boccaccio Le Muse Il Parnaso e L'Arno* (Florence: Olschki, 1978), 13; see also Vittore Branca, *Boccaccio medievale* (Florence: Sansoni, 1956). But this

for a different kind of writing. We have apparently moved from the garden and the realm of imagination to history and the world of the physical senses. The narrator acknowledges that he once thought as Fiammetta did. But Graziosa's hypothetical question in the *Filocolo* here is figured as the narrator's actual experience buttressed by historical precedent. The "amara esperienza" of Filomena's removal to Sannio has taught him, as Criseida's removal to the Greek camp taught Troiolo, that thought's ability to "disporre la cosa amata" and make her "benivola e rispondente" according to his desires ("Proemio," 5) dissolves into nothing in the face of not being able to see her.[19]

The differing responses to the repeated question invite us to invent a history of Boccaccio's narrative development. A youthful erotics of the imagination now yields to the more material demands of the senses. The superiority a naive poet would grant to the mind's fancies will be proved an illusion by the real pain his lady's absence causes him. No longer will recourse to the fictions of romance or the pretty dialectics of idealized love debates offer consolation; the narrator must rather seek the more substantive solace of history to face life. Only the temporal distance of events that really happened can serve as an adequate analogue to the heartfelt despair that the spatial distance of Filomena's absence has caused him.

And yet if we wish to weave a tale out of these contrasting outlooks

---

does not mean that Boccaccio was deaf by temperament to the metaphysical or theological overtones of the *stil novo*, as such critics seem to think, based (not unreasonably) on their readings of Boccaccio's *Trattatello* and *Esposizioni*. Quite apart from his reference in the *Teseida* not only to Cavalcanti's "Donna me prega" but to Dino del Garbo's commentary on it, Boccaccio's language here in the *Filocolo* and *Filostrato*, and throughout his *Rime*, shows that he understood quite well the *stil novo*'s metaphysical superstructure. It was simply of limited use to him. Like Mazzotta, I think that Boccaccio (from the start) thought of literature as a rhetorical meditation on the claims and procedures of a series of discourses (from philosophy, medicine, ethics, theology, law, etc.) that it appropriates. It follows that to reduce Boccaccio to the social conditions he assimilated in Naples and then in Florence (and especially to read his embrace of popular forms as a reflex of his social and economic class, as Chaucerians are fond of doing), is plausible and unconvincing at once. It is plausible because such a reading calls attention to a cultural complex of production and ideology that cannot be ignored. It is unconvincing, at least to me, on three counts: because it fails (in most cases) to historicize sufficiently; because it fails to theorize sufficiently the connection between the literary text and cultural production; and because it privileges the social over the linguistic by assuming without argument that the former causes the latter. The situation in *trecento* Italy at least is more complicated: Erich Auerbach is not entirely wrong when he says that through the *Comedy* "Dante created a public not for himself alone but for his successors as well" (*Literary Language*, 312).

19. My text is Boccaccio, *Tutte le opere*, vol. 2.

and call it, approvingly or not, a move toward naturalism, we still must ask what exactly has changed from the *Filocolo* to the *Filostrato*. Actual pain we assume makes love something different from Fiammetta's intellectualized conception of it, but the narrator's tortured experience, by his own account, is reducible to switching sides in a rhetorical debate. For the description of the miserable life he has led since Filomena's departure to Sannio has as its culminating point just this: that instead of thought, the narrator now knows he should have said that sight affords the greatest pleasure to the lover ("e con mia gravissima noia sono divenuto certo di ciò che io prima, non certo, in contrario disputava," "Proemio," 22). As a conclusion this seems inappropriately bloodless, since talk about the travails of life is as removed from them as ideas are. To make the heart's grief resolve itself as the retraction of an argument in a disputation, itself argues against the position he now advocates, the priority of experience and the senses over the mind. The setting may have shifted to the court of love ("Proemio," 1), but how far are we from Fiammetta's garden?

It might therefore be equally persuasive to say that there is little to choose between the *Filocolo*'s psychology of love and the rhetoric of desolation in the *Filostrato*. The narrator tells us that in order to suffer less his eyes twisted away as if by their own accord from the temples, balconies, and *piazze* where he has seen Filomena, so that in their sorrow they constrained his heart to cry out in Jeremiah's woeful words: "how solitary sits the city, which was once full of people and mistress among nations":

> quante volte per minor doglia sentire si sono essi [i.e. his eyes] spontanamente ritorti da riguardare li templi e le logge e le piazze . . . e dolorosi hanno il cuor costretto a dir con seco quel misero verso di Geremia: "O come siede sola la città la quale in qua addietro era piena di popolo e donna delle genti!" (12)

With Filomena gone, the narrator has become a sightseer who wanders through a city half present, half absent; his life is now little more than a narrative of the things he can no longer observe in the things he beholds. To represent the ghostly effects of these evacuations, which make him and his surroundings as remote in their way from reality as Fiammetta's imaginative abstractions are from the senses, the narrator offers a statement—the cry of grief from Jeremiah. This lament isn't descriptive or mimetic, for what is there for it to describe or imitate except vacancy and things that have ceased to be? Rather, the effusion signifies its speaker's condition by being a quotation, words that express his emotions but are not his own, that locate him not in Naples, or Jerusalem, or someplace else, but somewhere in between. Even the emotion, one notices, resides not in him but in the verse ("quel misero verso di Geremia"). Words do not betoken what he feels so much as the feelings arise from the words and have no extension beyond them. The narrator has come to occupy the same ontological space as the poem he will write: he gives language the same status and force as actions and emotions because his life apart from Filomena is marked by the same distance that separates writing from speech, speech from the objects the words refer to.

Thus it is not unexpected that the lamentation the narrator inscribes from *Lamentations* bespeaks less the anguish of having been forsaken than the rhetoric of anguish. But it is shocking nonetheless, twice so, once for its disproportion and again for its two-facedness. Readers of the *Vita nuova*, of whom Boccaccio was one, would immediately recall that Dante had used these same words to herald Beatrice's death.[20] The invitation to equate her passing from Florence and Filomena's passage to Sannio is deliberately outrageous, an outrageousness Boccaccio seems to underline when he immediately has the narrator admit that there is such a thing as degree: "Certo io non dirò ogni cosa parimente attristandoli" [Certainly I will not say all things equally sadden (my eyes)]. The allusion to Beatrice's death is meant, of course, to express the magnitude of the narrator's grief, but if he seems aware that it is exaggerated in relation to its cause, he should also realize that by likening Filomena to Dante's beatified madonna he will either trivialize his beloved or hold her to an ideal of love more akin to Fiammetta's ethereal conception than to his own. Even so, one still wants to believe that the impropriety of the quotation is nothing more than the ingenuous embellishment of a love-struck poet. There is, however, an insidious side to his citation. In light of the story he is about to tell, Filomena's departure makes Naples not only Jeremiah's widowed city but a latter-

---

20. See *Vita nuova*, 27 and 30. Boccaccio in fact alludes to the *Vita nuova* throughout the *Filostrato:* indeed, the first sentence of the work, when the narrator says he has been love's servant since youth, recalls *Vita nuova* 12.7. See Branca's note, *Filostrato*, 846–47, and the discussion of allusions to Dante in Smarr, *Boccaccio and Fiammetta*, 45ff.

day Troy as well. Yet if we remember how Troy was brought low, we remember a series of betrayers and acts of deception. By granting himself the author's privilege of future-perfect retrospection, the narrator can conceal within his compliment to his lady—see, these are the dimensions of the suffering you have caused me, so great is the love you have inspired in me—an angry warning that his love will have its vengeance if she proves to be a treacherous Criseida.[21]

The proem to the *Filostrato* in fact consistently gives contradictory responses to two kinds of issues. One is intellectual: as we have seen, the speaker contends that in love, sight is superior to thought, yet in championing the priority of the senses, he makes his lady a creature less of flesh and blood than of thought and reduces his own experience to a position in a rhetorical debate. These discrepancies seem to me to correspond to the moment of aporia in the intellect that Thomas points to when he establishes the propositional nature of faith. The other issue deals with desires and intentions, which are matters of the will: Filostrato desperately wants to persuade Filomena to return to Naples, yet he also seems ready to condemn her for not returning. Indeed, he says his life depends on his poem's ability to induce Filomena to return, but his anger peeps through his supplications, and anger has no desire at all to persuade. Rather we begin to suspect that under the guise of persuasion, Filostrato wants to upbraid Filomena, not for not having returned, but for having left in the first place.

What seems to me most remarkable about these conflicting impulses, which constitute the narrator and establish the character of his poem, is that they too are not passions of the heart so much as an eroticizing of rhetorical decorum. Rhetoric in the Middle Ages had both a cognitive and a judicative function: its primary goal was to persuade

---

21. In this regard, note the arch suppression of a key trope in Jeremiah: "Quomodo sedet sola civitas plena populo. Facta est quasi vidua domina gentium," Lamentations 1:1. In the *Filostrato* this appears as "O come siede sola la città la quale in qua addietro era pieno di popolo e donna delle genti!" The city in Jeremiah sits solitary like a widow: the narrator cannot afford to allow this to appear, since it would too openly invite the reader to relate his beloved to the Criseida, also a widow, who is the emblem of the fallen Troy. But rhetorical silences, such as this one, can speak as loudly as words. The silence is a real threat that Filomena not turn out to be the faithless sensualist the rhetoric of the poem will make the Criseida she has already been identified with. Rhetorical silences can also be ironic; if Filomena, through Criseida, is like a widow, the narrator can only be the dead spouse. He is happy to figure himself dead, or near to it, but the idea of having been married would cause more difficulties.

an audience to judge a particular act right or wrong, but before one can adjudicate, one must understand.[22] Prior to deciding whether one should approve or reject an allegation, in other words, one has to comprehend whether it is true or not. The question of truth, therefore, was one rhetoric always was concerned with, and a number of techniques were developed to determine its probability. Chief among them for Boccaccio, I would argue, was the argument *in utramque partem*.[23] It was, in fact, precisely this method of disputing both sides of a topic to arrive at the probable truth of an assertion that prompted Boccaccio both to frame the *Filostrato* within the confines of a *quistione d'amore* and to link it to the *Filocolo*. But these works, separately and together, show that the give-and-take of pro and con in rhetorical debate tends to leave matters as hard to judge after each side has had its say as they were before. Fiammetta's arguments about the superiority of thought are as difficult to falsify as the narrator's about sight are to verify. It all depends on the circumstances, and for Boccaccio these are always shaped by the ulterior motives of the arguers.

Boccaccio's particular point, in fact, is that the very means that were supposed to produce an adequate knowledge of the truth gain ethical neutrality only ironically, through selfish misuse for partial ends.[24] In the *Filocolo*, Graziosa and Fiammetta argue for their positions in the philosophical language of the *stil novo*, but the abstract psychology of that discourse serves Fiammetta's own purposes with respect to Caleon just as much as the presumably unprejudiced historical account of Troiolo and Criseida will serve Filostrato's. Similarly, in the *Filostrato*, the narrator proposes to frame his experience as a love debate because he is unable to judge the truth or falseness of his lady. It may turn out that Filomena remains faithful, just as events proved

---

22. For a thorough analysis of the principles of rhetoric in the classical and medieval world, see Wesley Trimpi, *Muses of One Mind* (Princeton: Princeton University Press, 1983), 73–79 and passim. The cognitive and judicative aspects of rhetoric have as their goal only the probable, unlike the scientific discourse of dialectic, which aims at certainty. As such, Boccaccio would claim that rhetoric is the appropriate discourse to represent the workings of the inner senses.

23. For an analysis of Boccaccio's use of the rhetorical argument *in utramque partem* throughout his works, see my *The Cast of Character*, 98–133; and Trimpi, *Muses of One Mind*, 287–95; 384–87.

24. Among the theorists of rhetoric who claimed such neutrality, besides Aristotle and Augustine, is Boccaccio himself. See Trimpi, *Muses of One Mind*, 384–87. The disclaimers we find at the beginning of the *Decameron*, and again at the beginning of the fourth day, are part of Boccaccio's rhetorical stance from the start of his career.

Criseida did not. But Filostrato is motivated neither by fairness nor by equity to hold his hopes and doubts in unbiased balance; his seeming evenhandedness toward Filomena actually masks his use of the protocols of rhetorical disputation to accuse her of betrayal at the same time that he swears he believes in her fidelity. Rather than determining the truthfulness of Filomena's love, arguing *in utramque partem* in fact has become a way for Filostrato to prosecute the proddings of his divided soul. His truth is the *modo di dire* he has fashioned to determine it, to say to Filomena "odi et amo," which he would translate as "I hate, I love, it depends on you."

Once one knows the truth, rhetoric becomes judicative. It would now move the audience to act *de expetendo fugiendoque*, by presenting the true as a good to be sought and the false as an evil to flee.[25] Once again the narrator of the *Filostrato* stands ready, this time to bend the ethics of judgment to his own ends. Though he may cast his love for Filomena as a refined *demande d'amour* in the cultivated language of the sweet new style, his identification of himself with Troiolo makes it clear that his desires are blatantly sexual. Her return, we realize, is not his ultimate goal, but only a means to it: he wants to sleep with her, just as Troiolo slept with Criseida. The persuasiveness of the story he will tell, therefore, from which Filomena can infer her goodness by the extent of his ardor for her, is a blind for his own exercise in salacious wish-fulfillment.

Similarly self-serving is the moral of the story, which would argue that false women like Criseida must be avoided. We know, of course, that Criseida was untrue because history has told us she was. But in Filostrato's hands, history is not an uninflected recitation of what was, and only incidentally does it provide the hindsight that makes knowledge certain and the action that follows from it exemplary. History instead merely becomes the narrator's excuse for telling the story backward, so that by positing Criseida's guilt from the start, he can vilify Filomena for leaving or hector her into rejoining him.

Filostrato, of course, does qualify his identification with Troiolo, just as he qualifies Filomena's with Criseida. The Trojan prince can stand as his surrogate only when he weeps and laments for Criseida. Nothing else, especially not the happiness Troiolo found with Criseida preceding her departure, has any reference to him. Such things are included,

---

25. On this aspect of rhetoric, see Trimpi, *Muses of One Mind*, 366–69.

he explains, for two reasons: first, because once one has seen happiness, one can understand far better how much and how great the misery is that succeeds it ("perché la felicità veduta d'alcuno, molto meglio si comprende quanta e quale sia la miseria sopravvenuta," "Proemio," 30); second, because the story of noble young lovers demands it ("perciocché la storia del nobile e innamorato giovane ciò richiede," "Proemio," 35). The first argument appeals to reason, the second to the requirements of desire: both seek their justification in the proprieties of literary decorum. But we have already seen how the narrator eroticizes the usages of rhetoric; here, in very much the same way, the procedures of allegory become a screen for pornography and spleen.[26] Allegory is continuous, not selective: its identities are made not in parts but in wholes. Everywhere else Filostrato has suggested that because he lives in longing, he lives in and through what he writes, that literature and his experience coincide because his life has become identical to his ability to persuade Filomena. The logic behind his contention is that since desire presupposes not possessing the object desired, he has effectively become a creature of imagination, which also operates in the absence of the object. Writing generally, and allegory in particular, similarly registers the nonpresence of the things it represents, and writers write by means of the imagination. So when the narrator claims his poem contains events that have not happened to him, he is saying that in relation to him, they are fictive. But as poet whose life is the story he sends to Filomena, those parts of the *Filostrato* that are "fictitious" are as actual as those that derive from his life, precisely because they too have been fictionalized by the conceit that makes Troiolo's history an allegory of his own. His disclaimer notwithstanding, the events based on the workings of his imagination can be no less real than those that he and Troiolo have undergone because both exist as extended tropes of his desires.

In the same way, Filomena is invited to associate Criseida with herself whenever she finds her beauty depicted, or her manners, or any

---

26. In this regard, see especially Mazzotta's "Allegory and the Pornographic Imagination," 105–30. To see how close the *Filostrato* actually is to the *Decameron*, one should note that at the end of the latter, Boccaccio defends its ethics by recalling the reasons he gave in the former for including the love scenes: if there are words that seem offensive, Boccaccio says, "la qualità delle novelle l'hanno richesta" (*Conclus.* 4–5). Clearly he echoes *Filostrato*, "Proemio," 35: in both instances, ethics have been reduced to the offensiveness of words. And Boccaccio's justification is also a matter of style: the nature of the work demands it.

other laudable quality in a woman ("e quante volte la bellezza e' costumi, e qualunque altra cosa laudevole in donna, di Criseida scritta troverete . . ." "Proemio," 34). But Criseida's "costumi" do not change all that much after she has left Troy, and the fact that Filomena no longer is in Naples suggests that she most resembles her Trojan counterpart not in her beauty or praiseworthy manners but in her capacity to forsake lovers and widow cities.[27]

This insistent recursion to personal motive constitutes an incipient critique not only of the "otherness" of allegory but also of its ideological use to exalt the loves of the nobility. To Boccaccio, the fleshlessness of French psychological allegory cannot stand as a surrogate for the body's own drive to delight itself, while the Italian refinements of the *stil novo* do not ignore the body so much as they naively idealize its gratifications by dressing them in the dignity of abstract scholastic terminology. By contrast, when Troiolo considers whether to fall in love, he vacillates between revealing his passion, which "were it ever known by any, would be greatly praised," and keeping it secret, since love "made known to many gains trouble as its reward, not joy" (1.35, 36). This appeal to allegory's dialectics of concealment and revelation, however, itself reveals and conceals a strange sexual politics. Troiolo would negotiate between his hope for praise and fear of blame (both of which, we notice, are the conventional topics of rhetorical discourse), by declaring himself Love's servant: "Signor, omai / l'anima è tua che mia esser solea" [Lord, now the soul is yours that used to be mine] (1.38). His prayer, which lasts a mere two stanzas, is a set piece; it invokes all the flat platitudes of courtly love lyrics. But it hardly marks a moment of ethical awareness of another. Troiolo does not directly cede his autonomy to Criseida—that is, to a woman who, because she really is someone else, could jeopardize Troiolo's self-possession. Rather, in anticipation of Pandaro, he yields to Love, a male God, as a way of retaining mastery and preserving manhood at the very moment when his surrender puts him in Criseida's position. Troiolo makes his love brave by making himself one with this God, who will then exert his

---

27. In much the same way that allegory is eroticized in the *Filostrato,* so too is medical discourse. In agreement with medical treatises, which promoted the therapeutic effects of literature, the narrator claims writing the poem has allowed him to find "great relief." But these arguments were generally used to defend literature as something salutary; in Boccaccio, the restoration of health comes about by writing to satisfy his narrator's prurient interests. On the therapeutic uses of literature, see Glending Olson, *Literature as Recreation in the Later Middle Ages* (Ithaca: Cornell University Press, 1982), esp. 134–232.

power to gain Criseida. In this way, by manipulating the concept of generic unity to suggest that extremes are actually covert extensions of the means that join them, Boccaccio's protagonist rewrites the personified narcissism of the *Roman de la Rose*. Instead of presenting the beloved as a congeries of ideational projections of the lover's desire, however, the narrator makes his poem the material form of selfish motives that, declared or disguised, at various moments go by the names of Troiolo, Creseida, and Amore. In his hands allegory has become a discourse of self-interest that takes mediation as its own end and writing as its mode of meaning, a development the narrator soon confirms when he slyly interjects himself into his description of Criseida's reaction to Troiolo's falling in love with her:

> E qual si fosse non è assai certo:
> o che Criseida non se n'accorgesse
> per l'operar di lui ch'era coverto,
> o che di ciò conoscer s'infignesse.
>
> (1.48)

[And it isn't certain whether Criseida was not aware (of Troiolo's condition) because he masked how love (for her) had affected him, or whether she feigned knowing.]

An "or" divides her response not because either explanation might tell us something about Criseida's feelings, as Troiolo's oscillations did communicate something about his, but because Filostrato, by inventing alternatives, can make her attitude, whatever it may have been, a metaphor of his uncertainty about Filomena. Under rhetorical scrutiny, the kind of difference that allegory seems to deploy cannot remain unmotivated. After the *Filostrato*, neither the language of Guillaume de Lorris nor of Dante can serve as the natural expression of qualities indigenous to an entire class of people. In Boccaccio's skeptical version, talking otherwise is only a way of speaking for oneself in particular.

The *Filostrato*, then, is something more than Boccaccio's meditation on the continuities and discontinuities of intellect and desire. By locating his love-epic in the juncture between faith and faithlessness, Boccaccio is able to explore the ambiguous middle ground that rhetoric creates between the discourses it poses as extremes. Like Aquinas, Boccaccio realizes that his writing will be of the same genus as the writings it is situated between; unlike Aquinas, however, Boccaccio suggests that the nature of the extremes is shaped by the nature of the means that mediates between them. When the means is literature itself, the genus the work belongs to consists of those compositions that participate in the genres of discourse they contain without belonging to them, that disinstall their generic attributes by translating their manners of meaning. Thus the disinterested, exemplary purpose that convention had assigned to psychological allegory and history is colored by the narrator's appropriation of them to further his own romance. When language becomes subject to intention, when the scholastic proposition is transformed into a rhetorical question of love, philosophical distinctions lose their purchase: thesis becomes hypothesis, hypothesis thesis, universal principle and particular motive each stand as the other's cause. The aristocratic identification with the courtliness of love allegories no longer will be able to pass unchallenged, nor will the confident equation many make of the lascivious with the popular traditions of the *cantare*.[28] Boccaccio included both *modi di dire* because "la storia ... ciò richiede." But he did not merely make his double-voiced, translational revision of means and ends the theme of the *Filostrato*, he inscribed them in his poem, lent them flesh and gave them a name: Pandaro.[29]

As middle man, Pandaro is the site within the poem where its extremes meet: it is his nature as pander, therefore, that will disallow too facile a judgment both of him and of Troiolo and Criseida. For since the means partakes of the nature of the end it is directed toward, at least generically, it would be easy enough to say that Pandaro reflects the differences in the lovers he has served: what's good in him is good because he shares it with Troiolo, and what's bad is bad because he shares it with Criseida. But Boccaccio complicates these assumptions

---

28. The tendency to equate the sexual in Boccaccio with popular literature is extremely common; see, for instance, Padoan, "Mondo aristocratico," 15. Without arguing against this, I do want to point out that to Boccaccio courtly literature is just as sexual. It should be noted as well that the "stilnovists" were themselves very concerned to redefine the nature of nobility as a product of virtue rather than of blood. The tendency to reify qualities in social classes runs counter to the ideology of the literature itself.

29. "Double-voicedness," of course, is an idea central to Bakhtin. In many respects, I would number the *Filostrato* among the forerunners of Bakhtin's conception of the novel; it does not present, however, an artistic image of language's diglossia so much as it inscribes rhetoric's ability to destabilize the monologic. See Mikhail Bakhtin, *The Dialogic Imagination,* ed. Michael Holquist, trans. Caryl Emerson and Michael Holquist (Austin: University of Texas Press, 1981).

by raising the question of what actually enables Pandaro to broker the affair between them.

Within the walls of Troy, of course, Pandaro is a perfect go-between, linked to Criseida by the bonds of kinship and to Troiolo by shared presuppositions of class and sex. Like his friend, he is "un troian giovinetto / d'alto legnaggio e molto coraggioso" [a young Trojan, of high lineage, and very courageous] (2.1). But superficial likenesses such as these can hardly be the reason Troiolo confides in Pandaro; after all, as Troiolo points out, Pandaro has been totally thwarted in love. His friend's response is fascinating, for even though he could not know it, Pandaro bases his credentials as an intermediary precisely on Aquinas's principle that the mean is of the same genus as the extremes. He does not argue that he will be able to bring Troiolo's affair to a successful conclusion despite his own failures. He argues that he will succeed as a go-between because of them: the person, he tells Troiolo, who has not been able to keep himself from poison can give good counsel that will save others from it, just as a blind man can sometimes go where the sighted stumble (2.10).

These statements at once constitute an ethics of mediation and call it into question. By positing his misadventures as one extreme, and Troiolo's triumph as the other, Pandaro distances himself from any possible experiential participation in love. He creates the impression of selflessness, of an absolute lack of personal interest that permits him to call his offer of service a legitimate act of friendship.[30] In effect, he defines himself as Troiolo's simulacrum, an ironic calque on the imaginative aspects of Dante's animal spirit in the *Vita nuova*, as removed from sexual gratification as Fiammetta would say intentions are from sense perception.

But Pandaro cannot act disinterestedly, though he himself as yet is not aware of this fact. From a practical point of view, his arguments are self-defeating; one wonders whom they were meant to persuade.[31] Cer-

---

30. However we take Pandaro, Ovid's counsel at the end of the first book of the *Ars Amatoria* definitely stands behind his actions. There Ovid warns the lover to be wary about praising too much his beloved to a friend who, believing what he hears, will strive to take his friend's place ("cum tibi laudanti crediderit, ipse subit," 1.742).

31. His terms, in fact, seem to recall Gorgias's when he asks Socrates who is more useful, the doctor who can prescribe a cure or the rhetor who can persuade the patient to take the medicine? Indeed, their evident sophistry corresponds, I would maintain, to that moment of unbridgeable intellectual distance Thomas establishes when he determines the nature of faith by appealing to the generic continuity of means and extremes.

tainly not Troiolo, for the prince knows that Pandaro's qualifications as an effective intermediary lie not in his fiascoes but in the fact that he is Criseida's cousin. Indeed, Troiolo is perfectly aware that consanguinity gives Pandaro leverage that makes his functioning as dispassionate middleman impossible. The prince sighs bitterly and blushes from shame when he tells Pandaro he is in love with his kinswoman (2.15): these outward signs of moral quandary, however, are quickly put aside when Pandaro himself says he would help even if it were his sister. Troiolo then reveals that he is in love with Criseida by saying:

> Altri, come tu sai, aman le suore,
> e le suore i fratelli, e le figliuole
> talvolta i padri, e suoceri le nuore,
> le matrigne i figliastri talor suole
> anche avvenir; ma me ha preso Amore
> per tua cugina . . . Criseida.
>
> (2.20)

[Others, as you know, love their sisters, and sisters their brothers, and sometimes daughters their fathers and fathers-in-law their daughters-in-law, and sometimes it happens that stepmothers love their stepsons, but love for your cousin Criseida has taken me.]

With these words, Troiolo explicitly points to the consequences of employing Pandaro as his middleman. All the loves he lists are illicit because they are within the family; to use Pandaro is to make him, as much as himself, Criseida's lover. Pandaro's previous professions of gratuitous service in the name of friendship, which establish, as I say, the only grounds that warrant the morality of his assistance, are compromised almost as soon as they are spoken.[32]

The implications of this crucial colloquy are worth lingering over. When Pandaro first finds Troiolo in tears, he asks in an oblique way whether it is the war that has so vanquished his spirit ("Hatti già così vinto il tempo amara," 2.1:8). Troiolo seizes on the idea that he is at

---

32. Of course, one could say that Troiolo wants to be certain that Pandaro fully understands the implications of his pandering; if this is the case, he morally warns his friend of the immorality of the agreement they are about to enter into. Or does Troilus ironically want to extend the duties of friendship so that it includes sharing the blame as well as the joy and pain? In either instance, Pandaro is compromised as a go-between.

death's door but emphatically rejects the notion that fear of battle has brought him there; whatever the cause of his hebetude, however, he begs Pandaro to drop the matter in the name of amiability ("Se la nostra amistà ha forza alcuna," 2.2–3). The way Troiolo parries the thrust of Pandaro's surmise is intriguing. He acknowledges the ultimate truth of his confidant's conjecture about his condition but swiftly denies that any want of courage is responsible for it. Then, as if to seal his rebuttal and bring the exchange to an end, he appeals to the canons of friendship. In truth, however, Troiolo must know that he has obliged Pandaro to press on and discover the cause of his distress, since a friend, according to Pandaro's own definition, is someone who amends his companion's woe if he can, or shares it with him if he cannot (2.4–5). Within two stanzas Troiolo has managed, not once but twice, to reposition a topic he initially invoked as an end in itself so that it becomes a means of maneuvering Pandaro into continuing the conversation on allied yet more advantageous grounds. He first converts his comrade's concern about his death into a reaffirmation of the bonds that join them; he now stands ready to expand that intimacy to include his passion for Criseida. Even before Pandaro volunteers for the job, Troiolo has turned his friend into his pander.

Troiolo proves equally adept at engineering subtle shifts of direction and intention when he discloses that he is in love:

> Amore, incontro al qual chi si difende
> più tosto pere ed adopera invano,
> d'un piacer vago tanto il cor m'accende,
> ch'io n'ho per quel da me fatto lontano
> ciascheduno altro, e questo sì m'offende,
> come tu puoi veder, che la mia mano
> appena mille volte ho temperata,
> ch'ella non m'abbia la vita levata.
>
> (2.7)

[Love, against whom he who defends himself perishes soonest and acts in vain, has so kindled my heart with a delightful beauty that for it I have put far off from me every other. This Love so assails me, as you can see, that I have scarcely stayed my hand a thousand times from taking my life.]

Troiolo begins in the elevated register of the *stil novo*; his conception of Amor, however, bears less resemblance to Dante's than to Francesca da Rimini's. "Amore, incontro al qual chi si difende / più tosto pere ed adopera invano": Troiolo's declaration echoes the self-warranting of Francesca's "Amor, che a nullo amato amar perdona" (*Inf.* 5.103) but in terms that transpose the ideas he floated in his previous reply. He again raises the specter of his own death and with it the hint of cowardliness he was quick to discredit in Pandaro's opening sally. Now, however, Troiolo admits that he does find the thought of defending himself daunting, not, though, because he must grapple with Achilles or some other Greek hero, but because it is Love who strides forth in all his might to confront him. As before, Troiolo will not have Pandaro think he is fainthearted. This time he checks the insinuation before it can arise by implying that in the face of so powerful a god, recreancy lies not in capitulation but in opposition, since to resist would be tantamount to committing suicide.

One cannot help admire a suppleness of mind that can so effortlessly discover valor in surrender before the battle has been fought; nevertheless, these are incredible sentiments to hear any prince utter during the Trojan War. Even Troiolo seems to think so, since by the end of the stanza he has contradicted himself. He moves to reassert the self-control he just appeared to cede; he *has* fought manfully against Amor's offense, he now maintains, by not killing himself: "This Love [or this beauty—"questo" can refer to both "Amor" and "piacer"], so assails me," he tells Pandaro, he has a thousand times been on the point of running himself through with his sword. Even though he again finds courage in a deed he does not commit, Troiolo's concluding conceit that he has stood against Amor is sufficiently at odds with his initial suggestion that he never would do so to make one wonder how the same sentence can accommodate both thoughts without being contradictory. Troiolo, though, has already negotiated the inconsistency by describing himself as victim and victor in love. Amor, he says, has so inflamed him with a "piacer vago," that for it he has banished every other such "piacer." If we understand "piacer vago" abstractly, as something akin to "gracious delight," Troiolo is suggesting that he has been seized by a lofty passion not unlike the magnanimous affection of friendship. So it may be; but Troiolo's response to the pleasure he feels has little of that riveted-to-the-spot, awestruck astonishment we might expect. This "piacer" does not overwhelm all others by the sublime force of its attraction; instead, calmly and fully self-possessed, Troiolo has set the other pleasures aside for this one ("per quel"). Because he remains so much in control of himself, Troiolo's love rapidly loses whatever idealized aura his language seemed at first to grant it. More and more "piacer" resonates with its Provençal overtones of "corporeal beauty" *(plazer)*.[33] The enchantment Troiolo is talking about, one realizes, is the charm of Criseida's physique; the delights it has caused him to put in storage are the images of every other beautiful woman Troiolo sees or, we must assume, has known. Ultimately, Troiolo's word echoes Francesca's use of it when she says that Love seized her so strongly with "delight" in Paolo ("mi prese del costui piacer sì forte"), it does not leave her even now *(Inf.* 5.104–5). Indeed, "vago," the word that modifies this "piacer," can mean "mobile" as well as "desirous." If we catch in it some sense of motion, the adjective nicely translates the irony of Francesca's statement. Dante asked his readers to measure the steadfastness of the love she asserts against her unalterable doom to be forever tossed haphazardly about the second circle of hell by an infernal whirlwind. In the *Filostrato*, "piacer vago" as "moving beauty" accurately describes both Criseida's effect on Troiolo now and forecasts her future vagrancy.

As a result of his rhetorical dexterity, Troiolo has smoothed the way for Pandaro's tenders of friendly service to be translated into an opportunity to advance his carnal desires. He is therefore in good position to assess the worth of Pandaro's persuasions that his own bungled affairs have made him a perfect mediator for Troiolo's; their mode of argument—converting ends into means—follows the same logic Troiolo had just deployed. Pandaro cuts closer to the bone, though, when he says that perhaps Troiolo's inamorata is someone with whom he will be particularly effective. In response to this gambit, the prince sighs bitterly and says that the reason why he has kept the name of the woman from his dear friend ("Amico caro") is a highly honorable one ("cagione assai onesta"): she is his relative (2.16).

From this moment on, the colloquy becomes peculiarly Italian. Pandaro replies that too little faith ("poca fidanza") has planted such distrust ("cotal sospetto"—another Francescan allusion) in his dear friend

---

33. See Michele Barbi, "Con Dante e coi suoi interpreti: II: Francesca da Rimini," *Studi danteschi* 15 (1932): 10–11.

("Amico fino"), for although his life depended on it ("s'io non sia ucciso"), he would act to satisfy his desires even if it were his sister he loved (2.16). The phrase Pandaro uses to authenticate his dedication is important because it indicates his understanding of what Troiolo has told him. By repeating his companion's pattern of linking death and friendship, Pandaro makes explicit his belief that the undying fidelity he owes his comrade in arms takes precedence over the loyalty a brother owes a sister. He then underlines the point by asking if the lady lives in his house ("È ella donna che sia 'n casa mia"), and by promising that he will be able to bring Troiolo relief before six days have passed if the woman turns out to be the one Pandaro thinks it is (2.17).

By now, both men have stretched the ideas they discuss far enough to include their opposites: amity has come to sanction betrayal, love has hired death as its purchaser. Troiolo, weeping, summarizes these strategic transformations of intent when he finally tells Pandaro it is Criseida he loves. Once again he rehearses the themes he has sounded. He says first that when he ponders what Love has driven him to, he wishes he were dead; then that if he could have kept her name hidden without wronging his friend he would have continued to dissemble forever. Wherefore, Troiolo continues, Pandaro can see that

> Amor non ha qual uom ami per legge,
> fuor che colei cui l'appetito elegge.
>
> (2.19)

[Love does not suffer a man to love by law except her whom desire chooses.]

With this couplet, a marvel of concision one needs to paraphrase to unpack, Troiolo both confirms the Boethian precept that no law governs lovers and contends that Love's law always compels a man to hunger for the woman he desires. By establishing Amor as lawful to itself and outlaw to everything else, Troiolo legitimates all passions, no matter how extreme, by placing them under the god's jurisdiction; more particularly he sanctifies his sodality with Pandaro, who, by forcing Troiolo's confession, has enabled the prince to prove that his love for Criseida is undeniable, yet who, by hearing it, instantly makes that love illicit. Troiolo's listing of all the variations of incestuous passion follows immediately.

One might think that for any Christian audience, well schooled in the degrees of propinquity allowed by the church for marriage, Troiolo's and Pandaro's casuistry would seem so obvious, their arguments would be their own refutations. Yet many Italian readers, however perverse they thought the Trojans' ethics, may well have paused before they condemned them, since they would be likely to hear in Troiolo's words an offer of terms to form a *consorteria*. The principle that had spurred the formation of these family corporations was the partition of the inheritance *(sors)* among all male heirs; by banding together, they could prevent the loss of landed property, which normally had occurred during the earlier Middle Ages as the result of the marriage of daughters. By the twelfth century, such "tower societies," as they had come to be called, were already common in northern and central Italian cities and towns; by Boccaccio's day they frequently included important members who were not related by blood to the founding family.[34] However shocked, then, the honest citizenry of a Florence or Bologna may have been by Troiolo's muster of forbidden liaisons, they would have been equally surprised to find that he had made Troy more familiar as well. To them, Troiolo would be saying that he proposes to join himself to his friend's household, not as kin or husband, but as a partner.[35] Just as a distinguishing characteristic of *consorteria* was the collective control the group exercised over property that belonged to individuals in it, so Troiolo in effect suggests to Pandaro that they think of the widowed Criseida as a legacy they will possess in common.[36]

From this point of view, of course, Criseida, like her Homeric counterpart, is little more than chattel; the actual status of widows in *trecento*

---

34. On the *consorteria*, see David Herlihy, *Medieval Households* (Cambridge: Harvard University Press, 1985), 88–92; see also Franco Niccolai, "I consorzi nobilari ed il comune nell'alta e media Italia," *Rivista di storia del diritto italiano* 13 (1940): 116–47, 292–342, 397–477.

35. In response to Pandaro's revelation that a highborn Trojan has fallen in love with her, Criseida says, "Who should take such complete pleasure in me unless he had already married me?" [Chi deve aver di me piacere intero / se già non divenisse mio marito?] (2.45). From the moment Florentine readers heard these words, they would find it difficult not to conflate Troiolo's incestuous implications with the church's strictures on marriage.

36. Speaking of the *consorteria*, David Herlihy and Christiane Klapisch-Zuber note: "Plus frappante encore, une autre des leurs caractéristiques est d'avoir imposé un droit de regard collectif sur le biens appartenant en propre à leurs membres." *Les Toscans et leurs familles* (Paris: Presses de la fondation nationale des sciences politiques, 1978), 534.

Italian cities was not much higher.[37] But as a cultural marker, Criseida serves interests far greater than those that benefited from Troiolo's reduction of her to the level of a partible patrimony. As we have seen, Boccaccio lived through a time when the axiology of social association was changing. Especially before the upheavals of 1341–42, the moral merchant or magnate who rejected Troiolo and Pandaro's collusion may also have been an enthusiastic supporter of the form of allegiance that determined how they would gain Criseida's love. By the end of the *Filostrato,* Criseida has been made to negotiate these tensions by simultaneously functioning as totem and taboo for the prosperous Florentine arriviste and established patrician alike.

As Pandaro's cousin, as the beloved of a royal prince of Troy, Criseida at the story's start would allow any Western medieval audience to recollect the old manner of noble alliance, in which agnate kinship determined familial membership and descent betokened gentility. When Pandaro asserts that he would even help Troiolo love his sister, however, he calls into question the usages and values of this system: his willingness to join his relation to someone outside the family controverts the practice of endogamy, which was the method the aristocracy had chosen to keep the *sors* within it; his exaltation of friendship provides as well an effective ideology to substitute for the glorification of blood, which was the preferred way highborn inbreeding had acculturated itself. Of course, the alacrity with which Pandaro abdicates his responsibilities to kith and kin still smacks of rank opportunism. Nevertheless, whatever his motives, Pandaro's tender of his sister could not be dismissed out of hand, since it implicitly aligned him with the church's pronouncements on this matter; even after the Fourth Lateran Council reduced the number of degrees from seven to four, marriage among near relatives was still proscribed as a form of incest.

Because Pandaro is someone who ought to uphold the customs of the noble clan but instead abandons them in order to aid his princely companion, he allows Criseida to take on the qualities of a fetish for both the long-standing city dweller who, like Dante, venerated the antique virtues of the old families, and for the *nova civis* who, having

---

37. Widows in many urban centers found themselves in increasingly desperate circumstances in *duecento* and *trecento* Italy because of the restrictions placed both on the portion husbands contributed to the dowry and on the portion the wife could recover after his death; see Herlihy, *Medieval Households,* 98–100. At the tale's start, Criseida would have seemed even more vulnerable to a Florentine audience than to one in London.

grown great, wrote his *recordanze*, a memorial account of familial deeds for the edification of future generations. By extending her his sympathy in the face of Pandaro's maneuverings, either man could believe his family still maintained the ideals that ennobled the ancestral domestic covenant, even if kinship no longer was its chief compacting agent. At the same time, however, the same reader would have agreed that intermarriage had corrupted ancient families from within. For the "consortialist," Criseida's subsequent treachery would be a validation of the morality of more recent forms of communal alliance that avoided the faults that bondings by blood had been heir to. By taking her betrayal of Troiolo as a comment on the flawed nature of his "incestuous" relationship with her, he could conveniently forget that Pandaro's arrangements and commitments, which are his commitments and arrangements as well, were equally egregious violations of primary bonds of trust. Her breach of faith makes his seem minor by comparison.

On his side, when Troiolo redefines the idea of "a friend of the family," he becomes Pandaro's inverted image. By explicitly raising the issue of incest, he reinstalls the old seignorial observances within the new model of association; in effect the proffer of brotherhood he extends to Pandaro gives Troiolo the chance to play the part of new husband to his own widowed cousin.[38] Once again, for the Italian audience, the implication of Troiolo's proposal would have been scandalous and unavoidable: consortial friendship is in essence just as incestuous as dynastic mating had been in fact. And once again Criseida comes to serve as the lightning rod that discharges the repercussions of such a traumatic insinuation. To many readers, her moral delinquency will be sufficiently grave to make the dissipation Troiolo attaches to his courtship of her seem an overly fastidious peccadillo; more importantly, for those unwilling to discount the gravity of the transgression Troiolo goes out of his way to acknowledge here, Criseida's surrender to Diomede afforded the chance to shift blame back onto the benighted mores of past ages. Her betrayal, after all, only repeats in a different key Troiolo's and Pandaro's betrayal of her, which began the moment they introduced overtones of inbreeding into a form of relationship in which they no longer were tolerated.

---

38. Because the Justinian Code and Gratian's *Decretum* held that the groom's *donatio* and the bride's *dos* had to be equal, the part that reverted to widows in the earlier Middle Ages was much larger; consequently, they were often remarried to their former husband's kin in aristocratic households.

The *Filostrato* is traversed by the conflicts and contradictions that marked competing modes of confederation in Italy during the later fourteenth century. Troiolo's love for Criseida is in no way incestuous; the suspicion that Pandaro's aid would make it so makes sense only in a land in which the notary's document authorizing a consortial brotherhood was as accepted and carried as much social sanction as the blood feud or marriage ceremony.[39] To realize the extent to which these conflicts were, in Anthony Giddens's phrase, interpretive schemes, we need only recall Boccaccio's letter to Mainardo Cavalcanti, which I discussed last chapter.[40] Within the same paragraph the repentant author twice associates his vernacular works with the idea of incest: although he holds that his stories do not impel illustrious women to commit incestuous acts ("etsi non ad incestuosum actum illustres impellantur femine"), in the end he fears that the women who read him will think he is a "filthy pimp, an incestuous old man" [Existimabunt enim legentes me spurcidum lenonem, incestuosum senem]. Boccaccio not only sees himself as a member of the family that possesses his texts, he clearly conceives of that family in both consortial and traditional terms. It is equally clear that he expects Mainardo to share his outlook; otherwise the self-accusation that his books are all Troiolo-Pandaros, incestuous "prencipi galeotti," would seem too bizarrely inappropriate to be taken seriously.[41]

Troiolo, however, is not the only character who undermines the possibility of Pandaro's acting as an ethical mean in such complicated and fascinating ways. The narrator does as well, for he makes Pandaro as much his proxy as Troiolo's. In this instance, Pandaro's surrogacy is rooted in more than the mere fact that his disappointments in love locate him in the same region of absence and desire where we found the narrator. If we compare the rhetorical question of the *Filostrato* with that of the *Filocolo*, we notice that the poem proposes a third choice,

---

39. Chaucer's excision of these references to incest is thus cultural as much as it is ethical; it is an instance of the difference that made Chaucer's reception of Italy a translation.

40. We should also recall the use of the Ordinamenti di giustizia to police the violence of the magnate clans. The extension of culpability by degrees of relation to the offender clearly was patterned after the church's proscriptions against incest.

41. From a different perspective, Boccaccio's "meditation" on incest, if one can call it that, is both an aesthetic and cultural probing of the category of the natural. In this particular instance, Boccaccio's position seems to me close to the radical stance that Gregory Stone argues he advances in the *Decameron*. See *The Ethics of Nature in the Middle Ages* (New York: St. Martin's Press, 1998).

speaking to the lady, in addition to sight and thought, as the greatest delight in love. This is the very function the narrator gives his poem: he hopes its words will prove as effective with Filomena as Pandaro's turn out to be with Criseida. In Troy, however, Pandaro panders by speaking to his cousin face to face. Because Filomena has left Naples, the *Filostrato* will be able to act as go-between only by addressing her indirectly, not as the narrator's speech but as his writing, as the pleadings of an absent supplicant. In the end, there is no difference between Pandaro's mediations and the poem's because Pandaro is the *orality* of its writing. He is the unargued option that actually subsumes both sight and thought, since each of these concludes in a kind of "inscribed" speech. The narrator's eyes, we remember, force his heart to quote scripture; in intellection, the articulation of the *verbum mentis* takes on the "deference" of writing when it stands as the predicate in a proposition. Pandaro thus is something more than the intermediary Andreas Capellanus says the lover, having first seen his lady and then contemplated her beauty, should procure to help make his desires actual.[42] Far from being a function of the plot, Pandaro is the embodiment of the *Filostrato*'s manner of meaning; as vocalized notation he is the means by which Boccaccio makes the poem palpable as a means, the personage through whom it goes signifying its inbred life as "prencipe Galeotto."[43]

Pandaro, in other words, is what *this* story of young and noble lovers requires; he is the figure the narrator directs our attention to when he says he must include some scenes of Troiolo's happiness. Indeed, when Pandaro goes to woo Criseida, he knows he must get her to think kindly about the Trojan prince before she would ever agree to see him. Criseida therefore will be moved first not by Troiolo himself, but by how Pandaro represents him. To fall in love with Troiolo, she must fall in love with Pandaro's words, even as Filostrato hopes Filomena will fall in love with him (again) through the words of his poem. (Yet this, we remember, is the same narrator who holds that sight supersedes thought in love!) The whole affair revolves about Pandaro: he is the lan-

---

42. See *The Art of Courtly Love*, trans. John Parry (New York: Ungar, 1959), 1.1. That Boccaccio knew Capellanus's treatise seems certain.

43. And if the narrator, like Pandaro, is unsuccessful, then let Filomena take note. Pandaro says the reason he has failed in love is because he did not keep it secret. Given the structure of the narrator's rhetoric, it is hard to see how this is not a veiled threat to Filomena of publication of their secret unless she returns.

guage of the story, hardly a man without qualities but the intrusive yet necessary notary whose diplomatics qualify the character of everyone and everything else.

These are some of the issues I think Boccaccio raises in the *Filostrato*; for him the choice of means determines the nature of the extremes. Indeed, the technical term for the choice of means to gain an end was *intention*, and intention was an act of the will.[44] Boccaccio's will was to scrutinize the intellectualized literature of his predecessors under the glass of his more rhetorical conception of writing. In particular, he radically transformed the ontological claims of Dante's poetics by restoring irony to allegory. In the *Comedy*, we saw how Love's breath effects an erasure when Dante notes it. This moment comes as close as any in medieval literature to embracing Benjamin's idea of allegory as effacement: "Und zwar bedeutet es genau das Nichtsein dessen, was es vorstellt" [Allegory means precisely the nonexistence of what it represents].[45] Dante immediately hastens to repair this negation by constituting himself as an allegory in the theological sense; he becomes an embodied representation that follows the mode in which Amor signifies. But the trace of irony that forever attends this incarnation of flesh as meaningful word is the silencing of Ovidian transformation. The narrator of Boccaccio's allegory of existence, by contrast, constitutes himself not as referentiality made tangible by an act of imitation but as the body and soul of writing that means to persuade. Once he makes history an agent of desire, absent voices can speak for present ends, even if they are in opposition, because allegory coordinates each voice as a translation of the other's intentional mode. For Boccaccio, "pure language" is less the sheer disfigural materiality of the word than writ-

---

44. Aristotle had distinguished human action from that of brutes by noting that in addition to willing an end, humans also choose the means to attain it. From this Aquinas inferred that the will is a rational appetite for the good. When the intellect affirms something is good, it also deliberates about the way it may be attained, which the will then puts into action. This deliberation about the means that the will chooses to gain an end that is good was called an act of intention. Intention, in other words, is tantamount to the will's choice of means.

Thomas's views about the superiority of the intellect in the determining of intention were challenged, largely in the context of debates on free will, by Franciscan thinkers, who insisted on the will's independence. But even in Scotus and Ockham intention remains what it was in Aquinas: the freedom of the will to choose the means to its goal.

45. Walter Benjamin, *The Origin of German Tragic Drama*, trans. J. Osborne (London: NLB, 1977), 233; *Ursprung des deutschen Trauerspiels* (Frankfurt am Main: Suhrkamp, 1961), 105. See in addition Cohen's discussion, *Ideology and Inscription*, 105ff.

ing's infinite openness to rhetorical revocalization. From this perspective, the *Filostrato* may be thought of as an experiment in what we today might call discourse theory; perhaps more than anything else, it was this aspect of the poem that I think Chaucer pondered most deeply.

When Fiammetta says in the *Filocolo* that her ideal lover "can embrace his lady in his thoughts without any fear and sport with her according to his desire," she sublimates erotic passion the moment she acknowledges it. To our ears Fiammetta may sound coy. If she is, however, she could respond that it is no crime, for hers is the coyness of the aesthetic. Like any good "stilnovist," she relies on us to know that the inner senses performed their operations by progressively stripping the phantasm from its material accidents. The term Avicenna passed on to the Latin West for this process was *denudatio* (disrobing). The senses effect an imperfect unclothing of the sensible form; only the phantasm the imagination extracts from that form has been truly denuded ("denudatione vera"). At this point, we remember, the phantasm is still individuated; to discover its inherent goodness or other insensible intentions, the estimative sense must disrobe it yet again. Once the phantasm is totally naked, the intellect acts on it; as Avicenna says, even "if it were not nude, nevertheless it would become so, because the contemplative virtue strips it such that no material affection remains in it."[46]

In Dante's prose elaboration of the first vision of the *Vita nuova*, Love carries Beatrice, naked except for a red cloth, in his arms. By representing Beatrice in this way, Dante signals that she already exists in his mind at that phantasmic juncture between the sensitive and rational souls. Though different in tone, Fiammetta stages her romance in the same place by presupposing the same psychological operations. In the *Filostrato*, however, the *denudatio* of the image gives way to literal disrobings in the bedroom. As advocate of sight over thought, Boccaccio returns to the senses the mental protocols that lie at the heart of the *stil novo*. In doing so, he created a new *modo di dire*, a rhetorical aesthetic whose territory is less the intersecting fields of understanding than the arena in which ethical principles and personal intentions translate one another when opposing contentions compete for minds and hearts.

Criseida becomes her own Pandaro when she devises a plan that allows Troiolo to come in secret to her house. While he was waiting in

---

46. I have taken this description of Avicenna from Agamben, *Stanzas*, 79.

a dark and remote place, Criseida coughed to let him know where she is ("acciò ch'ei la 'ntendesse / com'era posto, ella aveva tossito," 3.26). After everyone had gone to bed, Criseida, holding a burning torch in her hand, descended the stairs all alone to Troiolo's hiding place: "Avea la donna un torchio in mano acceso, / e tutta sola discese le scale" (3.28). Criseida apologizes for keeping Troiolo's royal splendor ("splendor reale") so confined; Troiolo takes up her image and responds that she is "the glorious lady of his mind":

> Donna bella,
> sola speranza e ben della mia mente,
> sempre davanti m'è stata la stella
> del tuo bel viso splendido e lucente.
>
> (3.29)

[Beautiful mistress, sole hope and good of my mind, the star of your beautiful, splendid, brilliant face has always been before me.]

The lovers kiss; then they mount the stairs to Criseida's chamber. Still clad in one last shift, she enters her bed and asks Troiolo, "Shall I remove this? New brides are bashful the first night" [Spogliomi io? Le nuove spose / son la notte primiera vergognose.] Troiolo encourages her: "My soul (Anima mia), I beg you be naked in my arms just as my heart desires." Criseida then tells Troiolo to see how she casts off her shift. That whole night, as they lie in each others arms, they scarcely can believe they are not dreaming: "Hotti io in braccio, o sogno, o sei tu desso?" they each ask the other [Am I holding you in my arms, or am I dreaming; is it really you?]

If Cino da Pistoia, whose "La dolce vista e 'l bel guardo soave" Boccaccio incorporates into book 5 of the *Filostrato*, ever read this scene, he certainly would have savored its wit. Criseida's coquetry, as Branca calls it, is not only a *jeu d'amour* Boccaccio could have derived from *romanzi bretoni*;[47] her striptease is also the climax of a series of gestures whose provenance is the soul's reception of the phantasm generally and Dante's conception of Beatrice in particular. Criseida's cough is as much Beatrice's in paradise (*Par.* 16.13–15) as it is the Lady of Malehaut's in Gallehault's castle; her emphasis on Troiolo's royal station

---

47. *Filostrato*, ed. Branca, 854. Branca points to the *Tristano riccardiano* as an analogue.

recalls Beatrice's disapproval of "our petty nobility of blood," just as her disrobing reminds us that Dante had compared birthright's rank to "a mantle that soon shrinks" (*Par.* 16.1–16). Criseida's descent of the stairs to Troiolo, lit torch in hand, deftly plays off Dante's conceit of Beatrice as the angelic light of the intellect ("Donne ch'avete") that miraculously comes down from heaven to earth ("Tanto gentile"). When Troiolo calls Criseida "his soul," "the sole hope and good of my mind," we would not be surprised to find these words on Cino's own lips;[48] yet when he goes on to offer his metaphor of Criseida as star, the language of *stil novo* modulates into that of the *cantare*.[49]

Throughout the *Filostrato* Boccaccio juxtaposes carnal impulses and refined yearnings, high styles and popular forms; the sincerest and the most self-serving professions of love coexist in the same space. Though poised between the claims of the body and those of the mind, however, this space is not the site of aesthetic knowing, as I have argued that it is in the *Vita nuova*. We do not make a progress through the hierarchies of knowledge, passing from lower to higher and back again, to come to a full understanding of the nature of love. Nor is this space the site of parody, where the body mocks the mind's forms by perplexing them with the enigmas of flesh and blood. Boccaccio rather invokes the idea of rhetorical decorum and its method of presenting first one and then the other side of a proposition to let sight and thought argue their superiority without appearing to decide for either beforehand. This is a legitimate debate for Boccaccio, even though his narrator subverts the idea that the *Filostrato* will provide neutral ground on which to argue it. As we have seen, by attaching all pronouncements to the person who makes them, Boccaccio makes us attend to the question of motives. And because motives often answer the demands of both the body and the soul, we quickly discover that judgment and persuasion, far from being disinterested and distinctly consequent acts, may be conjunct and partisan from the start. Through his narrator's double desire to induce

---

48. In the same way, Troiolo's and Criseida's not knowing whether they dream or are awake recalls the role of the *spiritus phantasticus* in dreams.

49. As Branca notes (*Filostrato*, 854), even the dittology of "la stella del tuo bel viso splendido e lucente" is a traditional fixture of the *cantare*. This does not mean a "stilnovist" would ban such expressions from his poetic vocabulary: Guinizzelli's "Io voglio del ver la mia donna laudare," for instance, is a veritable catalog of roses, lilies, and other commonplaces that the *cantarini* were fond of comparing to their ladies, yet is a poem entirely in the new manner. Guinizzelli's *donna* in particular "shines and appears brighter than the morning star" [più che stella diana splende e pare].

Filomena to return and to upbraid her if she does not, Boccaccio testifies that in his mode of meaning we can no more assign priority to cognition or volition, to sight or sound, than we can determine whether Criseida's boudoir savoir faire burlesques the disrobing of the phantasm or is ennobled by it, or whether a French romance, a *stil novo canzone*, or a *cantare* lyric was its model. The world Boccaccio's characters play and die in already is the world of Melchizedek, Saladin, and the three rings (*Decameron*, 1.3), a tale, appropriately enough, told by Filomena, the dedicatee of the *Filostrato*.

The space that rhetoric opens between the truth and rightness of action on one side and the vagaries of accident and self-interest on the other parallels the space that the interpenetration of sense and intellect creates in the *Vita nuova* but is, as I say, very different from it. The ethic of love the "stilnovist" generates when he identifies his lady with the processes that recognize her as a supernal good is absolute and certain. Dante established the rectitude or improbity of his conduct by measuring it against Beatrice's embodiment of universal virtue. Even Cavalcanti could claim that the alternatives he posits as love's outcome—dying or loving someone else—are equally ethical and unconditional, for all their dark irony, since both are underwritten by the impossibility of any lady proving to be the transcendental beauty he initially takes her for. The witty defense Cino once sent to Dante to justify his falling in love again is a perfect case in point: since one and the same infinite Beauty has always bound him, Cino claims his love has always been constant, even when he "delights in whatever is like it in beauty in different women."[50]

Boccaccio's literary translation of rhetoric, by contrast, produces a circumstantial ethics whose morality is constituted by its refusal to prejudge what is moral. One acts by listening now to this and now to that argument, always taking into account the conditions at hand and the motives of the speaker. This stance of impartiality, whether sincere or a pose, amounts to a disposition Boccaccio maintains throughout his vernacular works; in almost all of them, we find the material and personal in human affairs shaping the abstract and typical and being shaped by them. It is this disposition, for example, that prompts Boccaccio in the *Teseida* first to translate Palemone and Arcita into emblems of the concupiscible and irascible appetites, and then to ask us to discriminate

---

50. I discuss this poem in *Dante's Aesthetics of Being*, 4–6.

between them. In the soul, one appetite cannot be divided from the other, since to want something is to choose the means to gain it. In life, however, things are not so clear-cut; Palemone and Arcita's mutual dependence becomes the source of strife and their differing fates. The *Teseida* therefore makes the case for their inseparableness and for their individuality.[51] For Boccaccio, in other words, rhetoric was more than a practical art whose resources he reproduced in his fiction; it was a mode of meaning. It was rhetoric's embrace of the hypothetical that led him to view history as a discourse somebody writes for some purpose. It was rhetoric's propensity to scrutinize principles through the lens of motives and occasions that enabled him to make Dante a spokesman for his changing social and cultural commitments. Through the counterpositionings of rhetoric Boccaccio developed the capacity to acknowledge the imperatives of the past and adjust them to meet the needs of the present; this flexibility was a habit of mind that made him Petrarch's disciple long before he really knew his preceptor's work.

Chaucer may have had special insight into the scope and power of Boccaccio's rhetorical vision since he appears to have known at least portions of the *Filocolo*. An arranged meeting between Florio and Biancifiore (*Filocolo*, 2.165–83) seems to have furnished many of the incidents Chaucer added to those that lead to the consummation of Troiolo and Criseida's love in the *Filostrato*. More intriguing for my argument, however, is the fact that many critics think a story in book 4 of the *Filocolo* was the source of "The Franklin's Tale." Menedon's narrative comprises the fourth of the thirteen love-questions Florio hears in the garden at Naples; I find it hard to resist imagining that Chaucer turned over the leaf and read Graziosa's *quistione* as well. If he did, a door to the *stil novo* opened for him—a door, though, that Boccaccio and Petrarch at the same time were shutting for good. If Chaucer saw how Fiammetta's abstract determinations had been personalized in the *proemio* of the *Filostrato*, he may have also sensed just how obsolescent those *canzoni* composed in what Dante had called "l'uso moderno" (*Purg.* 26.113) had become. Of course, by the time Chaucer visited Florence, the usages of the *Filostrato* had themselves lost some of their modernity; even when they were new, however, they declared the *stil novo* a style whose time had passed. If Chaucer connected the manner in which Graziosa and Fiammetta conduct their *quistione* with

---

51. I elaborate this reading of the *Teseida* in *The Cast of Character*, 107–17.

Guinizzelli's "dolci detti" and the Dante of "Donne ch'avete," he could see that the inevitability of change "in forme of speche"—a Dantesque observation he poignantly repeated in the *Troilus*—had begun to overtake the poet of the *Comedy* himself. But whether or not Chaucer read the passage in the *Filocolo*, he certainly did pay careful attention to the way Boccaccio had transformed the pro and con of rhetorical disputation into the double-purposed psychology of the narrator in the *Filostrato*. Even if Boccaccio's works did not make Chaucer aware of the historicity of Dante's poetics, we can be sure he was conscious of the challenge they posed to Dante's aesthetics from the way he shaped the narrator of the *Troilus*.

This extraordinary figure, whose extraction is quite Italian yet whose character is entirely Chaucerian, can trace his pedigree chiefly to the combination of two narrative strategies, one of which Chaucer took from the *Comedy*, the other from the *Filostrato*. By means of the first Chaucer constructed the commentator whose verdict as Christian and historian continually joins in debate with his compassion for the pain and joy of the lovers he loves. In this posture he is the child of Dante's division of himself into the pilgrim who hangs on Francesca's every word and the poet who condemns her (and through her, himself) because she was seduced by a language of love that echoes his own. But mediating between these extremes of retrospective "auctoritee" and readerly experience is the narrator's willingness to defer judgment, his constant reminders that we need to gauge actions against intentions, his inclination to take up the cause of those "falsly . . . apeired / Thorugh wikked tonges, be it he or she" (1.38–39). In his readiness to speak now for Troilus, now for Criseida, now for Pandarus, and now, when it seems necessary, against them, the narrator shows he is the fraternal, rather than the identical, twin of Filostrato.

Chaucer's narrator is like Boccaccio's in that the benefit of hindsight does not fix his response to the story he tells. The poet of the *Filostrato*, as we saw, capitalizes on history to prosecute his ulterior design. He uses his knowledge of Criseida's betrayal as a strategic instrument to present Filomena with the choice of being a madonna by contrast or whore by imitation. The narrator of the *Troilus* is just as invested in his poem as his Italian confrere, but his desires are not directed toward judging or prevailing upon anyone in particular. In fact he is so completely uncommitted, he commits himself to everyone possible. Thus he begs in his prologue not only for prayers from those who take pleasure in his efforts but from those in whom he evokes sorrow. In partaking for himself by taking the part of all the other characters, Chaucer's narrator restores to rhetoric the disinterested impartiality it was supposed to proceed from. His adoration of Criseyde's every virtue and regret for her faithlessness are not made servants of narrow self-concern, as in the *Filostrato;* instead they become point and counterpoint in a larger dialogue about the delight and distress of earthly love, a dialogue in which the narrator speaks with great force for each side. Precisely because the tears he weeps are tears of anger and tears of pity, he makes the past, like everything else in the poem, equivocal and multivocalic. Knowing what happened offers the moralist in the narrator strong reasons to fault Criseyde and to call on his audience to give up the vanity of this life; the same knowledge also gives the apologist in him sufficient cause to set these faults against her good qualities, from which, he suggests, they may stem, but which somehow remain untainted by her lapses. In his famous valedictory description of Criseyde, the narrator says

> She sobre was, ek symple, and wys withal,
> The best ynorisshed ek that myghte be,
> And goodly of hire speche in general,
> Charitable, estatlich, lusty, and fre;
> Ne nevere mo ne lakked hire pite;
> Tendre-herted, slydynge of corage.
>
> (5.820–25)

What Shakespeare said of Wolsey applies to Criseida here: her faults lie gently on her. Without question she is "slydynge of corage," but would she have been, as Donaldson aptly wondered, had she not been (perhaps too) charitable and tenderhearted?[52]

Unlike Filostrato, who reduces his Trojan surrogates to ventriloquists of his double-edged message to Filomena, Chaucer's narrator truly is a creature of the dialogic imagination. To be sure, he is not a full-fledged Bakhtinian mouthpiece through whom the diglossia of different social discourses is heard, but he is the organ Chaucer speaks through to give pitch and volume to a multiplicity of independent per-

---

52. E. Talbot Donaldson, "Criseide and Her Narrator," in *Speaking of Chaucer* (New York: Norton, 1970), 65–83.

spectives. I do not mean that in being all things to all people he is no less a product of his times than Boccaccio's speaker is of his. Certainly the narrator's comprehensive tolerance becomes more topical the more one relates it to the Merciless Parliament of 1386, the year in which Chaucerians customarily date the composition of the *Troilus*. Of particular note was the trial and execution of Nicholas Bembre, erstwhile mayor of London, in that year. After the peers had cleared him of the accusation of treason, the Lords Appellant called on two representatives of every London guild to testify against him. On the basis of charges as flimsy as his plot to change the name of London to New Troy, he was condemned to death and hanged. If a London poet writing about Troy wanted to place himself far from the fray, it would be politic of him to call for judgment and for mercy, for the restitution of their good name to those, "be it he or she," whom wicked tongues had falsely slandered.[53] But as a translation of the Italian tradition, Chaucer's narrator owes his ecumenicalism chiefly to his creator's reading Dante and Boccaccio in conjunction with one other. Indeed, Chaucer endows the narrator with enough facets to make us think, in a fanciful moment, that he formed him with something like Beatrice's "tre specchi" (*Par.* 2.97) in mind. In the mirror Chaucer held up to Boccaccio, however, he saw Dante: the ever more expansive contexts Chaucer brings to the story, which make Troilus and Criseida at one moment emblems of the philosophical debate between free choice and the necessities of fate, at another exemplary figures in a historical meditation on the virtues of pagans and the forlorn inevitability of their ruin, and at a third character witnesses in a trial about the ethical qualities of fiction, which ultimately finds for "sentence" and against "solas"— these perspectives all urge us to see the narrator's "litel ... tragedye" in the light of the *Comedy*. The mirror Chaucer held before Dante, though, gave back the image of Boccaccio; the continual shifting between and among views, which complicates our determining even the probability of truth, much less the manner in which we should act on it, Chaucer transported from the author of the *Filostrato* and the *Teseida*. In the

---

53. Besides tempering one's readiness to make Chaucer a wholesale supporter of the guilds, incidents such as Bembre's trial point to appreciable differences between Italian and English values. The duke of Gloucester's resentment of the mayor stemmed from the fact that a merchant had presumed to meddle in the affairs of state. Though Florentines were certainly capable of the same level of indignation, they would have been puzzled by its cause. See A. R. Myers, *London in the Age of Chaucer* (Norman: University of Oklahoma Press, 1972), 98–101.

Troilus, perhaps the most Boccaccian moment is one that gives us the greatest pause about our ability to reach incontestable judgments: when Criseida's infidelity is no longer open to doubt, she elicits Pandarus's hate, and Troilus's abiding love, and the emotional convulsions of the narrator, which corroborate both. The third mirror, of course, would be the *Troilus* itself, in which the intermingled images of the other two are reflected and joined to that Machaut-like, bookish figure who had been Chaucer's alter ego in earlier poems. Together they form a unique amalgam, one perfectly suited to mediate the concerns, centripetal and centrifugal at once, that the poem holds in taut resolution.

Readers of the *Troilus* often analyze, in C. S. Lewis's phrase, what Chaucer really did to the *Filostrato;* what the *Filostrato* did for Chaucer is an issue that has provoked far less extensive discussion.[54] This perhaps is not surprising; Lewis was right to say that Chaucer did not accept the ethos of Boccaccio's poem, and critics are right to define the changes he made. But while Chaucer undoubtedly deepened and refined that ethos, he did not eliminate it; frequently we find the amendments and reductions Lewis categorizes, which "medievalize" the *Troilus* by making it much more French, side by side with the Italian heterodoxies they temper. Love remains spiritual and carnal, a balance between sublime influence and self-gratification. More than anything else, their counterplay is Boccaccio's invention; it is what Chaucer took from the *Filostrato* and what prompted him to make the *Troilus* his most transcultural poem. In it he reads the tradition of *fin amour* he knew, from de Lorris to Deschamps, against Boccaccio's harder-edged love; in it he measures the bliss and disenchantments of both against the eternal love that moves the sun and stars of Dante's universe. At the very end of the *Troilus* the narrator invokes Mary, just as he had invoked Tesiphone at the start. The Fury is a fitting proleptic Muse for his "woful vers," since the tears he weeps in sorrow will mix with those he must weep in exasperation at the treachery and deceit he has to relate. Mary's double nature as virgin and mother inevitably evokes and subsumes Criseida's double role as lover and betrayer. In the light of the final juxtaposition of the two women, Criseida's faults admit of neither denial nor mitigation—so much so that even the narrator's

---

54. C. S. Lewis, "What Chaucer Really Did to the *Filostrato,"* in *Selected Literary Essays* (Cambridge: Cambridge University Press, 1969), 27–44.

uncertainty whether she had children in retrospect seems a dire indictment against her. But if Mary justifies a reader's angry verdict against Criseyde, Chaucer would expect his audience to remember that she also is "mayde and moder" of mercy and pity; she is the person to whom all the narrator's opening prayers for compassion for the ill-used must ultimately be addressed if they are to avail. Those who would defend Criseyde, and give her better refuge than she ever found in Troy, shelter her in Mary's name. Even when the *Troilus* turns from "worldly vanyte" and looks to an unchanging God, "oon, and two, and thre, eterne on lyve," we remain with the narrator, earthbound. And on earth, what we know of the absolute and the unequivocal cannot always secure our judgment of the provisional and the "slydynge." We have seen that the spirit, even the words, that close the poem are Dante's, but the tension that accompanies them and becomes the medium of their representation is Boccaccio's. In the triune God of Chaucer's invocation, in the Father, Son, and the Spirit that joins them in love, we see the paradigm of the love that Troilus, Criseyde, and Pandarus unknowingly emulate and inevitably fall short of. They are to be condemned for their transgressions; their failures merit our pity as well. It is in this tension, a tension that is both cultural and aesthetic, that Chaucer's Italian tradition begins.

6

Boccaccio, Chaucer, and Early Italian Humanism: The *De casibus virorum illustrium*

Over the next two chapters I want to offer an assessment of Chaucer's encounter with the Latin humanism of Boccaccio and Petrarch. The central focus of this chapter will be Boccaccio's *De casibus virorum illustrium*, whose short introduction I will assume Chaucer knew, both because Boccaccio's compendium was the guiding inspiration, if not the chief source, of "The Monk's Tale," and because I will guess that Chaucer, like Petrarch reading the *Decameron*, paid particular attention to the beginning of the work. In the next chapter, I will discuss the Latin Griselda, most likely the only text Chaucer knew from which he could assess Petrarch's humanism. Three large arguments will run through both chapters. The first is that Boccaccio's humanism is to a large extent Petrarchan. The accounts in the *De casibus* are riven with inconsistencies; even those that speak vehemently against tyranny endorse the hegemony of a deserving elite. The second argument is that Petrarch's humanism is no less divided in its allegiances than Boccaccio's. As a political narrative, his tale of Griselda is a justification of autocracy; as an ethical meditation, however, his story insists on the liberty and independence of the soul. My third argument is the outgrowth of the first two: Chaucer responded to Petrarch's and Boccaccio's humanism poetically; he translated their texts' contradictions much more than he endorsed or rejected their political or social ideologies.

The cultural topography of Boccaccio's *De casibus virorum illustrium* is difficult to chart, primarily because the discursive fields that traverse it are so diverse. At the start of his prologue, Boccaccio conflates literature and the political order in a remarkable way by juxtaposing the private space of his study against a cityscape grown rank and perfidious:

Exquirenti michi quid ex labore studiorum meorum possem forsan rei publice utilitatis addere, occurrere preter creditum multa; maiori tamen conatu in mentem sese ingessere principum atque presidentium quorumcunque obscene libidines, violentie truces, perdita ocia, avaritie inexplebiles, cruenta odia, ultiones armate precipitesque et longe plura scelesta facinora. Que cum ductu scelestium viderem nullo coercita freno evolantia undique, et inde honestatem omnem fedari publicam, iustitie sacratissimas leges solvi, labefactari virtutes omnes, et—quod infandum est—detestandis exemplis in mores impios ignare multitudinis ingenia trahi, ratus eo me a fortuna deductum quo appetebat intentio, festinus arripui calamum scripturus in tales. (1–2)[1]

[In asking myself what I might perhaps add from my scholarly exertions that might be of use to the state, many things beyond what I believed occurred to me; but my mind was struck with particular force by the obscene lusts of princes and rulers, their savage acts of violence, time lost to indolence, insatiable greed, bloody feuds, sudden vendettas, and a great many more wicked crimes. When I saw these things set in motion by the wicked, bridled by no rein and flying about everywhere, and the probity of the state thereby befouled, the most sacred laws of justice unknit, all virtues undermined, and— what is unspeakable—impious habits inculcated in the minds of the ignorant multitudes by their detestable examples, I realized that fortune had led me where my desire intended, and immediately seized my pen to write against such men.][2]

---

1. My text is *De casibus virorum illustrium*, ed. and trans. Pier Giorgio Ricci and Vittore Zaccaria, in *Tutte le opere di Giovanni Boccaccio*, ed. Vittore Branca, vol. 9 (Milan: Mondadori, 1983). References are cited by book, chapter, and sentence number in parentheses. I am translating from the second version of the *De casibus*, which Boccaccio published in 1373 or 1374. He had completed the first edition around 1360 but released it only in 1373: see Zaccaria's introduction to the Mondadori edition, xv–xx. See also his "Le due redazioni del 'De casibus,'" *Studi sul Boccaccio* 10 (1977–78): 1–26; Branca, *Boccaccio*, 109–10; Bergin, *Boccaccio*, 269–72. One cannot be sure which version Chaucer saw.

2. The earlier version of the *De casibus* opens in the following manner:

> As I was casting about for a means of doing some service to public government with my scholarly labors, I was particularly struck by the way in which great men conducted themselves. I saw how immoral they were and how vile they had become through filthy lust; they carried on without check, acting as if they had drugged Fortune into lasting sleep by herbs or incantations, and as if they had anchored their princedoms with iron supports to an adamantine rock. I saw that their attitude not

The commonplace analogy that likened the well-regulated state to the harmoniously disposed soul underlies these introductory remarks. To counter the ruin that dissolute and nefarious rulers have visited on the republic, however, Boccaccio does not invoke medievalized precepts from Aristotle's politics, even though he knew the *Policraticus* and Aquinas's *De regimine principum;* he offers instead the redemptive virtues that Petrarch would crystalize in his meditations on the *vita solitaria*.³ In contrast to the *Decameron*, where the *brigata* escaped civic

> only caused them to oppress other men with all their might, but also led them to rise up with a foolish kind of temerity even against the very Creator of all things. When I beheld all this I was stupefied.
>
> The translation is from Henry Ansgar Kelly, *Chaucerian Tragedy* (Cambridge: Brewer, 1997), 26. The changes Boccaccio made from first to second version are notable; chief among them is the conversion of lethargy into a civic vice. Instead of believing they had administered a sleeping potion to Fortune ("so[m]pnum perpetuum soporassent herbis aut cantato carmine"), the princes in the revised prologue are themselves "slumbering in idleness in lethal sleep," as Boccaccio will say in his next sentence. This "desidia" is then transferred to the masses, who model their behavior after that of their leaders. For Boccaccio, this dereliction of political responsibility is so great, it actually substitutes for the accusations of godlessness he leveled against the magnates in the first version. The increased separation of church and state in the second edition is, I think, an effect of Petrarch's influence on Boccaccio's humanism. Not only does it reinforce the distance Boccaccio puts between the *De casibus* and academic discussions of politics; when God appears later in the introduction (and in the account of Gualterius), he virtually serves as the principle of necessity Petrarch believed ruled the public realm.
>
> 3. In Boccaccio's day, the primary site for discussion of the political was the university. As a form of prudential knowledge, *scientia politica* was the culminating course of arts curriculum, whose subject was practical moral philosophy. By studying grammar and logic, one learned how to analyze the texts of the church fathers and classical moralists who taught self-discipline; by learning rhetoric, one learned how to rule oneself in relation to others. Politics subsumed both by focusing on the cultivation of the virtues necessary to rule the communal whole. Hugh of St. Victor thus neatly summarizes the branches of moral philosophy: "Practica [ars] dividitur in solitarium / monasticum, privatam / oeconomicam, et publicam / civilem (*Didiscalicon*, 2.19). For an excellent discussion of these and many other aspects of "political thought" in the Middle Ages, see Janet Coleman, "The Science of Politics and Late Medieval Academic Debate," in *Criticism and Dissent in the Middle Ages*, ed. Rita Copeland (Cambridge: Cambridge University Press, 1996), 181–214. Coleman suggests that "the real debate concerning politics as a 'science' in the late Middle Ages was between the academicians and civilian lawyers, who already in the thirteenth century were calling themselves 'politici'" (192). In this regard, it is important to recognize that Boccaccio distances himself from both sets of disputants. The political in the *De casibus* is literary; it is not a species of knowledge but the exercise of the moral imagination on the will. Its propaedeutic context does not consist of texts like Aristotle's *Categories, Posterior Analytics, Topics,* and *Rhetoric*, as was the case at Paris and Oxford, but Boccaccio's own earlier works and the medieval exemplum. Its scene is not the classroom or the notarial chamber but the forum that is the scholar's library. In each of these respects, Boccaccio again is more "Petrarchan" than not.

chaos by withdrawing to the fantasy world of a garden, Boccaccio here suggests that the humanist's cultivation of moral probity in the solitude of his cell *can* inoculate the city against ills every bit as infectious and deadly as the plague's:

> Nam, quid satius est quam vires omnes exponere, ut in frugem melioris vite retrahantur errantes, a desidibus sopitis letalis somnus excutiatur, vitia reprimantur et extollantur virtutes? (3)

> [For what is better than to exert all one's strength to bring back erring souls to enjoy a better life, to shake lethal sleep from those slumbering in idleness, by repressing vice and extolling virtue?]

Yet at the very moment that Boccaccio prepares to unsay the unspeakable effects ("quod infandum est") that the grandees' degeneracy has produced in the minds of the masses, inconsistencies and contradictions infiltrate his efforts to articulate values that support what we might call a communal humanism:

> Nec me terruit maiorum nostrorum in hos ingentia vidisse volumina, et illa novisse stili suavitate et pondere sententiarum meis literulis preponenda plurimum, cum meminerim non nunquam rudem voculam excivisse non nullos quos tonitrua movisse non poterant. Bona igitur pace talium, quo inpellit dicendi impetus tendam, si forsan saxea hec corda tenui spiritu oris mei in salutem suam mollire saltem paululum queam. Sane cum tales, obscenis sueti voluptatibus, difficiles animos demonstrationibus prestare consueverint, et lepiditate hystoriarum capi non nunquam, exemplis agendum ratus sum eis describere quid Deus omnipotens, seu—ut eorum loquar more—Fortuna, in elatos possit et fecerit. (4–6)

> [Nor was I afraid to see the prodigious volumes that our forebears wrote against them or to know that their graceful style and weighty thought make these books far superior to my jottings, once I remembered that sometimes the poor, homespun voice has awakened some whom thunder could not move. Therefore I bid them good day; I will direct the impetus of my speech where it seeks to go, and see whether I can perhaps soften, at least a bit, their stony hearts for their good with the tender breath of my mouth. Since, of course, those

grown used to obscene pleasures are wont to follow rigorously reasoned arguments with difficulty and sometimes are taken by the charm of stories, I have decided to make use of examples to describe what almighty God—or, to speak in their manner, Fortune—can do and has done against the high and mighty.]

In order to distance himself from the despots he will chronicle, Boccaccio takes special care to profess his humbleness. His "spiritus" is tender, his language plain, a *sermo humilis* to mollify "saxea . . . corda." At the same time, as if to deflate the vanity of iniquitous sovereigns by denying them title to the magnificence they craved, he acknowledges the prodigiousness only of the volumes that have been written about them. Indeed, the degeneracy of the highborn is so catastrophic, it seems to have contaminated greatness itself; Boccaccio feels compelled to dissociate himself even from the "stili suavitate et pondere sententiarum" that graced the "ingentia . . . volumina" of his predecessors.

These effusions of modesty work hard to mute the emulation that the topos presupposes; they make no effort, however, to mask either their crafted eloquence or the high status Boccaccio thinks such rhetorical mastery confers on him. "Cum meminerim non nunquam rudem voculam excivisse non nullos quos tonitrua movisse non poterant": the attention-catching deployment of negative expressions—"non numquam" for sometimes, "non nullos" for some, both of which can be dropped from the clause—paradoxically certifies Boccaccio's diffidence by conspicuously displaying the stylistic polish the sentence forswears. Boccaccio then further warrants his want of pretension by appropriating the language of the least of the apostles. But the spirit that moves him to move stony hearts, he makes clear, is at least as much Roman as it is Christian. Boccaccio's purpose is to persuade princes; accordingly, he adopts a *modus scribendi* that appeals rather more to the protocols of Ciceronian oratory than to the mysteries of biblical allegory, which is what Paul is talking about when he contrasts revelations inscribed on the fleshy tables of the heart and the stony blindness of Jews whose eyes see not (2 Cor. 3). Instead of saying that his simple words cloak deep truths, Boccaccio invokes *teneritas* ("tenui spiritu oris mei"), the attenuated mode of gentle gracefulness, just as the precepts of the *genera dicendi* advised the speaker who needed to win his audience's ear.⁴ To evangelical humility Boccaccio has added the rhetor's sincerity. As a result, at the same time that he lowers his language, thereby acknowledging how far he is beneath the potentates he writes for, Boccaccio invests himself in classical authority, not only raising himself far above the "ignare multitudinis ingenia," but elevating his discourse to the point where, like Anchises committing Rome to the task of pulling down the pride of the mighty, he can address contemporary rulers on equal terms.⁵ Though the words Boccaccio uses to characterize his writing are socially coded ("rudem voculam," "tenui spiritu"), they do not consign him to a single class, because they simultaneously identify him as commoner and member of a cultural elite.

Such divided commitments crisscross the *De casibus* from start to finish: they are virtually a signature of Boccaccio's humanism. Whenever he wrote in the vernacular, Boccaccio hesitated to translate his sense of literary worthiness into social terms. In the *Decameron*, for instance, whose cognomen, "*prencipe* Galeotto," seems in retrospect one of many signals that mark it the Italian counterpart of the *De casibus*, Boccaccio took care to insulate his stories from history by establishing an area of play in which he could explore the dangers that literature posed to the social and political order.⁶ Once Boccaccio undertook to write in Latin about real princes for the edification of their peers, however, his goal was to make the poet's engagement with history part of public dis-

---

4. In this regard, one might add that the exempla Boccaccio will tell, which counterbalance the "detestand[a] exempl[a]" of the magnates, achieve a double-voicedness that again is more rhetorical than it is allegorical. The wreck and ruin of the puissant are not shadow-bearing prefaces of salvation history, as they would be if Paul had written the *De casibus*; putting aside philosophical demonstration for the charm of stories ("lepiditate hystoriarum"), Boccaccio instead constitutes the down and up of Fortune's wheel as a metaphor of his reproof of vice and commendation of virtue.

5. Anchises' injunctions to the caretakers of the Roman *imperium* precisely constitute the lesson that the *De casibus* wants to teach: "tu regere imperio populos, Romane, memento / (hae tibi erunt artes), pacique imponere morem, / parcere subiectis et debellare superbos" [You, O Roman, remember to rule nations by your authority; these shall be your arts, and to impose the ways of peace, to spare the defeated and make war against the proud] (6.851–53). Virgil creates an extraordinary collision of words whose semantic vectors move in opposite directions in order to present power as an agent for peace; the analogous conjunction in Boccaccio's work is its mixture of elevated and humble registers.

6. On the stylistic parallels between the *Decameron* and the *De casibus*, see Giuseppe Chiecchi, "Sollecitazioni narrative nel *De casibus Virorum Illustrium*," *Studi sul Boccaccio* 19 (1990): 103–49.

course. When the venue and the subject matter changed—when his study replaced the rooms that confined the women for whom he wrote his *cento novelle*, and historical narratives about the fall of the great, told with the civic-mindedness of a Livy, replaced fictions that pandered to desire—Boccaccio dared to make his political, cultural, and literary values interchangeable. In the event, his allegiances were continually splintered. An outspoken opponent of tyranny, he nonetheless held the artisanal classes in seigniorial contempt; Florentine of the middle stratum, he disdained the mercantile habits of mind of his fellow citizens with a hauteur worthy of an intellectual autocrat; author of a vernacular "merchant epic," tireless supporter of Dante, he firmly believed in the superiority of Latin as the language of *civitas*.

Boccaccio began the *De casibus* in the mid-1350s, a decade during which he undertook various important diplomatic missions for Florence; no doubt this service prompted him to think of his work as a new way to incorporate literature into the civic discourse of the commune. Perhaps this is why Boccaccio framed the stories of the *De casibus* by pretending that its famous figures appeared before him as he sat at his desk and asked that he record their sad downfalls for posterity. By making the imaginary an integral part of his mise-en-scène, Boccaccio indicated not only that the illustrious cohabit two worlds, one literary, the other historical, but that each was a necessary condition for the other. But by 1373, when Boccaccio issued a revised and expanded version of the *De casibus*, he had long since discovered that his aesthetic and political convictions were not as fungible as he had hoped. After the disappointments of the 1360s, he had, I think, moved closer to Petrarch's view: in the arena of public affairs, all was predetermined and the most one could do was suffer one's fate patiently; only in the privacy of the study was an individual free to will into being the autonomous moral soul. The dangers of the day had forced the literary imagination to retreat again, not, as in the *Decameron*, to the fictional consolations of stories told in gardens, but to the instructing stringencies of codex, candle, and quill in the scholar's workshop.[7]

---

7. Boccaccio's political pessimism late in life is clear in the epistle he wrote in 1373 when he dedicated the revised *De casibus* to Mainardo de' Cavalcanti. Boccaccio describes how he searched for an illustrious patron for his book; but when he thought of eminent churchmen, such as Cardinal Albornoz or Pope John XXII, he realized that they had grown so corrupt, not one would be appropriate; nor would any of the emperors or kings, among whom Boccaccio includes Edward III, "serus Brittanus, elatus novis successibus" [puffed up by his recent successes], against France. Almost in Nietzschean

We simplify matters too much, therefore, if we make Boccaccio exclusively the *defensor Florentiae libertatis* and set him against a Petrarch who is solely the official mouthpiece for Viscontian despotism. Part of Boccaccio the humanist—a large part—is a member of the Petrarchan academy, and it is the humanist Boccaccio, we should remember, whom Chaucer would have heard about, or met, when he was in Florence. In order to support these arguments, I want to offer an analysis of perhaps the most political narrative in the *De casibus*, the account of Walter of Brienne, duke of Athens, who was tyrant of Florence from 1342 to 1343.

Boccaccio prefaces his history of Gualterius by inventing an arresting scene: amid an innumerable troop of men bewailing their fate, Boccaccio sees Dante Alighieri coming toward him.

[E]t venientem cernam clarissimum virum et ampliissimis laudibus extollendum Dantem Aligherii, poetam insignem. Cuius cum reverendam faciem atque conspicua patientia refulgentem aspexi, surrexi illico et obvius factum inqui:—Quid, civitatis nostre decus eximium, has inter lacrimas dolentium merito spectabilis mansuetudine veteri, gradum trahis? (9.23.6–7)

[And I saw Dante Alighieri, the most illustrious man and famous poet, worthy of the greatest praise. When I saw his revered face glowing with conspicuous forbearance, I arose and went to him and said: "Why, O great glory of our city, do you walk among these tears of the sorrowful, you who are justly regarded for your antique patience and meekness?"]

---

despair, "nausea quadam vexatus," he had nearly decided to commit his book to the hands of fortune when God took pity on it and caused Boccaccio to recognize that he would rather dedicate his work to a friend than to a prince, however splendid he might be. And just as this thought came to his mind, so did Mainardo's name. Cavalcanti's past kindnesses, the fact that Boccaccio held Mainardo's son Carlo at his baptism, his support of men devoted to study, his distinguished lineage, all made him the ideal dedicatee. These are private and personal rather than public virtues; the values that shape Boccaccio's work, as well as its tone, are Petrarch's.
 One cannot tell whether Chaucer read this dedication to Mainardo. It did circulate separately and came to be attached to the earlier version of the *De casibus;* in the fourteenth century manuscripts that have survived, however, it is lacking.

"Is it that you want," Boccaccio continues, "that I should write about your own fate: how despite your distinguished birth and composition of the most memorable works you were exiled by ungrateful Florence and died in foreign parts?" If that is the case, "You know, O excellent father *(pater optime)*, that my abilities are too weak to shoulder such a task." Dante, however, replies that his concern is quite otherwise:

> Siste, fili mi, tam effluenter in laudes meas effundere verba, et te tam parcum tuarum ostendere . . . Verum non ille michi nunc animus quem tu reris, nec tanquam a Fortuna victus describar advenio, sed fastidiens civium nostrorum socordiam, ne illatorem, perpetui eorum dedecoris preterires, ostensurus accessi. Ecce, igitur, vide postergantem me domesticam pestem et inexplicabilem florentino nomini labem. Hunc, moresque eius et casum, si quid michi debes, describas volo, ut pateat posteri quosque expellant quousque suscipiant cives tui. (9.23.7–10)
>
> [Stop, my son, pouring out such a flow of words in my praise and showing how sparing you are of your own . . . My mind is not at all set on what you think: I come not so that I might be described as overcome by Fortune; rather, hating the negligent inactivity of our citizens, I have appeared so that you do not pass by in silence one who brought them everlasting shame. Look, then, and see behind me that homebred plague and inexpungible disgrace to the name of Florence. His habits and fall I want you to describe, if you owe me anything, so that it will be clear in ages to come whom it is your citizens expel and whom they clasp to themselves.]

Boccaccio was about to answer, but Dante had already vanished ("sed iam ab oculis abierat"). He then turned and saw Gualterius, the once deadly tyrant of Florence, who approached with "brows lowered, eyes set on the ground, face lugubrious, so soul-sad and vigorless from lament, you would scarce say he was the person you saw. O how changed he was from the man who first had dared with treachery to trample on the free necks of Florentines" (9.23.11–12) [Qui quidem, demissa fronte, deiectis in terram oculis, lugubri facie, adeo remisso animo et exhausto vigore querulus incedebat, ut non eum dicas quem videras. O quam mutatus ab illo qui primus ausus est dolo liberas Florentinorum calcare cervices!].

Certainly Boccaccio conjured up this tableau in order to contrast the poet and the despot: unshaken by exile, Dante radiates dignity because he would not compromise the principles of civic liberty ("civitatis nostre decus eximium"); Gualterius, who suppressed them, is all hangdog pusillanimity ("illatorem perpetui eorum dedecoris"). Yet to identify Dante for his "conspicua patientia" and "mansuetudo vetus" is startling; patience and meekness, from whatever age, were hardly the qualities that marked the man. Temererity seems a more appropriate trait for Boccaccio to have chosen to emphasize: to cite only one instance among the many that he knew, Dante did not hesitate to castigate Henry VII for delaying his attack against the hydra-headed monster that Florence had become.[8] As he had in the *Trattatello*, Boccaccio has bent the historical record far enough to force us to ask why. One reason is clear: he wants no one to mistake Dante for the "queruli" he writes about. Though as much a victim of fortune's rebuffs as any of them, Dante has no need to secure his fame by lamenting the history of his own wreck. A less apparent reason is that Boccaccio wants his readers to take Dante as a prior version of himself. Just as in the prologue to the *De casibus* a public-minded Boccaccio had chastised the "perdita ocia" of princes (*Prohemium*, 1), his Dante here would provoke Florence to rouse itself from civic torpor by rebuking the hateful neglectfulness ("fastidiens civium nostrorum socordium") that once had invited and welcomed Walter of Brienne's tyranny.

Underlying Dante's validation of the republican allegiances of the *De casibus*, however, is a scripting of fatherhood and sonship that is at least as hierarchic and conservative, politically and aesthetically, as it is associational and transgressive. "Pater optime," Boccaccio says to Dante; "Fili mi," Dante says in response; with this paternal benediction, Dante assumes his place in a household crowded with progenitors, among whom we find Boccaccio's own father and, greater than all of them, Petrarch.

---

8. The letter is dated April 17, 1311. For a recent assessment of the political allegory of these epistles, see Lino Pertile, "Dante Looks Forward and Back: Political Allegory in the Epistles," *Dante Studies* 115 (1997): 1–17. Pertile points to the pronounced reactionary character of these letters; they are aimed at precisely the *gente nova* whom Boccaccio celebrates in the *Decameron*. Boccaccio mentions the letters to Henry in the *Trattatello;* throughout this work Dante appears as a man whose passionate devotion to his commitments hardly allowed him to suffer injustice patiently. A further example: Dante did not hesitate to write to the cardinals in conclave at Carpentras to advise them what sort of pope they should choose to succeed Clement V. This Epistle (Ep. 8) was copied in a manuscript Boccaccio owned.

Just before Dante's appearance, Boccaccio had told the story of Jacques de Molay, grand master of the Templars, who was burned at the stake on March 18, 1314. The great wealth that the Templars had acquired, not without contaminating the virtue and spirituality that distinguished the order when it was new and poor, had caught the avaricious eye of Philip the Fair. The French king accused the knights of denying Christ and of engaging in idolatry; ignoring established judicial procedure, he then engineered the torture and slow immolation of a number of them. As their leader, de Molay had been imprisoned separately; at the urging of Pope Clement V, he admitted in a moment of weakness to some of the charges that had been brought against him, knowing that the king had promised he would be freed if he did. But when the time came for him to confirm his confession, Jacques renounced it in plain sight of the king, "with intrepid and constant heart." He soon suffered the same excruciating death as his fellow Templars.

Boccaccio describes the moving denouement of this sad drama with great precision; he heard about it, he says, from his own father, who told him that he had witnessed the grand master's last hours ("et se his testabatur interfuisse rebus," 9.21.22).[9] Boccaccio di Chellino was in Paris at the time, "a businessman engaged in increasing his household resources through honest labor" [ut aiebat Boccaccius, genitor meus, qui tunc forte Parisius negotiator honesto cum labore rem curabat augere domesticam]. Boccaccio thus notarizes his account by deferring to his father, whose oral testimony authenticates its truthfulness; at the same time, Boccaccio takes noticeable pains to discriminate between his father's honorable acquisition of wealth and the greed that equally shamed Philip and the Templars. Both the deference and the distinction are acts of filial piety: Boccaccio "fils," who would gain fame by writing about the illustrious but is too humble to be confused with them, attaches himself to Boccaccio "père," who works to make money but remains uncorrupted by it. Yet the very fact that Boccaccio felt the need to publicly vouch for his father's probity hints at an underlying tension

---

9. For Ricci, the elder Boccaccio's presence as an oracular witness is certain: see his note (1055); Branca is less sure (*Boccaccio*, 4), primarily because, as he demonstrates fully in *Boccaccio medievale*, 2d ed. (Milan: Sansoni, 1996), 235–38, Boccaccio took many details from the chronicle of Giovanni Villani. For me, the actual presence of Boccaccino is not really what is at stake here; indeed, the fact that Boccaccio has introduced his father is all the more striking because he relied on Villani.

between them. It is, of course, tempting to see the emphasis on the "honesty" of the senior Boccaccio's labor as his offspring's way of negotiating his illegitimacy. Boccaccio, however, is not Edmund; whatever distance we sense he interposes between himself and his parent is there not because he resents his birth but because the repute a merchant can gain for his fair dealing, while of no small value, cannot secure the fame that Boccaccio covets. That prize only the assiduous industry of the writer can procure.[10]

How much familial standing and economic respectability will have to defer to artistic authority becomes apparent in the homily in praise of patience ("Auctor patientiam commendat et suadet," 9.22) that Boccaccio appended to the history of de Molay. Antiquity provides many famous instances of perseverance in suffering, but neither an Anaxarchus nor a Scaevola ever showed greater resolution than the Templars who endured their agonizing auto-da-fé. Who will say, Boccaccio wonders, that he marvels at the patience of those condemned to die in days gone by if he has seen that of men of today? ("Quid inquient de patientia suppliciorum veterum mirabundi, si nostrorum inspexerint?" 9.22.7). Learn, then, he urges his readers, to imitate the Templars' example; heed the admonishments of resignation and forbearance and a virile strength will support you and make you disdain feminine fickleness ("Discite suis monitis virile robur assumere, et levitatem dedignari femineam," 9.22.11).

---

10. Implicit in the tension that marks Boccaccio's relation with his father here are the competing claims of oral and written testimony as documentary evidence in the later Middle Ages. In acknowledging the relative status of both, Boccaccio epitomizes the phenomenon of simultaneity in the *De casibus*, whereby he confirms and revises his commitments at the same time. Boccaccino's testimony is oral: on the one hand, it authenticates his son's account of de Molay; on the other, it survives its own assertion only because Boccaccio has inscribed it in the history. Writing makes the oral available to posterity; for this reason, Dante's poetry gives him greater fame than Boccaccino's good name. In fact, however, merchants were writers in Boccaccio's day; see Christian Bec, *Les marchands écrivains: Affaires et humanisme à Florence 1375–1434* (Paris: Mouton, 1967). Viewed culturally, by associating his father and orality Boccaccio attempts to distinguish his Latin compilation from the vernacular *ricordanze* and chronicles businessmen produced, which were also highly moral but were concerned more with the cultivation of commercial than civic virtues. As such, Boccaccio's distinction inscribes its own contradiction in much the same way that the fame that Dante's written poetry brought him is essentially something "spoken"—*fama*, talk, good repute. On the interpenetration of orality and written culture, see Brian Stock, *The Implications of Literacy: Written Language and Models of Interpretation in the Eleventh and Twelfth Centuries* (Princeton: Princeton University Press, 1983); and most recently Janet Coleman, *Public Reading and the Reading Public in the Late Medieval England and France* (Cambridge: Cambridge University Press, 1996).

This exhortation, which stands as prelude to Dante's entrance, also prepares for Boccaccio's acknowledgment of him as father. Dante's face shines with the patience Boccaccio has just praised; his poetry, a labor of heroic persistence, has gained him a renown ("poetam insignem") that eclipses the elder Boccaccio's, whose own good name, certified by his testimony of de Molay's fortitude, is also the fruit of truthful language. Yet even as Boccaccio gently ushers his father from the paternal stage, without repudiating him in any way, he also moves away from the Dante whom he now addresses as "pater optime." The same sermon on patience also makes legible Boccaccio's surprise, reflected in his questions, when he sees Dante, "merito spectabilis mansuetudine veteri," among the likes of the very Philip who made the Templars martyrs to his rapacity.[11] If we take "vetus" in the phrase I just quoted to mean something like "old-school," we can perhaps say that Boccaccio sees Dante as Dante saw his own ancestor Cacciaguida. But the context makes it clear that the words "mansuetudine veteri" connect Dante to the ancients, whose capacity for resoluteness ("patientia suppliciorum veterum") Boccaccio had just qualified. In the same way that his commendation of his father's labor was real, but conditional, so Boccaccio's commendation of the poet's mildness is heartfelt but limited by the antiquity and by the femininity that he has just associated it with.

In the *De casibus*, however, Dante's "mansuetude," as Chaucer would have called it, is not primarily an indication of character.[12] While sensual love may have overly swayed the youthful poet, the mature man scorned "levitas feminea." The lightness Boccaccio links to old "mansuetudo" is rather a social and cultural trope.[13] Though clearly

---

11. Boccaccio implicitly asks his audience to compare as well Dante's heated denunciations of "il novo Pilato," as he calls Philip in the *Comedy* for his depredation of the Templars (*Purg.* 20.91–93), with the more temperate counsel of patient resolution he derives from de Molay's experience in the *De casibus*.

12. In *The Canterbury Tales* (I.654), the Parson translates "mansuetude" as "debonairetee": "The remedie agayns Ire is a vertu that men clepen mansuetude, that is debonairetee; and eek another vertu, that men callen patience or suffrance." The connotations of gentle acceptance, mildness, and restraint are precisely what made Dione call the women he addresses in the *Decameron* "mansuete mie donne" (10.10.1). Though the Parson goes on to define "debonairetee" as a quality that men sometimes are endowed with by nature, it is clear that he, like Boccaccio, feels it necessary to save the concept by masculinizing it.

13. Boccaccio again distances himself from Dante when he puts the tag "siquid michi debes" in his mouth. Dante's Virgil had adopted this phrase, which itself alludes to Dido's "si bene quid de te merui" (*Aeneid*, 4:318), when he addresses Ulysses in *Inferno* 26. Virgil speaks to Ulysses instead of Dante because the Greek hero perhaps would scorn the lowliness of the Italian language. Boccaccio, I would argue, re-creates the clash between vernacular and classical idioms but reverses Dante's valuation of each.

beneficial, Dante's concern for the well-being of the republic will seem self-involved and driven by the passions of his exile, especially if we compare it to Petrarch's more disinterested, philosophical command of himself and his pursuit of fame through study. Though undoubtedly virtuous, Dante's vernacular, the language he acquired without any rule from his nurse (*De vulgari eloquentia*, 1.2), could never have the weight or mature virility that Petrarch had given Latin, the language he had astonishingly reinvigorated by marrying classical elegance to Christian morality.[14]

At the beginning of the eighth book of the *De casibus*, Boccaccio relates that he had sunk into such torpor and sloth, he abandoned himself to complete indolence ("in amplissimum ocium") and fell into a sleep so profound he appeared even to himself to be one of the unmoving dead. After he awakened, still drowsy and propping himself up on his elbow, he asked himself why he foolishly persisted in burdening himself with unremitting work ("assiduo . . . labore") by writing the *De casibus*. The palm of fame he thought he would win is vanity; even if everyone now or in years to come were to sing paeans to his name alone, what good would such celebrity do him when he is dead? No one will know what he looked like; many others will go by his name;[15] he is actually toiling for others as much as for himself. Better to spend the short time that remains by giving himself to the pleasures of the moment (8.1.1–4).

While indolence ("desidia") sought to persuade him with these words and others like them, Boccaccio again lay his head on his pillow, when suddenly there appeared standing before him

> nescio quibus missum ab oris, hominem astitisse aspectu modestum et moribus, venusta facie ac miti placidoque pallore conspicua, virenti laurea insignitum et pallio amictum regio, summa reverentia dignum. (8.1.5)

---

14. Boccaccio discusses the greater distinction of learned languages in his refutation of those chatterboxes who garrulously deny the worth of rhetoric in book 6 of the *De casibus* (13). One should recall as well Boccaccio's belief that the *Comedy* would have carried greater gravity if Dante had written it in Latin; see chapter 4, note 26.

15. In his refutation, Petrarch calls this argument particularly ridiculous. Why then would Boccaccio make it? I find it hard not to see in his concern another instance of Boccaccio's simultaneous affirmation of and separation from his father, with whom he shared his name.

[a man, sent from who knows what region, modest in mien and manner, whose face was graceful and conspicuous for its mild and gentle pallor; he was distinguished by green laurel and clothed in a royal cloak. He was worthy of the highest reverence.]

The figure remained silent; when Boccaccio had shaken himself completely awake, reopened his eyes, and looked more carefully, he recognized that before him stood Petrarch, "optimum venerandumque preceptorem meum," whose admonition ("cuius monitus") always spurred him to virtue and whom he esteemed above all others once he was no longer a youth (8.1.6). Petrarch then delivers a long speech in which he chastises Boccaccio's sloth, refutes each of his arguments about fame, and revives his determination to complete the *De casibus*.

Petrarch's reproof obviously had its effect: Boccaccio's own commendation of the Templars' determination amid doubt and tribulation in book 9 ("Discite suis monitis") reformulates the advice his master gives here. The thematic similarity of the passages will also spur the reader to recall Petrarch's appearance and to measure Dante's against it. Boccaccio goes to Dante as soon as he sees his "revered face shining with conspicuous patience" ("conspicua patientia"); when he saw Petrarch, he was struck by the pleasing elegance of his preceptor's face, conspicuous for its mild paleness ("miti placidoque pallore conspicua"). Dante is called "poetam insignem"; Petrarch's poetic laurels likewise marked him out as "insignitum." These resemblances obviously equate the poets insofar as they are able to attract Boccaccio's regard; they do not, however, conceal the differences between the men and what they say. For all his distinction, Dante comes amid an endless troop of grumblers: "Cum nec numero dolentium finis appareat, et venientem cernam clarissimum virum . . ." (9.23.6). Petrarch appears alone, unconnected with the unfortunate great who are Boccaccio's subject. Although Dante does not want Boccaccio to write about his own fate, he nevertheless introduces it into the lesson he wants Boccaccio to emphasize: the tyrant Walter personifies the kind of stranger Florence invites to lead it, Dante the kind of citizen it banishes. By contrast Petrarch's indignation transcends the personal. He does not materialize to urge on Boccaccio a moral his own misfortunes exemplify but rather to insist that he finish a book that makes ethical demonstration, whether political or individual, possible.

Both men visit Boccaccio to enjoin him to overcome lethargy. The idleness his Dante excoriates, however, is civic; he clearly remains the poet of the city, still moved by its perturbations. His patience, we realize, is distilled from the tumult of earthly involvements he continues to feel. The torpor Boccaccio's Petrarch defeats is deeper, more fundamental. He knows that long before the path to virtuous fame passes through the hurly-burly of the *piazza della Signoria*, a man must gain the self-mastery that comes from disciplining the soul in private. This Petrarch is not without his political attachments, as his "royal mantle" acknowledges.[16] But Boccaccio has entirely subsumed the public in the private man. He is the exemplar of humanism, the poet-scholar who appears in Boccaccio's study because that is the fit place for him to convince his disciple that one becomes great not in "feminine" dissipation ("voluptatibus deditus"), as Boccaccio had resolved, but by manfully submitting oneself to the soul-enriching rigors of reading and writing, which cause the body to grow beautiful ("venusta") by growing pale through devotion to learning.

Boccaccio endorses this ascetic practice of the aesthetics of selfhood, which anticipates Foucault's in many respects, by representing Petrarch as his Lady Philosophy. His numinous advent echoes hers: just as Boccaccio seemed to see a man standing before him in his study ("Sed ecce visum est michi . . . hominem astitisse," 8.1.5), so the imprisoned Boethius suddenly became aware of a woman who seemed to stand above his head ("adstitisse mihi supra verticem visa est mulier"). Just as Petrarch's visage evokes the greatest reverence in Boccaccio ("summa reverentia dignum"), so Philosophy's countenance filled Boethius with the utmost awe ("mulier reverendi admodum vultus").[17] Like Petrarch, Philosophy will argue that justice abides not in the

---

16. Petrarch's "pallium regium" refers to the mantle that King Robert of Naples gave him to wear at his coronation at Rome. It must also have carried ironic overtones Boccaccio both muted and probably meant Petrarch to catch: how different the standards of royalty Petrarch has known, first King Robert, now the tyrant archbishop Giovanni Visconti. Still, it is significant to note that Boccaccio's portrait of Petrarch, composed in the heyday of his disillusionment with his master's decision to remain in Milan, remains completely flattering.

17. *The Consolation of Philosophy*, 1.pr.1. I quote from Boethius, *The Consolation of Philosophy*, ed. and trans. S. J. Tester, Loeb Classical Library (Cambridge: Harvard University Press, 1973). As Joachim Gruber points out, Boethius uses the word "adstitisse" to communicate that Philosophy's advent is godlike. See *Kommentar zu Boethius De Consolatione Philosophiae* (Berlin: Walter De Gruyter, 1978), 58. After Philosophy dispels some of Boethius's misery, he again looks at her; now he recognizes who she is by looking at her face ("faciem," 1.pr.3), just as Boccaccio recognizes Petrarch. Boccaccio's lament at the start of book 8 nicely corresponds to Boethius's self-pitying elegiacs, which open the *Consolation;* like Petrarch, Philosophy upbraids Boethius for his lethargy ("lethargum," 1.pr.2).

marble halls of the senate but in the single mind that is willing to fight for it; she girds Boethius for this struggle to return to his "true country" by reminding him that he once was a "man who, nourished with my milk, brought up on my food, went forth with the strength of a virile soul" [Tune ille es, . . . qui nostro quondam lacte nutritus nostris educatus alimentis in virilis animi robor evaseras] (1.pr.2). For Boccaccio, Petrarch clearly is Philosophy, but in man's form. His face may be "mitis," "placidus," and "venusta," but the objurgation ("obiurgatio") he delivers against neglectfulness has nothing Boccaccio could call womanly about it. He is entirely composed; he speaks without a hint of the anger Philosophy shows when she sees the Muses of Poetry, nor do his rebukes carry the emotional voltage of self-vindication that crackles in Dante's. Instead of mother's milk, a standard figure for the vernacular, Boccaccio has Petrarch offer more substantial fare: a robust rhetoric, founded on the ethics of the classics and fortified by Christian virtue, that prompts a man to honor the obligations he owes to himself so that he may be able to discharge those he owes to his city. Because he does, he, not Dante, stands forth as the greater father in Boccaccio's paternal order.[18]

Whenever the privileges of blood, political temperament, and poetic authority are simultaneously asserted, the mix will be volatile. Boccaccio's elevation of Petrarch does not cancel his commitment to Dante. As we have seen, even before Boccaccio recognizes Petrarch, he knows he is in the presence of someone "summa reverentia dignum." This phrase repeats Dante's description of Cato's appearance on the shores of Purgatory:

vidi presso di me un veglio solo,
degno di tanta reverenza in vista,
che più non dee a padre alcun figliuolo.

(1.31–33).

---

18. When Boccaccio says that Petrarch is the man whom he esteemed above all others once he was no longer a youth, his qualification again illustrates how he positions himself between his two poetic fathers. In the *Trattatello*, written about the same time as the *De casibus*, we have already seen Boccaccio misinterpret for his own ends Dante's assessment of the *Vita nuova* in the *Convivio*; now he invokes Dante's trope of passing from passionate youth to the more sober pursuits of maturer years to establish Petrarch's superiority to him. Boccaccio's strategy is as contradictory here as it is when he invokes Lady Philosophy to establish the virility of Petrarch's language.

[I saw close to me an old man alone, worthy in his looks of such great reverence that no son owes more to his father.]

In the *Comedy*, Cato's actions underscore the need for the total reformation of the relationships that Dante invokes. His reproof of Virgil's appeal to him in the name of Marcia shows that no familial bond can have any hold on the soul that declares itself ready to become Jesus' bride;[19] his dispersal of the souls rapt by Casella's song—a scene itself laced with references to the beginning of the *Consolation*—shows that no earthly art can furnish nourishment for the sodality of saints. The scandal of Cato's very presence as guardian of Purgatory is perhaps the most dramatic way Dante signals his belief that the only city in which liberty prevails is that "Rome where Christ is Roman" (*Purg.* 32.102). In each of these respects, Petrarch can more or less comfortably be identified with Cato. But the Cato who mattered for Petrarch and Boccaccio both was Lucan's Cato, the man who so despised tyranny, he took his life rather than submit to it. As long as Petrarch continued to reside with the Viscontis, Boccaccio could ask him to gauge the truthfulness of the compliment he has paid him. Petrarch may play the central role in the final act in the *De casibus*'s drama of fathers and sons, but the inspiration to stage the play comes from Dante, whose own performance in the part Boccaccio never permits the reader to forget.

According to the complex chemistry of paternity that introduces the account of the duke of Athens, then, we should expect Boccaccio to affirm the communalism he associates with Dante but temper it with Petrarch's rejection of the forum as the locus where the moral soul is free to fashion itself. Like Dante Boccaccio therefore will loathe the indolence and neglect of Florence's citizenry ("fastidiens civium nostrorum socordiam"); as Petrarch advised, he will overcome his own inactivity by writing the tyrant's rise and fall for the *De casibus*. But however carefully Boccaccio calibrated and balanced his sentiments, he could not make his Dante and his Petrarch cease to pull in different directions. He needed to create a narrative alembic of peculiar strength to withstand the antagonistic pressures they exerted when both

---

19. Dante emphasizes the revision of familial relationships in the afterlife by making Cato's appearance foreshadow Virgil's vanishing at the top of Purgatory. Dante poignantly catalogs his guide's failures as poet of love and Rome at the very moment he acknowledges him his "dolcissimo patre" (*Purg.* 30.50).

presided over the same political exemplum. Fortunately, Boccaccio had at hand a story in which he had already mapped the fault lines that traverse any attempt to make public policy an extension of the private dispositions through which a soul exerts its power to form itself. Long before Petrarch rewrote Dioneo's story of Gualtieri and Griselda, Boccaccio made the last tale in the *Decameron* a calque that his history of Gualterius of Brienne translates into Latin.

Boccaccio alerts us that the stories are linked by more than the name the two tyrants share. In the *De casibus,* Dante identifies Gualterius by calling him a "homebred plague." "Domesticam pestem" relates the duke of Athens not only to the plague that begins the *Decameron,* but more particularly to the domestic dictator who dominates the story that ends it. Similarly, by making Dante's patience so conspicuous, Boccaccio evokes the virtue for which Griselda has become a synonym. Equally pertinent is Dante's "mansuetudo," since Griselda very nearly personifies this trait as well. Giuseppe Mazzotta has shown how her mildness, precisely in ways that Aristotle and Aquinas had formulated, counteracts the "matta bestialità" that Dioneo says characterized Gualtieri.[20] Yet throughout the history of Gualterius, we never will quite be certain how to value these qualities, or even with whom we are to associate them: forbearance sometimes seems Petrarchan, sometimes Dantesque; at one moment, it is commendable; at the next, a dereliction of the responsibilities of citizenship.

Both narratives begin with a glance at ancestry. As "maggior della casa," Gualtieri succeeded to the marquisate; instead of ensuring his succession by marrying and producing an heir, he spent his time hunting and hawking. This gained him the reputation, Dioneo says, of being a very wise man: "di che egli era da reputar molto savio" (10.10.4). His remark is worth worrying a bit, since it brings into focus the interlinking of figural language, moral judgment, and epistemological certainty that his tale encourages and challenges. Does Dioneo agree that Gualtieri should be reputed wise? Or, as seems more likely, does he

---

20. Mazzotta, *World at Play,* 122–30. Mazzotta establishes the moral link between *bestialitas* and *mansuetudo* in Aristotle and Aquinas. For Aristotle, *bestialitas* is "a kind of madness, the occurrence of cruelty, folly, and tyranny in exaggerated forms." Aquinas linked bestiality to intemperance; as an aspect of temperance, *mansuetudo,* which Aquinas defines as the bridling of one's own excesses, directly counteracts bestiality.

think the marquis's indulgences are thoughtless and those who think them otherwise are fools? If he thinks the latter, his aside is ironic, which would be fitting, since Dioneo has been irony's standard-bearer throughout the *Decameron*. But in this instance, his irony would place Dioneo on the same side as Gualtieri's advisors, who are entirely serious when they in effect tell the marquis that by failing to make provision for the future he will foolishly erase his past, since his line will end with his death. During the previous nine days of storytelling, Dioneo has always undermined or excused himself from seignorial presumptions; to find him agreeing with these arguments now would be disconcerting. In the event, however, Gualtieri's actual response is even more unsettling, for it shows the marquis *is* wise, or at least that he is as wise as his counselors are. In a voice Dioneo could easily call his own, Gualtieri tells them that if they think the past determines the future, they are as shortsighted as they think he is, for bloodlines are no guarantee of nobility. Most disturbing of all, though, is Gualtieri's revelation after he has mercilessly tested Griselda that he was acting according to a design he had foreseen from the beginning ("ad antiveduto fine operava," 10.10.61). Once again Dioneo reports that he was accounted a very wise man: "e savissimo reputaron Gualtieri" (10.10.66). Wise when he takes no thought for the future; wise when he plots out everything in advance; perhaps the situations do not precisely cancel one another, but the repeated phrase suggests that ultimately the difference between foresight and caprice doesn't amount to much.

Such a suggestion consigns epistemology to chaos, unless, of course, we think that Dioneo's point may merely be that knowledge is not absolute or timeless, but relative and as subject to uncertainty as the contingencies it judges. He seems to imply as much in his final comment on the tale; Boccaccio will offer a similar reading of the *Decameron*'s moral propensities in the *conclusione dell' autore*. But it is difficult to dress up Dioneo as spokesman for this view. If Gualtieri's self-indulgence before his marriage can elicit exactly the same response as his cruel tempting of Griselda during it, Dioneo would make no distinction between even the most disparate of events. His irony would be unconditional; relentless in its discovery of grounds for opposition from within, it would prove as uninflected by circumstance as Gualtieri is single-minded in his determination to satisfy his will. Just as the marquis collapses past and future, memory and anticipation, into the gratifications of the present moment, for which he never ceases to live, Dioneo would enthrone irony as the master figure whose power to subvert is so irresistible no occasion can withstand it.

Such a Dioneo would not savor the irony that he is as obsessive and authoritarian in the pursuit of his predilections as Gualtieri is in his. Perhaps we should therefore entertain the possibility that Dioneo does feel the marquis deserved his reputation; instead of viewing him ironically, in other words, Dioneo considers Gualtieri's desire to avoid the yoke of marriage, and his actions once he did wed, exemplary. Before he begins, Dioneo specifically says he wants his tale not to be too removed from his companions' own experience. Once the tale has been told, however, one wonders which character the *brigata* will be able to say is near them? Not Griselda; the plague her husband visits on her is no less real because it is a metaphor than the one Fiammetta and the others have sought to escape by flight and fiction. For the company to legitimately read Griselda as their proxy, they would have had to stay in Florence and suffer the pestilence in patience. It must be Gualtieri, then, whom they are not too distant from. But surely this cannot be: even those within the story who affirm the marquis's wisdom after he has revealed his purpose say his proofs of Griselda were too harsh and intolerable ("come che troppo reputassero agre e intollerabili l'esperienze prese della sua donna," 10.10.66). If his means were objectionable, can the wisdom they brought about be reasonable? It is hard, then, to imagine any among the *brigata* who would not join Dioneo in rejecting the slightest suggestion that their behavior and Gualtieri's were cut from the same pattern. Yet neither can they honestly say that Griselda's was. A tale that bids its audience to gauge the pertinence of the characters' conduct and then short-circuits any connections they might make is a strange tale indeed.

In fact, however, the marquis's determination to live in the pleasure of the moment by whatever means is not so different from the *brigata's* decision to leave Florence and gambol in gardens. Gualtieri, not Griselda, *has* been made the ethical touchstone against which they must evaluate the wisdom of their own actions. If they feel they have behaved judiciously, they have to explain how Gualtieri has not; if they think the marquis swinish, they need to wink hard to avoid seeing how close his inclinations are to theirs. The only way the storytellers can put some space between themselves and Gualtieri is for them to say that the plague makes their revelries a form of prudence.[21] But to argue this requires them to justify the probity of their comportment by appealing to the Black Death, whose effect, as Boccaccio's prefatory description makes inescapable clear, is to annul all standards of morality and render patience a form of lunacy.

In either case, it seems, judgment and knowledge are ironic: Gualtieri is wise in his folly, a beast in his wisdom; he is yet cannot be the figure the troop is nearest to. Only Griselda would appear to be exempt from such contradictions: her steadfastness could not be more thoroughgoing. Her undeviating consistency should be what enables her to be exemplary; in truth it makes her as unknowable and as problematic to imitate as her husband. Within the tale, Gualtieri never stops trying to fathom her; he never succeeds because the sheer transparency of Griselda's obedience to her promise to obey makes her impenetrably opaque to him. Outside the tale, the plague makes it absurd for anyone to emulate her forbearance; indeed, the relentless way the disease afflicts its victims causes the reader to wonder whether Griselda's repeated submissions are not themselves a kind of tyranny of suffering she imposes on herself and her children. Without in any way reducing Gualtieri's culpability, Dioneo hints that Griselda does more than endure her husband's unfeeling implacability; she introjects it.

One could, I suppose, conclude from this perspectival and conceptual imbroglio that Boccaccio wants to drive home at the end of the *Decameron* an idea he has emphasized throughout: to be heard in the real world, the ideals and certitude that allegory and the exemplum would secure rely on the same rhetorical strategies of figuration as the fabular and the fantastic. A less benign reading would point out that as soon as Dioneo raises the possibility of moral application, ethical valuation and the discourses that seek to stabilize it are thrown into irreparable disarray. For both these reasons, as scaffolding for a political parable, Dioneo's story offers far less sturdy support of communal republicanism than it at first appears to. The disgust he feels toward Gualtieri is clear, but Dioneo's own need to stand outside the rules that govern the rest of the company, in association with their quest to master each day and make it delightful, gives rise to the discomfiting suspicion that the desire to live with others in liberty and the desire to

---

21. Medical lore in the Middle Ages commended the therapeutic effects of those activities the company engages in for their pleasure, as Glending Olson has shown in *Literature as Recreation*. Dioneo's tale complicates this argument without invalidating it.

exert one's will over them, far from being contrary, are actually complicitous. Indeed, Dioneo's tale works to prevent his companions from taking comfort in the fact that they, unlike Gualtieri, who is coercive, freely choose the hierarchical arrangements they live by. Griselda chooses freely as well, and the way she keeps her vow implies that each choice not only can but perhaps should be an invitation to subservience: beyond relinquishing the freedom to reconsider one's commitment, the exercise of virtue willfully seeks out tribulation to prove itself. In his concluding remarks, Dioneo drives the tale in precisely these conflicting directions:

> What more is there to say but that celestial spirits drop like rain from heaven on both the houses of the poor and the palaces of those who were worthier to keep swine than rule men. Who but Griselda could have endured, not only without tears but happily, the cruel and unheard-of proofs Gualtieri devised? It perhaps wouldn't have been unjust if he had bumped up against a woman who, after he had driven her out of their home in her shift, had gotten herself someone else to shake her skin-coat, and so have come out of it with a fine robe. [Al quale non sarebbe forse stato male investito d'essersi abbattuto a una che quando, fuor di casa, l'avesse in camiscia cacciata, s'avesse sì a un altro fatto scuotere il pilliccione che riuscito ne fosse una bella roba.]

In his first sentence Dioneo acknowledges that divine blessings are gratuitous but scornfully objects to the impartiality of their distribution. In the second, he grants that Griselda's fortitude is unmatched, but denounces the circumstances that elicited it; if Gualtieri's tests were sadistic and entirely uncalled for, then her passivity in submitting to them seems at least questionable. In the final sentence, Dioneo develops these implications to the point that they become so incompatible, he has to dismiss both his characters. Griselda would have been a fit mate for Gualtieri if she had answered his outrages with one of her own. The pun on *vestire* in "non sarebbe stato investito" links the marquis to Dioneo's alternative Griselda, who in finding someone to shake her "pilliccione" might have gained "una bella roba" to wear.[22] This

---

22. The connotations of "pilliccione" (skin, pelf, fur) play on the sexual implications Dioneo finds in Panfilo's story of Messer Torello, which immediately precedes the Griselda. It is all very well to praise Messer Torello when he regains his wife, Dioneo says before he begins his tale, but what of the man who was about to marry her, "che aspettava la seguente notte di fare abbassare la coda ritta della fantasima" [who was expecting

sort of woman would satisfy Dioneo's sense of justice, which God's apportioning of celestial spirits seems to have frustrated, but her act of resistance transforms her into the kind of wife who would give the misogynist reason to think Gualtieri was wise when he took no thought for marriage. In the end, Dioneo tells the *brigata* that they will ignore the lesson of Griselda and Gualtieri at their peril, but that neither character has much to teach them.

When Boccaccio turned to Gualterius's lineage in the *De casibus*, the exfoliation of ironies that had constituted the qualities of fiction in the *Decameron* reappears to complicate the very idea of advocacy in political invective. Gualterius's ancestors "were noble by blood and degenerate by custom." His father was beheaded by enemies who captured him while he was trying to increase his possessions by force ("dum possessionem genitor armis posceret," 9.24.2); the phrasing intentionally points to the contrast between Boccaccio's own father and the duke's. Gualterius subsequently tried to avenge his death by mustering support among various nobles and making preparations for war; in the event, he was betrayed by the Greek mercenaries he had recruited, who killed his only son.

Greed, vengeful fecklessness, improvidence, disloyalty: these are the attributes that seem to have steered the counts of Brienne into misadventure and treachery from one generation to the next. With just a few pen-strokes, Boccaccio sets his narrative in motion by presenting a Gualterius who is as dissolute as his namesake in the *Decameron* and in even greater danger of dying without an heir to preserve his family name.[23] We can guess, then, that like Gualtieri, whose early tendencies

---

to lower the werewolf's erect tail the following night] (10.10.2). The Griselda he imagines at the end of his tale is just the wife for this disappointed bridegroom. He can be the "bella roba" that covers her.

23. It is instructive to compare Boccaccio's portrait of Walter with those one finds in the "Cronache" of Giovanni Villani and Stefani. Near the midpoint of the latter's account, for instance, we learn that the duke "was short in stature, dark complected, and not handsome. He delighted in furs, and sported a large beard. His answers lacked graciousness; he was not given to gluttony" [La statura di questo signoree si fu bassa, e fu di pelle bruna e non grazioso aspetto. Dilettossi in peli, la barba avea grande. Nelle sue risposte non grazioso, la vita assai onesta di mangiare e di bere] (567). Just prior to this description, Stefani reported that the duke had begun to associate with lesser guildsmen and people of the middle strata; he also gradually fortified himself and disarmed the citizens of Florence. Immediately after it he speaks of the duke's counselors, and especially of Guiglielmo d'Asciesi, whose particular cruelty Boccaccio will highlight at the end of his narrative. Rather like Chaucer's description of Diomede in the *Troilus*, Stefani's portrait suggests that physiognomy recapitulates ontogeny; as much by placement and asso-

to indulge himself were monstrously magnified after he married, Gualterius's career as tyrant will repeat and intensify the experiences of his father and his son. The duke's rise to power began when Pisa laid siege to Lucca in 1341. Florence, which had just gained jurisdiction over the latter city by paying some 250,000 florins, sent an army to defend it; it was defeated. A few months later, in April 1342, a new expedition was launched; the count, who had been trying to shark up soldiers to avenge his own losses, pretended that he wanted to make a pilgrimage, left Naples in secret, and joined the Florentine army. This campaign also ended in failure: Lucca fell to the Pisans; Gualterius returned to Florence with the disconcerted troops.

The contractual obligations that bound Florence to Lucca form an ambiguous backdrop for the negotiations that led to Gualterius's seizure of the commune. On one side, we see a city that honors its pledges; in this the agreements Boccaccio refers to in the *De casibus* recall those Gualtieri and his subjects entered into when they discussed his taking a bride in the *Decameron*. On the other, the first and the second defeat at Lucca come too soon after rapacity kills the elder Gualterius and an abortive vendetta costs his grandson his life for the reader to ignore the parallels. The "buying" of Lucca reveals a society already bankrupted by its own avaricious yearning to increase its possessions and extend its power. No wonder, then, that Florence would court the duke of Athens as its savior; the man, whose title should have always branded him an insult to democratic aspirations of the state, was someone the city, to its discredit, all too easily could consider a native son.[24]

---

ciation as by ocular proof, one discerns an inherent baseness in Walter's appearance that extends to his manners. By contrast, Boccaccio omits these personal details; his portrait of Gualterius, with which his account begins, is at once more "historical," in the sense that Walter's depravity is generational, and more socially generic, in the sense that the duke and Florence's magnates are linked by the depravities peculiar to their class. Boccaccio returns to these themes at the end of his narrative. All citations from Stefani, which are identified by their rubric number, are from *Marchionne di Coppo Stefani Cronaca fiorentina,* ed. Niccolò Rodolico, *Rerum Italicarum Scriptores,* vol. 30, part 1 (Città di castello, 1903).

24. Boccaccio is so intent on establishing discrediting similarities between the citizens of Florence and the man they would invite to rule it, he doctors the record. He says Gualterius fought without distinction in the skirmishes outside Lucca (9.24.4). Stefani, however, although no friend to the duke, reports that in fact Walter fought valiantly and was the only member of the Florentine forces who did so. He notes that Walter's victory over superior forces led by one Bruschino, a German mercenary, was thought to be miraculous (550), and that his bravery figured greatly in the priors' decision to offer him the offices of "Conservadore," "Capitano di guardia," and "Capitano di guerra" (553). Villani does not mention Walter's conduct in battle.

In 1342, the commune Boccaccio had only recently returned to from Naples was afflicted by its recent defeats, overburdened by the intolerable expense of paying for its acquisition of Lucca, and riven by sedition. On May 26, after a series of parleys in which Gualterius and the city's priors maneuvered as if they were two families bargaining over a wedding contract, the Signory voted to name the count the protector and keeper of the state, captain of war, and guardian of the commune until the following Easter. In his account, Boccaccio lays the blame for this momentous decision chiefly on the city's magnates, who were looking for an opportunity to overturn the Ordinances of Justice, and on the *popolani grassi*, who needed relief from their creditors:[25]

> Et ignaviter eligentes potius exteri hominis tyramnidem, quam ignorabant, quam civilium legum quarum consuetudine noverant iugum ferre, minus de se confidentes, sibi cives alieno obligatos eri iunxere, quorum ea tempestate ingens erat copia. (9.24.8)

> [And listlessly choosing the tyranny of a stranger, whom they did not know, rather than to bear the yoke of civil laws that they knew from experience, trusting little in themselves, (the magnates) joined with citizens, of whom there were a great number at that time, who were pressed by their foreign investments.]

The slippage that occurs in this sentence is worthy of Dioneo. By their own determination, the citizens of Florence, through the free operation of their representational government, turned their backs on their own civic traditions and delivered themselves into the hands of an outsider they knew nothing about. They acted, that is to say, rather like the *Decameron's* Gualtieri both before and after he agreed to submit to the yoke of marriage. Perhaps Boccaccio intended to imply that Florence's nobility lies in its democratic institutions; to have chosen to abandon them was to elect to suffer historical amnesia. But at the very moment when Florence's magnates were subverting the values he cherishes, the categories Boccaccio deploys to register his censure, knowledge and self-esteem, join the humanist to the aristocrat. In chiding his compatri-

---

25. As Ricci notes (862), both Stefani and Villani say that many among the *popoli minuti* supported the conferral of power on Gualterius because they had been angered the year before by the stacking of a powerful *balìa* with *popolani grassi*.

ots for not remembering who they were, Boccaccio constructs the city's past as if it were a noble lineage whose greatness they sullied by allying themselves to the duke of Athens.

Although Boccaccio clearly finds his fellow citizens' dereliction stupefying, he nevertheless ascribes it to "ignavia." Because he means a laziness that is one part self-forgetfulness and two parts cowardice, presumably no one would mistake the commune's passivity for the conspicuous patience of a Dante or a Griselda. But what reader of the *Decameron* who also read this account would not rebel at the thought of associating the poet's perseverance and her nonresistance? Dante's defiant, unbowed republicanism in fact does more than underscore his difference from the tyrant and the people who appoint him; it emphasizes how they are like Griselda, whose husband's exercise of power over her was also unjust but not in violation of the agreement by which she took him (all unknown) as her lord. In the *De casibus* Boccaccio has raised the stakes at play in Dioneo's disturbing idea that those who choose to suffer may actually be covertly exercising their drive to dominate. From this point on, it will become increasingly difficult to tell whether patience comes from a failure or an excess of will, whether resignation consorts with tyranny or is its foe.[26]

However much these inconsistencies concerned Boccaccio, he was prepared to risk a far greater one: making Dante and Petrarch share the same civic vision. As we have seen, when Boccaccio wrote this account, he had already bitterly chided "his illustrious master" for abandoning Florentine liberty to take up residency with the Visconti in Milan.[27] Yet by chastising his countrymen's "ignavia," Boccaccio connects his criticism of their lassitude with Petrarch's criticism of his: "You have begun a race," Petrarch had admonished his disciple, "and now when you are near the finish, you stop, led astray by foolish languor *(stulta seductus ignavia)*" (8.1.9).[28] As a citizen, Boccaccio's aversion to tyranny remains

---

26. We should remember that Boccaccio was not unaware of Dante's own imperial ambitions for Henry VII.

27. In taking leave of the *De casibus,* Boccaccio places it under the correction of the wisest philosophers of his age; preeminent among them is "insignis preceptor meus," Franciscus Petrarca (9.37.6).

28. Boccaccio links his rebuke to Petrarch by a more circuitous route when he suggests that if Florence's magnates and merchants had been better grounded in rhetoric, they never would have succumbed to this fit of moral hebetude. By choosing to ally themselves to an unknown dictator instead of submitting to the laws they and their parents had lived under, they showed the same excessive credulity Boccaccio had explicitly

unabated; as a scholar, he remains in need of his master's exhortation to overcome the one fault that in the public arena most befriends despotism. The task Boccaccio assigned himself as a humanist in mid-*trecento* Florence, it would seem, was to produce a civic discourse that was loyal both to autocratic, Petrarchan models of self-government and to the associational forms of communal life. In terms of its rhetoric, the *De casibus* is a signal success; as a politics, however, it is unable to reconcile these antagonistic positions.

Boccaccio's merging of ruler and ruled intensifies until Gualterius, at the urging of all the enfranchised classes of Florence, accepted dictatorship for life and immediately proved himself the canonical tyrant. The duke had seen from the moment a group of magnates had met with him in secret that he could realize his ambitions if in effect he, unlike them, did not forget himself and merely continued to be kind of man he always had been:

> Qui, honestate sua atque fide postposita, seva regni cupidine agitatus, infaustas prebens aures, cernensque si animus esset, non defuturum verbis effectum, ne armis temptaret quod, gradatim incedens, per dolum obtinere posse arbitratus est. (9.24.10)

> [He, having put honesty and fidelity aside, driven by his savage avidity for rule, listened menacingly, and, perceiving that the outcome would not differ from the words, if only he had the spirit, he thought that he would not attempt to gain by arms what he could get by proceeding slowly through guile.]

Gualterius is quite as ready as his father was to aggrandize himself by subjugating others; he thinks twice, however, about gambling on a direct assault, perhaps because he remembered that the erstwhile count had lost his head as a result of just such a foray. Instead the duke dis-

---

reproved earlier in the *De casibus*. When Theseus believed Phaedra, whom he hardly knew, but not his own son Hippolytus, he showed, according to Boccaccio, how one always must guard against precipitous judgments by taking into account "who speaks, for what end, who it is who has been charged and who has accused him, the time, the place, and the quality of the man, whether he is even-tempered or irascible, friendly or hostile, a scapegrace or honorable" (1.11:4). These are the traditional rhetorical circumstances, as Boccaccio makes clear later when he specifically commends the art: "In garrulos adversus rethoricam" (6.13). Petrarch's invective against Boccaccio is the remedy that can prevent such lapses of judgment and character as the Florentines exhibited in 1342.

cerned that he could satisfy his lust for lordship by deceiving his allies in Florence, even as he had been deceived by the Greek mercenaries who killed his son and heir. In this Gualterius showed that he did not want for spirit ("si animus esset"), but that his deeds, like Guido da Montefeltro's, would be "not those of the lion but of the fox" (*Inf.* 27.74–75). To a man of his perverse temperament, Boccaccio implies, plotting a path to lifetime rule by subterfuge and fraud would seem a fit way to avenge the dishonor his line had suffered.

These maneuverings, passive and aggressive at once, set the pattern that Gualterius's every action in the *De casibus* conforms to; throughout the narrative, the structures Boccaccio feels best express the dastardly, grasping man he is are familial and aristocratic. We now also will discover that the citizens whom the duke gulls are equally passive and aggressive; they, however, furiously chase after their own subjection by parliamentary decision. Walter soon asked the priors to expand his powers so that he could remove certain dangers that threatened the city (9.24.10); they agreed in July 1342. Encouraged by their timidity, the duke then demanded further authority to deal with seditious factions in the city (11); although the priors were astounded by the request, by the end of August Gualterius had been granted the control he wanted. Finally, in a belated effort to place some curb on his prerogatives, the city fathers proposed that the duke assume full command ("potestas omnis . . . in cives") for one year. He readily consented and swore to relinquish his tenure after the year had passed. On September 8, at nine o'clock in the morning, all the citizens of Florence met in a general "parlamento" (the word is Stefani's) before the doors of the palace of the priors to hear the public reading of these agreements and stipulations. Suddenly an armed troop of mounted and foot soldiers appeared, whom Ranieri di Giotto, captain of the soldiers assigned to guard the priors' palace, had surreptitiously admitted into the city on previous nights. Gualterius ascended to the high seat of counsel; a group of magnates drove the elected magistrates from him, and the orator, a judge named Francesco Rustichelli, proclaimed the accords to the people. As soon as he came to the passage in which the duke was given plenipotentiary power for a full year, the people, especially the lowest among them ("imo vulgi fex," 16), began to shout and ask that his rule be perpetual. "And immediately, through the handiwork of the traitor Ranieri, the doors of the palace were opened to the tyrant and his armed men" [Et evestigio proditoris Raynerii opere, tyramno armatisque suis palatii patuere fores] (16).

When Gualtieri took Griselda from her poor home and bought her to his castle, he upset all the assumptions that ordered the social hierarchy. The laying open of the fortress of Florentine liberty ("florentine libertatis arce"), as Boccaccio calls it, is a comparable moment of crisis; in the *De casibus,* however, it is the civic order that is turned topsy-turvy. An act of treason, notarized by armed guards, whose sudden appearance all but trumpeted in classic fashion Gualterius's assumption of the mantle of tyranny, instead of evoking terror and dismay, was welcomed by the entire populace:

Eam igitur urbem, quam non solum a progenitoribus liberam orbem intrantes suscepimus, sed nec ullius unquam memoria cuiquam, exceptis imperatoribus Romanorum, subditam, his artibus iniquissimi cives exteri ac scelestissimi hominis tyramnidi subiecere; et quasi non sue sed alterius tantum libertati iniecissent vincula, cepere magnates tripudiis subacti populi celebrare triunphos; et qui alienum es debuerant, in creditorum pauperiem debachari; sic et plebs inferior discurrere undique, et ignotum sibi Capitolium conscendere, rimari cuncta, scomatibus ignominiosis et cantibus diem agere celebrem, et eo quod nulli sit die illa negatus ingressus aut clause fores, et patebant omnia omnibus, sibi inertes non tyramno arbitrabantur quesisse dominium. (18)

[Thus that city, which not only was free when we received it from our parents at our birth but, with the exception of the Roman emperors, was never in recorded memory subject to anyone, by such connivance of iniquitous citizens was placed under the tyranny of a foreign and wicked man. And as if they had put in chains someone else's liberty and not their own, the exultant magnates began to celebrate the triumph of a suppressed people. And those who owed money reveled in the impoverishment of their creditors. And the common people likewise ran about everywhere; they entered the palace they did not know, pried into and ransacked everything, and celebrated the occasion with scabrous and indecent songs. And because that day the doors of the palace were not closed nor entrance denied to anyone—everyone went where he pleased—the sluggish rabble did not think they had acquired a tyrant but had gained lordship for themselves.]

In the wake of Gualterius's ascension, everyone in Florence behaved as if he believed the city had just been emancipated; for Boccaccio, however, they were in truth all partners in its sack. To convey the grotesqueness of their actions, he constructs a carnival of inverted values and identities. Magnates thought of themselves as an oppressed people released from long persecution; merchants who lived by extending credit rejoiced in the nonpayment of debts; the craftworkers of the lesser guilds fancied themselves kings for a day. Having done the despot's work for him, each class joined in revelries that confirmed their city's torpor. United by the shackles these lords of misrule had placed on themselves, all of them, in a very real sense, became "cives inertes."

As we have seen, till now Boccaccio has held the great families primarily responsible for Florence's deterioration; in this passage, however, he directs his greatest scorn at the "plebs inferior." He obviously appears to find their helter-skelter lurchings through the "palazzo dei Priori" particularly objectionable; their loutish curiosity about and hostility toward things that are above them, the coarse songs they sing, all seem meant to suggest that they saw the duke's pact with the priors as a kind of marriage, which they would celebrate with skimmington and shivaree and every other vulgarity common to their nature.[29] I have little doubt that Boccaccio wished readers of the *Decameron* to contrast

---

29. These details are not reported in Villani or Stefano. Indeed, in both chroniclers' accounts, the only revelries are those of the magnates. Villani reports that the duke and grandees held riotous revels ("Il duca e i grandi feciono grande festa d'armeggiare," 12.3); the next day (September 8), he held a grand and solemn festival at Santa Croce, during which he freed 150 prisoners and the bishop of Florence preached his magnificence to the people. (All quotations from Villani refer by book and chapter number to *Cronica*, ed. F. G. Dragomanni, 4 vols. [Florence: Sansone, 1844–45].) In Stefani, the common people comport themselves in a far more dignified manner than they do in Boccaccio:

> Li Grandi ... feciono grande festa ed armeggiata e falò e luminare ricche. Ma pure gli scardassieri, che furono quelli che molto favorirono alla piazza gridando, fatta la festa, tornarono a scardassare ed a guadagnare lo pane. (556)

> [The magnates held a great celebration, fumbling about in their arms amid bonfires and lavish lightshows. But even the wool carders, the very people who had shouted in favor of (the lifetime appointment of) the duke in the Piazza of the Priors, once the festivities were over, returned to their carding and earning their livelihood.]

the effrontery of these boors to Griselda's humility at her own wedding to her lord. But even if his present audience did not know Dioneo's tale, Dante's tutelary spirit still would force them to pause at this moment of union and consider the politics of Boccaccio's shift in disapproval. After all, is the forbearance he commends in Dante the proper response to the prospect of tyranny? Shouldn't the people have run riot, occupied the houses of power, burned down the Italian equivalent of the Savoy?[30] Compared to the idle merrymaking of the magnates and *popolani grassi*, the more energetic escapades of the *popoli minuti* seem almost called for; they may know not what they are doing, but they act in ways that Boccaccio will applaud when the commune finally does rise to cry havoc against its oppressor.

At first glance, one might think Boccaccio's contempt for the ignorance of the masses is merely a reflex of his humanism. To some extent it is, but in this instance his superciliousness is strategic as well: by scorning the mob, Boccaccio forecloses the possibility that someone might associate their inertia with his patience; by spurning their mindless surges, which can only parody principled acts of resistance, he safeguards the integrity of the *De casibus*'s torrents of impassioned reproof, which are founded on moral precept. In the process, of course, Boccaccio seems less high-minded than highhanded; the incongruence of conscripting a divisive social anthropology to validate his authority to speak against princes in the name of freedom for the entire commune does not appear to trouble him. But it is the timing of Boccaccio's class prejudices, rather than their self-defeating logic, that marks them as something more than an expression of Petrarchan snobbery. As soon as the language of celebration begins to edge toward the language of insurrection, Boccaccio rushes to declare his belief in autarky and the whip. As vociferously as he castigates freeborn Florentines for acquiescing in the forfeiture of their liberty, he is equally adamant that the "meno potenti," as Stefani calls them, should be kept in their place. All

---

30. According to Villani, after "certain carders and *popolazzo minuto* and henchmen (*certi masnadieri*) of great families had shouted, 'Sia la signore del duca a vita, sia il duca nostre signore,'" the magnates took Walter and bore him to the palace, where they shouted for axes because the doors were closed (12.3). In Stefani, it is the commoners who bear Walter to the palace and shout, "Alle scure, alle scure; al fuoco, al fuoco" [Get the axes, get the fire] (555). On cue, Ranieri had the door opened, and with great pomp and fanfare, Walter was carried into the palace and took his place as lord while the psalm "Te deus laudamus" was played and sung ("sonato e cantato"). Boccaccio's version of the scene is even more weighted against the lower classes than Stefani's.

too quickly the most ardent republican sounds as coercive as Gualterius. All too suddenly Boccaccio's disdain seems designed to protect him against a charge that Dante's conspicuous example would constantly bring to mind: by writing the *De casibus* he too risked accusations of treason and the possibility of exile. Florence, it would seem, did not have to look to the Viscontis in Milan for instruction in the elements of tyranny; there was enough of an inclination toward the dictatorial already afoot within the city walls to make anyone who demanded liberty a secret partisan of those who would be happy to suppress it.

When the commune finally does bestir itself, these antithetic energies coalesce to produce a paradoxical political ideology: patient rebelliousness. With the speed of peripety, Gualterius reveals his true depravity in Boccaccio's account only a sentence or two after he gains absolute power.[31] Having decried the fact that many surrounding cities followed Florence's lead and took the duke as their lord, Boccaccio then says the tyrant cowed the people by appointing men of exceeding cruelty to be ministers of justice. He began to cultivate flatterers, nurture pimps, and name the most evil and wicked men as his counselors. He imposed heavy taxes, confiscated goods, took everything for himself, showed mercy to no one. Then, with blandishments, gifts, threats, and violence, he drew virgins and even their mothers to his bed, corrupted innocent youths, and permitted every iniquity. "In short," Boccaccio summarizes, he "befouled things both human and divine with his filthiness" [et breviter spurcitiis suis humana pariter et divina fedare] (21–23).

This last phrase puts one in mind of Dioneo's assessment of Gualtieri, whom the heavens favored even though he was better suited to keep pigs than to rule men. That Walter, of course, changed abruptly after he married; an equally abrupt change of heart now occurs in Boccaccio's chronicle, not, though, in its Walter, who remains the scoundrel he always has been, but in the people of Florence:

> Quibus miseri cives initio anxii, pavidi et elingues effecti, ingemiscere male cognitam deiectamque libertatem cepere, mortem deiectionemque tyramni cupere, desidiam suam damnare, et, si via daretur, se in libertatem redigere pristinam exoptare. (24)

---

31. As one would expect, in both Villani's and Stefani's chronicles many events intervene between the duke's assumption of lordship, the revelation of his depravities, and the resolution to unseat him.

[At first (Gualterius's outrages) frightened the wretched people, filled them with dread and made them mute; they began to weep for the too little prized liberty that they had lost, to desire the death and overthrow of the tyrant, to condemn their indolence and want to recover their former freedom, if there were a way.]

Distrust of each other, however, prevented them from taking any action, "wherefore they stood listlessly bearing the yoke far longer than was right" [Quam ob rem, diutius quam oportunum fuerit passi iugum, tepentes stetere] (25). Finally, however, "God took pity on their indignities, and, as if having opened their eyes to the baseness of their servitude, he invigorated their tepid hearts with his virtue." A group of magnates met to plot Gualterius's ouster; they eventually confided in a number of *popolani grassi*. The duke learned of the intrigue and had some of the conspirators tortured; fearing that the same fate would befall them, the other rebels had no choice but to arm themselves and take to the streets, raise the cry of liberty, and call for the tyrant's death, in the hope that the people would support them. "O bone Deus, quam mirabilia sunt iudicia tua!" (30), Boccaccio exclaims. Few knew of the plot, but as soon as they heard the clamor and outcry, the whole city, as if aware of what was happening ("tanquam gestorum conscia"), rushed to get their weapons and march against the duke (31):

> Fit ergo concursus civium armatorum undique, fit clamor ingens, panduntur crimina, postulatur vindicta et Gualterius ipse in victimam tot scelerum totis votis optatur ab omnibus.
>
> [Thus it was that armed men ran about everywhere, the clamor was tremendous, (the duke's) crimes were revealed, vengeance was demanded, and everyone said with one voice that Gualterius himself should pay for so many wicked deeds.]

The people gad about as riotously now as they had when the duke assumed his office, but because they precipitate Gualterius's overthrow, Boccaccio can commend deeds he had condemned before. Yet the citizenry are strangely divorced from the release they are poised to bring about. Bemired in the slough of their lassitude, the free men of Florence bore the yoke of tyranny much longer than Boccaccio says they should have; yet when they do move to right their wrongs, he pulls back from them, even after they have acknowledged culpability for their plight. Rather than endorsing their revolt without reservation, Boccaccio instills what we must suppose is a form of patience in the newly aware people by making them largely unwitting agents of God's will, from whom all sanction for the uprising derives and to whom all credit for its success accrues. Gualterius was stunned by the unexpected turn of events; he was advised to leave the palace at once and launch an attack against the crowd while they were still disorganized and leaderless; effeminate man that he was, crazed, and conscious of his guilt ("Ipse vero, effeminatus homo, vecors, et sue perfidie conscius," 32), he broke down in tears instead. Thus it pleased God to avoid a slaughter in the streets of Florence, "not at all as a result of the merits of the Florentines, but because the iniquity of the prince had long since offended heaven" [Sic Deo placuisse manifestum est, non equidem Florentinorum meritis, sed nequitia imperantis, que iam celum premebat et superos] (33).

So Boccaccio concludes, but not before the values he wished to censure have again contaminated those he wished to promote. God may have been the rebels' unseen commander, but they are disadvantaged enough without an earthly "duce" ("absque duce," 32)—the word is too close to Gualterius's title as "Athenarum dux" to ignore the similarity—for us not to hear Boccaccio endorsing the need for one. The denunciation of Walter's effeminacy certainly reconfirms his spineless enervation; at this juncture, however, his womanish weeping saves many lives. Boccaccio more than implies that the duke has sold his birthright as man and lord, but his slur virtually begs a question: against whom, then, does he think the tyrant should have proved his courage, if not the people of Florence, whom Boccaccio has continually berated for being as pusillanimous as the wretch they chose to oppress them? Boccaccio clearly feels citizenship demands a virile valor that his countrymen have failed to exercise. Along with his desire to rehabilitate them as responsible republicans, however, he seems to want to scourge them for their own lack of fortitude. He cannot afford to wield the lash too forcefully, though, not only out of fear of reprisals but because to do so would expose a will to rule uncomfortably similar to Gualterius's. So Boccaccio accommodates his twofold desire to punish and reform by transposing the conflict between them into the less risky arena of sexual convention. When the listless populace at last rouses itself, the only restitution of manhood Boccaccio allows the insurgents is to dissociate them from the duke by associating him with women, a group every male in the commune would agree is rightly disenfranchised, properly subservient, and very much in need of masculine supervision. By emasculating Walter, Boccaccio can administer the thrashing Florence required yet largely spare the slackers who deserved it. But his discipline purchases its patience dearly; the moment before the city's emancipation, Boccaccio's antifeminism discloses one mode of subjugation that supported both its freedom and his authority to admonish the forfeiture of it.

For all his approval of forbearance, however, Boccaccio still seems unable to appease the itch for civic retribution, which the association of Walter with long-suffering women only defers. Despite the fact that the Ordinances of 1293 were promulgated to check the blood feuds of the great clans of Florence, despite the fact that Gualterius's own attempts at vendetta emblematized his worthlessness and the extinction of his family, Boccaccio ends his account by applauding two instances of vengeance.

Once Walter saw that he had lost the chance to escape, he in effect bought his way out of the city. He promised to restore the commune's right to self-determination if he and his people were allowed to leave; to assuage the citizens' fury, he turned over to them one William of Assisi, "more cruel than any beast," and his children, who were "fiercer even than their father." This Guilielmus had caused many families to mourn the loss of their sons; God's justice now permitted ("Cuius ob meritam passus est Deus...," 36) bereaved fathers to have the satisfaction of seeing William see his own heirs torn to pieces before he was killed in the same fashion. Later, however, "so that the innocent city would not remain entirely unavenged against the obnoxious tyrant" [ne omnino innocua civitas ex nocuo tyramno preteriret inulta] (41), God, in Boccaccio's opinion ("Dei iudicio, arbitror"), brought it about that Gualterius fought with John the Good against Edward III at the battle of Poitiers. When John was captured, the duke realized that combat in the field was not the same as struggling in bed with ladies ("cerneretque rem aliter agi quam in thalamis matronarum," 41), and so, frightened, he abandoned the king and fled. Some Florentine mercenaries who were fighting for John stopped Walter and, following a barrage of taunts and insults, forced him to return to the battle. There, thrown from his horse and exhausted from a chest wound, it seems ("ut fama fert") he was recognized by a Florentine soldier of fortune in

Edward's service and forced to submit his neck to the sword ("iugulum dare coactus est"). "So it was," Boccaccio says by way of peroration, "that a Florentine hand let loose the blood and life of a man who had so cruelly shed Florentine blood. Thus was Gualterius, a deadly, deceitful, iniquitous man, ejected, put to flight, and killed, rather more happening on the day he merited than coming to it" [Et sic exitialis, dolosus, scelestusque Gualterius, deiectus, fugatus atque oppressus est, in diem potius quam meruerat deveniens quam venisset] (42).

To maintain the conservation of forms appropriate to Fortune dramas, Boccaccio makes the execution of Gualterius's henchman and his sons recall the demise of the fifth count of Brienne and his grandson. He then has the duke finish his scrofulous career much the way he began it, disgraced in battle, again the weary victim of a vengeful swordstroke rather than its source. Even though some thirteen years separated Walter's deposition and the battle of Poitiers, these two vendettas immediately follow one another in the narrative. One suspects that no gap in time, however great, could have prevented their suturing, since by juxtaposing them Boccaccio firmly fixes our parting image of the duke as a craven, inert, anile man brought down by his own devices. Earlier Boccaccio had ignored Gualterius's bravery outside Lucca; now, entirely indifferent to how Walter was wounded, he allows the duke only to submit phlegmatically to the blow that kills him. How unlike this fall, Boccaccio seems to imply, and Arcita's unfortunate demise from a similar wound in the *Teseida;* how disparate the dignified obsequies Theseus accorded the Theban knight and the words of scorn that are this latter-day duke of Athens's epitaph: "in diem potius quam meruerat deveniens quam venisset."

Walter may well have been effete, but by continually reverting to his passivity, even after he is dead, Boccaccio effectively disestablishes himself as a conspicuous example of the patience he tells the story to commend. Each disparaging iteration becomes an evasion of forbearance that tries to mark itself as an instance of it; together they reveal a Boccaccio who only half believed that vengeance was a perquisite of honor and manhood, in the act of washing his hands of someone he felt had neither but whose rank and station obliged him to embody both.

The correspondences that Boccaccio deliberately created to knit together beginning and end are not, therefore, limited to Walter.[32] The

---

32. One indication that Boccaccio intended to join these acts of vengeance together is the fact that neither Stefani nor Villani mentions how Gualterius dies. We can measure the distance that separates the *De casibus* from the chronicles by this difference.

Florentine adventurers who have chosen to auction themselves to one or the other warring party inevitably recollect the disastrous purchase of Lucca, the first and the second discomfiture of the armies Florence sent there, and the subsequent dealings that surrendered the city to Gualterius. Instead of bringing his tyranny to an end, these mercenaries, who defame him and kill him, exemplify the causes that brought it about.

Perhaps for this very reason, Boccaccio again describes the men of Florence as the agents of retaliation but leaves no doubt that the vengeance they effect is the Lord's. The aspersion of Walter as effeminate once more assures the potency of the city's males, while the repeated ascription of their deeds to God's disposition (or, for that matter, to hearsay ["ut fama fert"]), distances them from their bloodletting without discrediting or making them appear inept—no one would take these Florentines for Gualterius, who lost his son in his effort to avenge his father. Or so, one suspects, Boccaccio hoped it would seem. By again endorsing his compatriots' actions while counseling patience, he extends to them the same gratifications of vengeance he has allowed himself, but simultaneously records his opposition to the vendetta when it subverts the operation of civic institutions. Progressive and absolutist, Boccaccio thus manages to hate tyranny and embrace force in the name of justice and order.

In the end, though, no matter how staunch his defense of communal forms of governing, no matter how committed he is to the necessary regimentation of the classes, Boccaccio's politics are chiefly defined by the way he disconnects himself from the issues he raises. Patience is more than the moral he draws from this story; it is its manner of meaning. By lifting him above the desolations of "ignavia," by inoculating him against the passions of magnates and commoners, patience allows Boccaccio to engage his city's public history and to shield himself from the consequences of doing so. As well as any document could, his account of the duke of Athens encapsulates the ambivalent and contrary convictions of the humanist-citizen of mid-*trecento* Florence.

With the appearance of John Lydgate's *The Fall of Princes*, by the middle of the fifteenth century the *De casibus* was well known in England. It was especially popular, as Seth Lerer notes, among aristocratic readers.[33] One can understand why. Starting with his title, Lydgate domesticated

---

33. Seth Lerer, *Chaucer and His Readers* (Princeton: Princeton University Press, 1993), 40. On *The Fall of Princes*, see especially Derek Pearsall, *John Lydgate* (London: Routledge and Kegan Paul, 1970), 223–54.

the work by changing the arena in which it was to have its effect from the city to the nobleman's court; Lydgate's moral didacticism, moreover, was sufficiently monochromatic to filter out whatever strange or troubling notions of communal republicanism or civic autonomy he may have noticed.[34] At a time when Lancastrians were assiduously working to legitimate their rule, a monk who sought their patronage might be expected to reproduce Boccaccio's ideological tilt toward the great but few of the considerations that complicate it.[35] When, for instance, Lydgate describes the negotiations between the priors and Gualterius that resulted in his assuming the Signory, he ignored Boccaccio's explicit explanation of the purpose and effect of the Ordinances of Justice. According to *The Fall*, the duke was chosen governor by a parliament made up exclusively of magnates, whose intent was to rob the commons of their liberty and plunder merchants of their riches:

> The gret estatis, reulers of the toun,
> Callid magnates tho daies in sothnesse,
> To Gaulteer gaff this domynacioun,
> Of entent the comouns to oppresse
> And marchauntes to spoille of ther richesse,
> Streyne men of crafft be froward violence
> Ageyn the libertes vsid in Florence
>
> (9.2595–2601).

In its disposition of power, this parliament already resembles the one that met at Westminster far more than its Florentine counterpart. In both the earlier and later versions of the *De casibus*, Boccaccio had insisted that the magnates secured the duke's rule by working with, not against, the *popolani grassi*; by misrepresenting their aims, at least in

---

34. In his prologue, the closest Lydgate comes to recognizing the civic environment of the *De casibus* is when he says: "And so as myn auctor list to comprehende,— / This Iohn Bochas, bi gret auctorite,— / It is almesse to correct and a-mende / The vicious folk off euery comounte" (204–7). All citations are from *Lydgate's Fall of Princes*, ed. Henry Bergen, Early English Text Society 121–24 (1924; rpt. Oxford: Oxford University Press, 1967). Of course, whenever one discusses *The Fall*, one must take into account that Lydgate is really translating Laurent de Premierfait's translation of the earlier version of the *De casibus*; one again is reminded how much the early English reception of Italy was mediated by France.

35. Lydgate dedicated his translation of *The Fall* to the younger brother of Henry V, Humphrey, duke of Gloucester; the duke does not appear to have been as forthcoming with pecuniary support as Lydgate had hoped. See Pearsall, *John Lydgate*, 223–30.

part, Lydgate turns the Italian lords into a party of despots. Indeed, as if to call attention to this transformation, Lydgate then seems to associate them with Ranieri di Giotto, whom the poet elevates from the traitor he is in the *De casibus* into a second tyrant: Rayneer

> With soudiours hadde stuffid ech hostrye . . .
> For to susteen of Gaulteer the partie.
> And traitourli for to fortefie
> Thentent of Gaulteer . . .
> . . . the cas was pereilous,
> Whan too tirauntis be bothe of oon assent
> With multitude tacomplisshe ther entente.
>
> (2649–57)[36]

For those who were inclined to remember, say, Richard's quarrels with London in the mid-1390s, noblemen such as these might easily stand in for the money-hungry king and his grasping associates.[37] To have opposed them, to have deposed the oppressor they mimicked, was to take up arms in the name of righteousness and liberty.

While Lydgate's retelling of the duke of Athens's tyranny is undoubtedly political, there is nothing in it that reflects the civic ideology of Florentine protohumanism. Despite its geographical specificity, the moral he draws is transhistorical; it applies to any number of other illustrious downfalls: "Thus he loste be his insolence / Al his poweer and domynacioun / Bothe of Tuscan and also of Florence" (2784–86). The question I would like to consider, then, is the extent to which Lydgate speaks for the London reader some sixty or so years earlier. Let us imagine that someone like John Gower had acquired a copy of the *De casibus* and had scanned the manuscript before he undertook a serious reading of it. For argument's sake, let us also assume that he overlooked at its very end the brief appearance of John of France, who curses his execrable misfortune at Poitiers when Edward III overran

---

36. Lydgate significantly expands Ranieri's role in the story; Boccaccio only briefly reports his fraud in admitting the duke's armed supporters into Florence (sentence 12 in the latter version) and his treachery in opening the doors of the priors' palace to the troop (16). He never calls Ranieri a second tyrant.

37. On Richard's quarrel, see Caroline Barron, "The Quarrel of Richard II with London, 1392–97," in *The Reign of Richard II*, ed. F. H. R. Du Boulay and Caroline Barron (London: Athlone, 1971), 173–201; and Sylvia Federico, "A Fourteenth-Century Erotics of Politics: London as a Feminine New Troy," *Studies in the Ages of Chaucer* 19 (1997): 121–55.

and ravaged his kingdom. Even a man as willing as Gower was to criticize his countrymen most likely would not have returned to the book's beginning once he had seen Boccaccio characterize the English as "a worthless, sluggish, cowardly race" [ab Anglis, inertissimis atque pavidis et nullius valoris hominibus] (9.27.3).[38] Let us suppose instead that the rubric "De Gualterio, Athenarum dux" had caught this reader's eye, and that he stopped to peruse the history with the Uprising of 1381 still fresh in his mind.

Gower himself would have found much he could applaud in Boccaccio's narrative. He certainly would have been struck to discover another Walter and William linked by an act of vengeance; in the *Vox clamantis*, when Guillelmus (William Walforth, the mayor of London) kills Wat Tyler, Gower calls the rebel leader "Walterus, furiarum Capitaneus."[39] In facing the madmen's captain, however, this William, like the Florentines in the *De casibus*, seems much more God's instrument than self-motivated avenger. Gower in fact dispatches Walforth in two brief clauses: moved by a righteous spirit, he is the man who "held the sword by which that proud Jay fell."[40] Tyler is the figure on whom Gower's attention is fixed:

Qui ferit ex gladio periit gladiator in illo,
Et magis infelix imbuet auctor opus:

---

38. At the end of the prologue of the *Vox clamantis*, Gower's deprecation of the English far outstrips Boccaccio's; one may doubt, though, that he would have appreciated hearing similar sentiments coming from "foreign" lips, especially when the occasion that prompted them was Edward III's victory over King John. I imagine his response would have been closer to Lydgate's, who in fact was so upset by Boccaccio's partisanship, he attacked him by saying that though he fought with pen and ink, he not only gave no mortal wound, but shamed himself: "His fantasie nor his oppynioun / Stood in that caas of noon auctorite: / Ther kyng was take; ther knihtis did flee; / Wher was Bochas to helpe at such a neede? / Sauff with his penne he made no man to bleede" (9.3178–82). Boccaccio had also made *amor patriae* a function of virility, but to a completely different end. Lydgate's swipe at Boccaccio's courage arises from a fit of pique; in the *De casibus*, manliness is a trope, a mode Boccaccio employs in his effort to articulate a political ideology. In any event, Lydgate's sentiments are all the more remarkable to hear after he has spent more than thirty thousand lines commending the authority of master "Bochas."

39. Wat Tyler is called Gualterius in the argument that introduces the nineteenth chapter of book 1 of the *Vox clamantis*; all citations are from *The Complete Works of John Gower*, ed. G. Macaulay, vol. 4 (Oxford: Clarendon, 1902). The translations are from *The Major Latin Works of John Gower*, trans. Eric Stockton (Seattle: University of Washington Press, 1962). Wat is, of course, also called Walter in the *Anonimalle Chronicle*, the *Eulogium Historiarum*, etc.

40. "Vnus erat Maior Guillelmus, quem probitatis / Spiritus in mente cordis ad alta mouet; / Iste tenens gladium quo graculus ille superbus / Corruit..." (1859–62).

In scelus addendum scelus est, in funera funus,
Sic luet exactor quod tulit ante malum.

(1869–72)

[The swordsman who struck with the sword perished by it, and the wretched leader got a taste of his own work. Crime had to be piled on crime, corpse on corpse, so that the tyrant might pay for the evil he had committed before.]

Through repetition and rhyme ("ferit," "periit"), through wordplay ("auctor," "exactor") and the balancing of contraries, through the duplication of rhythms and cadences, Gower delivers here, rhetorically and syntactically, the blows he had left suspended between the mayor's raised sword and Tyler's fall. As much as Boccaccio, Gower savors the gratifications of vengeance. But immediately after he has deployed *traductio, contentio, adnominatio,* and his other figures to participate stylistically in the execution of Wat's doom, Gower abruptly changes register:

Inque leues abiit morientis spiritus auras,
Si petat inferius antra scit ipse deus.

(1873–74)

[The spirit of the dying man departed into the gentle breezes, and God knows whether it reached the pits below.]

The shift in tone is so unexpected, one wonders whether Gower suddenly awoke to the implications of the reciprocity that his repetitions create and decided he had better judge not, lest he be judged.[41] Few who read "Qui ferit ex gladio periit gladiator in illo" would have failed to recognize its source: "omnes enim qui acceperint glaudium gladio peribunt" (Matt. 26:52). The poet's problem was that the biblical verse equates Tyler and Walforth more than it distinguishes them. The very eloquence that was supposed to separate Gower from rabble he mocks identifies him with it.[42] Yet once he has established to his satisfaction

---

41. According to the chronicles, Wat struck at Walforth with a dagger; the mayor's armor deflected the blow. William then wounded Wat in the neck and head; rather like Boccaccio's Gualterius, he was borne by his horse some eighty paces until he fell, half dead.

42. Steven Justice has argued that Gower's virtuoso transformation of the rebels into beasts keeps his voice from being too similar to theirs; the verbal mastery of this passage functions in the same way. See *Writing and Rebellion: England in 1381* (Berkeley and Los Angeles: University of California Press, 1994), 208–14.

that this vendetta is God's work, Gower remusters his troop of tropes (*repetitio, conclusio*, etc.) and strides forth again in support of God's judgment:

> Sic quia miliciam transumsit ymagine monstri,
> Irrita decepti vota colonis erant.
> Cum magis est quicquid superi voluere peractum,
> Desinit a furiis sors maledicta suis.
>
> (1875–78)

[Since he had taken to warfare in the shape of a monster, the deluded peasant's prayers were ineffectual. Since everything the gods wished was carried out, his cursed lot came to an end because of such follies.]

But then he again reverses himself and very nearly erases the deed itself: "Fortisan illa dies erroris summa fuisset, / Si deus in tali morte negasset opus" [But perhaps that day would have been the last of the confusion even if God had denied the necessity of this man's death] (1879–80).

Gower shuttles between resignation and retribution as rapidly as Boccaccio, but in the *Vox* neither patience nor vengeance functions the way both do in the *De casibus*. Revenge in London was not the civic act the vendetta was in Florence; precisely because the English city never had to promulgate statutes like the Ordinances of Justice, the ultimate provenance of Gower's language of requital is the Bible. For him, the chaos of the Revolt, though unloosed in London, was not specific to it:

> O the degenerate nature of our former city, which allowed the madly raging rabble to take up arms! O what a backward state of affairs it is that the unarmed knight shakes with fear and the barbarous mob has the leisure for fighting. (980)

With exactly the same lamentation, a Jeremiah in Paris could have bemoaned these failures of heart and the inversion of the ordained roles of the estates they occasioned. By contrast, when Boccaccio berated his fellow citizens' "ignavia," he reminded them of their history as Florentines; though his ethics are as Christian as Gower's, their contextual backdrop includes both the municipal chronicle and Roman political philosophy.

In the *Vox*, the private counterpart of the Uprising's social turmoil is the inner desolation Gower experiences as he flees London. He grows lean from lack of food, and his thin skin scarcely covers his bones. Fear made him suffer in his mind as well; he kept to himself, for "there was hardly a single friend to be trusted then" (1498). Whenever he did meet someone and was on the point of speaking to him, he "considered [him]self to be in ambush." He never could speak his mind; indeed, to prevent his death he often had to speak agreeable words to those who questioned him (1500–1520). As he walks the very land the rebel peasants may have left to march on London, Gower seems entirely unaware that he is suffering their lot. The fact that his bid for sympathy simultaneously reveals his want of it gives these lines a disconcerting power. Once again, however, his deprivations, intense and ironic as they are, are not the deprivations a Boccaccio or a Dante would represent. To be sure, Gower configures himself a stranger in a strange land; more muted, but nonetheless present, is the sense that the alien territory he wanders through is his own. But Gower's loss of himself neither arises from nor ever seems connected to his exile from his city. He certainly would claim he understands Dante's distillation of his experience as outcast: "how salt is the taste of another's bread, and how hard the path to descend and mount by another man's stairs" (*Par.* 17.58–60). But Gower, like Lydgate, lacks the civic habit of mind, to say nothing of Dante's power of expression, to conceive of saying, as Cacciaguida does, that the poet will gain fame for having been "parte per se stesso" [a party by yourself] (*Par.* 17.69).

Even when Gower does focus specifically on London, he generates an erotics rather than a discourse of politics. Sylvia Federico has shown how in the *Vox* Gower links deviant political to deviant sexual behavior.[43] When the peasants enter London, he depicts them as rapists of New Troy, thereby ambiguously joining the city to its lascivious eponym; he likewise encourages readers to compare the town's opening herself to the rebels to a prostitute plying her trade in Southwerk. London also becomes the widowed city, whose protectors sacrificed their masculinity to cowardliness.[44] The ideological purposes such mythological and sexual displacements serve in Gower's poem do not differ much from those they serve in Boccaccio's account of Walter. But

---

43. Federico, "Fourteenth-Century Erotics," 121–55.
44. Federico, "Fourteenth-Century Erotics," 138. The trope of the womanish man was common; Federico cites Knighton, who in his *Chronicle* also chides knights "struck as if by womanish fear" [quasi timore femineo].

the mode of meaning in the *Vox* is very different. Gower dehistoricizes the voice that cries out in it; the dream framework, the transformation of the peasants into beasts, the very fact that Gower implicitly locates his exhortations in the wilderness, all reveal that his escritoire in London and Boccaccio's *scrittoio* in Florence were separated by much more than distance.

Unlike Gower, Chaucer did know at least parts of the *De casibus*. One would like to think that when he acquired a copy of the *Vox clamantis*, Chaucer read his friend's *cri(se) de coeur* with Boccaccio's text in mind. Indeed, one would like to think that, in addition to noting the similarities between the works, Chaucer also began to sense that Gower's vision, although set in London, does not really take place there, at least not in the way Boccaccio's takes place in Florence. As he read, Chaucer would see that the walls of Gower's "noua Troia" are more fabulous than fortified; he would understand that, compared to the communal rhetoric of the *De casibus*, the language of the *Vox* never aims to be part of the ongoing deliberations of public life. Remembering Boccaccio's *prohemium*, Chaucer would become aware that in Gower's prologue, history is regressive, the occasion for moral condemnation, rather than forward-looking in its concern for the ethical formation of the polis. He would see that, unlike Aesop, Gower did not use the beast fable to enlarge the arena of human interaction but to disqualify the rebels from participating in it. He would perceive how, in presenting their uprising as a sort of circus animals' desertion, the *Vox* validated established class hierarchies by rendering the peasants an alien species by definition unqualified to challenge them.

We would like to say, in other words, that it was Boccaccio who inspired Chaucer to rescue his fiction from the Monk's monocularly tragic determinism; that it was the competing, polyvalent allegiances of the *De casibus* that prompted him, at least in part, to parody the social reductions of Gower's prologue in "The Nun's Priest's Tale."[45] But if we do say these things (and I think we should), we also need to acknowledge that at the same time Chaucer multiplied audiences with

---

45. See Steven Justice's full elaboration of this argument in *Writing and Rebellion*, 207–18. If Chaucer read Boccaccio's account of the duke of Athens, he may also have recognized in its depiction of the *popoli minuti* rummaging about the priors' palace the "writing lesson" Susan Crane has elucidated in the Wife of Bath's prologue. See "The Writing Lesson of 1381," in *Chaucer's England: Literature in Historical Context*, ed. Barbara Hanawalt (Minneapolis: University of Minnesota Press, 1992), 201–21.

the Knight, Host, and his "sweete preste" and "goodly man sir John," he entirely ignored the civic element of Boccaccio's humanism. None of Boccaccio's works provided Chaucer greater incentive than the *De casibus* to contemplate the connections between and among political language, Latin, and vernacular fiction in England. In the Monk's and the Nun's Priest's tales, he accepted and declined the challenge. He accepted it by translating the public discourses of Italy into the socially diverse ethics of reading that he foregrounds nowhere in *The Canterbury Tales* more prominently than in the sequence of tales that runs from the "Melibee" to Chaunticleer's tragicomedy. But he declined the challenge as well when he returned learning to the clergy by associating the *De casibus* with the Monk. In place of the scholar-citizen's study and the public piazzas of Florence Chaucer substituted the cell and the cloister of the monastery. These transpositions are not merely sops to tradition; they belong to a notable tendency in Chaucer to sidestep any direct engagement with the communal life of his city. Despite his exposure to Florentine politics, despite his knowledge of Boccaccio's republicanism, Chaucer seems to have remained aloof from both.

After the domestic education of the "Melibee," no one would have been surprised if the proper government of the state were in fact the subject of the next tale. Instead of using the link to prepare his audience to hear a mirror for princes or a meditation on the *vita civile*, however, Chaucer describes Harry Bailly's overheated wish that his Goodelief would behave more like Prudence. For "whan I bete my knaves," the Host laments, his wife

> bryngeth me forth the grete clobbed staves,
> And crieth, "Slee the dogges everichoon,
> And brek hem, bothe bak and every boon!"
> And if that any neighebor of myne
> Wol nat in chirche to my wyf enclyne . . .
> Whan she comth hoom she rampeth in my face,
> And crieth, "False coward, wrek thy wyf!
> By corpus bones, I wol have thy knyf,
> And thou shalt have my distaf and go spynne!"
> (B2.3087–97)

Although Goodelief's tirades remain housebound, the venue that prompts them does become more public; yet the forum Chaucer finally chose when he wanted to move the issues of counsel and conduct outside the home was not the Guildhall or Westminster but the parish church.[46] By questioning Harry's manhood, Goodelief's disparagement would seem to translate Boccaccio's disdain for an effeminate "ignavia" that robs the citizenry of their virility. But Chaucer's politics are sexual and familial; neither the Baillys' incivility between themselves, nor the violence with which they treat their servants, ever becomes a counterexample for civic comportment. Harry's wife's ramping instead virtually foreordains that he will look to the Monk, a "manly man" (A.167), as someone who can refurbish the standing of his sex. Of course, to compensate for Goodelief's browbeating, Harry must also exercise his own authority over the Monk, even though he acknowledges that this exemplar of masculinity makes him a "shrympe" by comparison. He first jocularly asks whether he should call the Monk Daun John, Daun Thomas, or daun Albon; he then mock-bemoans his withdrawal from the world:

> I pray to God, yeve hym confusioun
> That first thee broghte unto religioun!
> Thou woldest han been a tredefowel aright.
> Haddestow as greet a leeve as thou hast myght
> To parfourne al thy lust in engendrure,
> Thou haddest bigeten ful many a creature.
>
> (B2.3133–38)

Like the narrator in "The General Prologue," Harry worries, "How shal the world be served?" (187). Removing the Monk from social circulation, he suggests, has stymied the process of natural selection and threatened the survival of the species.

No doubt the Host's bantering is meant in part to divert attention from his recent admissions, but as he himself says,

> But be nat wrooth, my lord, though that I pleye.
> Ful ofte in game a sooth I have herd seye!
>
> (3153–54)

---

46. One can gauge the latent political potency of this tableau by recalling the similarity between Goodelief's attitude and that of the wives of the "Haberdasshere" and his fellow guildsmen, or, for that matter, the debates in "The Parliament of Fowles." The fact that the scene seems to be a transposition of "The Host's Stanza" at the end of "The Clerk's Tale" is further evidence, as we shall see next chapter, that Chaucer dealt with the protopolitical discourses of early Italian humanism by domesticating them.

This irony, which makes "ernest" of "game," just as the Monk is about to do, in an entirely different mode, coincides with the manner of meaning of his previous high jinks. To balance the public disclosure of the "privitee" of his marriage, Harry calls on a man who, instead of staying married to Christ within the walls of his abbey, has divorced himself by being an "outridere," a hunter, and a glutton:

> And whan he rood, men myghte his brydel heere
> Gynglen in a whistlynge wynd als cleere
> And eek as loude as dooth the chapel belle.
>
> (A.169–71)

The Monk, who was supposed to personify the life "inside," ambles abroad as a horse-borne contradiction; instead of hearing the "tin tin sonando," as Dante had called it, "at the hour when the Bride of God rises to sing matins to her Bridegroom" (*Par.* 10.140–43), he hears the bridle bells' call to nature's pastimes.[47] When the Host simultaneously elevates and deflates him, he reenacts the incongruities of the man by judging him against the expectations of the social world he actually inhabits rather than those of the spiritual world he should.[48] In the process, however, the two worlds penetrate and merge with one another. When Harry makes the difference between his wife and Prudence the basis of his jokingly serious acknowledgment of the difference between himself and the Monk, the boundaries that distinguish the sexes blur, the distinction between "sentence" and "solaas" fades, and the very ground for making judgments disappears. We are already in the realm of burgeoning senses and open-ended invitations to gloss that is "The Nun's Priest's Tale." As a reply to the *De casibus,* then, the interchange between Harry and the Monk suggests that more than anything else Chaucer transported into his work the jagged seam of the stitching by which public and private domains were joined in Boccaccio's.

---

47. The possibility of punning on "bridal"-"bridle" was certainly available to Chaucer. Since his simile provocatively inverts tenor and vehicle—we would have expected the Monk's chapel bell to be the thing something else is compared to—it does not seem far-fetched to think Chaucer is substituting the secular for the religious here as well.

48. In this regard, Harry's word "tredefowel" generates an extraordinary array of polyvocal resonances that will counteract the Monk's reductivism. Besides continuing the idea that the Host is "henpecked," which "The Nun's Priest's Tale" will soon make literal, it announces a permeability that contradicts the demarcations of genre and species. To speak of "tredefoweles" and "shrympes" when discussing human generation is already to have entered the discursive world of the beast fable.

Like many others, I think "The Monk's Tale" itself is an experiment in reductivism. The best of these readings, to my mind, is Winthrop Wetherbee's, who argues that the Monk's compulsion to limit fortune to his narrow definition of tragedy allows Chaucer to expose how the "arbitrary moralism, the pathos of popular religious literature, or the optimism and idealism of chivalric romance . . . can distort or obfuscate social and political reality in the process of 'interpreting' it."[49] Certainly the vibrant interchanges of opinions in the prologues to the Monk's and Nun's Priest's tales mark the monochromatic complexion of the Monk's gloom as alien to Chaucer's Canterbury poetics.[50] For my purposes, however, the transformation of Fortune into tragedy, whose implications have occasioned almost all the critical dissension about the tale, is not nearly as important as the fact that Chaucer made "the Monkes Tale De Casibus Virorum Illustrium," as a number of manuscript subtitles have it, part of a *literary* debate. This debate, which is essentially about the mode of meaning of *The Canterbury Tales*, is a translation of Boccaccio to the extent that it disarticulates the connection he would forge between the exclusive idioms of humanism and those of communal republicanism. By reformulating the civic tensions of the *De casibus* as a conflict between the estates, in which the church does not compete with the state, as it very much did in Italy, but with secular society, Chaucer responded more to Boccaccio's contradictoriness than to specific forces or ideologies that are at cross-purposes in the *De casibus*. The frontloading of technical and literary terms in the Monk's prologue—"versified," "exametron," "six feet," "prose," "meetre," "endited," not to mention the explanation of "tragedie" itself—are all formal indications that suggest Chaucer read the *De casibus* primarily as a poet. Compared to Boccaccio, he seems timid and backward-

---

49. Winthrop Wetherbee, "The Context of the Monk's Tale," in *Language and Style in English Literature: Essays in Honour of Michio Masui* (Hiroshima: English Research Association of Hiroshima, 1991), 159–77. Other readings of the tale in relation to the *De casibus*, which vary in their attention to Boccaccio, include Piero Boitani, "The *Monk's Tale:* Dante and Boccaccio," *Medium Aevum* 40 (1976): 50–69, and *The Tragic and the Sublime in Medieval Literature* (Cambridge: Cambridge University Press, 1989), 20–55; Renate Haas, "Chaucer's *Monk's Tale:* An Ingenious Criticism of Early Humanist Conceptions of Tragedy," *Humanistica Lovanensia* 36 (1987): 44–70; Monica McAlpine, *The Genre of "Troilus and Criseyde"* (Ithaca: Cornell University Press, 1978), 93–103; Michaela Paasche Grudin, *Chaucer and the Politics of Discourse* (Columbia: University of South Carolina Press, 1996), 135–48; Kelly, *Chaucerian Tragedy*, 65–79.

50. I agree with Wetherbee that "The Monk's Tale" is actually an "anti–*De casibus*" as well. See "Context," 167.

looking; he is very willing to see practical moral philosophy, to use the language of Hugh of St. Victor's *Didiscalicon*, as an "economic" virtue, but extremely reluctant to explore the possibilities of a confederation between politics and fiction. Rather than advancing from the "Melibee" to a discussion of the place of prudence in civil, public discourse ("publicam / civilem"—the terms again are from Hugh), Chaucer retreats; the Monk, who patiently abides Harry's barbs, would return judiciousness to its monastic, solitary uses ("solitarium / monasticum"). Compared to the *Vox clamantis*, however, Chaucer's creation of multiple readerships and his embrace of the problematic responsibilities of interpretation in the final tales of Fragment 7 carry the force of a political critique. This clash of perspectives, which will grow more pronounced when Chaucer encounters humanism's high priest, Petrarch, is one sign of his Italian tradition.[51]

---

51. Only after I had completed this chapter was I able to read Richard Neuse's new, spirited essay "The Monk's *De casibus:* The Boccaccio Case Reopened," in *The Decameron and the Canterbury Tales*, ed. Leonard Koff and B. Schildgen (Teaneck, N.J.: Fairleigh Dickenson University Press, 2000), 247–77. Neuse treats many of the passages I discuss; he also makes use of a work by Benjamin (the *Ursprung des deutschen Trauerspiel*) to reconfigure the debate on the nature of tragedy in Boccaccio's and Chaucer's texts. His conclusions differ considerably from mine; I have not, however, addressed the differences here.

7

Petrarch, Chaucer, and the Making of the Clerk

When Harry Bailly calls on the Clerk to tell a tale, he attempts to construct the identity of the man from a variety of discourses that can be associated with him:

> "Sire Clerk of Oxenford," oure Hooste sayde,
> "Ye ryde as coy and stille as dooth a mayde
> Were newe spoused, sittynge at the bord;
> This day ne herde I of youre tonge a word.
> I trowe ye studie aboute som sophyme;
> But Salomon seith 'every thyng hath tyme.'"
>
> (E.1–6)

Uppermost in the Host's mind, it seems, is his desire to have this clerk be like the clerks he knows from literature. Perhaps the Clerk's retiring demeanor has reminded Harry of the characters of courtly romance; he describes the pilgrim's reserve in terms that would not be inappropriate for a lady such as Emilye. Harry's simile in fact recalls the man who describes her; according to "The General Prologue," the Knight's comportment makes him "as meeke as is a mayde" (A.69). Or perhaps the Host is thinking instead of the witty student of the fabliau, someone like Nicholas, the Oxford prognosticator in the Miller's tale; Harry's attitude, with its implicit jibes at the Clerk's manliness, recalls Robyn's, who seems to think all intellectuals are simpering and effeminate.[1] But

---

1. Absolon's effeminacy goes without saying, but even Nicholas, "Ful fetisly ydight with herbes swoote; / And of himself as swette as is the roote / of lycorys, or any cetewale" (A.3205–7) does not escape the Miller's typecasting. Compare the anecdote Old John later relates about the astronomical clerk who walked with his eyes so fixed on the stars he fell into a "marle-pit" (A.3457–61).

whether the cleric Harry envisages is abstemious or risqué, by reconstituting the verbal requiting of the first two *Canterbury Tales*, Chaucer's filigree of suggestion and allusion has prepared his readers for the Clerk's impending skirmish with Alice of Bath.[2]

Harry, however, also knows that clerks are schoolmen, given to philosophy and disputation, both of which he apparently prefers less than the "solas" of fiction. By urging the scholar to remember that everything has its time, he calls on the Clerk to attend to the present moment with its concrete demands and preoccupations. Now is not the time, he suggests, for the "sophyme" he imagines the Clerk has silently pondered all day; such head-in-the-clouds speculation distances him as far from his fellow pilgrims as the rarified fancies of romance remove its personages from the real world. At any rate, when Harry quotes Ecclesiastes to induce the cleric to join the company's tale telling, he signals as well his knowledge that clerks preached—something Harry wants to forestall most of all: no lengthy, lenten sermon, if he can avoid it.

Even before he says a word, then, literary, philosophical, and spiritual discourses compete to define the subjectivity of the Clerk. In *The Canterbury Tales*, each is a social language that comes already marked by contexts that will enter into dialogue with the meanings and intentions the Clerk will bring to his utterances. Yet as much as these discourses "speak" the Clerk, the way Chaucer has represented them—as expressions of his pilgrims' tendency to construct others according to their own motives and desires—shows that they are also always spoken by someone in particular for specific purposes. When Harry pictures the Clerk as a newly married maid sitting at the board, he has positioned him between two worlds. With its evocations of virginal chasteness and demure obedience, the scene has an out-of-time delicacy that arrests it against his knowledge of its approaching loss. Wife-nagged publican that Harry is, he is aware that his wedding tableau, like the deferential sublimations of courtly romance, exists in an idealized space that will vanish with the consummation of the marriage,

---

2. The allusive equating of the Knight and Clerk also seems to me a forecast of the upcoming rebuttal of the Wife of Bath. As readers of poems such as the "Altercatio Phyllidis et Florae" know, clerks traditionally maintained their superiority to knights in matters of love. Part of the fundamental wit of the "Marriage Group" is that Chaucer has relocated a conventional courtly love debate to the precincts of wedlock, even though theorists like Andreas proscribed *fin amour* from the bridal chamber. See further my "The Lineaments of Desire: Wish-Fulfillment on Chaucer's Marriage Group," *Criticism* 25 (1983): 197–210.

which is imminent. He knows that "every thyng hath tyme," that after the board there is the bed, after mirth, a reckoning that must be paid. Yet for all his workaday acumen, to talk the Clerk back down to earth Harry fabricates a figure out of his own masculine fantasies who is every bit as detached from the world as a scholar lost in thought. The Host's clerk could be the fulfillment of his own swagger; if he wants the man to be more Nicholas than Aristotle, Harry, a virile fellow ("of manhod he lakkede right naught," A.756) yet henpecked at home, may see the Clerk as a more assertive and verbally resourceful version of himself. But because he has learned the "wo that is in mariage," Harry could also be concocting a different clerkly surrogate to play his part in an equally wishful vision of his own postnuptial life—not Nicholas but Jankyn, another Oxford man, who was the Wife of Bath's fifth husband. Jankyn may have suffered a fate similar to Nicholas's when Alice knocked him into their hearth-fire, but he, unlike Goodelief's milksop, struck back. As if to compensate for his submissive meekness under his own roof, Harry, who is "boold of his speche, and wys, and wel ytaught" (A.755), quotes Solomon's precept to the Clerk he has outfitted as a coy bride; he uses biblical texts, that is to say, in the same way the Wife has used them, to establish authority over a man of authority. Forward and forbearing at once, both Harry and the clerks he fancies himself as look back to Alice of Bath and ahead to Griselda.[3]

Chaucer's Clerk, however, is a man who "hadde geten hym yet no benefice, / Ne was so worldly for to have office" (A.291–92); for him the sexual innuendoes of the Host's gentle raillery, together with its implied alternatives of and confusion between not so gentle manly aggression and womanly submission, can be reformulated as a set of choices conditioned more by historical institutions than by the conventions of literary genres. In the rawer world he returns to at Harry's bidding, the Clerk will find his "sophismatic" self-abstraction translated into the abstinence required of clerks, who, if at university, were in orders, and who would remain celibate if they became priests. Or he will find more secular quarters in which to put his knowledge to use.

---

3. Especially in their emphasis on the textuality of masculinity, Harry's clerks look ahead as well to the Monk. Most critics think that Chaucer canceled the Host's stanza at the end of "The Clerk's Tale" (E.1212a–g) when he wrote the Merchant's prologue; he then reworked the canceled link when he wrote the introduction to the Monk's tale. The same themes appear in both passages; more importantly the link they establish between Clerk and Monk is further evidence that Chaucer associated learning with the clergy.

But whether he becomes a "lerned . . . clerk" like the Parson or a clerk of the king's works like Chaucer, he will discover that here too, in the realm of social intercourse, he has been spoken for. The Clerk will certainly bring to his calling a grammar and logic to master the instabilities of time and death and meaning, all of which he refers to repeatedly in his answer to Harry. But he will have already learned enough on the way to Canterbury to know that neither time nor death nor meaning will be subject to his dialectical arts alone. For he has heard the Wife of Bath seize upon the liberty of widowhood to argue that her experience gives her as strong a claim to authority as his celibacy or education. First in her *sermon joyeux* and then in the dream she related to Jankyn, Alice had suggested that the chaste virgin and the chastened widow are virtually the same woman. The idea, she happily acknowledged, wasn't original with her; Paul had said he preferred that these women who stand on either side of wedlock maintain a continence equal to his own. The Wife merely exploited the saint's equation to hint with a blink and a smile that she reclaimed her maidenhood each time she "overbade" her husband. But her point is serious. In effect, by advising the widow to wear "virgin weeds," Paul was telling her to erase her history as a wife. Alice's reply, in effect, is that it is no more illogical for men to ask this of women whom they continue to define by their relation to marriage than to ask the widow to recover her virginity. The Wife has seen that under the name of accommodation, Paul's distinction between apostolic and married life is absolute and unremitting; Alice is never more Pauline than when she remains absolute and unremitting in her demands for sovereignty despite the satisfaction she professes to feel from her give-and-take with Jankyn. More than anyone else, in other words, St. Paul is the clerk who has taught the Wife how to generate rhetorical authority when speaking of marriage; just as the apostle's fierce asceticism underwrites his right to counsel husbands and wives, Alice makes her equally zealous embrace of sensuality her license to champion woman's mastery. Precisely because she has learned that "Diverse scoles maken parfyt clerkes" (D.44c), this Clerk of Oxenford, who rides as maidenly as a bride, had to know that clerkly honor made it necessary for him to oppose the usurpations of the Wife's sexual politics.

As a man who "unto logik hadde longe ygo," however, the Clerk would understand that Alice's preacherly revelation of the linkages between sex and "auctoritas" was not the only challenge she posed to his sense of self. Her recourse to what Louise Fradenburg has emphasized as the "pastness" of her tale raised an appropriately literary provocation as well.[4] Chaucer may well have meant to neutralize the disruptions and reversals the Wife has practiced in life by consigning them to a fairy-tale world of long ago, but he also made Alice fully aware that her legend is an anachronism. By opening an irreparable rift between then and now, the Wife located herself in history; her "joly body" raised a specter that must haunt the idea of authority, whose strength lies in its claim to transcend historical difference.[5] For all these reasons, then, the Clerk had no options; free to tell what he would, to be the Clerk he had to dispute the Wife.

This proliferation of intersecting discourses suggests Bakhtin's dialogism; like his tale, the Clerk himself may be read as a compound of style, the artistic image of various social languages which he speaks and is spoken by.[6] In this the Clerk is not unlike many other pilgrims. More than other pilgrims, however, the Clerk affords us an opportunity to view the discourses that fashion him historically. For whatever else he is, the Clerk is the product of Chaucer's intellectual encounter with Petrarch, a poet like himself, but a man whose ideological and literary commitments differed considerably. To understand why Chaucer assigned the story of Griselda to the Clerk, we must ask what Chaucer understood of Petrarch, what he could not have understood, and how what he did and did not comprehend are translations. For it is in the figure of the Clerk, I think, maybe even more than in the story he tells, that we see Chaucer as a reader of his transcultural experience.

In the last two decades, Anne Middleton, Charlotte Morse, and espe-

---

4. See Louise Fradenburg, "The Wife of Bath's Passing Fancy," *Studies in the Age of Chaucer* 8 (1986): 31–58.

5. See Lee Patterson, "'For the Wyves Love of Bathe': Feminine Rhetoric and Poetic Resolution in the *Roman de la Rose* and the *Canterbury Tales*," *Speculum* 58 (1983): 656–95.

6. Recently, a number of critics have read "The Clerk's Tale" in light of Bakhtin. John Ganim has stressed the carnivalesque elements of the "Envoy" in "Carnival Voices and the Envoy to the *Clerk's Tale*," *Chaucer Review* 22 (1987): 112–27; Lars Engle, "Chaucer, Bakhtin, and Griselda," *Exemplaria*, 1 (1989): 429–59, and William McClellan, "Bakhtin's Theory of Dialogic Discourse, Medieval Rhetorical Theory, and the Multi-voiced Structure of the Clerk's Tale," *Exemplaria* 1 (1989): 460–88, have stressed the dialogism of the tale. I see the Clerk's character as being similarly structured. Other studies, while not invoking Bakhtin, approach the tale in not incompatible ways. I have found especially useful Judith Ferster, *Chaucer on Interpretation* (Cambridge: Cambridge University Press, 1985), 94–121; and Peggy Knapp, "Knowing the Tropes: Literary Exegesis and Chaucer's Clerk," *Criticism* 27 (1985): 331–45.

cially David Wallace have written about the ideological suppositions and political commitments that underwrite Petrarch's translation of Griselda and the subsequent reception of it.[7] Each of these important studies breaks new ground; each in its way theorizes the Clerk's tale by locating it in the contestatory space that translation inevitably opens. As we have already seen, in this space the mastery and authority of a source is paradoxically affirmed by another text whose different language both displaces that of the original and makes it subject to cultural appropriation. The differing ends this act of appropriation serves, of course, effectively constitute the historicity of the translation. In Petrarch's case, these ends cannot be separated either from the elitist predisposition of his humanist project or from the tyrannical political regimes that supported him. As Wallace in particular has shown, when Petrarch first agreed to stay in Milan, he defended himself from the outrage of Florentine friends by saying that he found the Viscontis' offer to free him from the vulgarities of the forum too seductive to resist. In the event, he never did gain the *otium* he had stipulated as the precondition for the higher *studia* of poet and philosopher. Far from being removed from the petty affairs of the day, Petrarch served as spokesman for the territorial ambitions of the Viscontis; his professions of devotion to the *vita solitaria* became no more than a shibboleth to mask the political power that secured it. This power then reproduced itself in two forms. One was primarily cultural: the masculine, learned cliques called into being by Petrarch's writings, whose members were arbiters of judgment. The other was literary: the ideology of authority that drives Petrarch's translation of the last tale of the *Decameron*.

For the most part, this critique of Petrarch seems to me well founded. The Boccaccio of the mid-1350s certainly would have agreed with it; the *Trattatello* brilliantly exposed how residing with the archbishop in Milan converted Petrarch's rhetoric into so much imposture. But by 1373, Boccaccio had long since reconciled with Petrarch, and Florence had actually allied itself with its northern rival not too many years before. One can doubt, then, that during the months Chaucer visited

---

7. Anne Middleton, "The Clerk and His Tale: Some Literary Contexts," *Studies in the Age of Chaucer* 2 (1980): 121–50; Charlotte Morse, "The Exemplary Griselda," *Studies in the Age of Chaucer* 7 (1985): 51–86; David Wallace, "'Whan She Translated Was': A Chaucerian Critique of the Petrarchan Academy," in *Literary Practice and Social Change in England, 1380–1530,* ed. Lee Patterson (Berkeley and Los Angeles: University of California Press, 1990), 156–215, now in *Chaucerian Polity,* 261–98. Morse is concerned preeminently with the reception of the Griselda, Wallace with its ideology. Middleton discusses both.

Florence he heard many complaints about Petrarch's choice of associates. Still, Chaucer speaks of the "tyraunts of Lumbardye" (*Legend of Good Women*, G 354); he may well have gained enough knowledge on his visits to Italy to fathom the general political implications of Petrarch's Griselda. His version of the tale shows that such implications interested him. But I want to enter into dialogue both with Wallace's reading and with the other studies I mentioned because I do not think they pay enough attention to how Petrarch represents his allegiances. Everything Petrarch wrote he wrote about himself: if any claim can be called Petrarchan, it is that literature is unique in its capacity to spur the formation of the independent, moral self. The process by which this self was created, however, was highly complex, a double act of burial and disinterment, of rupture with the past so that the present might be made continuous with it. The translation of the Griselda is especially driven by this humanist hermeneutic of history, as Thomas Greene has called it; the tale is a meditation on the role of imitation in the ontology of the self, a critique of the social world and the place of the individual seeking truth in it.[8] As a political statement, his retelling is a self-justifying escape from history. Petrarch, however, presents the tale primarily as an ethical manifesto, and ethics, he insists, is the product of our engagement with history. The epistemological issues the Griselda raises, its deep concern for moral and spiritual values, for the effects of time and death on the progress of the soul: these matters were at the center of Petrarch's humanism, and they, as much as the politics of the tale, determined Chaucer's translation of it into terms he, and his audience, might understand.

The tale of Griselda Chaucer read was part of a discussion Petrarch conducted with Boccaccio across two decades about the nature and purpose of literature. In its most immediate context, the Griselda is a counter-example to the *Decameron*, which Petrarch both faults and defends in the first part of the letter that contains the translation.[9] Its proximate context

---

8. Thomas Greene, "Petrarch and the Humanist Hermeneutic," in *Italian Literature: Roots and Branches*, ed. G. Rimanelli and K. J. Atchity (New Haven: Yale University Press, 1976), 201–24; expanded in *The Light in Troy* (New Haven: Yale University Press, 1982), 81–146. Unless otherwise noted, I quote from *Light in Troy*.

9. For the Latin letter to Boccaccio, I follow the text established by J. Burke Severs, *The Literary Relationships of Chaucer's Clerkes Tale* (1942; rpt. New Haven: Archon, 1972). No critical edition of the *Epistolae Seniles* exists; unless otherwise indicated, all translations are from *Letters from Old Age*, trans. Bernardo Levin, 2 vols. (Baltimore: Johns Hopkins

is the previous letter of *Seniles*, in which Petrarch had vigorously rejected Boccaccio's request that he put aside his exhausting literary pursuits in deference to his age; it is his writing, Petrarch had responded, that gives his life its virtue and meaning. The exemplary tale therefore occupies a crucial position in the overall argument of the four letters, all addressed to Boccaccio, that together comprise the seventeenth book of the *Epistolae Seniles:* it demonstrates in literary form the answer Petrarch had just given rhetorically. Beyond this, as the last complete book of the *Seniles*, these letters assume special importance as a group, comparable to that which the Griselda occupied in Boccaccio's book; they are Petrarch's valedictory remarks in another conversation he had begun with his friend in his earlier collection of letters, the *Familiares.* Together, the epistles expressed Petrarch's final conviction, which was the conviction of Renaissance humanism, that literature, more than any other discourse, created the independent moral self and the pious Christian soul. Indeed, Petrarch ultimately justified his criticisms of the *Decameron* by implicitly offering the relation that joins yet distinguishes his two compendia of letters as a contrasting model.

These issues are encapsulated in the animadversions on the *Decameron* that serve as Petrarch's preface to his translation of Griselda. Petrarch says he has seen Boccaccio's book; like a hurried traveler, however, he has only leafed through it since it is very long and written in vernacular prose for the common herd; moreover, when he took up the volume, he was distracted by the wars that were breaking out in Italy in 1373. Among the things Petrarch says he did note with approval, though, was how Boccaccio had defended himself from attacks against the *Decameron.* Some parts of the work may be lewd, but Boccaccio's youthfulness, as well as the literary demands of the book, its style, idiom, subject matter, and audience, excuse them. Most of all, however, Petrarch commends the beginning and end of his friend's work. The description of the plague is perfect, he says, not least for the way in which Boccaccio magnificently deplored the condition of the country. And the concluding story of Griselda so impressed and delighted him, he desired to memorize and translate it, "something I would not have readily undertaken for anyone else."

University Press, 1992). For the Latin text of the *Familiares,* see *Le Familiari,* ed. V. Rossi, 4 vols. (Florence: Sansoni, 1933–42); all translations are from *Rerum familiarum libri,* trans. Aldo Bernardo, 3 vols. (vol. 1, Albany: State University of New York Press, 1975; vols. 2–3, Baltimore: Johns Hopkins University Press, 1982–85).

With his opening sentence, Petrarch set in motion a complex comparison between his own writing and Boccaccio's. He has invited his younger friend to read the *Decameron*, the product of a youth long since passed ("Librum tuum, quem . . . olim, ut oppinor, iuvenis edidisti"), from a maturer perspective, the very perspective that age gives the *Epistolae Seniles*. Perhaps Petrarch issued the invitation because he recognized that the different tenor of the last tale ("et multis precedencium longe dissimilem") gave the *Decameron* a sense of alterity similar to that of the *Canzoniere*, Petrarch's own large collection of youthful lyrics in the vernacular.[10] He had opened his cycle of 365 poems by saying he was estranged from the experiences it records: he confesses in his introductory sonnet that his hopes and griefs have proved his passion vain and have made him "a different man from the one he was" (1.1–4). But simply clearing a space for retrospective regret of former excesses is not what Petrarch implies he wanted his friend to undertake now. He was asking that Boccaccio join in nothing less than a hermeneutical revision of his authorial self. The Latin letter Boccaccio has before him will provide a model for this reformation: the slack and low style of youthful indulgence will be transfigured into the exemplary discourse of moral and religious fervency. In offering the Griselda to Boccaccio, Petrarch offered him as well the opportunity to translate himself.

A complicated theory of reading history lies behind Petrarch's remarks, a theory whose documents include letters in the *Familiares* and *Seniles* that Petrarch had sent to Boccaccio. As Thomas Greene has shown, Petrarch was acutely aware that the antique culture he so admired and desired to emulate was inescapably alien to him. Early in life, an active mind let Petrarch animate landscapes so that they would grant him access to the spirit of former times that remained in them. In a letter addressed to Virgil, for instance, Petrarch described how, visiting Mantua, he sought glades, fields, and streams, not for their own sake, but to question them: "I constantly wonder by what path you were wont to seek the unfrequented glades . . . what streams to visit . . . Such thoughts as these bring you back before my eyes."[11] Nature is not diminished when her creatures change and pass away; for a mind sufficiently invested to evoke his presence, Virgil, in the manner of the genius loci, is still part of the Mantuan countryside. But when Petrarch

---

10. Petrarch may also have remembered Dante's own words about the maturity of the *Convivio* in relation to the *Vita nuova*, and Boccaccio's comments in the *Trattatello*.

11. *Familiari*, 24.11. Quoted and discussed by Greene, *Light in Troy*, 89–90.

looked on the ruins of antiquity, or still more at the manuscripts in which classical culture is inscribed, he did not confront the past as a perceptible immanence but as a textual presence written with the ink of decay. This antiquity was not something he could see or summon directly; it was something he had to read. Thus, in that crucial moment when, as Greene says, "the poet turn[ed] from landscape to the literary remains," he became an archaeologist who "struggles to pierce their verbal surfaces to reach the living particularity of the past they bear within them."[12]

Because this past was latent, or hidden, or indecipherable, however, it could be constituted only as the object of historical, not experiential, knowledge. As a consequence, a certain ghostliness attended this past and whoever attempted to recover it. In his conversations with antiquity, Petrarch continually acknowledged the gap that exists between the factuality of classical culture and the facticity of his mental reconstruction of it. For him, knowing the past meant knowing his own temporal relation to it, the distance that the passage of centuries had placed between the impoverished present and the greatness of an age that is no more. This disquieting alertness led Petrarch to reconceive the nature of epistemology. In Aristotelian psychologies, the mind's utterance defined the rational substance of particular entities by setting them in the form of a proposition. Petrarch instead made mental discourse a sign of the difference between the reality it represents and the remote, far more estimable world it has replaced. No longer a transparent expression of the essence of the object it comprehends, the Petrarchan *verbum mentis* established its truthfulness only by registering its historicity as a signifier.

The hermeneutic consequences of such a theory of knowledge were considerable, both for the soul and for literary aesthetics. From Plato on, understanding had presupposed a likeness between knower and what is known: an analogy was thought to link the ways sensible, imaginative, and intellectual knowing were arranged in the mind and the hierarchy of material, mathematic, and rational realities they had as their objects. Guinizzelli had rooted the *stil novo* in these analogies; though Dante revised them radically in his explanation of himself to Bonagiunta, he still depended on them. With Petrarch, however, the likeness between the self and the past it desires to know was con-

---

12. Greene, *Light in Troy*, 93.

structed not by analogy but by a dialectic of mutual subordination: each subjected and was subject to the other. Antiquity, though prodigious, exists only as absence; the present, though real, is dwarfed by the magnitude of prior achievements.

Out of such an interplay of forces, one the necessary condition for the formation of the other and the herald of its dissolution, Petrarch generated the moral, historical subject. Always attending to himself because he was forever endeavoring to make himself better than he was, his soul almost needed to be divided to express itself truthfully. Forever exiled, Petrarch thus sought a permanent home in the autonomy and freedom of solitude; sovereign of himself because removed from the vulgar squabble of the forum, he nevertheless chose to live under an emperor; confident of his own superiority because of his knowledge of the past, he continually feared to be eclipsed by the eminence and renown of writers he discovered and communed with.

To understand "a voice from the depths of time," however, is one thing: to converse with it, as Greene says, Petrarch had to find an outward style to catch the inner movements of his soul. Unlike Dante, he needed a mode of writing that would fortify his own sense of selfhood even as he acknowledged its dependence on earlier exemplars. He found this style by simultaneously imitating ancient authorities and seeking to surpass them. By imitating them, Petrarch deferred to his models; by emulating them, he reburied them.

Petrarch had described what we might call his elements of style in a number of earlier letters to Boccaccio. In *Familiares* 22.2, written in 1359, Petrarch discussed how his writing reflected his soul:[13]

> I much prefer that my style be my own, rude and undefined, perhaps, but made to the measure of my own mind, like a well-cut gown, rather than to use someone else's style, more elegant, ambitious, and ornamented, but suited to a greater genius than mine . . . Certainly each of us has naturally something individual and his own in his utterance and language as in his face and gesture. It is better and more rewarding for us to develop and train this quality than to change it.[14]

---

13. For dating Petrarch's letters, see Ernest H. Wilkins, *Petrarch's Correspondence* (Padua: Antenore, 1960).

14. With this image of a well-cut gown, Petrarch virtually defines his style as a kind of translation. As Carolyn Dinshaw has shown, translation nearly became synonymous with a whole range of sartorial tropes in Rome and during the Middle Ages. The image is

Some six years later he developed his thought further: it is incumbent, he says, that an imitator "take care that what he writes resemble the original without reproducing it":

> we writers must look to it that with a basis of similarity there should be many dissimilarities. And the similarity should be planted so deep that it can only be extracted by quiet meditation. The quality is to be felt rather than defined. Thus we may use another man's conceptions and the color of his style, but not his words. In the first case the resemblance is hidden deep; in the second it is glaring. The first procedure makes poets, the second makes apes. (*Fam.* 23.19)[15]

These precepts can be extended to everything Petrarch authored. Style is an act of imitation, analogous to the intellectual process that discovered it, by which antiquity gains presence in the world, both at the level of representation and at the level of experience. In his poems, Petrarch made Virgil, in his prose, Cicero and a host of other authorities, subtexts that, though lying beneath the surface, gave his own writing its shape. In his life, Petrarch gave random events a style through the constancy of his response to them. No matter the occasion, Petrarch would maintain that his resolute consideration of every ethical imperative provided the pattern that ordered his experience.[16]

When Boccaccio read his comments about the *Decameron* and his translation of the tale of Griselda, Petrarch fully expected him to acknowledge the differences between their texts and to recognize their consanguinity as writers. Though he deprecates Boccaccio's book

---

especially prominent in Petrarch's version of the Griselda. See *Chaucer's Sexual Poetics* (Madison: University of Wisconsin Press, 1989), 132–55 and passim. See also Kristine Gilmartin Wallace, "Array as Motif in the *Clerk's Tale*," *Rice University Studies* 62 (1976): 99–110.

15. I follow here Greene's fine discussion of these passages in *Light in Troy*, 95–99.

16. As we have seen, when Petrarch chose to stay with the Viscontis in Milan, it outraged his friends in Florence, who viewed their city as the defender of liberty. However contradictory it seemed to Boccaccio, however, Petrarch's decision would have seemed consistent to him: how could the poet of the *Africa*, in which Virgil lived again, not reside with a latter-day Augustus, whom he might help bring an era of peace to Italy's warring factions through his poetry? See further Wallace, "Whan She Translated Was," 173ff. In one sense, I agree with Wallace that Petrarch desired to escape history entirely (161); this is balanced, however, by his intense desire to experience history through his own consciousness, which is the basis of his hermeneutic of the self. From this perspective, we can see Petrarch's Griselda as his delayed answer to Boccaccio's anguished letters of 1353; it is also his response to the more subtle criticisms of the *Trattatello*, though it is doubtful Petrarch read this work.

because it is in the vernacular, the product of his youth, and in prose, Petrarch honors it by according its final story the same status he granted Cicero, whom he also on occasion had simultaneously imitated and criticized at once. Just as Virgil's spirit breathes beneath the *Africa*, so the different style ("stilo . . . alio") of Petrarch's translation will reform the spirit of Boccaccio's tale and be animated by it. Though Petrarch considers his style and the purpose it supports nobler than Boccaccio's, they are united in their conviction that literature is exemplary.

This balancing of conflicting commitments is nowhere more evident than in Petrarch's approval of Boccaccio's defense of the *Decameron*: though detractors bit at it like dogs ("librum ipsum canum dentibus lacessitum"), Boccaccio repulsed them with his walking stick ("baculo") and yells ("tuaque voce"). Presumably Petrarch is referring to the introduction to the tales of the fourth day, where Boccaccio answered critics of the first part of his book by telling the story of Filippo Balducci and his son, who continues to hanker after women even after he is told they are geese. Petrarch, however, does not mention the tale; instead he substituted a different defense. There is a class of insolent and lazy men, he explains, who are eloquent only in chastising in others what they themselves do not want, or know, or are unable to do.

Of course Petrarch rides the hobbyhorse of his own haughtiness here. Boccaccio's apology appears as much impugned as praised. Reduced to "sticks and shouts," his story is made to seem a "vulgar" thing in itself, especially when compared to the stately dignity of Petrarch's own measured reproof. Yet while he scorns the style of Boccaccio's response, Petrarch clearly approves its form: the only way Boccaccio should have answered his maligners was by means of a story.[17] Indeed, Boccaccio's point was that by vindicating the moral innocence and inherent goodness of natural passion the *Decameron* justified itself, since vernacular fiction is the proper medium to deliver such a message to "graziosissime donne." In Petrarch's translation, the argument is that a story that apologizes for animal desire by claiming it is part of human nature is the proper reply to the doggy rabble who missed the point because they were deaf to its style. Though their reasons differ, Petrarch and Boccaccio would agree that literature, even prose in the mother tongue, has its place in the education of the soul.

17. See Glending Olson's perceptive comments about Petrarch's criticism of the *Decameron* in *Literature as Recreation*, 217–22.

It was in fact precisely the various ways different texts can reform the soul that Petrarch stressed in his letter to Boccaccio. While he was reading it, Boccaccio might well have recalled another his preceptor had sent to him ten years earlier, in which Petrarch had passionately defended his own style against captious faultfinders. That epistle Petrarch had begun without greeting, by itself an indication of his indignation:

> I ought either to have said nothing or gone into hiding, or better still, not to have been born so as to avoid these barking Scyllas. To come out into the open is not a game. Strong dogs rage with their teeth, weak ones with their bark. (*Ep. Sen.* 2.1)

He continued in a similar state of high dudgeon, discharging every weapon his invective had in its arsenal. When he repeated himself a decade later, Petrarch implied that just as Boccaccio had given an apposite answer to those hounds who disparaged the natural pleasures of the senses, so his previous emotional outbursts in Latin, the language of knowledge, had given a fitting answer to those curs who had claimed his writings were ignorant and untruthful. By contrast, Petrarch's censure in the preface to his translation of Griselda is dispassionate; at the end of his life he has put fustian aside in favor of moral philosophy. Once again, the level and purpose of these discourses differ: together Boccaccio's fable of Balducci, Petrarch's Latin screed, and his translation of Griselda, which integrates the best qualities of the other two, form a virtual paideia for perfecting the self and soul. Yet they all say the same thing about the role of literature in that process of amelioration: because the censors blinded themselves to its exemplarity, they did not understand its style; because they did not understand its style, they failed to be transformed by it. To underscore this point, Petrarch exemplified it one last time in his final letter to Boccaccio (17.4): he described how a friend from Verona remained unmoved as he read the translated Griselda because he thought it untrue. Though he did not respond, Petrarch says to Boccaccio, "The answer was simple." He then repeated the precept he had used to defend the *Decameron:* "there are some who consider whatever is difficult for them impossible for everyone."

The *Decameron*, in short, does cultural work; Petrarch may denigrate the culture, but he never devalued the work. Petrarch could therefore present the retelling the tale of Griselda as his own version of Boccaccio's story of Balducci's son without contradicting himself: it too is an argument, a defense of his writing and the motives that have driven it. We have already seen how in the preceding letter (17.2) Petrarch had rejected his friend's counsel to put aside the toils of composition, now that he has surpassed the fame of Virgil and Cicero, in order to preserve his health. Writing, Petrarch had said, sustains his life, because through it he exercises his virtue, which is the only reason to live. By placing his recasting of Griselda after this letter, even though he tells Boccaccio he wrote the translation first, Petrarch does not merely give the substance of experience to what might otherwise have remained a bromide. He implicitly grants to the tale of Griselda the same standing and power to instill knowledge and move readers to honorable action as his great invective *On His Own Ignorance*.

In this Petrarch repeated a note he had long sounded: because rhetoric and poetry solicit the emotions and engage the will, these discourses, far more than the empty formalistic analyses of dialecticians, provide the ground that makes the imperatives of philosophy and theology real, authentic, and knowable. As Petrarch had said earlier in the *Secretum*, when contemplating death, the entire soul needs to be engaged to prevent one's thoughts from "flying past, and not sinking in": "We must picture to ourselves the effect of death on each several part of our bodily frame, the cold extremities, the breast in the sweat of fever, the side throbbing with pain."[18] The cataloging of ailments goes on until their combined weight gives the meditation the heft of a lived event.

This particular passage helps us understand why Petrarch admired the description of the plague that opens the *Decameron*. Boccaccio's ability to embody the suffering of that wretched time corresponds to the feeling reflection on mortality Petrarch made one of the cardinal points of his spiritual exercises. Certainly the middle letters of *Seniles* 17 suggest that Petrarch thought the Griselda performed the same service in the face of death. In addition to this, however, the translation provided Petrarch a final opportunity to address two allied issues that had long preoccupied him: the cultivation of virtue in the face of the miseries brought by fortune; and the salvation of the soul. In the *Secretum*, Augustinus, speaking for piety, had proposed that the three concerns

---

18. *Secretum*, book 1, in Francesco Petrarca, *Opere*, ed. G. Ponte (Milan: Mursia, 1968), 460, quoted in Charles Trinkaus, *The Poet as Philosopher* (New Haven: Yale University Press, 1979), 62. I follow here two of Trinkaus's chapters, "Petrarch's Critique of Self and Society" and "Theologia Poetica and Theologia Rhetorica in Petrarch's Invectives."

are interrelated: one should continually contemplate death, because doing so will make one realize that true happiness depends on virtue rather than on fortune's transitory goods. Since for Augustinus no goal is meritorious unless it is spiritual, striving to achieve an end should be a manifestation of Christian devotion; a man works well only when what he does makes him fit to receive the gift of grace. From this point of view, Petrarch's pursuit of fame, love, and glory is a chasing after phantoms. But if qualities honored in the city of man find no place in the city of God, Petrarch wonders, how then is one to advance to worthiness? As Augustine's own experience proves, to sequester oneself from the world avoids that full engagement of will and the self-conscious mind that makes the choice of living piously truly commendable. One must be in the world to meaningfully transcend it. This line of thought concerned Petrarch enough that he made it the burden of a separate book, the *De otio religioso,* in which he considered the life his brother Gerardo was leading with his fellow monks in a Carthusian monastery.

For Franciscus, who speaks for Petrarch's ambitions, the struggle for virtue poses the same problem in a different form. He remains convinced of the worthiness of his aspirations. The palms he craves, however, are fundamentally civic virtues, yet like spiritual attainments, they must be gained through an intensely private inner battle to determine the constitution of the self. Only the man who has made himself estimable in solitude, shut off from the public, will be able to win the public's esteem. This tension also merited further inquiry; it became the subject of the *De vita solitaria.* Out of the press and pull of these conflicting beliefs Petrarch developed, in Charles Trinkaus's words, a twofold ethic:

> In one sphere of life (the external, public, social) men act according to certain necessary conventions or compulsions. There is no freedom there, and the best advice is to "submit patiently to circumstances." In the other sphere (the internal, private, spiritual and moral) men have power and freedom to change their feelings as they please, to accept divine grace when proffered or spurn it. (83)

Throughout his life Petrarch sought a means that could accommodate the contesting impulses of this "double consciousness." The Griselda represents his maturest attempt to reconcile the demands of the personal will and communal duty.

At the end of the story, Petrarch says he has told the tale "in a different style not so much to move women of his time to imitate [Griselda's] patience, which scarcely seems imitable to me, but to urge readers to imitate her constancy, that what she took on herself for her husband, we might dare to take on ourselves for God." When Griselda married Walter, she exercised the autonomy of her will by choosing to bury it, once and for all. From that moment on, the obedience she promised put her outside time and beyond the need for words: her patience collapsed every situation into the all-encompassing moment she swore her vow; no matter the circumstance, she would say only what she had said then. By making Griselda's submission the center and circumference of her universe, Petrarch equipped her to be an allegory of the soul's total surrender of self when it is folded forever in God's embrace.

But in itself her voluntary relinquishing of will could not serve as an example for the public or the private soul, because with her oath Griselda surrendered the freedom to choose to obey or disobey in the future. When she converted contingency into necessity, Griselda's patience became scarcely imitable, not because it is unattainable; as Petrarch's reaction to his reader from Verona shows, he allowed it the possibility of occurring in the real world. Her patience is inimitable because it is scarcely historical, since with her "I do" she sacrificed the power to reenact her choice; never again would she take into account the shifting occasions of time and place that make each decision a different decision, even if the conclusion reached is always the same.

If Griselda's patience is not exemplary, however, her constancy is, because constancy presupposes the historicity of choice. Even though her pledge froze Griselda in the instance of its utterance, she did continue to exist in time; the various predicaments Walter devised to tempt her proved Griselda's steadfastness again and again. It is this proof over time that Petrarch urges his readers to imitate: what he finds praiseworthy is the resolution to affirm one's choice in full recognition that changed conditions could have led one to decide otherwise.[19]

---

19. In this regard, compare Greene's remarks about the difference between Christian allegoresis and Petrarch's hermeneutic: "the older method presupposed a fullness of knowledge awaiting the successful interpreter":

> This method aligned author and reader in a single universe of discourse wherein no cultural distance could exist because, with the sole exception of the Christian revelation, historical change was virtually unknown. The new "archeological" hermeneutic, on the other hand, presupposed a considerable distance. . . . Instead of a relation

Griselda's exemplarity therefore depends on our ability to translate her patience into her constancy. Petrarch asks us to read her dateless devotion temporally, according to the same hermeneutic by which he has read antiquity, constructed his style, and shaped his selfhood. Now, in the ripeness of age, the remoteness of a privileged past does not concern him; he is intent instead on creating a new language that will posit and bridge the distance between this world and the next. To devise this language, he aligned the dialectic whereby he has understood himself in history with an allegorical understanding of himself in eternity. Amid the disparate goals that divide the soul in this transient life, constancy can enable the will to transform its fragmented but continual activity into an image of the unceasing unity of salvation. The power to choose reveals itself to be a palimpsest, under which Petrarch found written the choice of absolute submission to the will of God. In the event, Griselda's constancy became not only an analogy of faith but its discursive imitation, its style.[20]

For many readers, these repositionings, which inaugurate the aesthetics of Renaissance self-fashioning, actually intensify the totalitarian impulses of Petrarch's translation. They preempt protests against Walter's marital cruelty and political tyranny by making them part of an

---

between "veil" and "truth" that, once discovered, is easily grasped and formulated, there emerges an interplay of entities that resists total description because it operates in the elusive domain of style.

In the Griselda, Petrarch has defined exemplarity as the temporal dimension of allegory. Morse, "The Exemplary Griselda," therefore makes the division between exemplariness and allegory too stark, at least insofar as Petrarch is concerned.

20. It is in this spirit that Petrarch bid Boccaccio read his masterpiece against the two collections of letters, the *Seniles* and the *Familiares,* that are its counterparts. Like the *Decameron,* both of Petrarch's compendia begin with the plague. The *Familiares* opens with a (brief) lament to Petrarch's Socrates, Ludwig van Kempen, about the desolation the outbreak in 1348 has caused; the *Seniles* starts with the resolution, delivered to his Simonides, Francisco Nelli, that Petrarch will bear stoically the depredations of 1361, when the Black Death robbed him of everything the earlier eruption had left, including his Socrates. Like the *Decameron,* each collection ends with a meditation about its own style. The *Familiares* concludes with a series of letters to Horace, Virgil, and Homer; the *Seniles* with the four letters to Boccaccio and the unfinished letter to posterity. Both collections are engaged in the same project of the formation of the moral soul, yet the difference between them, signaled by the names of the dedicatees, constitutes a significant transformation. The *Familiares* chronicle the formation of the moral self out of the archaeological excavation of the ethical authority of antiquity. The *Seniles* begin there, with professions of stoic resignation in the face of fortune and death, but end by aligning this soul with Christian revelation. Socrates was a philosopher; Simonides, as Petrarch notes (*Sen.* 3.1), both poet *and* priest.

unexceptionable call to submit to the will of God; they purchase Griselda's efficacy as an icon of spiritual patience by making her the welcoming victim of each trespass against her, the thief of her own voice as a woman. Through this foreclosure of dissent and extenuation of violence, Petrarch's moral collaborates with his ambition to establish Latin as the proper vehicle for dignified communication. His Griselda works to shut down the arena of cultural contestation that the *Decameron* and translation of texts into the vernacular had opened. Both as a literary and as a social document, Petrarch's translation seeks to expand the hegemony of humanist authority.

I agree. But I think we also need to acknowledge that other forces are in play that pull against these autocratic tendencies. Although Petrarch does muffle the mutter of the quotidian to have Griselda speak for timeless truths, the qualities that make her worthy to imitate she evinces in specific, purposeful acts. From beginning to end, Petrarch's narrative moves toward the synchronic and the diachronic simultaneously; for this reason, as his first two readers confirm, it resists being read from one controlling perspective. In the *Decameron*, Dioneo's ironic postscript prevents his final tale from being solely an allegory, despite the clear references to Job and other biblical texts in it. In Petrarch's retelling, Griselda's exemplarity substitutes for Dioneo's skepticism but is just as much a translation, in the full Benjaminian sense, of her allegorical progress as his disbelief is. Her constancy is a this-worldly mode of meaning that follows the way her patience makes her a model of how things mean in the next; at the same time, however, her patience is no more convertible with her constancy than heaven is with earth. As a parable of the spirit, Griselda's subservience converts her into a Job and Walter into God's surrogate. But in the actual world, Petrarch says, God, unlike Walter, does not tempt. He does, however, test us:

> Probat tamen et sepe nos multis ac gravibus flagellis exerceri sinit, non ut animum nostrum sciat, quem scivit ante quam crearemur, sed ut nobis nostra fragilitas notis ac domesticis indicijs innotescat.

> [He does, however, test us and often allows us to be vexed with many heavy scourges, not that he might know our souls, which he knew before we were created, but that he might make us aware of our frailty through known and familiar signs.]

Insofar as Griselda remains constant, her travails give the will the reason it needs to endure even unmerited suffering: to become virtuous, God allows us to note our fragility with each sunrise and sunset. But insofar as Griselda bears her trials patiently, the lesson she teaches is the lesson Job learns from the whirlwind: God knows our purposes completely; we know nothing of his. For Petrarch, two modes of knowledge, how to live in life and how to live by leaving life, mingle in Griselda. Neither mode is subordinated or folded into the other, nor does one cancel the other; Griselda is more than their trope or the body on which they are inscribed. She is their translation.

A similar pattern of disarticulation amid correspondence contours the topographical prologue Petrarch wrote to introduce the tale:

> There stands in Italy, toward the western side, Mount Vesullus, one of the highest of the Apennines, whose summit, surpassing the clouds, thrusts itself up into the pure ether. This mountain, noble in itself, is most noble as the source of the Po, which, issuing from a little spring in its side, flows eastward toward the rising sun. Descending in its course, swelling quickly with great tributaries, so much so that Virgil calls it not merely one of the greatest but the king of rivers, it cuts through Liguria violently with whirling waters; then, bounding Emilia, Ferrara, and Venice, it empties at last through many great mouths into the Adriatic Sea.

The mountain exhibits its nobility by rising to the heavens, as if ether, not earth, were its proper element. Its elevation, which is a measure of its greatness, seems less a quality of the peak than a virtue it has achieved by overcoming the downward drag of natural propensities. Vesullus "casts itself up" to the skies ("liquido sese ingerit etheri"); it practically aspires to grandeur. To the extent that its loftiness should stand as an emblem of magnanimity and uprightness, Petrarch's message to noblemen like Walter or the Visconti is thus double-edged: he bows to their social prominence by presenting it as something massive, enduring, an expression of nature's glory; at the same time, he stipulates that the highborn are truly distinguished only if they raise themselves to the height of their distinction every day.

Petrarch's critique quite willingly supports the social hierarchies it simultaneously challenges; this tension increases when he adds that Vesullus is most noble because the Po issues from its side. Instead of rising up, the Po descends; instead of remaining an immovable solidity, it changes as it goes, growing from its unassuming source into the "fluviorum . . . rex" until it reaches the sea and loses its name. To the extent that its course charts Griselda's path from poor peasant to illustrious marchioness, the river's flow restates in terms of movement and time the ethical meaning of the mountain, which Petrarch had expressed in terms of space. The wellspring of merit, he will seem to say in retrospect, is constancy; the noble are themselves ennobled when they, like Griselda, reaffirm their resolve to remain unmoved come bad fortune or good. But the Po's own excellence has nothing to do with the fluctuations it undergoes; whether turbulent or majestic, while it is a river, it is always the Po. Its virtue, Petrarch implies, is deep-seated, unalterable, like the fixity of Griselda's patience and sacrifice of will, which unmake her as a person so that she can be made Christ-like. The Po issues humbly from Vesullus's side ("latere"), like the water and blood that flowed from Jesus' ("latus") when he, always God even dying, voluntarily suffered the humiliations of crucifixion.

By having the river translate the mountain the way constancy translates patience, by making Griselda both moral model and as inimitable as a pinnacle or stream, Petrarch's prologue exemplifies the manner in which his story translates both Boccaccio and himself. At the beginning of the *Decameron*, Boccaccio had asked his audience of "gracious ladies" to think of the plague as a rugged and steep mountain ("una montagna aspra e erta") beyond which lies a beautiful and delectable plain: the pleasure a traveler will enjoy there will be greater the more difficult the climb has been (*Intro.* 4). The transparency of Boccaccio's homage to the *Comedy* is matched by his flagrant rewriting of its intentional mode. Only a "prencipe Galeotto" would blithely transform Dante's allegory of salvation into an inducement to turn the page—Boccaccio turns the soul's hard ascent of Mount Purgatory to reach the Garden of Eden into a short season in hell that the persevering reader should suffer for the sake of one hundred delightful fictions told in lovely gardens that await her.[21] Petrarch's homage to Boccaccio in turn flagrantly reformulates the recreational poetics of the *Decameron* according to the precepts Petrarch set forth in his letters to its author; Vesullus "restyles" the rhetorical mountain of his friend's prologue so that it corresponds to the ethical and spiritual imperatives he saw in the tale of Griselda.

---

21. Boccaccio's figure, of course, also invokes the hellish depravities of the plague by recalling the "erta" of the first canto of the *Inferno*.

Petrarch's conversion of Boccaccio's "bellissimo piano e dilettevole" into his description of Vesullus and the Po marks the Latin Griselda a self-translation as well. Petrarch had composed his polemic *De ignorantia* in 1367 while "sitting in a small boat amid the whirling waves of the Po" as he returned to Pavia from Venice. Writing in 1373, he would expect Boccaccio to notice that instead of sailing against the current, he now follows the natural flow of the river to the Adriatic. From immersion in life's agitations Petrarch has moved to patient acceptance of them. This change in mind and attitude, which allows Petrarch to imply that the Griselda triumphs over his invective without denying it, also provides the occasion for him to tell Boccaccio that politics never influenced his devotion to moral philosophy. Petrarch had returned to Pavia in response to an invitation from Galeazzo Visconti; six years later, in the letter immediately preceding his version of the Griselda, he made a point of answering Boccaccio's charge that he had wasted too much time in the service of princes. The truth of the matter, Petrarch replies, is that "I was with the princes in name, but in fact the princes were with me; I never attended their councils, and very seldom their banquets."[22]

No less than Boccaccio's Gualterius, then, the convictions that drive Petrarch's Griselda are themselves driven by their own internal antagonisms. These antagonisms are translated rather than resolved, and occupy discrete linguistic and cultural registers; however much Petrarch strove to unify them, his language is more stratified than it is monovocal. To a large degree, Chaucer records his response to early Italian humanism in the ways he translated the fractures that run through Petrarch's discourse.

We should not underestimate the obstacles Chaucer faced as he read the Latin Griselda. Severs has shown that Chaucer's manuscript of the tale almost certainly contained Petrarch's preface to it.[23] Even if he did know that the book Petrarch was talking about was the *Decameron,* unless Chaucer read the previous letter (17.2), it would have been difficult for him to see that Petrarch's critique and his translation were driven by the same principles. Indeed, without knowing the *Familiares* and *Epistolae Seniles,* or more generally his historical construction of the self, Chaucer

---

22. *Ep Sen.* 17.2, p. 650.
23. Severs, *Literary Relationships,* 41–46.

would not have understood how Petrarch's Griselda exemplified his own understanding of himself as a writer. Similarly, without knowing the *De vita solitaria* and *De otio religioso,* Chaucer might have found Petrarch's equally intense abhorrence and involvement in the political affairs he mentions a strange, perhaps troubling, contradiction.

Despite the visits to Florence and Milan, despite the consistent praise, Petrarch remained for Chaucer a man more heard of than read. Some aspects of the "lauriat poete['s]" project clearly escaped him. Petrarch often heaped contempt on scholastic dialecticians, and on sophistic "Brittani" in particular; an Oxford clerk who "unto logyk had longe ygo" was precisely the wrong person to make his disciple.[24] Someone who dismissed the geographical prohemium to the tale as a "thyng impertinent" clearly did not see in landscape what Petrarch saw.

Just as clearly, however, Chaucer was in position to comprehend a great many of the issues Petrarch raises—not in the forms and contexts he raised them, which spoke to his own poetic self-fashioning and cultural ideologies in Italy, but in contexts Chaucer did know. The idea, for instance, of public poetry in the reign of Richard II, as Anne Middleton has called it, with its call for poems to aid the establishment of peace, could have prompted Chaucer to ponder the politics of Petrarch's translation, as well as the place a detached, retiring Clerk, who proves himself a master of rhetoric, should occupy in the common profit.[25] When Harry Bailley asked the Clerk to keep his high style "in stoor," he had two figures in mind, both of whom were indeed defined by their public use of language: the scribe who writes with due ceremony to the king ("as whan that men to kynges write"), and the preacher whose bombast made him hard to comprehend.[26] Harry, we remember, had just silhouetted the Clerk against the realms of romance and fabliau; the venues he now has the Clerk shuttling between are secular and religious. But whether he's imagined a secretary in West-

---

24. On Petrarch's contempt for dialecticians in general, and British logicians in particular, see Trinkaus, *The Poet as Philosopher,* 57; and Neil Gilbert, "Richard of Bury and the 'Quires of Yesterday's Sophisms,'" in *Philosophy and Humanism: Renaissance Essays in Honor of Paul Oskar Kristeller,* ed. E. Mahoney (New York: Columbia University Press, 1976), 228–57; Eugenio Garin, *L'eta nuova* (Naples: Morano, 1969), 148–52.

25. See Anne Middleton, "The Idea of Public Poetry in the Reign of Richard II," *Speculum* 53 (1978): 94–114.

26. This last species of cleric is the kind Wyclif had opposed when he demanded that sermons avoid "heroic declamation." See John Wycliffe, *Sermones,* part 4, sermon 31, p. 231. See further my "'And Speketh so Pleyn,'" 319–20.

minster or a priest in his parish, Harry pointedly bids this Clerk to shelve the style that made clerks political in either domain. Away from London, not yet near Canterbury, the Host wants "straight talk" that dispenses with the contorted verbiage of crown and miter:

> Speketh so pleyn at this tyme, we yow preye,
> That we may understonde what ye seye.
>
> (19–20)

Harry's call for the clear language of daily conversation, of course, is itself political. The knotty questions involved in determining the proper relationship between ecclesiastical and civil power, problems a Langland needed his whole life to shuck and bolt, the Host would simply dodge in the name of communal "solaas." Like Chaucer, Harry thinks that "men shal nat maken ernest of game"; for both of them, however, the associational polity that storytelling creates is a polity to the extent that it avoids association with the controversies of the day. As an ideology, it would seem that fiction is for Harry (and his maker) much what humanism was for Petrarch: a mode that engages the ethics of history by deflecting the consequences of its demand for public commitment.

The Clerk responds to the Host's prayer by reperforming its odd attitude of deference and command. He defers to Harry by replying neither as civil servant nor as churchman; he overrules him by continuing to speak from the more private realm of his studies:

> "Hooste," quod he, "I am under youre yerde;
> Ye han of us as now the governance,
> And therefore wol I do yow obeisance,
> As fer as resoun axeth, hardily."
>
> (E.21–25)

Instead of a simple "I am at your service," he says to the Host, as only a logician would, "I acknowledge your authority by my own free will as it is informed by reason." This answer, like the solicitation that prompts it, also moves in two directions: while the exercise of free choice is always the outgrowth of a dialogue between reason and the will, the Clerk's "now" stresses how provisional this particular decision to yield is. Like Petrarch, the Clerk is a man drawn to contemplative seclusion and fully ready to clear a space for himself in the social fray; self-possessed yet tractable, he has been well suited to register the ambivalences that tug at Petrarch's Griselda.

Indeed, as a schoolman educated by the nominalists of Oxford, who came of age during the period of "Franciscan hegemony," he would appreciate the rhetorical emphasis of Petrarch's humanism and applaud the primacy he accorded the will, no matter what he thought of the notion that a poet's musings could lead the soul to virtue.[27] Such a cleric would readily acknowledge the temporal difference that at once distinguishes Griselda's constancy from her patience and establishes a connection between them. Chaucer's Clerk shows that he is well aware of the effects of time on voluntary actions and that he is as preoccupied by death as Petrarch was. In the prologue, he underlines the fact that the man who taught him his tale is "deed and nayled in his cheste" (29), for all the fame "rethorike sweete" brought him:

> But Deeth, that wol nat suffre us dwellen heer,
> But as it were a twynklyng of an ye,
> H[y]m . . . hath slayn.
>
> (36–38)

These musings, in and of themselves, are clerical platitudes, but the Clerk's deployment of them has nothing commonplace about it. A moment before he had simultaneously agreed to Harry's "governance" and declared his independence from it. Now he proclaims Petrarch the living authority whose words he attentively committed to memory at Padua and a ghost whose textual remains he will presume to edit and comment upon. Paul used the trope "in ictu oculi" to foretell the speed with which the body will rejoin the soul at the Resurrection (1 Cor. 15:51). The Clerk uses the phrase to signify a separation of author from work that instantaneously enables him to become a second husband to the words that survive as Petrarch's relict.[28] The long *occupatio* that fol-

---

27. "Franciscan hegemony" is Heiko Oberman's phrase to describe fourteenth-century Christian theology; see his "Fourteenth-Century Religious Thought: A Premature Profile," *Speculum* 53 (1978): 80–93. See also Oberman's *The Harvest of Medieval Theology* (Cambridge: Harvard University Press, 1963); Charles Trinkaus, *In Our Image and Likeness*, 2 vols. (Chicago: University of Chicago Press, 1970).

28. As a figure of the ultimate metamorphosis in Christianity, the Clerk's use of Paul's "twynkyng of an ye" also prepares his audience both for the sudden change in Walter's behavior within the tale, and for the Clerk's equally sudden conversion of the tale from an allegory of the soul's submission to God to a handbook for wives directed at Alice of Bath.

lows, in which the Clerk proceeds to summarize Petrarch's prologue and then pronounce it irrelevant, perfectly combines his compliance as copyist and assertiveness as magister. With this singular act of self-invention, so reminiscent yet so unlike Petrarch's excavation and reburial of the manuscripts of antiquity, the Clerk becomes the first English Petrarchist and his first English critic.

Despite the Host's request, the Clerk, already a Griselda and a Walter, seems intent on remaining "sophismatic." He is a character, that is to say, in whom assurance and humility disarticulate and follow one another as modes of meaning. As such, he is not simply a response to or translation of Petrarch but the performance of translation as I have understood it in this book. His passing in an eyeblink from reverence to emulation puts readers on notice that Walter's abrupt decision to devise cruel proofs of Griselda's known virtue neither contradicts nor repeats his initial insight into her goodness so much as it transcribes the relationship between her submission and her unyielding determination to persevere in it.[29] His transformation of Harry's badinage into the student's deference and teacher's sureness before a text explains in advance why Walter's appearance before Griselda's hut, and hers before the people as his bride, have all the trappings of sudden materializations in high romance and all the solemnity of a biblical miracle, why Griselda's trials after her marriage locate Walter in an ur–"Tale of Ill-Advised Curiosity" while for her they are chapters in a martyr's biography. More than in Boccaccio and Petrarch, fairy-tale marvel and hagiographic mystery in "The Clerk's Tale" reveal the mode by which each acknowledges and defers the hardships and depredations of toil, of age, of death.[30]

The Clerk performs as translation again at the end of the tale when

---

29. Because I believe Griselda's resolve translates Walter's, I also would argue that Linda Georgianna simplifies the apparent distinction Chaucer draws between Walter's prudence, characterized by his "avysement," and Griselda's "grammar of assent." See Linda Georgianna, "The Clerk's Tale and the Grammar of Assent," *Speculum* 70 (1995): 793–821. I do think, however, that the collision of prudential and spiritual wisdom in "The Clerk's Tale" is a Chaucerian translation of Petrarch's mode of conjoining patience and constancy, allegory and exemplarity.

30. Long ago Severs noted that Chaucer's most prominent additions to Petrarch intensified both the spiritual and the affective aspects of the tale. Allusions to the Annunciation and Nativity are especially notable (*Literary Relationships*, 215–50). Elizabeth Salter's classic analysis is still trenchant; see *The Knight's Tale and the Clerk's Tale* (London: Arnold, 1962). Chaucer's additions, I would note in passing, have much in common with the juxtaposition of romance marvel and spiritual miracle in the Wife of Bath's prologue and tale. I think it likely that one was made with the other in mind.

he suddenly converts Petrarch's allegory of the soul's surrender to God into an ironist's handbook for wifely comportment. Before the "Envoy" begins, the Clerk rehearses not so much his conversation with Harry as its dynamics.[31] The Host had asked for lighter fare that might appeal to the community of pilgrims, regardless of their learning or degree of familiarity with the different social languages of England. The Clerk will now give Harry what he wanted: donning a docility that associates him with both the heroine of the tale of obedience he has just related and the timorous bride of Harry's initial words to him, the Clerk says that "for the Wyves love of Bathe" he will now "stynte of ernestful matere" and the "heigh stile" that he had been asked to avoid. Yet at the same time that he presents himself as the soul of complaisance and companionship, he is preparing to launch his satiric squibs at the Wife. The Clerk may in truth be a patient man, but his imitation of Griselda's humility here is part of a strategy of requital: under the guise of agreeing with Alice of Bath by exhibiting the meekness she so prized in the later Jankyn, he moves to check her from charging, when he does attack, that he has merely imitated her attacks on clerks. He affiliates himself with Walter's wife, in other words, in order to show the Wife's a Walter; five stanzas of repeated rhymes in "-ence" and "-aille" later, he has persisted in driving home his point with both Walter's aggressiveness *and* Griselda's constancy amid the "wo that is in mariage." By the end of the "Envoy," the Clerk has sufficiently differentiated himself from Alice for him to think he has rescued clerkhood from her definition of it; in fact, however, he and the Wife have translated one another the way Walter and Griselda do in the tale.

The Wife is not the only authority figure the Clerk engages in his "Envoy"; he manipulates Petrarch in the same manner he manipulates Alice. He first identifies himself with the "worthy clerk" of "Padowe" by identifying him with Griselda. Like him, she "is deed, and eek hire pacience, / And bothe atones buryed in Ytaille." In the prologue, however, the imminence of mortality had excited thoughts of the frailty of all human life; in the "Envoy," the Clerk rescores Griselda's death into a clarion call for uxorial domination:

---

31. For a recent reading of the "Envoy," as well as a full review of the scholarship on it, see Howell Chickering, "Form and Interpretation in the *Envoy* to *The Clerk's Tale*," *Chaucer Review* 29 (1995): 352–72.

Lat noon humylitee youre tonge naille,
Ne let no clerk have cause or diligence
To write of yow a storie of swich mervaille.

(1177–86)

With this counsel, the Clerk manages to contravene Petrarch's *moralitas* and to read it literally. He ignores the caution against taking Griselda's patience as a guide to conjugal behavior yet also advises wives that they should indeed take Petrarch's recommendation and not "folwen Griselde as in humylitee." The Clerk tells them they should follow the Wife instead and covet "maistrye." Meek as Griselda, and man enough to beat the Wife at her own game, the Clerk thus stands forth as the most supportive of misogynists; in order to secure the allegory of his irony, however, he reads Petrarch in the same manner that Alice reads Scripture.

Once Petrarch suggested wifely obedience could signify steadfast submission to God's will, he could no longer claim the heuristic model that made the analogy possible was restricted or confined to himself; when he made Griselda exemplary, the intensely personal ethic whereby he discovered his private and public soul became a paradigm of moral philosophy for everybody.[32] In repeating Petrarch's peroration, the Clerk endorses this aspect of the tale. But when he added the "Envoy," Chaucer subjected its drive toward comprehensiveness to rhetorical scrutiny. With all the suddenness of the transformation of the hag in Alice's tale, or, from a different perspective, Walter's determination to test his wife, we realize that the Clerk himself, like Troiolo or Dioneo, has spoken with motive aforethought; moreover, because he does, he proves that Petrarch's is only one among many possible readings of the tale.[33] Allegory allowed Petrarch to make Griselda an occa-

---

32. Petrarch's use of the Letter of St. James makes clear the extent to which Griselda's exemplarity relies on his hermeneutics of the self. Griselda's obedience becomes an emblem of the soul's steadfast devotion to God because James had said that God tempts no man (1.13). As we have seen, Petrarch then supplies his own commentary: God does allow us to be tested, "not that He may know our spirit, which He knew before we were begotten, but that we might be made aware of our frailties through known and familiar signs." For Petrarch, Griselda is a way to know himself.

33. In retrospect we also realize that the Clerk is as much a fantast as Harry. I have argued elsewhere that he sees Griselda as a projection of himself ("The Lineaments of Desire," 206–7; *The Cast of Character*, 141–42, 163–65).

sion for the disciplined language of an exemplary soul and the Word without end to translate each other; with the Clerk, both allegory and Griselda, in the "twynklynge of a ye," become the foil of irony. The Aristotelian logician who learned her story from Petrarch at Padua is never more Boccaccian than when he introduces Griselda of Saluzzo to the Wife of Bath on the road to Canterbury.

Ultimately, because Petrarch represented them imaginatively, Chaucer responded to the poetic and the political challenges of the Griselda aesthetically. He translated the competing forces at play in Petrarch's construction of himself into those discourses that negotiated the boundaries between the secular and the ecclesiastical, between worldly experience and scholarly authority. In England, the university was one site where these discourses especially intersected; the Clerk was born when Chaucer juxtaposed them "sophismatically" as both motivated and unmotivated speech. At once an uncanny compound of insight into and ignorance of Petrarch and his culture, the Clerk is also the most "Italian" of the Canterbury pilgrims. We need only compare him to the clerks in *Piers Plowman*, or, even more to the point, to measure Langland's use of the graduate curricula to represent his clerks against the less scholastic knowledges that constitute Chaucer's, to feel the effect of the Italian tradition generally, and of Boccaccio in particular. But to the extent that the Clerk at the same time signifies the difference of Italy, as well as the problems history poses to epistemology, he also testifies to Chaucer's ability to use the tradition he made to create a figure we will not find in Petrarch, in Boccaccio, or in Dante, but who translates the figures we do.

8

Envoy / *Congedo*

I have heard that Charles Muscatine once was asked why he hadn't written a book on the Italian tradition to complement his famous study of Chaucer and the matter of France. He answered, in effect, "Because it isn't there." The story may be apocryphal; its point, however, is pertinent and one I have tried to remember throughout this study. Although Florentine merchants were active in London throughout the fourteenth century, although some members of Richard's court were part of an international network of literary exchange, although a poem like the *Alliterative Morte Arthure* could invoke Genoa, Milan, and Rome for complex cultural purposes, before Chaucer there was no Italian tradition in England.[1]

Precisely because Dante's, or Boccaccio's, or Petrarch's customs and conventions were not part of English literary culture the way Froissart's were, I have argued that the transnational dialogue Chaucer inaugurated had to have differed both in its construction and in our comprehension of it from the French tradition he could "gather from

---

1. See Michael Hanly, "Courtiers and Poets: An International System of Literary Exchange in Late Fourteenth-Century Italy, France, and England," *Viator* 28 (1997): 305–32. In this important article, Hanly shows that multilingual courtiers were able to transmit the themes and some of Boccaccio's and Petrarch's humanistic texts at least a generation earlier than commonly believed. Obviously the Italian tradition that emissaries such as Philippe de Mèziéres and Honorat Bovet helped to create in France impinges on the cultural reception of Italy that French poets in England, such as Grandson and Deschamps, were promoting there. But the fact remains that no record of Italian-language poetic manuscripts has been found in English library catalogs in the fourteenth century. See Hanly, *Boccaccio, Beauvau, and Chaucer: Troilus and Criseyde: Four Perspectives on Influence* (Norman: University of Oklahoma Press, 1990), 27–31. Even though Chaucer, who had direct or indirect ties to each of these courtier-poets (except possibly Bovet), should be included in this network of transmission, his Italian tradition, it seems to me, can only be considered a translation of the French counterpart. At the very moment when Grandson and Deschamps were making Italian literary developments known at Richard's court, Chaucer had turned away from court poetry for good.

the air," as Pound once put it.[2] In truth, of course, the usages and assumptions that England shared with France were not at all like the air Chaucer breathed; they were social and semantic fields, whose interpenetrating values one could map, as Muscatine did, by plotting the differences in style and direction between "The Book of the Duchess" and Machaut's "Jugement," by setting "The Miller's Tale" alongside "Bérenger au long cul." These values and practices gained the genealogical impress that made them traditional within the crosshatching of contemporary axiologies that emanated from the courts of Richard II and Charles V; their ideological frontier was bordered by the public worlds of London and Paris. This was the tradition of which Deschamps was right to say that Chaucer was a "grant translateur."

But Italy was not France. No journey to Paris could have lessened the sense of disconnectedness a Londoner would feel as he learned about the political and social organization of Italian city states; an English poet would discover very quickly that Florentine vernacular literature had developed in ways he had not anticipated. The interpretive schemes or habitus (in Bourdieu's sense) that made civic and literary forms traditional in the commune, of course, differed greatly from those in seignorial Milan; however acutely Chaucer interpreted these schemes in either city, one thing he would not register was any sense of their "transmittedness." The absence of traditionality is in fact the key feature of Chaucer's Italian tradition: it is what prompted him to read the texts he acquired in relation to one another; it is the reason why, from *The House of Fame* to *The Canterbury Tales*, everything new he imported from Italy bears markings of how uncomfortably it fit his idea of what was old.[3]

To acknowledge these differences, I have maintained that, in contrast to the French, Chaucer's Italian Tradition does not inhere in his translations of the *trecentisti* but is a translation of these translations. As I said at the outset, I have not, therefore, for the most part, sought this tradition by asking what Chaucer took from Dante, why he did what he did to Boccaccio, or how he changed Petrarch. I have sought it instead

---

2. In *The French Tradition and the Literature of Medieval England* (Toronto: University of Toronto Press, 1994), William Calin has examined narratives in great detail; as James Wilhelm has said, equally massive volumes could be written on drama, lyric, and religious texts. See Wilhelm's review, *Speculum* 71 (1996): 706.

3. On tradition and traditionality, see David Shils, *Tradition* (Chicago: University of Chicago Press, 1981); and Clare A. Lees, *Tradition and Belief: Religious Writing in Late Anglo-Saxon England* (Minneapolis: University of Minnesota Press, 1999).

by asking how, after Chaucer had read these authors, the modes of meaning in the poems he wrote corresponded to, yet disarticulated, the modes that determined ways in which the Italian works translated each other.

I hope my readers will bear with me, then, if in the form of a valedictory envoy or *congedo* I belabor a point they will have long since grasped. As an inquiry into tradition, this book is not about sources or the ascription of influence as such. The burden of my argument, let me insist, has not been that Chaucer imitated the allegory of the *Comedy*, or that the *Filostrato* was the source of his analysis of the ironies of motive in the *Troilus*, or even that the origin of their combination in the Manciple's prologue was his reading Dante and Boccaccio together. I believe each of these statements is true. I believe as well they are not proven less true by acknowledging that Chaucer knew Latin, French, and English texts in which allegory and irony were deployed to explore the connections between language, ethics, selfhood, and salvation. Demonstrating their truth, however, has not been my main intent.

I have tried instead to address Chaucer's Italian tradition as a translation of manners of meaning. I have found Benjamin useful for this project precisely because he redefined standard explanations of source and influence. For him, as we have seen, the originating text had nothing primary or authoritative about it; it was rather a signature of its language's intention, compounded out of the material differences of speech itself, which became legible when set beside another text that has been signed in a different language in a corresponding way. Although I feel a language may have many intentions, some of which are culturally determined, Benjamin's central premise, that translation is the expression of how the correspondence reveals and, as it were, smudges the signatures that comprise it, does offer a way to read both the resistances and the changes that occur when cultures cross.

Interstitial though it may be, Chaucer's Italian tradition still needs a far longer book to do it justice. I claim no more for my chapters on the Manciple and the Clerk or my brief comments about the *Troilus* than that they represent an approach to the topic. But neither those chapters, nor a book that would include any like them, could be written without establishing the Italian tradition that is the horizon of the one Chaucer made. I am well aware that by charting the readings and counter-readings that inform Dante's poetics, and Boccaccio's, and Petrarch's, I have left Chaucer offstage for long stretches; as much as his journeys, however, these dialogues are crucial because they are what enable us to recollect Chaucer's Italy as a translation.

In light of this attention to Italian literary history, it may seem odd that I have said little about the *Decameron* and nothing about Chaucer's relation to it. Helen Cooper, writing for the new edition of *Sources and Analogues*, Nigel Thompson in his *Chaucer, Boccaccio, and the Debate of Love*, and the various contributors to *The Decameron and the Canterbury Tales*, have all recently stressed the imprint of Boccaccio's masterpiece on *The Canterbury Tales*.[4] I have been silent in part because I think the matter needs a book dedicated entirely to it; I do believe, however, that the persuasiveness of any attempt to read the two collections together depends on the way it theorizes the dissimilarities between their intentional modes. Those who have denied Boccaccio's influence, often for tendentious purposes of preserving Chaucer's morality or enhancing his genius, have grounded their denial in the fact that Chaucer, who rendered lengthy passages from the *Filostrato* and *Teseida*, never put into verse a single sentence that unquestionably came from one of Boccaccio's stories. From advocates this textual absence has provoked a variety of explanations, the most prominent of which has been Chaucer's "memorial" reconstruction of the *novelle*. To my mind, however, precisely because it discomfits efforts to hard-wire the connection between Boccaccio's prose and the *Tales*, Chaucer's failure to echo the *Decameron* is crucial for reclaiming its importance to him. Rather than reason it away, we should, I am convinced, take Chaucer's muteness as an injunction to rethink the dynamics of cross-cultural translation. Instead of asking what Chaucer did to Boccaccio or Boccaccio to Chaucer, instead of drafting lists of narrative or thematic correspondences (which often rely on the logic that if a is x and b is x, then a is b), we might more profitably ask what sort of work *The Canterbury Tales* would be if its tale telling began with the Pardoner and ended with the Clerk. By assessing the extent to which modes of making meaning differed in Italy and England, and why, we can analyze the preoccupations both authors shared without running into the cul-de-sac of intentionality or erasing obliquities of history in the name of influence. That at least is the way I would want to discuss the relations between the

---

4. Helen Cooper, "*Sources and Analogues of Chaucer's Canterbury Tales*: Reviewing the Work," *Studies in the Age of Chaucer* 19 (1997): 183–210; Nigel Thompson, *Chaucer, Boccaccio, and the Debate of Love* (Oxford: Clarendon Press, 1996); Koff and Schildgen, *The Decameron and the Canterbury Tales*.

Tales and Boccaccio's *capolavoro*. But, as I say, I did not think this book, lengthy enough as it is, was the proper venue for that discussion. Perhaps I am wrong; if I am, I ask pardon, for this and for my other indiscretions, in words I translate untranslated from "myn auctor": "arrette it nat to my wyl, but to myn unkonnynge."

Bibliography

Sources and Ancient Texts

Albert the Great. *Alberti Magni . . . Opera Omnia*. Ed. August Borgnet and Emile Borgnet. Paris: Ludovicum Vives, 1890–99.
Ambrose. *Expositio Evangelii secundum Lucam*. In *Traité sur l'Évangile de S. Luc*. 2 vols. Sources Chrétiennes 45, 52. Ed. G. Tissot. Paris: du Cerf, 1952.
Aristotle. *The Complete Works of Aristotle*. 2 vols. Ed. Jonathan Barnes. Princeton: Princeton University Press, 1984.
Augustine. *Quaestionum evangeliorum libri duo*. Patrologia Latina 35:1323–64.
———. *In Iohannis Evangelium tractatus*. Corpus Christianorum series latina 36. Turnhout: Brepols, 1954.
Averroes. *Commentarium magnum in Aristotelis De anima libros*. Ed. F. S. Crawford. Cambridge, Mass.: Medieval Academy of America, 1953.
Boccaccio, Giovanni. *Il Filocolo*. Ed. Salvatore Battaglia. Bari: Laterza, 1938.
———. *The Life of Dante*. Trans. Vincenzo Z. Bollettino. Garland Library of Medieval Literature. New York: Garland, 1990.
———. *Opere in versi: Corbaccio, Trattatello in laude di Dante, Prose Latine, Epistole*. Ed. Pier Giorgio Ricci. Milan: Ricciardi, 1965.
———. *Opere latini minore*. Ed. Aldo F. Massèra. Bari: Laterza, 1938.
———. *Le Rime, L'Amorosa Visione, La Caccia di Diana*. Ed. Vittore Branca. Bari: Laterza, 1938.
———. *Tutte le opere di Giovanni Boccaccio*. Ed. Vittore Branca. 12 vols. Milan: Mondadori, 1964–.
Boethius. *The Consolation of Philosophy*. Ed. and trans. S. J. Tester. Loeb Classical Library. Cambridge: Harvard University Press, 1973.
———. *The Consolation of Philosophy*. Trans. R. H. Green. Indianapolis: Bobbs-Merrill, 1962.
Bonaventure. *Opera omnia*. Ed. PP. Collegii a san Bonaventura. Quaracchi, 1882–1902.
Capellanus, Andreas. *The Art of Courtly Love*. Trans. John Parry. New York: Ungar, 1959.

Cavalcanti, Guido. *The Poetry of Guido Cavalcanti*. Ed. and trans. Lowry Nelson Jr. New York: Garland, 1986.

Chaucer, Geoffrey. *The Complete Poetry and Prose of Geoffrey Chaucer*. Ed. John H. Fisher. 2d ed. New York: Holt, Rinehart and Winston, 1989.

———. *The Complete Works of Geoffrey Chaucer*. Ed. William Walter Skeat. Oxford: Clarendon, 1894–97.

———. *The Manciple's Tale*. Ed. Donald C. Baker. Vol. 2, part 10 of *A Variorum Edition of the Works of Geoffrey Chaucer*. Norman: University of Oklahoma Press, 1984.

———. *The Minor Poems*. Ed. George Pace and Alfred David. Vol. 5, part 1 of *A Variorum Edition of the Works of Geoffrey Chaucer*. Norman: University of Oklahoma Press, 1982.

———. *The Riverside Chaucer*. Ed. Larry D. Benson. Boston: Houghton Mifflin, 1987.

———. *The Works of Geoffrey Chaucer*. Ed. F. N. Robinson. 2d ed. Boston: Houghton Mifflin, 1957.

Cicero. *De officiis*. Ed. and trans. W. Miller. Loeb Classical Library. Cambridge: Harvard University Press, 1928.

———. *De Oratore*. Ed. and trans. H. Rackham. Loeb Classical Library. Cambridge: Harvard University Press, 1960.

Contini, Gianfranco, ed. *Poeti del duecento*. 2 vols. Milan: Riccardo Ricciardi, 1960.

Dante Alighieri. *Dante's Lyric Poetry*. Ed. and trans. Kenelm Foster and Patrick Boyde. 2 vols. Oxford: Clarendon, 1967.

———. *De vulgari eloquentia*. Ed. Pier Vincenzo Mengaldo. In *Opere Minori*, vol. 2. Milan: Riccardo Ricciardi, 1979.

———. *La Divina Commedia secondo l'antica vulgata*. Ed. Giorgio Petrocchi. 4 vols. Società dantesca italiana. Milan: Mondadori, 1966–67. Translated as *The Divine Comedy* by Charles Singleton. Princeton: Princeton University Press, 1970–76.

———. *Vita nuova*. Ed. Domenico de Robertis. Milan: Riccardo Ricciardi, 1980.

Gower, John. *The Complete Works of John Gower*. Ed. G. Macaulay. 4 vols. Oxford: Clarendon, 1902.

———. *The Major Latin Works of John Gower*. Trans. Eric Stockton. Seattle: University of Washington Press, 1962.

Guillaume de Lorris and Jean de Meung. *Le Roman de la Rose*. Ed. Daniel Poirion. Paris: Garnier-Flammarion, 1974.

Guinizelli, Guido. *The Poetry of Guido Guinizelli*. Ed. and trans. Robert Edwards. New York: Garland, 1987.

Hugh of St. Cher. *Opera omnia in universum Vetus et Novum Testamentum*. Lugduni: J. A. Hugvetom and G. Barbier, 1669.

Hugh of St. Victor. *Didascalicon.* Ed. and trans. by Jerome Taylor. In *The "Didascalicon" of Hugh of St. Victor.* New York: Columbia University Press, 1961.
Isidore of Seville. *Etymologiarum sive originum libri XX.* Ed. W. M. Lindsay. 2 vols. Oxford: Clarendon. 1911.
Langland, William. *Piers Plowman.* Ed. J. A. W. Bennett. Oxford: Clarendon, 1972.
Latini, Brunetto. *Li livres dou tresor.* Ed. F. J. Karmody. Berkeley and Los Angeles: University of California Press, 1958.
———. *Tesoretto.* In *Poeti del duecento,* ed. Gianfranco Contini, 2:169–284. Milan: Riccardo Ricciardi, 1960.
Lydgate, John. *The Fall of Princes.* Ed. Henry Bergen. Early English Text Society 121–24. 1924; rpt. Oxford: Oxford University Press, 1967.
Machaut, Guillaume de. *Oeuvres de Guillaume de Machaut.* Ed. E. Hoepffner. 3 vols. Société des anciens textes français. Paris: Firmin-Didot, 1908–21.
Ovid. *P. Ovidi Nasonis Amores . . . Ars Amatoria, Remedia Amoris.* Ed. E. J. Kenney. Oxford Classical Texts. Oxford: Oxford University Press, 1961.
———. *P. Ovidii Nasonis Metamorphoses.* Ed. W. S. Anderson. Leipzig: Teubner, 1977.
Patrologiae cursus completus [*Patrologia Latina*]. Ed. J. P. Migne. 221 vols. Paris, 1844–64.
Petrarca, Francisco. *Canzoniere.* Ed. Alberto Chiari. Milan: Mondadori, 1985.
———. *De sui ipsius et multorum ignorantia.* In *Opere latini di Francesco Petrarca,* vol. 2, ed. Antonietta Bufano, 1025–1151. Turin: UTET, 1975.
———. *De vita solitaria.* Ed. Guido Martellotti. In *Prose,* ed. Guido Martellotti et al. Milan: Ricciardi Editore, 1955.
———. *Le Familiari.* Vols. 1–3 ed. Vittorio Rossi, vol. 4 ed. Umberto Bosco. Florence: Sansoni, 1933–42.
———. *Letters of Old Age: Rerum senilium libri I–XVIII.* Trans. Aldo S. Bernardo, Saul Levin, and Rita Bernardo. 2 vols. Baltimore: Johns Hopkins University Press, 1992.
———. *Letters on Familiar Matters.* Trans. Aldo Bernardo. 3 vols. Baltimore: Johns Hopkins University Press, 1975–86.
———. *The Life of Solitude.* Trans. Jacob Zeitlin. Urbana: University of Illinois Press, 1924.
———. *Opere.* Ed. Giovanni Ponte. Milan: Mursia, 1968.
———. *Opere latine di Francesco Petrarca.* Ed. Antonietta Bufano. 2 vols. Turin: UTET, 1975.
———. *Prose.* Ed. Guido Martellotti et al. Milan: Ricciardi Editore, 1955.
———. *Rerum familiarum libri.* Trans. Aldo S. Bernardo. Vol. 1, Albany: State University of New York Press, 1975. Vols. 2 and 3, Baltimore: Johns Hopkins University Press, 1982–85.
———. *Secretum.* In *Opere,* ed. Giovanni Ponte, 432–597. Milan: Mursia, 1968.

Pliny, *Naturalis Historia*. Ed. and trans. H. Rackham and W. Jones. 10 vols. Loeb Classical Library. Cambridge: Harvard University Press, 1957.
Quintilian, *Institutio Oratoria*. Ed. and trans. H. E. Butler. 3 vols. Loeb Classical Library. Cambridge: Harvard University Press, 1953.
Stefani, Marchionne di Coppo. *Marchionne di Coppo Stefani Cronaca fiorentina*. Ed. Niccolò Rodolico. Rerum Italicarum Scriptores, 30, part 1. Città di castello: 1903.
Thomas Aquinas. *Aristotle's "De anima" in the Version of William of Moerbeke and the Commentary of St. Thomas Aquinas*. Trans. Kenelm Foster and Silvester Humphries. New Haven: Yale University Press, 1954.
———. *Commentary on the Nicomachean Ethics*. Trans. C. I. Litzinger. 2 vols. Library of Living Catholic Thought. Chicago: Regnery, 1964.
———. *De regimine principum ad regem Cypri*. In *Opuscula philosophica*, ed. R. M. Spiazzi. Turin: Marietti, 1954.
———. *Summa theologiae*. Ed. Dominicans from the English-speaking Provinces. 61 vols. London: Blackfriars, in association with Eyre and Spottiswoode, 1963–76.
Varro. *De Lingua Latina*. Ed. and trans. R. G. Kent. Loeb Classical Library. Cambridge: Harvard University Press, 1957.
Villani, Giovanni. *Cronica*. Ed. F. G. Dragomanni. 4 vols. Florence: Sansone, 1844–45; rpt. Frankfurt am Main: Minerva, 1969.
Villani, Matteo. *Cronica: con la continuazione di Filippo Villani*. Ed. Giuseppe Porta. 2 vols. Parma: University of Guanda, 1995.
Virgil. *P. Virgili Maronis Opera*. Ed. R. A. B. Mynors. Oxford: Clarendon, 1969.
Wycliffe, Johannis. *Sermones*. Ed. Johann Loserth. London: Trübner, 1887–90.

Modern Works and Studies

Agamben, Giorgio. *Stanze*. Turin: Einaudi, 1977. Translated as *Stanzas: Word and Phantasm in Western Culture* by Ronald Martinez. Minneapolis: University of Minnesota Press, 1993.
Allen, Mark. "Penitential Sermons, the Manciple, and the End of *The Canterbury Tales*." *Studies in the Age of Chaucer* 9 (1987): 77–96.
Astell, Ann. *Chaucer and the Universe of Learning*. Ithaca: Cornell University Press, 1996.
Auerbach, Erich. *Literary Language and Its Public in Late Antiquity and the Early Middle Ages*. Trans. Ralph Manheim. Princeton: Princeton University Press, 1965.
Badel, Pierre-Yves. *Le Roman de la Rose au xive siècle*. Geneva: Droz, 1980.
Bakhtin, Mikhail. *The Dialogic Imagination*. Ed. Michael Holquist. Trans. Caryl Emerson and Michael Holquist. Austin: University of Texas Press, 1981.

Balbi, Giovanna Petti. *L'insegnamento nella Liguria medievale. Scuole, maestri, libri.* Genoa: Tilgher, 1979.
Barbi, Michele. "Con Dante e coi suoi interpreti: II: Francesca da Rimini." *Studi danteschi* 15 (1932): 10–11.
Barolini, Teodolinda. "Dante and the Lyric Past." In *The Cambridge Companion to Dante,* ed. Rachel Jacoff, 14–33. Cambridge: Cambridge University Press, 1993.
———. *Dante's Poets: Textuality and Truth in the Comedy.* Princeton: Princeton University Press. 1984.
———. *The Undivine Comedy.* Princeton: Princeton University Press, 1992.
Barron, Caroline. "The Quarrel of Richard II with London, 1392–97." In *The Reign of Richard II,* ed. F. H. R. Du Boulay and Caroline Barron, 173–201. London: Athlone, 1971.
Beardwood, Alice. *Alien Merchants in England, 1350–1377.* Cambridge: Medieval Academy, 1931.
Bec, Christian. *Les marchands écrivains: Affaires et humanisme à Florence 1375–1434.* Paris: Mouton, 1967.
Becker, Marvin. *Florence in Transition.* 2 vols. Baltimore: Johns Hopkins University Press, 1968.
Benjamin, Walter. "The Task of the Translator." In *Illuminations,* trans. Harry Zohn, 69–82. New York: Schocken, 1969.
———. *Ursprung des deutschen Trauerspiels.* Frankfurt am Main: Suhrkamp, 1961. Translated as *The Origin of German Tragic Drama* by John Osborne. London: NLB, 1977.
Bergin, Thomas. *Boccaccio.* New York: Viking, 1981.
Bestul, Thomas. "Chaucer's Parson's Tale and the Late-Medieval Tradition of Religious Meditation." *Speculum* 64 (1989): 600–619.
Billanovich, Giuseppe. "La leggenda dantesca del Boccaccio dalla lettera di Ilaro al Trattatello in laude di Dante." *Studi danteschi* 28 (1949): 45–144.
Blake, Norman. *The Textual Tradition of the Canterbury Tales.* London: Edward Arnold, 1985.
Boitani, Piero. *Chaucer and Boccaccio.* Oxford: Society for the Study of Mediaeval Languages and Literatures, 1977.
———. "The *Monk's Tale:* Dante and Boccaccio." *Medium Aevum* 40 (1976): 50–69.
———. *The Tragic and the Sublime in Medieval Literature.* Cambridge: Cambridge University Press, 1989.
———. "What Dante Meant to Chaucer." In *Chaucer and the Italian Trecento,* ed. Piero Boitani, 115–39. Cambridge: Cambridge University Press, 1983.
———, ed. *Chaucer and the Italian Trecento.* Cambridge: Cambridge University Press, 1983.

Boli, Todd. "Boccaccio's *Trattatello in laude di Dante,* or Dante Resartus." *Renaissance Quarterly* 41 (1988): 389–412.
Bömer, Franz. *P. Ovidii Nasonis Metamorphosen: Kommentar.* 5 vols. Heidelberg: Winter, 1969–86.
Boyde, Patrick. *Perception and Passion in Dante's Comedy.* Cambridge: Cambridge University Press, 1993.
Branca, Vittore. *Boccaccio: The Man and His Works.* Trans. Richard Monges and Dennis McAuliffe. New York: New York University Press, 1976.
———. *Boccaccio medievale.* 2d ed. Milan: Sansoni, 1996.
———. *Il cantare trecentesco e il Boccaccio del Filostrato e del Teseida.* Florence: Sansoni, 1936.
Brewer, Derek. "Towards a Chaucerian Poetic." Sir Israel Gollancz Memorial Lecture. *Proceedings of the British Academy* 60 (1974): 219–52.
Brinkmann, Hennig. *Mittelalterliche Hermeneutik.* Tübingen: Niemeyer, 1980.
Brucker, Gene. *The Civic World of Early Renaissance Florence.* Princeton: Princeton University Press, 1977.
Bruyne, Edgar de. *Études d'esthétique médiévale,* 3 vols. Bruges: De Tempel, 1946.
Calabrese, Michael. *Chaucer's Ovidian Arts of Love.* Gainesville: University of Florida Press, 1994.
Calin, William. *The French Tradition and the Literature of Medieval England.* Toronto: University of Toronto Press, 1994.
Cardini, Franco. "Intellectuals and Culture in Twelfth- and Thirteenth-Century Italy." In *City and Countryside in Late Medieval and Renaissance Italy,* ed. Trevor Dean and Chris Wickham, 3–24. London: Hambledon Press, 1990.
Cerquiglini-Toulet, Jacqueline. *La couleur de la mélancolie: La fréquentation des livres ai XIVe siècle, 1300–1415.* Paris: Hatier, 1993.
Chickering, Howell. "Form and Interpretation in the *Envoy* to *The Clerk's Tale.*" *Chaucer Review* 29 (1995): 352–72.
Chiecchi, Giuseppe. "Sollecitazioni narrative nel *De casibus Virorum Illustrium.*" *Studi sul Boccaccio* 19 (1990): 103–49.
Childs, Wendy. "Anglo-Italian Contacts in the Fourteenth Century." In *Chaucer and the Italian trecento,* ed. Piero Boitani, 65–87. Cambridge: Cambridge University Press, 1983.
Cohen, Tom. *Ideology and Inscription.* Cambridge: Cambridge University Press, 1999.
Coleman, Janet. *Public Reading and the Reading Public in the Late Medieval England and France.* Cambridge: Cambridge University Press, 1996.
———. "The Science of Politics and Late Medieval Academic Debate." In *Criticism and Dissent in the Middle Ages,* ed. Rita Copeland, 181–214. Cambridge: Cambridge University Press, 1996.
Coleman, William. "Chaucer, *Teseida,* and the Visconti Library at Pavia: A Hypothesis." *Medium Aevum* 51 (1982): 92–101.

Condren, Edward. *Chaucer and the Energy of Creation*. Gainesville: University of Florida Press, 1999.
Cooper, Helen. "*Sources and Analogues of Chaucer's Canterbury Tales:* Reviewing the Work." *Studies in the Age of Chaucer* 19 (1997): 183–210.
Copeland, Rita. *Rhetoric, Hermeneutics, and Translation in the Middle Ages*. Cambridge: Cambridge University Press, 1991.
Copleston, Frederick. *A History of Philosophy. Medieval Philosophy*, vol. 2, part 2. Garden City: Doubleday, 1962.
Cornish, Alison. "Getting There: The Physics of Moral Advancement in Dante's *Paradiso*." *Dialoghi: Rivista di Studi Italici* 1 (1997): 73–85.
Crane, Susan. "The Writing Lesson of 1381." In *Chaucer's England: Literature in Historical Context*, ed. Barbara Hanawalt, 201–21. Minneapolis: University of Minnesota Press, 1992.
Crow, Martin, and Claire Olson, eds. *Chaucer Life-Records*. Austin: University of Texas Press, 1966.
Dameron, George. *Episcopal Power and Florentine Society, 1000–1320*. Cambridge: Harvard University Press, 1991.
David, Alfred. "Chaucer's Good Counsel to Scogan." *Chaucer Review* 3 (1968–69): 265–74.
Dean, James. "Dismantling the Canterbury Book." *Publications of the Modern Language Association* 100 (1985): 746–62.
Dean, Trevor, and Chris Wickham, eds. *City and Countryside in Late Medieval and Renaissance Italy*. London: Hambledon Press, 1990.
Delasanta, Rodney. "Penance and Poetry in the *Canterbury Tales*." *Publications of the Modern Language Association* 93 (1978): 240–47.
De Man, Paul. Introduction to *Toward an Aesthetic of Reception*, by Hans Robert Jauss, trans. Timothy Bahti. Minneapolis: University of Minnesota Press, 1982.
———. *The Resistance to Theory*. Minneapolis: University of Minnesota Press, 1986.
Denley, Peter. "Government and Schools in Late Medieval Italy." In *City and Countryside in Late Medieval and Renaissance Italy*, ed. Trevor Dean and Chris Wickham, 93–107. London: Hambledon Press, 1990.
Derrida, Jacques. "La Loi du genre/The Law of Genre." *Glyph* 7 (1980): 176–232.
Dinshaw, Carolyn. *Chaucer's Sexual Poetics*. Madison: University of Wisconsin Press, 1989.
Dionisotti, Carlo. *Gli umanisti e il volgare fra quattro e cinquecento*. Florence: Le Monnier, 1968.
Dobbs, Elizabeth. "Literary, Legal, and Last Judgments in *The Canterbury Tales*." *Studies in the Age of Chaucer* 14 (1992): 31–52.
Dobson, R. B., ed. *The Peasant's Revolt of 1381*. 2d ed. London: Macmillan, 1983.
Donaldson, E. Talbot. *Speaking of Chaucer*. New York: Norton, 1970.

Dyer, Christopher. *Standards of Living in the Later Middle Ages.* Cambridge: Cambridge University Press, 1989.
Engle, Lars. "Chaucer, Bakhtin, and Griselda." *Exemplaria* 1 (1989): 429–59.
Federico, Sylvia. "A Fourteenth-Century Erotics of Politics: London as a Feminine New Troy." *Studies in the Age of Chaucer* 19 (1997): 121–55.
Ferster, Judith. *Chaucer on Interpretation.* Cambridge: Cambridge University Press, 1985.
Fradenburg, Louise. *City, Marriage, Tournament: Arts of Rule in Late Medieval Scotland.* Madison: University of Wisconsin Press, 1991.
———. "The Manciple's Servant Tongue: Politics and Poetry in *The Canterbury Tales.*" *English Literary History* 52 (1985): 85–118.
———. "The Wife of Bath's Passing Fancy." *Studies in the Age of Chaucer* 8 (1986): 31–58.
Freccero, John. *Dante: The Poetics of Conversion.* Ed. Rachel Jacoff. Cambridge: Harvard University Press, 1986.
———. "Dante's Firm Foot and the Journey without a Guide." *Harvard Theological Review* 52 (1959): 643–72.
Fyler, John. *Chaucer and Ovid.* New Haven: Yale University Press, 1979.
Galloway, Andrew. "Marriage Sermons, Polemical Sermons, and *The Wife of Bath's Prologue:* A Generic Excursus." *Studies in the Age of Chaucer* 14 (1992): 3–30.
Ganim, John. "Carnival Voices and the Envoy to the *Clerk's Tale.*" *Chaucer Review* 22 (1987): 112–27.
Garin, Eugenio. *L'eta nuova.* Naples: Morano, 1969.
Georgianna, Linda. "Love So Dearly Bought: The Terms of Redemption in *The Canterbury Tales.*" *Studies in the Age of Chaucer* 12 (1990): 85–116.
———. "The Clerk's Tale and the Grammar of Assent." *Speculum* 70 (1995): 793–821.
Gerola, Giuseppe. "Alcuni documenti inediti per la biografia del Boccaccio." *Giornale storico della letteratura italiana* 32 (1898): 355–60.
Giddens, Anthony. *Central Problems in Social Theory.* Berkeley and Los Angeles: University of California Press, 1979.
Gilbert, Neil. "Richard of Bury and the 'Quires of Yesterday's Sophisms.'" In *Philosophy and Humanism: Renaissance Essays in Honor of Paul Oskar Kristeller,* ed. E. Mahoney, 228–57. New York: Columbia University Press, 1976.
Ginsberg, Warren. *The Cast of Character.* Toronto: University of Toronto Press, 1983.
———. *Dante's Aesthetics of Being.* Ann Arbor: University of Michigan Press, 1999.
———. "The Lineaments of Desire: Wish-Fulfillment on Chaucer's Marriage Group." *Criticism* 25 (1983): 197–210.
———. "Ovid and the Problem of Gender." *Mediaevalia* 13 (1989): 9–28.

———. "Ovid and the Politics of Interpretation." *Classical Journal* 84 (1989): 222–31.
———. "Ovidius ethicus? Ovid and the Medieval Commentary Tradition." In *Desiring Discourse: The Literature of Love, Ovid through Chaucer*, ed. James Paxson and Cynthia Gravlee, 62–71. Selinsgrove, Pa.: Susquehanna University Press, 1998.
Green, Richard F. *Poets and Princepleasers: Literature and the English Court in the Late Middle Ages*. Toronto: University of Toronto Press, 1980.
Greene, Thomas. *The Light in Troy*. New Haven: Yale University Press, 1982.
———. "Petrarch and the Humanist Hermeneutic." In *Italian Literature: Roots and Branches*, ed. Giose Rimanelli and Kenneth J. Atchity, 201–24. New Haven: Yale University Press, 1976.
Grendler, Paul. *Schooling in Renaissance Italy: Literacy and Learning, 1300–1600*. Princeton: Princeton University Press, 1988.
Grennan, Joseph. "Saint Cecilia's 'Chemical Wedding': The Unity of the *Canterbury Tales*, Fragment VIII." *Journal of English and Germanic Philology* 65 (1966): 466–81.
Gross, Kenneth. "Infernal Metamorphoses: An Interpretation of Dante's Counterpass." *Modern Language Notes* 100 (1985): 42–69.
Gruber, Joachim. *Kommentar zu Boethius De Consolatione Philosophiae*. Berlin: Walter De Gruyter, 1978.
Grudin, Michaela Paasche. *Chaucer and the Politics of Discourse*. Columbia: University of South Carolina Press, 1996.
Guasti, Cesare. *Le feste di San Giovanni Battista in Firenze*. Florence: Cirri, 1908.
Haas, Renate. "Chaucer's *Monk's Tale*: An Ingenious Criticism of Early Humanist Conceptions of Tragedy." *Humanistica Lovanensia* 36 (1987): 44–70.
Hanly, Michael. *Boccaccio, Beauvau, and Chaucer: Troilus and Criseyde: Four Perspectives on Influence*. Norman: University of Oklahoma Press, 1990.
———. "Courtiers and Poets: An International System of Literary Exchange in Late Fourteenth-Century Italy, France, and England." *Viator* 28 (1997): 305–32.
Hanning, Robert. "Come In out of the Code: Interpreting the Discourse of Desire in Boccaccio's *Filostrato*." In *Chaucer's Troilus and Criseyde: "Subgit to alle poesie,"* ed. R. A. Shoaf, 120–37. Binghamton: Medieval and Renaissance Texts and Studies, 1992.
———. "The Crisis of Mediation in Chaucer's *Troilus and Criseyde*." In *The Performance of Middle English Culture*, ed. Lawrence Clopper, James Paxson, and Sylvia Tomasch, 143–59. Cambridge: Brewer, 1998.
Harwood, Britton. "Language and the Real: Chaucer's Manciple." *Chaucer Review* 6 (1972): 268–79.
Hawkins, Peter. "The Metamorphosis of Ovid." In *Dante and Ovid: Essays in*

Intertextuality, ed. Madison Sowell, 19–34. Binghamton: Medieval and Renaissance Texts and Studies, 1991.

Hazelton, Richard. "'The Manciple's Tale': Parody and Critique." *Journal of English and Germanic Philology* 62 (1963): 1–31.

Herlihy, David. *Medieval Households*. Cambridge: Harvard University Press, 1985.

Herlihy, David, and Christiane Klapisch-Zuber. *Les Toscans et leurs familles*. Paris: Presses de la fondation nationale des sciences politiques, 1978.

Hexter, Ralph. *Ovid and Medieval Schooling*. Münchener Beiträger zür Mediävistik und Renaissance Forschung, 38. Munich: Arbeo Gesellschaft, 1986.

Hill, John. *Chaucerian Belief*. New Haven: Yale University Press, 1991.

Howard, Donald. *The Idea of the Canterbury Tales*. Berkeley and Los Angeles: University of California Press, 1976.

Huot, Sylvia. *The "Romance of the Rose" and Its Medieval Readers*. Cambridge: Cambridge University Press, 1993.

Huygens, R. B. C. *Accessus ad auctores, Bernard d'Utrecht, Conrad d'Hirsau "Dialogus super Auctores."* Leiden: Brill, 1970.

Ives, E. W. *The Common Lawyers of Pre-Reformation England*. Cambridge: Cambridge University Press, 1983.

Jauss, Hans Robert. *Alterität und Modernität der mittelalterlichen Literatur*. Munich: W. Fink, 1977.

———. *Toward an Aesthetic of Reception*. Trans. Timothy Bahti. Minneapolis: University of Minnesota Press, 1982.

Justice, Steven. *Writing and Rebellion: England in 1381*. Berkeley and Los Angeles: University of California Press, 1994.

Kaske, Carol. "Getting Around the Parson's Tale: An Alternative to Allegory and Irony." In *Chaucer at Albany*, ed. Rossell H. Robbins, 146–77. New York: Franklin, 1975.

Kean, P. M. *Chaucer and the Making of English Poetry*. London: Routledge, 1972.

Kelly, Henry Ansgar. *Chaucerian Tragedy*. Cambridge: Brewer, 1997.

Klein, Robert. *La forme et l'intelligible*. Paris: Gallimard, 1970. Translated as *Form and Meaning* by Henri Zerner. New York: Viking, 1979.

Knapp, Peggy. "Knowing the Tropes: Literary Exegesis and Chaucer's Clerk." *Criticism* 27 (1985): 331–45.

Knight, Stephen. "Chaucer and the Sociology of Literature." *Studies in the Age of Chaucer* 2 (1980): 15–51.

Koff, Leonard, and Brenda Schildgen, eds. *The Decameron and the Canterbury Tales*. Teaneck, N.J.: Fairleigh Dickinson University Press, 2000.

Kolve, V. A. *Chaucer and the Imagery of Narrative*. Stanford: Stanford University Press, 1984.

Kretzmann, Norman, Anthony Kenny, and Jan Pinborg, eds. *The Cambridge History of Later Medieval Philosophy: From the Rediscovery of Aristotle to the Disin-*

tegration of Scholasticism, 1100–1600. Cambridge: Cambridge University Press, 1982.
Larner, John. *Culture and Society in Italy, 1290–1420.* New York: Scribners, 1971.
Lawton, David. "Chaucer's Two Ways: The Pilgrimage Frame of *The Canterbury Tales.*" *Studies in the Age of Chaucer* 9 (1987): 3–40.
Lees, Clare A. *Tradition and Belief: Religious Writing in Late Anglo-Saxon England.* Minneapolis: University of Minnesota Press, 1999.
Leicester, H. Marshall. *The Disenchanted Self.* Berkeley and Los Angeles: University of California Press, 1990.
Lenaghan, R. T. "Chaucer's *Envoy to Scogan:* The Uses of Literary Conventions." *Chaucer Review* 10 (1975–76): 46–61.
Lerer, Seth. *Chaucer and His Readers.* Princeton: Princeton University Press, 1993.
Lewis, C. S. "What Chaucer Really Did to *Il Filostrato.*" In *Selected Literary Essays.* Cambridge: Cambridge University Press, 1969.
Lloyd, T. H. *Alien Merchants in England in the High Middle Ages.* New York: St. Martin's Press, 1982.
Lopez, Robert. *The Commercial Revolution of the Middle Ages, 950–1350.* Englewood Cliffs, N.J.: Prentice Hall, 1971.
Mandicott, J. R. *Law and Lordship: Royal Justices as Retainers in Thirteenth- and Fourteenth-Century England,* Past and Present, Supplement 4. Oxford: Past and Present Society, 1978.
Mazzotta, Giuseppe. *Dante's Vision and the Circle of Knowledge.* Princeton: Princeton University Press, 1993.
―――. *The World at Play in Boccaccio's Decameron.* Princeton: Princeton University Press, 1986.
―――. *The Worlds of Petrarch.* Durham: Duke University Press, 1993.
McAlpine, Monica. *The Genre of "Troilus and Criseyde."* Ithaca: Cornell University Press, 1978.
McClellan, William. "Bakhtin's Theory of Dialogic Discourse, Medieval Rhetorical Theory, and the Multi-voiced Structure of the Clerk's Tale." *Exemplaria* 1 (1989): 460–88.
Middleton, Anne. "The Clerk and His Tale: Some Literary Contexts." *Studies in the Age of Chaucer* 2 (1980): 121–50.
―――. "The Idea of Public Poetry in the Reign of Richard II." *Speculum* 53 (1978): 94–114.
Minnis, A. J. *Medieval Theory of Authorship.* London: Scolar Press, 1984.
Morse, Charlotte. "The Exemplary Griselda." *Studies in the Age of Chaucer* 7 (1985): 51–86.
Muscatine, Charles. *Chaucer and the French Tradition.* Berkeley and Los Angeles: University of California Press, 1969.
Muscetta, Carlo. *Giovanni Boccaccio.* 2d ed. Bari: Laterza, 1974.

Myers, A. R. *London in the Age of Chaucer.* Norman: University of Oklahoma Press, 1972.
Najemy, John. *Corporatism and Consensus in Florentine Electoral Politics, 1280–1400.* Chapel Hill: University of North Carolina Press, 1982.
Nardi, Bruno. *Dante e la cultura medievale.* Bari: Laterza, 1983.
Neuse, Richard. *Chaucer's Dante.* Berkeley and Los Angeles: University of California Press, 1991.
———. "The Monk's *De casibus:* The Boccaccio Case Reopened." In *The Decameron and the Canterbury Tales,* ed. Leonard Koff and Brenda Schildgen, 247–77. Teaneck, N.J.: Fairleigh Dickinson University Press, 2000.
Niccolai, Franco. "I consorzi nobilari ed il comune nell'alta e media Italia." *Rivista di storia del diritto italiano* 13 (1940): 116–47, 292–342, 397–477.
Nolan, Barbara. "'A Poet Ther Was': Chaucer's Voices in the General Prologue." *PMLA* 101 (1986): 154–69.
Oberman, Heiko. "Fourteenth-Century Religious Thought: A Premature Profile." *Speculum* 53 (1978): 80–93.
———. *The Harvest of Medieval Theology.* Cambridge: Harvard University Press, 1963.
Olson, Glending. *Literature as Recreation in the Later Middle Ages.* Ithaca: Cornell University Press, 1982.
Owen, Charles. *Pilgrimage and Story-Telling in the Canterbury Tales.* Norman: University of Oklahoma Press, 1977.
Owens, Joseph. "Faith, Ideas, Illumination, Experience." In *The Cambridge History of Later Medieval Philosophy: From the Rediscovery of Aristotle to the Disintegration of Scholasticism, 1100–1600,* ed. Norman Kretzmann, Anthony Kenny, and Jan Pinborg, 440–59. Cambridge: Cambridge University Press, 1982.
Padoan, Giorgio. "Ancora sulla datazione e sul titolo del 'Corbaccio.'" *Lettere Italiane* 15 (1963): 199–201.
———. "Mondo aristicratico e mondo communale nell'ideologia e nell'arte di Giovanni Boccaccio." In *Il Boccaccio Le Muse Il Parnaso e L'Arno.* Florence: Olschki, 1978.
———. "Sulla datazione del 'Corbaccio.'" *Lettere Italiane* 15 (1963): 1–27.
Paparelli, Giocchino. "Due modi di leggere Dante: Petrarca e Boccaccio." In *Giovanni Boccaccio editore e interprete di Dante,* ed. Società dantesca italiana, 73–90. Florence: Olschki, 1979.
Patterson, Lee. *Chaucer and the Subject of History.* Madison: University of Wisconsin Press, 1991.
———. "'For the Wyves Love of Bathe': Feminine Rhetoric and Poetic Resolution in the *Roman de la Rose* and the *Canterbury Tales.*" *Speculum* 58 (1983): 656–95.
———. *Negotiating the Past.* Madison: University of Wisconsin Press, 1987.
———. "The Parson's Tale and the Quitting of the *Canterbury Tales.*" *Traditio* 34 (1978): 331–80.

———. "Perpetual Motion: Alchemy and the Technology of the Self." *Studies in the Age of Chaucer* 15 (1993): 25–57.
———. "'What Man Artow?': Authorial Self-Definition in *The Tale of Sir Thopas* and *The Tale of Melibee*." *Studies in the Age of Chaucer* 11 (1989): 117–75.
Pearsall, Derek. *The Canterbury Tales*. London: George Allen and Unwin, 1985.
———. *John Lydgate*. London: Routledge and Kegan Paul, 1970.
———. *The Life of Geoffrey Chaucer: A Critical Biography*. Oxford: Blackwell, 1992.
Peck, Russell. "Biblical Interpretation: St. Paul and the *Canterbury Tales*." In *Chaucer and the Scriptural Tradition*, ed. David L. Jeffrey, 143–70. Ottawa: University of Ottawa Press, 1984.
Pertile, Lino. "Dante Looks Forward and Back: Political Allegory in the Epistles." *Dante Studies* 115 (1997): 1–17.
———. "Il nodo di Bonagiunta, le penne di Dante, e il Dolce Stil Novo." *Lettere italiane* 46 (1994): 44–75.
Petrucci, Armando. "The Illusion of Authentic History: Documentary Evidence." In *Writers and Readers in Medieval Italy*, ed. and trans. Charles Radding, 236–50. New Haven: Yale University Press, 1995.
Picone, Michelangelo. 2000. "Ovid and the *exul inmeritus*." Paper presented at "Dante 2000," Columbia University, April 7, 2000. <http://www.italianacademy.columbia.edu/lectures/dante2000/index.html>.
Ricci, Pier Giorgio. "Per la dedica e la datazione del *Filostrato*." *Studi sul Boccaccio* 1 (1963): 333–47.
———. "Le tre redazioni del 'Trattatello in laude di Dante.'" *Studi sul Boccaccio* 8 (1974): 197–214.
Rickert, Edith. "Chaucer's Hodge of Ware." *Times Literary Supplement*, October 20, 1932, 761.
Robertson, D. W. *Chaucer's London*. New York: Wiley, 1968.
Robins, H. R. *Ancient and Medieval Grammatical Theory in Europe*. 1951; rpt. Port Washington, N.Y.: Kennikat Press, 1971.
Rosser, Gervase. *Medieval Westminster, 1200–1540*. Oxford: Clarendon, 1989.
Rudd, Jay. "Chaucer's *Envoy to Scogan*: 'Tullius Kyndnesse' and the Law of Kynde." *Chaucer Review* 20 (1986): 323–30.
Salter, Elizabeth. *The Knight's Tale and the Clerk's Tale*. London: Arnold, 1962.
Scanlon, Larry. "The Authority of Fable: Allegory and Irony in the *Nun's Priest's Tale*." *Exemplaria* 1 (1989): 43–68.
———. *Narrative, Authority, and Power*. Cambridge: Cambridge University Press, 1994.
Scattergood, John. "Old Age, Love, and Friendship in Chaucer's *Envoy to Scogan*." *Nottingham Medieval Studies* 35 (1991): 92–101.
Scattergood, V. J. "The Manciple's Manner of Speaking." *Essays in Criticism* 24 (1974): 124–46.
Schless, Howard. *Chaucer and Dante*. Norman, Okla.: Pilgrim Books, 1984.

Severs, J. Burke. *The Literary Relationships of Chaucer's Clerkes Tale*. 1942; rpt. New Haven: Archon, 1972.
Shaw, J. E. *Guido Cavalcanti's Theory of Love*. Toronto: University of Toronto Press, 1949.
Shils, David. *Tradition*. Chicago: University of Chicago Press, 1981.
Shoaf, R. A. *Dante, Chaucer, and the Currency of the Word*. Norman, Okla.: Pilgrim Books, 1983.
Shumaker, Wayne. "Chaucer's *Manciple's Tale* as Part of a Canterbury Group." *University of Toronto Quarterly* 22 (1953): 147–56.
Smarr, Janet. *Boccaccio and Fiammetta*. Urbana: University of Illinois Press, 1986.
Smith, James Robinson. *The Earliest Lives of Dante*. 1901; rpt. New York: Russell and Russell, 1908.
Steneck, Nicholas. "Albert on the Psychology of Sense Perception." In *Albertus Magnus and the Sciences: Commemorative Essays, 1980*, ed. James Weisheipl, 263–90. Pontifical Institute of Medieval Studies. Toronto: University of Toronto Press, 1980.
———. "Albert the Great on the Internal Senses." *Isis* 65 (1974): 193–211.
Stevens, John. "Dante and Music." *Italian Studies* 23 (1968): 1–18.
Stillinger, Thomas. *The Song of Troilus*. Philadelphia: University of Pennsylvania Press, 1992.
Stock, Brian. *The Implications of Literacy: Written Language and Models of Interpretation in the Eleventh and Twelfth Centuries*. Princeton: Princeton University Press, 1983.
Stone, Gregory. *The Ethics of Nature in the Middle Ages*. New York: St. Martin's Press, 1998.
Strohm, Paul. *Hochon's Arrow*. Princeton: Princeton University Press, 1992.
———. *Social Chaucer*. Cambridge: Harvard University Press, 1989.
Taylor, Daniel. *Declinatio: A Study of the Linguistic Theory of M. T. Varro*. Amsterdam Studies in the Theory and History of Linguistic Science, 3. Amsterdam: John Benjamins, 1975.
Taylor, Karla. *Chaucer Reads "The Divine Comedy."* Stanford: Stanford University Press, 1989.
Teskey, Gordon. *Allegory and Violence*. Ithaca: Cornell University Press, 1996.
———. "Irony, Allegory, and Metaphysical Decay." *Publications of the Modern Language Association* 109 (1994): 397–408.
Thompson, Nigel. *Chaucer, Boccaccio, and the Debate of Love*. Oxford: Clarendon, 1996.
Thrupp, Sylvia. *The Merchant Class of Medieval London*. 1948; rpt. Ann Arbor: University of Michigan Press, 1962.
Trexler, Richard. *Public Life in Renaissance Florence*. New York: Academic Press, 1980.
Trimpi, Wesley. *Muses of One Mind*. Princeton: Princeton University Press, 1983.

Trinkaus, Charles. *In Our Image and Likeness*. 2 vols. Chicago: University of Chicago Press, 1970.
———. *The Poet as Philosopher*. New Haven: Yale University Press, 1979.
Tupper, Frederick. *Types of Society in Medieval Literature*. New York: Holt, 1926.
Ussery, H. E. *Chaucer's Physician: Medicine and Literature in the Fourteenth Century*. Tulane Studies in English, no. 19. New Orleans: Tulane Dept. of English, 1971.
Wack, Mary. *Lovesickness in the Middle Ages*. Philadelphia: University of Philadelphia Press, 1990.
Wailes, Stephen. *Medieval Allegories of Jesus' Parables*. Berkeley and Los Angeles: University of California Press, 1987.
Wallace, David. *Chaucer and the Early Writings of Boccaccio*. Suffolk: Brewer, 1985.
———. *Chaucerian Polity: Absolutist Lineages and Associational Forms in England and Italy*. Stanford: Stanford University Press, 1997.
———. "'Whan She Translated Was': A Chaucerian Critique of the Petrarchan Academy." In *Literary Practice and Social Change in England, 1380–1530*, ed. Lee Patterson, 156–215. Berkeley and Los Angeles: University of California Press, 1990.
Wallace, Kristine Gilmartin. "Array as Motif in the *Clerk's Tale*." *Rice University Studies* 62 (1976): 99–110.
Wetherbee, Winthrop. *Chaucer and the Poets: An Essay on Troilus and Criseyde*. Ithaca: Cornell University Press, 1984.
———. "The Context of the Monk's Tale." In *Language and Style in English Literature: Essays in Honour of Michio Masui*, 159–77. Hiroshima: English Research Association of Hiroshima: Eihosha Ltd, 1991.
Wilkins, Ernest H. *Petrarch's Correspondence*. Padua: Antenore, 1960.
———. *Petrarch's Eight Years in Milan*. Cambridge: Medieval Academy, 1958.
Williams, Gwyn. *Medieval London*. London: Athlone, 1963.
Wimsatt, James. *Chaucer and His French Contemporaries*. Toronto: University of Toronto Press, 1991.
———. "Guillaume de Machaut and Chaucer's Love Lyrics." *Medium Aevum* 47 (1978): 68–87.
Windeatt, Barry A. *Chaucer's Dream Poetry: Sources and Analogues*. Cambridge: Brewer, 1982.
Wood, Chauncey. "Speech, the Principle of Contraries, and Chaucer's Tales of the Manciple and the Parson." *Mediaevalia* 6 (1980): 209–27.
Zaccaria, Vittore. "Le due redazioni del *De casibus*." *Studi sul Boccaccio* 10 (1977–78): 1–26.

Index

Accursio, Mainardo, 126n. 38
Agamben, G., 156, 180n
Albert the Great, 152, 154n. 11, 156n, 157n. 17
Albizzis, 131, 131n. 49, 146
Albornoz, Cardinal, 196n
allegory, ix–xi, 8, 11, 16–17, 31, 34, 59–65, 67–69, 74–76, 97–99, 128, 164–66, 179, 276, 268, and passim. *See also* irony
Allen, M., 89n. 45
Alliterative Morte Arthure, 269
Ambrose, St., 63n. 9, 66
Anderson, W., 40n. 23
Andrea dell'Ischia, 140
antiphrasis, 67–68, 85, 86, 103, 104. *See also* irony
Aquinas, St. Thomas, 66, 78n. 35, 148–49, 152, 153, 154n. 12, 155, 166–67, 168n. 31, 179n. 44, 192, 208
Aristotle, 54n. 41, 123n, 127n. 39, 148, 149, 162n. 24, 179n. 44, 192n. 3, 208
Arnaut Daniel, 106n, 107
Astell, A., 4n. 10
Auerbach, E., 20, 157n. 18
Augustine, St., 44, 66n. 19, 80, 81nn. 37, 38, 154n. 12, 162n. 24
Averroes, 151, 152
Avicenna, 151, 152, 156, 180

Badel, P.-Y., 109n. 8
Baker, D., 59n, 71n. 27, 73n. 30, 89n. 45

Bakhtin, M., 167n. 29, 186, 244
Balbi, G., 3n. 8
Barbi, M., 172n
Barolini, T., 11n. 26, 106n. 4
Barron, C., 229n. 37
Battaglia, S., 152n. 6
Bec, C., 201n
Becker, M., 130n. 47, 131n. 50, 132n. 51
Bede, 65
Bembre, Nicholas, 187
Benjamin, W., viii–ix, 8–10, 31, 34, 41, 43, 179, 239n, 271
Bennett, J. A. W., 82n
Bérenger au long cul, 270
Bergin, T., 150n. 4, 191n. 1
Berkeley, Edward, 2
Bestul, T., 78n. 35
Bible
   Acts 9, 70–71
   1 Chron. 29, 127n. 40
   1 Cor. 7, 194–95
   1 Cor. 15, 47
   Eccles. 3, 241
   Gen. 1, 98
   James 1, 267n. 32
   John 2, 80–81
   Lamentations 1, 159, 161n
   Luke 16, 62–69, 92n. 50
   Matt. 24, 76–77
   Numbers 21, 102
   1 Thess. 5, 73n. 30, 74–75
   Wisdom 16, 103n. 68
Billanovich, G., 114n. 17, 125n

Black Death, 131, 211, 247
Blake, N. , 58n. 2
Boccaccio, Giovanni, vii, viii, and
    passim
  works
    Ameto, 140
    Carme III, 119n. 3
    Carme IV, 127n. 40
    Corbaccio, 120n. 26, 126, 134n. 56
    Decameron, xi, 7, 120n. 26, 128,
        144, 162n. 24, 164n, 183, 190,
        192–93, 195, 202n. 2, 208–13,
        245, 247–48, 251, 252–53,
        254, 257–58, 260, 272–73
    De casibus virorum illustrium, x,
        14n. 68, 21, 190–208, 213–27
    Epistolaria consolatoria, 134n. 56,
        140–42
    Epistole, 119nn. 22, 23, 143–44
    Ut huic epistole, 120n. 26, 122n,
        124n. 32
    *Esposizioni sopra la Comedia di
        Dante*, 17, 23, 30, 110–11,
        118n. 20, 121n. 28, 127n. 39,
        142n. 67, 157n. 18
    Filocolo, 117n, 147, 150–52, 155,
        157, 158, 162, 184–85
    Filostrato, x, 11–14, 16, 18–19, 20,
        108–10, 111, 115–17, 124,
        125, 142, 144, 149–85
    Life of Petrarch, 119n. 23, 129
    Rime, 21–24, 157n. 18
    Teseida, 18, 19, 108, 110, 111n. 13,
        112, 125, 183–84, 188, 226
    Trattatello in laude di Dante, 21,
        30, 111–30, 133, 133n. 55,
        134–36, 139–40, 142–43, 147,
        157n. 18, 199, 206n, 245,
        248n. 10, 251n. 16
Boccaccio di Chellino, 200–202
Boethius, 128n. 41, 205
Boitani, P., 29, 238n. 49
Boli, T., 114n. 17, 119n. 23
Bollettino, V., 111n. 14, 114n. 16
Bömer, F., 40n. 25
Bonagiunta of Lucca, 21, 108

Bonaventure, St., 66, 67n. 21
Bourdieu, P., 270
Bovet, Honore, 269n
Boyde, P., 156n
Branca, V., 23n, 110n. 10, 115n. 18,
    120nn. 25, 26, 126nn. 38, 40, 144n.
    72, 150n. 4, 181
Brewer, D., 100
Brinkmann, H., 62n, 65nn. 14, 15,
    69n
Brucker, G., 128, 129n. 44, 132n. 52,
    133n. 55, 135n, 137n, 157n. 18,
    160n, 191n. 1, 200n
Brunetto Latini, 32
Bruni, Leonardo, 114

Calabrese, M., 55n. 42
Calin, W., 270n. 2
cantare, 110, 115n. 18, 167, 182, 183
canzone, 44n. 31
Capellanus, Andreas, 178, 241n
Cardini, F., 3, 133n. 56
Cavalcanti, Guido, 107, 138, 152,
    153n. 8, 155n. 14, 157n. 18, 183
Cavalcanti, Mainardo, 143, 177,
    197n
Cerquiglini-Toulet, J., 19, 109n. 9
Charles of Valois, 138
Chaucer, Geoffrey, vii, viii, and
    passim
  works
    Book of the Duchess, 109
    Canterbury Tales, 8, 17, and
        passim
    Canon Yeoman's Tale, 96
    Clerk's Tale, 236n, 240–46,
        263–68
    Cook's Tale, 91
    Franklin's Tale, 184
    General Prologue, 59–62, 71n.
        28, 82, 85n, 94, 97–99,
        240
    Knight's Tale, 19, 93, 108
    Manciple's Tale, ix, 17, 58–100
    Melibee, 235, 239
    Miller's Tale, 91–93, 94–95, 240

Monk's Tale, x, 160, 235–39, 242n
Nun's Priest's Tale, 100, 234, 235, 237
Pardoner's Tale, 71
Parson's Tale, 58, 60n, 83n, 93–94, 96, 98–100, 103, 202n. 12
Reeve's Tale, 92, 94–95
Retractions, 59, 75, 94n. 54, 95, 100–101
Second Nun's Tale, 96
Wife of Bath's Tale, 241, 243–44, 265n. 30
Envoy to Scogan, 21, 24–28
House of Fame, 18, 107, 270
Legend of Good Women, 3n. 5, 246
Parliament of Fowls, 137n, 236n
Troilus, x, 6, 14–16, 18, 19, 108–10, 147, 185–89, 213n. 23
Chickering, H., 266n
Chiecchi, G., 195n. 6
Childs, W., 2n. 2
Cicero, xi, 24, 36, 37, 65n. 15, 126, 127, 136, 252
Cino da Pistoia, 18, 145, 181, 182, 183
ciompi, 135
    Ciompi rebellion, 135n
Clement, V., 120n. 25, 199n, 200
Cohen, T., 9, 10, 179n. 45
Coleman, J., 192n. 3, 201n
Coleman, W., 111n. 13
Compagni, Dino, 138n. 61
Condren, E., 29n
consorteria, 132, 133, 174–76
Cooper, H., 273
Copeland, R., 4
Copleston, F., 154n. 12
Cornish, A., 49n
Crane, S., 234n
Cristiano, Luca, 126n. 38
Cronica fiorentina, 138n. 61

Dante, vii, viii, and passim
    works
        Comedy, ix, x, and passim
        Inferno 1: 260n; 4: 145n; 5: 171–72; 11: 46; 16: 11n. 26; 25: 32–33, 42, 101–3; 26: 202n. 13; 27: 218; 29: 22, 23
        Paradiso 1: 33; 2: 187; 14: 14–16; 16: 181–82; 17: 233; 18–19: 49–50; 25: 43, 47, 120; 33: 48n. 35
        Purgatorio 1: 27, 206–7; 12: 48–49; 13: 78n. 35; 14: 77–79; 15: 31; 20: 202n. 11; 22: 47–48; 24: 10–11, 43–47; 25: 43, 47; 26: 152, 184; 30: 207n; 32: 207
        Convivio, 32n. 10, 117, 118, 125, 153n. 8, 248n. 10
        De vulgari eloquentia, viiin, 30, 44n. 31, 203
        Donne ch'avete intelletto d'amore, 10, 102, 103, 182, 185
        Eclogue II, 44n. 31
        Epistle 8, 199n
        Epistle to Can Grande, 30, 121n. 28
        Poscia ch' Amor del tutto m'ha lasciato, 23
        Vita nuova, 7, 11, 17, 33, 56, 105n. 2, 107, 113, 117–18, 125, 142, 147, 156, 160, 168, 180, 182, 248n. 10
Dante da Maiano, 105, 105n. 2, 106
David, A., 24n. 39
Dean, J., 59
De Bruyne, E., 66n. 16
Defensor pacis, 129n. 44
Delasanta, R., 75n
De Man, P., 5, 9nn. 20, 22, 10, 41, 63n. 9
Denley, P., 3n. 8
denudatio, 180–83
Derrida, J., 6
Deschamps, Eustache, 1, 27, 44n. 31, 110, 188, 269n
Dino del Garbo, 157n. 18
Dinshaw, C., 250n. 14

Index

disputatio in utramque partem, 162–63
Dobbs, E., 92n. 49
Donaldson, E., 186
Donati, Corso, 138
Donati, Forese, 21, 45
Donati, Gemma, 125, 128n. 41
Dyer, C., 79n

Edward III, 20, 196n, 225, 229
Engle, L., 244n. 6

Federico, S., 229n. 37, 233
Ferster, J., 244n. 6
Fiamma, Galvano, 123n
fin amour, 106, 188, 241n
Fisher, J. H., 26n
Florence, x, 2–4, 7, 17, 20, 24, 31, 119, 124n. 33, 126, 127, 128n. 40, 143n. 68, 175–76, 214–15, 218–27, 235, 245–46
Foucault, M., 205
Fradenburg, L., 74n, 89n. 45, 244
Freccero, J., 56n, 102, 127n. 39
Froissart, Jean, 1, 19, 269
Fyler, J., 89n. 45

Galloway, A., 81n. 38
Ganim, J., 244n. 6
Garin, E., 262n. 24
gender, 40–41, 54
Genoa, 2, 3n. 8, 269
Georgianna, L., 92nn. 49, 50, 265n. 29
Gerola, G., 23n
Gervais of Melkley, 65
Giacomo da Lentini, 45
Giddens, A., 132, 177
Gilbert, N. , 262n. 24
Ginsberg, W., 7n, 11n. 25, 21n. 34, 35n, 36n. 16, 42n. 27, 45n. 33, 50n, 55n. 43, 102n. 65, 103n. 68, 106n. 6, 108n, 113n, 132n. 53, 152n. 7, 162n. 23, 183n, 184n, 241n, 262n. 26, 267n. 33
Giovanni del Virgilio, 117
Girolami, Remigio, 129n. 44
Gower, John, 19, 229–34, 239

Grandson, Oton, 269n
Green, R. F., 4n. 9
Greene, T., 246, 248, 249, 250, 251n, 256n
Grendler, P., 3n. 8
Grennan, J., 96n. 56
Gross, K., 42n. 28
Gruber, J., 205n. 17
Grudin, M., 238n. 49
Guasti, C., 138n. 61
Guiglielmo d'Asciesi, 213n. 23, 225
Guillaume de Lorris, 1, 166, 188
Guillaume de Machaut, 1, 17, 27, 107, 108–9, 110, 188, 270
Guinizelli, Guido, 21, 108, 182n. 49, 185, 249
Guittone d'Arezzo, 45, 106

Haas, R., 238n. 49
Halmo of Auxerre, 66
Hanly, M., 269n
Hanning, R., 150n. 3
Harwood, B., 89n. 45
Hawkins, P., 32n. 11
Hazelton, R., 89n. 45
Henry VII, 199, 216n. 26
Herlihy, D., 174nn. 34, 36, 175n
Hexter, R., 53n
Hill, J., 89n. 45
Howard, D., 91n. 47
Hugh of St. Cher, 63n
Hugh of St. Victor., 192n. 3, 239
humanism, xi, 7, 21, 24, 31, 118, 120, 121, 121n. 38, 125, 127, 133n. 55, 140, 143, 190–208, 215–16, 221, 227, 229, 235, 236n, 238–39, 263–64
Humphrey, Duke of Gloucester, 228n. 35
Huot, S., 30n. 8

imagination, 153, 154, 155, 157, 164. *See also* phantasm
impersonation, 69, 73–74, 90, 91
incest, 144, 173–76
Innocent III, 68n

intellection, 154–55
intelligible species, 154. See also *verbum mentis*
intention, 152–53, 155, 179, 180, 271
internal senses, 153–54, 155
irony, ix–xi, 59, 62n, 63–65, 67–69, 74–76, 88, 97–99, 267, 268, and passim. *See also* allegory, antiphrasis
Isidore of Seville, 62n, 65
Ives, E., 79n

Jacques de Molay, 200–202
Jauss, H., 5–6, 9
Jean de Luxembourg, 109n. 8
Jean de Meung, 1
John of Salisbury, 192
John the Good, 225, 229
John XXII, 196n
Justice, S., 231n. 42, 234n

Kaske, C., 100n. 63
Kean, P., 24n. 39
Kelly, H., 191n. 2, 238n. 49
Kennedy, T., 44n. 31
Klapisch-Zuber, C., 174n. 36
Klein, R., 16
Knapp, P., 244n. 6
Knight, S., 58n. 3
Kolve, V. A., 91, 153n. 9

Langland, William, 82n, 263, 268
Larner, J., 123n
Laurent de Premierfait, 228n. 34
Lawton, D., 58n. 2, 94n. 54
Lees, C., 270n. 3
Leicester, H. M., 89
Lenaghan, R. T., 24n. 39
Lerer, S., 227
Lewis, C. S., 19, 188
literacy, 3n. 8
London, x, 1, 2, 19–20, 27, 32, 147, 187, 229, 232–33, 270
Lopez, R., 2n. 3
Lydgate, John, 227–29, 230n. 38, 233

Mandicott, J. R., 79n
Map, Walter, 120n. 27
May Day, 138
Mazzotta, G., 110, 128, 150n. 3, 157n. 18, 164n, 208
McAlpine, M., 238n. 49
McClellan, W., 244n. 6
memory, 153, 154, 156
metamorphosis, 40–43, 48, 48n. 35. *See also* translation
  in Dante, 42–43, 46–47, 49–50, 56
  in Ovid, 34–42
Middleton, A., 244, 262
Milan, 2, 3n. 5, 7, 120, 122n, 124n. 33, 125, 127, 216, 222, 245, 269
Minnis, A. J., 58n. 2, 94n. 54
Morse, C., 244, 256n
Muscatine, C., 1, 269, 270
Myers, A. R., 187n

Nardi, B., 105n. 2, 153n. 8, 156
Neuse, R., 29, 239n
Niccolai, F., 174n. 34
Niccolò di Bartolo di Buono, 140
Nolan, B., 98
nominalism, 264
notaries, 45n. 32

Oberman, H., 264n. 27
Olsen, G., 165n, 211n, 252n
Ordinamenti di giustizia, 130–31, 133, 177n. 40, 232
Ovid, 1, 14, 32, 47, 56, 57, 101, 103
  works
    Amores, 53n, 55n. 43
    Ars amatoria, 14, 32, 34, 50–56, 83–85, 168n. 30
    Ex ponto, 33n. 12
    Heroides, 55n. 43
    Metamorphoses, 34–42, 46, 86n, 101
    Remedia amoris, 33, 55, 55n. 43, 105
    Tristia, 33n. 12
Owen, C., 58n. 2
Owens, J., 154nn. 12, 13

Padoan, G., 111n. 12, 120n. 26, 134n. 56, 150n. 4, 157n. 18, 167n. 28
Paparelli, G., 119n. 24
parables, 64–66, 69n. *See also* allegory
Parte Guelfa, 20, 136–37, 146
Patterson, L., 19, 58, 92n. 50, 96n. 57, 99n. 61, 244n. 5
Pearsall, D., 58n. 1, 227n, 228n. 35
Peck, R., 100n. 64
Petrarch, Francesco, vii, viii, and passim
works
  Africa, 145, 251n. 16, 252
  Bucolicum carmen, 120n. 27
  Canzoniere, 144, 145, 248
  De otio religioso, 255, 262
  De sui ipsius et multorum ignorantia, 254, 261
  De vita solitaria, 126n. 35, 142, 255, 262
  Epistolae seniles, xi, 246–61
  Familiares, 119nn. 22, 24, 120n. 27, 122n, 124n. 33, 126, 247, 250–51, 257n, 261
  Secretum, 254
Pertile, L., 48n. 35, 199n
Petrarch, Gherado, 119n. 22, 120, 142n. 67, 255
Petrucci, A., 45n. 32
phantasm, 153, 155, 156, 180, 181. *See also* imagination, intellection
Philippe de Mèziéres, 269n
Philip the Fair, 200, 202
Picone, M., 33n. 12
Pino de' Rossi, 140, 141, 142n. 65
Plato, 37, 168n. 31
Pliny, 38, 40n. 25
pneumatology, 155–57
propriety, 36–41, 48n. 35, 66, 67

Quintilian, 37, 64n. 11, 65, 67

Raniere di Giotto, 218–19, 221n, 229
rhetoric, 161–62
Ricci, P. G., 24, 111n. 14, 114n. 16, 118n. 21, 126n. 35, 134, 140n. 62, 150n. 4, 200n, 215n
Riccis, 131, 146
Richard II, 3n. 5, 4, 27, 229, 262, 269, 270
Richard of Bury, 99n. 60
Rickert, E., 93n. 51
ricordanze, 133n. 55, 176, 201n
Robert of Naples, 205n. 16
Robertson, D. W., 99n. 60
Robins, H. R., 37n. 19
Robinson, F. N. , 82n
Romance of the Rose, 30n. 8, 109n. 9, 166
Rudd, J., 24n. 39
Rustichelli, Francesco, 218

Sacchetti, Franco, 132
Salter, E., 265n. 30
Salutati, Coluccio, 132
Scanlon, L., 63n. 9
Scattergood, J., 24n. 39, 28n
Scattergood, V. J., 89n. 45
Schless, H., 30n. 8
Sennuccio del Bene, 145
Severs, J. B., 246n. 9, 261, 265n. 30
Shaw, J. E., 154n. 8, 155n. 14, 156n
Shils, D., 270n. 3
Shoaf, R. A., 29
Shumaker, W., 89n. 45
Singleton, C., 47, 48n. 34
Smarr, J., 150n. 3, 160n
Smith, J. R., 114nn. 16, 17
Sordello, 106n. 3
spirits, 155–57
Statius, 1, 107
Stefani, Marchionne di Coppo, 131n. 50, 213n. 23, 214n. 24, 215n, 218, 220n, 221, 221n, 222n, 226n
Steneck, N. , 153nn. 8–10, 154n. 11
Stevens, J., 44n. 31
Stevens, W., 72, 73
stil novo, x, 6, 7, 8, 17, 18, 20, 21, 106, 109, 110, 149, 157n. 18, 162, 163–65, 171, 180, 182, 183, 184, 249

Stock, B., 201n
Stone, G., 177n. 41
Strohm, P., 3n. 5, 4, 4nn. 9, 10, 24n. 39, 27

Taylor, D., 39n. 21
Taylor, K., 29
Templars, 200–202
teneritas, 194–95
tenzone, 21, 45, 145
Teskey, G., 63n. 9, 64, 64n. 11, 67, 72, 89n. 45
Thompson, N. , 273
Thrupp, S., 3n. 5
traditionality, 270–71
translation, viii, 4, 8–10, 34, 45, 49, 258, 265–66, 270–71
  and metamorphosis, 41–42, 49–50, 265
Treaty of Sanzara, 138n. 60
Trexler, R., 138n. 61
Trimpi, W., 162nn. 22–24, 163n
Trinkaus, C., 254n, 255, 262n. 24, 264n. 27
Tristan riccardiano, 181n
Tupper, F., 82n
Tyler, Wat, 230n. 39, 231n. 41

Ugolino, Luca, 140
Uguccione de' Ricci, 131
Uprising of 1381, 135n, 230
Ussery, H. E., 89n. 45

Valori, Filippo, 23n

Varro, 39, 40
Velluti, Donato, 129
verbum mentis, 154, 178, 249
Villani, Giovanni, 129, 130n. 48, 138, 200n, 213n. 23, 214n. 24, 215n, 220n, 221n, 222n, 226n
Villani, Matteo, 129, 129n. 45
Virgil, xi, 1, 47, 48, 56, 57, 195n. 5, 202n. 13
Visconti, Azzone, 123n
Visconti, Bernabò, 3n. 5, 146
Visconti, Galeazzo, 261
Visconti, Giovanni, 121, 124, 124n. 33, 127n. 40, 205n. 16, 216, 245

Wack, M., 156n
Wailes, S., 66n. 19, 67n. 21, 68n, 94n. 53
Walforth, William, 230, 231n. 41
Wallace, D., viin, xii, 3n. 5, 4, 110n. 10, 245, 246, 251n. 16
Wallace, K. G., 250n. 14
Walter of Brienne, 130, 143n. 68, 197, 245, 251n. 16
Weber, M., 89
Wetherbee, W., 17n, 29, 238
Wilkins, E. H., 121n. 29
Wimsatt, J., 27n. 41, 44n. 31
Windeatt, B., 109n. 8
Wood, C., 89n. 45
Wyclif, John, 43, 81n. 38, 262n. 26

Zaccaria, V., 191n. 1